Jurisprudence

Jurisprudence

JG Riddall MA (TCD)
of the Inner Temple, Barrister at Law
formerly Senior Lecturer in Law, University of Leeds

OXFORD
UNIVERSITY PRESS

OXFORD
UNIVERSITY PRESS

Great Clarendon Street, Oxford OX2 6DP

Oxford University Press is a department of the University of Oxford.
It furthers the University's objective of excellence in research, scholarship,
and education by publishing worldwide in

Oxford New York
Auckland Cape Town Dar es Salaam Hong Kong Karachi Kuala Lumpur
Madrid Melbourne Mexico City Nairobi New Delhi Shanghai Taipei Toronto

With offices in

Argentina Austria Brazil Chile Czech Republic France Greece
Guatemala Hungary Italy Japan South Korea Poland Portugal
Singapore Switzerland Thailand Turkey Ukraine Vietnam

Published in the United States
by Oxford University Press Inc., New York

First published 2005

British Library Cataloguing in Publication Data
Data available

Library of Congress Cataloging in Publication Data
Data available

ISBN-13: 978-0-406-90010-4
ISBN-10: 0-406-90010-8

1 3 5 7 9 10 8 6 4 2

Printed in Great Britain by
Antony Rowe Ltd,
Chippenham, Wilts.

Preface

The principal change in this edition has been the addition of chapters dealing with topics not previously treated. Topics so covered include Utilitarianism, Scandinavian realism, the New Critics; and the Hart v Dworkin debate. Dworkin's *Law's Empire* has been made the subject of a separate chapter. The chapter on Rights has been substantially rewritten. The chapter on Justice has been extended to cover Rawls's *Political Liberalism*.

In 1998 the book was translated into Spanish.

Howard Davies, of the University of Leeds, has again, as in the case of the first edition, given me valuable advice. Without his assistance this ship would have foundered before getting out of the harbour.

I express my thanks to the University of Sheffield for permission to use the Crookes Law Library.

The publishers have my thanks for all the detailed work that goes into the production of a book of this kind.

Once again my greatest debt is to my wife; for her help, and for her patience.

Derbyshire   J G Riddall
May 1999

Acknowledgments

Grateful acknowledgment is made for permission by the Oxford University Press to reproduce the following works:

FINNIS, JM   *Natural Law and Natural Rights*
HART, HLA   *The Concept of Law*

Contents

CHAPTER 1

'I hate jurisprudence'

And what can be done about it

'Most of us know people who seem to be effortlessly articulate and
can talk fluently and expressively without actually *saying* anything.'
Rita Carter[1]

Why do people hate jurisprudence? Or rather, since we are lawyers,
and should be precise, – why is it that some law students, at any rate
at certain stages, feel a lack of sympathy with the subject matter, or
the treatment of the subject matter, of certain aspects of
jurisprudence?

There can be several reasons, among which the following may
figure.

1. Suppose that a student is preparing for this first tutorial in a
jurisprudence course. He sits in the library with an article from his
reading list open in front of him. He reads as follows. 'The predictive
empiricism inherent in the neo-Thomist rejection of metaphysics
qua metaphysics typically characterises the substantive epistemology
so clearly demonstrated by Weberstrom's implicit acceptance of the
semantically normative assertions made by Haranmere in all his later
work on voluntarist teleology.'

'Um,' thinks the student, 'I never realised that.' He continues
reading.

'But the question arises as to why it was that Haranmere's
conceptualisation of Platonic ontology placed him so firmly in the
ranks of those who believed that cognitivism in its contractarian

1 *Mapping the Mind*, p 139.

form is no support for Weberstrom's analysis of the Kelsenian grundnorm. This is the question that must be faced.'

'Indeed it must,' the student thinks. At this point his attention is distracted by a friend who says, 'Feel like a cup of coffee?' Over coffee the friend asks, 'What were you reading?'

'The article by Plankhaffer in the MLR,' says the student.

'What's it like?' asks the friend.

'Very good,' the student replies, not having understood a word he had read.

This being so, why had he continued reading? Perhaps the reason was that he was unable to bring himself to admit that he had not understood the page of English in front of him. Or perhaps, while recognising that he had no idea of what the author was saying, he felt that if he persevered the words and their meaning would by some kind of osmosis be transferred into his brain. Or perhaps he had continued reading not knowing what else to do, his senses numbed by confusion and despair.

Whatever the reason, it is worth enquiring why law students sometimes fail to understand what they read when they come to jurisprudence.

(a) One reason can be that, not having studied philosophy, they do not know the meaning of certain words as common among philosophers as such words or phrases as 'fee simple', 'seisin', 'mens rea' or 'volenti non fit injuria' are among lawyers. Not knowing the meaning of words such as ontology, teleology, epistemology, cognitivism, neo-Thomism, they can have no reason to expect to understand much of what they will read. Osmosis from the page to the brain does not occur. (Had the student in the example above known the meaning of each of the words used in the above passage he would have realised that it was gibberish.)

(b) Nor may newcomers to jurisprudence have a proper understanding of certain other words, words of a more general nature not confined principally to philosophy. They might have met such words as deduction, ethics, prescription and efficiency. But they may be hazy about the distinction between deduction and induction, ethics and morality, prescription and proscription, efficiency and efficacy (and some might even think that infer was a superior way of saying imply). Not knowing the precise meaning of such words as these, it is not surprising that they fail to grasp what is being said.

(c) Being newcomers to jurisprudence law students are unlikely to realise that in this subject certain words carry a meaning different from that in general usage. For example, by convention the word 'magistrate' is used to mean the holder of any judicial office, 'municipal' is used to mean relating to a sovereign state (not merely a municipality in the context of local administration).

2. Much jurisprudence is written by philosophers, or by academic lawyers who have been influenced by the ways of philosophers. So the law student enters an alien realm. He has been used to a world of practicalities, where importance is attached to reaching, where ever possible, clear cut conclusions; of using as few words as are necessary to convey the meaning intended. The law student is used to reading judgments of the higher courts that carry a meaning that is capable of being summarised in a head note; to reading articles that end with a list of the conclusions drawn from the preceding discussion. The law student is used (at any rate during term times) to working under pressure. The study of law entails pressing on, finishing one job and getting on with the next.

So the world of the philosopher comes as a surprise. Here the pressures are off. Tangents can be longer than the treatment of the main subject. Discussion can switch from one topic to another without warning. A writer can make so many digressions and deal with so many irrelevancies that he ends up forgetting what it was he had set out to talk about. The steel thread that holds together the beads that make up a good judgment is missing. Meander replaces logical sequence. The beads lie scattered.

Another thing a law student soon appreciates is that some philosophers, learning from sociologists, like where possible to use off-track words rather than ones that are immediately familiar. So 'societal' is preferred to 'social', 'instantiations' to 'instances', 'characterised' to 'described'. Similarly, single words are replaced by phrases so that, for example, 'idea' becomes 'conceptualised notion'. Added length is obtained by sprinkling adverbs such as 'uniquely', 'typically', 'meaningfully', 'contingently', and adjectives such as 'normative', 'multicentric'. Indeed, it will soon seem that for some jurists every noun should have a qualifying adjective and every verb a qualifying adverb. For example, 'response' becomes 'structured response'; 'argument', 'conceptual argument'; 'illustrates', 'typically illustrates'; 'theory', 'conceptual theory'; 'validity', 'normative validity'. Great play too, it appears, can be had by the skilful juggling of 'subjective' and 'objective'. Simple phrases can be built into longer ones. For example, 'the idea is ...' can become 'the notional concept, *qua* concept, can be meaningfully characterised as ...'; '... indicates that ...' can become '... can validly be taken as a conclusively affirmative indication that ...'; 'How would

Hart fit the common law into his idea of the law being made up of rules?' becomes 'How would the notion of common law be conceptualised within a Hartian positivist schematic view of law as a framework of normative assertions?'

It is not long before the law student realises that the aim of some writers is not clarity but obfuscation. Opaqueness is the quality to be pursued. To this end the use of double negatives can be useful. Consider the following passage from a book published in 1987. 'Just as the earlier argument against Nozick's invocation of the Kantian maxim did not show that the moral views he is advocating are compatible with consequentialism, so the argument against Nagel's interpretation of personal projects and relationships is not meant to show that he is mistaken in claiming that they are irreconcilable with an agent-neutral view of practical reason.' There are in this sentence, as a reviewer[2] pointed out, six double negatives. 'Could not the number of these be cut down?' the reviewer asked. 'It is not,' he commented, 'as if the sentence is easy to understand once the negatives are mastered. After all one has to bear in mind Nagel's interpretation and Nozick's invocation, and one may be holding judgment on whether agent-neutrality means something clear. One may also be wondering what logical force "compatible" is intended to have here.'

3.   Law students expect a subject to have a recognised content. They expect a book on contract to deal with the various elements of contract law – offer and acceptance, consideration, misrepresentation and so on. They expect a book on tort to deal with the various forms of tort, the remedies of a plaintiff and the defences of a defendant. They expect that when the relevant material has been treated in a detail appropriate to the length of the book, the book will end. They expect a full stop. That's *it.* So when the law student comes to jurisprudence it is unsettling to find that while there are certain themes that are of recurring interest, there is no standard content. This is because jurisprudence consists of whatever anyone (anyone, that is, who manages to get his ideas promulgated) chooses to say about law. In this there are very few rules. One is that if someone has said the same thing before this should be acknowledged. But there is no rule about what can be said. Here the game is wide open. One can say what one thinks law is, its essential nature, or what a legal system consists of. One can analyse such concepts as 'ownership', 'possession' or that of a legal 'personality'. One can talk about the relationship, if

2   S Guest, (1987) 103 LQR 642.

it is believed that there is one, between law and morality. One can discuss whether an individual is ever justified in disobeying the law. One can explore why some people feel an obligation to obey the law. One can examine (a rich field here) the meaning of 'obligation', of what it means to be 'obliged'. One can scrutinise the way the law works in practice – how the courts operate, how judges reach their decisions. One can seek to distinguish between law and justice, and determine what justice consists of. One can consider whether law should fulfil a social function, and if so what this should be. In discussing such matters as these it does not matter whether what is said takes a few lines or many volumes. If it is about law (not law, but *about* law) it is jurisprudence. The fact that jurisprudence is wide open leaves the law student with the feeling that he wants to get up and shut the door.

4. Law students expect topics within a law subject to have sharp edges. They expect a chapter on easements to deal with easements, not to drift off into a discussion of adverse possession, or start regurgitating what had been said earlier about the rights of riparian owners to extract water, or even wander away into an examination of the effects of mistake in contract. So it is disturbing to find that in jurisprudence the boundaries that conveniently and conventionally delimit the areas of other law topics are missing. It is, though, in the nature of jurisprudence that this should be so. Jurisprudence is about ideas and ideas do not lend themselves to being sorted into mutually exclusive pigeon holes. Anything said on one matter (for example, the nature of justice) can well have a bearing on another matter (for example, obedience to the law). A book such as this is of necessity divided into chapters dealing with various topics that jurisprudence has been concerned with. But this treatment is one of convenience and should not obscure the fact that jurisprudence is not a series of separate topics. It is a mêlée of intermingling ideas, any of which may be as relevant as any others in considering any particular question.

5. Law students similarly expect subjects on a law syllabus themselves to have sharp edges. They will recognise that there may be areas of overlap, for example between land law and trusts. But generally they expect land law to be land law, contract to be contract, tort to be tort, and so on. (Perhaps, bearing in mind the complexities of everyday life, they should not expect this, but in the light of the way law books are written, and the law commonly taught, it is not surprising if this is the expectation.) So here also it is unsettling to find that the boundaries traditionally placed around law subjects are nowhere to be seen. Jurisprudence rubs shoulders with and

shares common ground with ethics, politics, history, theology and philosophy. It is only in a small number of instances that we can say that a topic is properly regarded as being exclusively the province of jurisprudence. Time and again we find that a subject is of mutual interest to jurists and the student of politics (for example, the nature of sovereignty), or to jurists and theologians (witness the influence of the Church on the doctrine of natural law, discussed in Chapter 5), or to jurists and moral philosophers (as over the relationship of law and morality), or to jurists and the students of more than one of these disciplines. The overlap between jurisprudence and other subjects in the world of ideas the student will find reflected in the titles of the books on his reading list. Books with such titles as *Morality and the Law*, *Law and Justice* have long been commonplace. In recent times authors have taken to triplication[3] and we have books with such titles as *Law, Morality and Religion*; *Law, Morality and Society*; *Law, Liberty and Morality*; *Law, Liberty and Legislation*; *Rules, Principles and the Law*; *Justice, Law and Rights*; *Law, Reason and Justice*. (Perhaps in time we shall come to have quadrupling, *Law, Liberty, Justice and Morality*.)

The fuzziness of the scope of jurisprudence can leave a law student disturbed.

6. Law students are used to reading comment, for example comment on new legislation or on cases that break new ground. They are used also to articles that deal with a particular aspect of law, for example an article on whether a right to roam at will over certain land can be acquired by the public from long usage, an article in which the case law would be reviewed and conclusions drawn. But what comes as a surprise to a law student is to find the same matters repeatedly, and seemingly endlessly, commented on. The reason for this is that while the scope of law is so wide, and expanding so fast (witness the burgeoning of environmental law) that more new law emerges than academic lawyers have time to comment on, the content of jurisprudence is, notwithstanding that new topics do from time to time arise, relatively speaking so limited that a great deal of retilling of the same ground goes on. Everybody, it seems, has to have his go at justice, at natural law, at 'obligation', at law and morality. (There comes a tendency to yawn.)

---

3   The fashion is not confined to jurisprudence. In philosophy we have such titles as *Contingency, Irony and Solidarity*; and in History, *Conquest, Coexistence and Change*, and *Recovery, Reorientation and Reformation*.

7. In writing on law there is no need for an author to produce an idea that has never been thought of before. Thus if someone who writes on the question concerning a right to roam mentioned above confines himself to a survey of the decided cases and from these draws conclusions as to the present state of the law, this is enough. But in jurisprudence the ideal is to think of something new to say. Sometimes this happens and instances are given later in this book, for example Professor Hart's notion of a legal system and Professor Rawls's idea of the nature of justice. But original ideas do not come easily, or often. Yet those who earn a living from jurisprudence need to write, at least if they are to stand a chance of promotion. So what happens is that even if someone (A) has no original idea about, say, justice, he may have an original idea about what someone else said about justice (most likely a criticism). So A writes an article pointing out what he believes to be a flaw in the view of justice expressed by, say, Rawls. Then B comes along. He has no original idea about justice, or about Rawls's view of justice. But he does detect a weakness in what A has written. So he writes an article pointing out the flaws in what A has written. Then C comes along ...

So when the law student starts reading an article he may find himself several steps away from the ideas of the thinker whose views he is meant to be studying. For example, in preparing for a tutorial on John Stewart Mill he may read Samek's discussion of McCloskey's views of Berlin's analysis of Mill's notion of liberty;[4] or Sartorius's comments on Dworkin's reaction to Devlin's opposition to Mill's attitude to the enforcement of morality;[5] or Reynold's views about Sartorius's re-formulation of Mill's argument so that it could meet the objection raised by Devlin while avoiding the difficulties inherent in the points raised by Dworkin and Hart.[6]

Now for the participants this is all good clean fun, part of a splendid game (more than a game, an industry) but the newcomer can be left dazed and depressed. (It is no wonder that our student accepts an invitation to go for a cup of coffee.)

What can be done about it?

1. Do not be side-tracked into reading comments on (or comments on comments on) a jurist's views until those views have been understood. Start with the master. (Do not read *Reading Rawls* until Rawls has been read.)

---

4 (1971) 49 Can Bar R 188.
5 (1972) 81 Yale LJ 891.
6 (1977) 11 Georgia LR 1325.

2. Recognise the foolishness of reading any passage without understanding the meaning of every word used. Read with a dictionary available of at least the size of a good desk top version such as the *Concise Oxford Dictionary*. Where several meanings are given, look for the meaning of the word as used in philosophy, usually introduced by an abbreviation such as 'Phil'. At the end of this chapter there is a list of certain of the words that crop up in jurisprudence with definitions or explanations. (It may be found helpful to note the meaning of the words marked with an asterisk before proceeding to the next chapter.)

3. Recognise that even if words of standard usage such as induction and proscribe, and Latin terms such as *qua, per se* and *a fortiori*, and words of a more specialised kind such as ontological and heuristic are all understood, if unnecessary double negatives are cancelled out, if superfluous words are disregarded – even if all these steps are taken, recognise that from time to time passages of such confusion will be met that, however much effort is expended, no intelligible meaning can be discerned. (Indeed whole *books* may be met from which no intelligible message can be extracted.) Always bear in mind the possibility that when difficulty is experienced in understanding a passage the cause may not be the reader's lack of intelligence but the writer's inability (or absence of intention) to express himself intelligibly (or his lack of anything actually to say).

4. Do not expect jurists, having posed a question, to give an answer.

5. Do not expect jurists to expound their theories in a logical sequence. The components of a theory may have to be re-ordered to produce a coherent scheme.

6. Accept that jurists adapt their ideas during the course of their lives, perhaps to meet criticisms that have been made. This may make it difficult to say what a particular writer 'said', since he said different things at different times. (Sometimes the most interesting and striking view is that expressed at the beginning, before the writer has begun to modify and water down his theory to meet objections that have been raised. An example is the work of Hans Kelsen.[7])

7. Take heart. Among the great jurists are some who write with a clarity and precision that matches the importance of what they have to say.

---

7 Chapter 9.

Whether the reader finds the content of jurisprudence of interest will depend on his own attitude. But the issues that the subject raises have been, and remain, of great practical importance in the conduct of human affairs. The issues are not 'puzzles for the cupboard, to be taken down on rainy days for fun'.[8] They 'nag at our attention, demanding an answer'.[9]

Some words

Appetition   The direction of desire towards an object or purpose; seeking after. (OED.)

* *A priori reasoning*   The method of reasoning that proceeds by reaching conclusions from what has gone before: '... since this, it follows that ...' Eg in order to become well educated children must be encouraged to do their best. Children do best what they like doing. Children do not like learning that involves hard work. Children learn most when they are not required to work hard.

Canon   A rule, law or decree of the Church; especially a rule laid down by an ecclesiastical council. (OED.)

Canonists   Those expert in the canon law.

Christianity   Religious faith based on the teaching of Jesus of Nazareth (in what is now Israel). Members of the faith are termed Christians. The essentials of the Christian faith are as follows. God made the world and everything in it, including mankind. God laid down rules for human conduct. Breaking the rules ('sin') resulted in a person, on his death, suffering punishment in Hell. From the beginning, people did break the rules, and so went to Hell. God was disappointed at this as he loved people and would have preferred them to go, on their death, to be with him in Heaven. But he was not prepared to change the rules. If there was badness, the price had to be paid. So God was in a dilemma. He resolved the dilemma by means of a scheme that would enable people to go to Heaven notwithstanding that they had been bad. The scheme was that he should have a son, who would take human form but, being the son of God, would be without sin. The son

8   D W Dworkin *Taking Rights Seriously* (1st edn) p 14.
9   Ibid, p 15.

would die a bad death and then go back to Heaven to be with his
father again. By this means God's insistence on punishment would
be satisfied and thereafter everyone could, subject to certain
conditions (see below), go to Heaven irrespective of what kind
of life they had lived.

And so it came to pass. God's son was born in BC 4. His
mother, Mary was a virgin, inception being effected not by Mary's
husband, Joseph, but by the Holy Spirit, which is another aspect
of God. He was named Jesus. He was a man without flaw. He
was executed by crucifixion in AD 29 or 30 by the Roman
authorities in control of the country at the time. Two days later
he came alive again and was seen by several people, some of
whom recognised him. After 40 days, he returned to Heaven.

The death of Jesus by itself did not, and does not, mean that
sinners automatically go to Heaven. To do so, it is necessary for
sinners to repent of their sins; acknowledge that Jesus is the son
of God and was sent into the world to save sinners from having
to go to Hell; request God to treat Jesus's death as a substitute
for the punishment that they deserve; and acknowledge that
Jesus came alive again, and is still alive both in Heaven and in
the hearts of those who believe. For Christians God is a
composite body consisting of God himself ('God the Father'),
Jesus ('God the Son'), and the Holy Spirit, the three making up
the 'Holy Trinity'.

* *Cognitivism*   From cognition, the act of knowing. (Cf recognition.)
The view that it is possible to know the absolute truth about things,
for example as to what constitutes truth, or beauty or justice. A
cognitivist may base his cognition on a truth considered to have
been revealed by a divine source. (Cf Non-cognitivism.)

* *Contractarian*   Relating to the view that the basis of a human
society rests on a contract, actual or hypothesised, under which
the original inhabitants of a community or group agreed to
surrender some of their powers either to a sovereign or to the
community as a whole, in order to achieve the benefits of orderliness and freedom from violence. 'No culture has a specific
starting point in time; yet in the operation of the first function it
is as though men were getting together and saying to each other,
"Look here! Let's have a little organisation or we'll never get
anywhere with this mess! Let's have a clear understanding of who's
who, what we are to do, and how we are going to do it!" In its
essence [this] is what the social-contract theorists recognised as
the foundation of social order.' (E A Hoebel.)

Deduction   The process of obtaining knowledge by drawing conclusions from a pre-existing premise or principle. (The process
of deducing from something known or assumed. OED.)

Deontology   The study or science of obligations, in particular moral
obligations. So, deontological, pertaining to morality or ethics.

* *Efficacy*   Effectiveness; capacity to achieve a particular result. Used
in jurisprudence in connection with efficacy of law, referring to
the extent to which law is obeyed. If the laws of a community are
observed the law is said to be efficacious.

Eleustic   Concerned with cross-examination.

Empiricism   The view that the only source of knowledge is experience,
eg by the observation of facts in the natural world. The empiricist
does not start from general principles assumed to be valid and make
deductions from these. The scientific method of modern times is
empirical, observations being made and from these hypotheses
formed to explain the observed facts, a hypothesis being assumed
to be valid unless or until further observation shows the hypothesis
to be inadequate. Empiricism operates by *induction*. For the
empiricist, truth is provisional and, to the extent that truth can ever
be known, is that which tallies with experience.

Epistemological   Relating to knowledge, in particular relating to
theories as to how knowledge is acquired, how things can be *known*.

Erastianism   Belief in the supremacy of the state in ecclesiastical
affairs. (From Erastus, Swiss theologian and physician, 1524–
1583.)

Eristic   Relating to disputation, controversial. (OED.)

Heuretic   The branch of logic which treats the art of discovery or
invention. (OED.)

Hermeneutic Relating to interpretation (as distinct from
explanation).

Hypostasis   That which lies at the basis of anything, its essence.
(From the Greek, 'that which lies under'.)

Idealism   The notion, expounded by Plato, principally in *The
Republic*, that qualities such as truth, courage, virtue, equality,
justice, have an existence distinct from, and pre-existing, actions
or objects that have such qualities. For example, the beauty of an
object on earth is no more than a manifestation, a pale reflection,
of the ideal quality of beauty that exists independently of, and

irrespective of the existence of, any beauty that is seen on earth. The nature of idealism is explained more fully in Chapter 5.

* *Imperative theory of law*   The theory that regards law as being in the nature of a command: see Chapter 2.

Induction   The process of inferring a general principle or law from the observation of particular instances. (OED.) Modern science, being empirical (*qv*), operates by induction, not deduction (*qv*).

Innativism   The view that certain principles are innate within human consciousness, being brought into the world by men from their first being. For the believer, the principles are those that God has inscribed in men's hearts.

Intuitional   Pertaining to the view that certain knowledge is, or can be, gained by intuition, as opposed to, eg observation.

Maieutic   Pertaining to (intellectual) midwifery, ie to the Socratic process of helping to bring into full consciousness conceptions previously latent in a person's mind. (OED.)

Monism   The view that there is only one, eg that mind and matter are one, or that there is only one Supreme Being (not a duality of powers of good and evil).

*Non-cognitivism   The view that it is not possible to know the final, absolute, truth about anything. The non-cognitivist may base his non-cognitivism on the view that values, eg in the sphere of morality, are relative, varying from one society to another and from one age to another.

Nominalism, Nominalist   See 'Universals', below.

*Obligation   That which exists when a person is obliged to do, or to refrain from doing, something. See 'Ought', below.

*Ought   When the word 'ought' is used a relationship is made between a certain act and a certain standard or objective. Commonly the standard implicitly referred to when the word 'ought' is used is a moral one, as in 'I ought not to have taken the money from the collecting box by the church door.' Here the relationship is between the taking of the money and the moral precept 'Do not steal'. The word 'ought' thus relates to the achievement of an objective or compliance with some standard: in order to comply with the moral precept 'Do not steal', it is required that I do not take the money from the box. The attainment of the objective of not hurting my neighbour is achieved by refraining from hitting him over the head, expressed by saying, 'I ought not to hit him over the head'. Here the act has not occurred. If the act has already taken place we would say 'I ought not to have hit him over the head', ie if I was to have complied with the moral precept that requires me not to hurt my neighbour.

The objective referred to need not be compliance with a moral precept. If I hit my neighbour over the head and then make the statement, 'I ought to have hit him harder', the objective implicit in the statement is the infliction of greater damage than was done by the blow that was struck. The objective referred to may be the satisfaction of a particular wish or intention, as in, 'If I am going to catch the 9.47am from Hope station to Edale, I ought to leave the house *now*.' The objective may be compliance with a legal requirement, as in 'An employer ought to provide safe tools, plant and equipment' (ie if he is to comply with the common law duty of care and avoid the penalties involved in failing to do so), or with the rules of a game, as in 'He ought not to have touched the ball'. Or the objective may relate to the avoidance of a non-legal penalty, as in 'You ought not to goad him too far' (ie if you are to avoid retaliation).

Sometimes when the word 'ought' is used, the speaker expresses the standard with reference to which the word ought is used, as in the statement, 'The government ought not to allow the export of arms to Burgundia if it wishes to place humanitarian considerations above economic interests'. More commonly, the standard is left to be deduced from the context in which the word appears.

The words 'obligation' and its relative 'obliged' similarly relate to the attainment of an objective. For example, suppose that staff in a law faculty have an arrangement under which a member of staff having a cup of coffee puts 10p in a saucer. A lecturer explains. 'I knew that I was obliged to put 10p in the saucer when I had a cup of coffee, but as I had put in 20p on the previous occasion and there had been no change for me to take, I did not feel obliged to put in 10p for the next cup. However, when I heard someone approaching, and wanted to avoid being thought to cheat, I felt obliged to put in a further 10p.' In each of the three occurrences of the word, 'obliged' refers to the attainment of a different objective. In Chapter 11 of *The Concept of Law* Hart illustrates the meaning of 'obligation' and 'obliged' by the example of a gunman demanding money from a bank clerk. The bank clerk was not obliged to hand over the money (ie in order to attain the objective of complying with the law) but nevertheless was obliged to do so (ie in order to achieve the objective of not being shot).

At first sight it might seem that 'ought', 'obliged' and 'obligation' are words that are used in different senses (as in 'I ought not to have hit him', and 'I ought to have hit him harder'). But it will be appreciated from what has been said that it is the objectives or standards that are impliedly referred to when the words are used that vary, not the meaning of the words ('ought', etc) themselves.

A word that is sometimes compared and contrasted with 'obligation' is 'duty'. Duty is that which is required of a person according to some authority, the word generally being used in a manner that indicates that the person accepts the authority's entitlement to impose the duty, as in 'It is my duty under God to tell you the truth' (a moral duty); 'It is my duty under the law to do jury service' (a legal duty); 'It is my duty to my country to serve under the colours' (a patriotic duty); 'It is my duty as a soldier to report the following breach of Queen's Regulations' (a military duty).

Philosopher   As in 'the Philosopher', Aristotle.

Platonist   One who subscribes to the views of Plato, in particular with regard to his theory of idealism (*qv*). (See Chapter 5.)

*Positivism   The view that regards law as being that which is decreed, irrespective of its content, in particular irrespective of its moral goodness or badness. (See Chapter 2.)

*Predictive theory of law   The view that law consists of commands by a sovereign or other supreme authority in respect of which it can be predicted that disobedience will result in punishment. (Sometimes, incorrectly and confusingly, used to refer to the view of certain American realists (see Chapter 13) that law consists of predictions of what judges will decide when a matter comes before the courts.)

Realism   (1) The term used in philosophy to mean a belief that some kind of thing, or state of affairs, or some kind of fact, has a real existence, ie independent of ourselves and not, eg existing solely in our minds or as no more than a word in our language. (2) Carrying the everyday sense of being realistic, concerned with practicalities, looking at the actualities of a situation, for example at what actually is responsible for causing a judge to reach a particular decision.

Schoolmen   Those scholars, almost exclusively ecclesiastics, who wrote and taught theology, logic and metaphysics in the medieval schools or universities.

Stagirite, as in 'the Stagirite' Aristotle, after his place of birth, Stageira.

Substantive Having substance, an existence; as in 'substantive justice', ie as opposed to, eg merely procedural justice (which consists of no more than complying with prescribed procedural rules); and in 'The attention that philosophers pay to the question of method is often inversely related to the substantive progress being made in the field.' (Soper (1982) 100 HLR 1166, 1168.)

Syllogism An argument taking the form of two propositions (termed premises) containing a common word or term, from which a conclusion is necessarily drawn. For example,
All dogs have four legs.
Abba is a dog.
Abba has four legs.
Syllogistic reasoning is one form of *a priori* reasoning.

Teleological Pertaining to the doctrine that everything has a pre-ordained end or purpose. (See Chapter 3.)

Thomism Views that accord with those of St Thomas Aquinas. (See Chapter 5.) Hence, Thomist, one who subscribes to those views.

Universals In Bradwell there lives a dog called Abba. Up the road there is a dog called William. On the other side of the village live Kim, Suzy, Rosie and Poppy. In Schmitten, in Germany, there lives Sophie. What makes all these entities *dogs*? The answer, surely, is that there is a quality of dogness that they all share. Similarly in the case of tables. There must be a quality of tableness (that of being a manufactured artefact consisting of a raised flat surface designed for putting things on) that all tables share. Similarly there must be a quality of beauty, a quality of which all beautiful things partake. Dogness, tableness and beauty are each an example of a 'universal' – a universal quality. Some philosophers have considered that universals have an existence distinct from that of the particular items that share the quality that constitutes the universal. One who subscribes to this view is in this respect a 'realist'. (See, 'realism', supra.) St Thomas Aquinas was a leading medieval realist in the sense of believing in the actuality of universals.

Those who consider that universals have no separate existence, that only the individual instances of a category have any real existence, a universal being no more than a name attached for convenience to instances of a class, are termed 'nominalists'. Nominalism gained ground during the later middle ages, a leading proponent being William of Ockham.

Utilitarianism[10]   The term stems from the word utility, meaning use or usefulness. Utilitarianism is a theory that lies principally in the field of ethics. At the core of utilitarianism lies the view that the proper end of a society is the attainment of what is sometimes expressed as 'the greatest good of the greatest number' of its inhabitants. Inherent in, and pre-supposed in, this notion is the view that a society should *have* an object. For the jurist the interest of utilitarianism arises from the fact that it is by its laws that a society to a large degree attains its objectives.

The leading proponent of utilitarianism was Jeremy Bentham (1748–1832). For Bentham the 'good' to be attained was to be measured in material (not spiritual or moral) terms. (It is for this reason that 'utilitarianism' is sometimes used, inaccurately and unfairly, in a denigratory sense to mean materialist, failing to pay due attention to spiritual, ethical or moral values; as, for example, in a reference to 'those who are guided by purely utilitarian considerations'.)

In seeking to show how the greatest good of the greatest number was in practice to be achieved Bentham examined a wide range of British institutions and conventions and proposed far-reaching reforms.

Utilitarianism is treated in Chapter 13.

10   See Davies and Holdcroft *Jurisprudence: Texts and Commentary* Chap 7.

CHAPTER 2

Teeth that can bite

John Austin[1]

'The legal, let it be repeated, has teeth that can bite.'

E A Hoebel

Since jurisprudence is the study of the nature of law, it might be thought that a question early to occur in men's minds was – what *is* law? Yet it was not until relatively recent times that this question received attention.

What answer would the reader give to the question? The chances are that he has never considered the question. Law is law. It exists. The question no more requires attention than the question, What is weather? or, What is a wheel? Yet the question 'What is law?' differs from these two questions in that in seeking to define the nature of law we are seeking to define an abstraction. Law may be manifested in physical objects or in physical deeds (a statute or the act of a policeman in arresting an offender). But law, being an abstract term, cannot, like a wheel, be defined in terms of its physical characteristics. How, then, would the reader define the term law? Someone who has studied law for two years will know a law when he sees one but he may nonetheless be hard put to it to describe law's essential nature. By the end of this book, when the views of a number of people on this matter have been considered, the reader may find himself in a position to decide whose views seem to him to come closest to providing the answer to this, and to certain other questions, the discussion of which forms the central theme of jurisprudence.

---

1 Davies and Holdcroft *Jurisprudence: Texts and Commentary* Chap 2; J W Harris *Legal Philosophies* (2nd edn, 1997) Chap 3; W L Morrison *John Austin*.

There is no logical, or conventional, starting point for a study of jurisprudence. Here we will begin with the views of one writer, John Austin who made the question 'What is law?' a focus of his attention.

Austin was born in 1790, the son of a flour miller in Ipswich. After serving in the army for five years he resigned his commission and spent seven years in study. He was called to the Bar in 1818 and was appointed to the Chair of Jurisprudence at London University in 1825. *The Province of Jurisprudence Determined* was published in 1832. His lectures were not well attended and he resigned in 1835 and devoted himself to further writing. After another unsuccessful period of teaching, at the Inner Temple, his health declined. His death in 1859 was little noted. The importance in his ideas was recognised by Sir Henry Maine, the Cambridge legal historian, and by the last quarter of the nineteenth century Austin's views were established as a dominant force in English legal thinking.

Austin's analysis of law

Before giving his definition of law, Austin identifies what kind of law it is he is seeking to define. There are, he says, various kinds of law in the broadest sense; for example God's laws, and the laws of science. (Austin's analysis is set out diagrammatically on p 29.) At the head of the tree comes a 'signification of desire' (a desire, for example, that someone should not travel faster than a certain speed). Significations of desire are of two kinds: a request (or admonition) in which the person signifying the desire has no power to inflict evil on the person to whom the desire is expressed in the event of the desire not being satisfied; and a command, in which a power does exist 'to inflict evil or pain in case the desire be disregarded'.[2] The 'evil which will probably be incurred in case a command be disobeyed ... is frequently called a sanction or an enforcement of obedience. Or ... the command ... is said to be sanctioned or enforced by the chance of incurring the evil.'

Commands are of two kinds. Where a command 'obliges generally to acts or forbearances of a class, a command is a law ..., but where it obliges to a specific act or forbearance, ... a command is occasional or particular ...'. Thus commands are either general, or particular.

---

2   All quotations from Austin in this chapter are from *The Province of Jurisprudence Determined*.

A command of the former kind is a law, a command of the latter kind is (although Austin does not use the term) an order.

Laws are of two kinds: laws 'properly so called' and 'laws not properly so called'. Every law 'properly so called' consists of 'a rule laid down for the guidance of an intelligent being by an intelligent being having power over him'.

Laws not properly so called are of two kinds: 'Laws by analogy' and 'Laws by metaphor'. Under 'Laws by analogy' Austin places such matters as the dictates of fashion, of honour, the 'laws or rules imposed upon gentlemen by opinions current amongst gentlemen' and also international law. These are 'rules set and enforced by mere opinion'. These matters, it will be noted, are 'laws' in that they are a species of command. The rule that a man should take his hat off in church is a command in that a person who disregards the law suffers the evil of the opprobrium felt towards him by his fellows. A state which, being a party to an international law, breaks that law suffers the disapproval of those states that uphold it. (A sanction will not be prevented from being a sanction because it is 'feeble or insufficient'.) By 'Laws by metaphor' Austin refers to 'laws regulating the growth or decay observed by lower animals; … laws regulating the growth or decay of vegetables; … laws determining the movements of inanimate bodies or masses'. Such laws do not fit happily into Austin's scheme as it is not easy to envisage such a law as being a species of command, or to imagine such laws being 'broken'. But Austin must have felt that the laws of science should have a place in his scheme and, perhaps for want of anywhere better, placed them under the head of 'laws not properly so called'.

'Laws properly so called' – rules laid down for the guidance of an intelligent being by an intelligent being having power over him – are of two kinds. 'Laws set by God to human creatures and laws set by men to men' – God's laws, and human laws. Human laws are of two kinds, laws 'strictly so called' and laws 'not strictly so called'.

Laws 'not strictly so called' comprise laws 'set by men not as political superiors'. These are not the commands of a sovereign and are not supported by legal sanctions administered by the state. Austin cites as examples the rules made by a parent for his children, or by a master for his servant. It is under this head that Austin places constitutional law, principally, it seems, because he did not consider constitutional law as being enforceable by sanctions imposed by a sovereign.

Law 'strictly so called' comprises law as the word is most commonly understood today. It consists of (a) laws set by men as political superiors to political inferiors; and (b) laws set by men as private individuals in pursuance of legal rights. Included within (a) are laws set by subjects as subordinate political superiors. These are 'set by sovereigns or states in the character of political superiors, although they are set by sovereigns circuitously or remotely. ... They are made through legal rights granted by sovereigns or states and held by ... subject authors as mere trustees for the grantors'. It would seem that delegated legislation, such as local authority bye-laws, should be placed in this category. Regarding (b), laws set by men as private individuals in pursuance of legal rights, Austin cites as an example a rule made by a guardian in pursuance of a legal duty imposed on him, for his ward.

Austin's analysis is complicated by the fact that in addition to the classification we have described, he proposes a second form of classification which cuts across the first. This second classification consists of the division into two groups (1) 'positive law', by which Austin refers to 'laws strictly so called'; and (2) 'positive morality'. Under this second head he places (a) laws not strictly so called (ie laws set by men not as political superiors) and (b) laws by analogy (eg the dictates of fashion, rules of honour, of 'the behaviour of gentlemen'). The laws under the second head differ from those under the first in that they are not set by men as political superiors to political inferiors, nor by men in pursuance of legal rights. By 'moral' in the term 'positive morality' Austin indicates what we would today understand as 'social'. Laws under the head of positive morality are positive in that they are set in place by men. But since they are not enforced by the sovereign, they are not laws strictly so called. The distinction he draws between positive law and positive morality is thus that between laws enforced by the state and laws (ie including customs, conventions) enforced by other pressures.

The analysis of laws into 'positive law' and 'positive morality' is incidental to Austin's main scheme. What matters is Austin's concept of 'laws strictly so called' – *these* are 'The Province of Jurisprudence ...'

Austin's concept of law

Having distinguished 'law strictly so called' from all other types of law, or rule, or command, Austin is in a position to give us his definition of what this law is. For Austin 'law strictly so called' consists of a command given by a sovereign enforced by a sanction. The definition would seem to work. The state decrees that no driver should exceed 70 mph on a motorway, subject to a maximum fine of a specified amount. A sovereign power, the state, has given a command, and enforced it by a sanction.

Sovereignty

To amplify his definition Austin goes on to examine the nature of sovereignty.[3] Sovereignty exists, Austin says, where the bulk of a given political society are in the habit of obedience to a determinate common superior, and that common superior is not habitually obedient to a determinate human superior. He amplifies certain aspects of this concept.

(1) The common superior must be 'determinate'. A body of persons is 'determinate' if ' *all* the persons who compose it are determined and assignable'. Determinate bodies are of two kinds. (a) In one kind the 'body is composed of persons determined specifically or individually, or determined by characters or descriptions respectively appropriate to themselves'. (In this category would be placed a sovereign such as 'the King'.) (b) In the other kind the body 'comprises *all* the persons who belong to a given class. ... In other words, *every* person who answers to a given generic description ... is ... a member of the determinate body.' (In this category could be placed a sovereign such as a supreme legislative assembly.)

(2) The society must be in 'the habit of obedience'. If obedience 'be rare or transient and not habitual or permanent' the relationship of sovereignty and subjection is not created and no sovereign exists. (But isolated acts of disobedience will not preclude the existence of sovereignty.)

(3) '... habitual obedience must be rendered by the generality or bulk of the members of a society to ... one and the same determinate person, or determinate body of persons.' ('For example: in case a given society be torn by intestine war, and in case the conflicting parties be nearly balanced, the given society is in one of two positions. If the bulk of each of the parties be in a habit of obedience to its head, the given society is broken into two or more societies. If the bulk of each of the parties be not in that habit of obedience, the given society is simply or absolutely in a state of nature or anarchy. It is either resolved into its individual elements, or into numerous societies of

3 For examinations of the nature of sovereignty, see W J Rees *The Theory of Sovereignty Restated*, in *Philosophy, Politics and Society* ed Laslett (1956); R V F Heuston *Sovereignty* in *Oxford Essays in Jurisprudence* ed Guest (1961); D Lloyd *The Idea of Law* pp 177–193.

an extremely limited size: of a size so extremely limited, that they could hardly be styled societies independent and political.')

(4) In order that a given society may form a political society, 'the generality or bulk of its members must habitually obey a superior determinate as well as common ... For ... no indeterminate body is capable of corporate conduct, or is capable, as a body, of positive or negative deportment.'

(5) The common determinate superior to whom the bulk of the society renders habitual obedience must not himself be habitually obedient to a determinate human superior. 'He may render occasional submission to commands of determinate parties. But the society is not independent ... [if] that certain superior habitually obeys the commands of a certain person or body ... Let us suppose, for example, that a viceroy obeys habitually the author of his delegated powers. And, to render the example complete, let us suppose that the viceroy receives habitual obedience from the generality or bulk of the persons who inhabit his province. The viceroy is not sovereign within the limits of his province, nor are he and its inhabitants an independent political society. The viceroy, and (through the viceroy) the generality or bulk of its inhabitants, are habitually obedient or submissive to the sovereign of a larger society. He and the inhabitants of his province are therefore in a state of subjection to the sovereign of that larger society. He and the inhabitants of his province are a society political but subordinate ...'

(6) The power of the sovereign is incapable of legal limitation. 'Supreme power limited by positive law is a flat contradiction in terms.' But what of the position of a sovereign in relation to a society's constitution? May a body be sovereign yet subject to the constitutional law? Austin answers, no. A sovereign is subject to no legal limitation. He explains that: '... when we style an act of a sovereign an unconstitutional act ... we mean, I believe, this: That the act is inconsistent with some given principle or maxim; that the given supreme government has expressly adopted the principle, or, at least, has habitually observed it: that the bulk of the given society, or the bulk of its influential members, regard the principle with approbation: and that, since the supreme government has habitually observed the principle, and since the bulk of the society regard it with approbation, the act in question must thwart the expectations of the latter, and must shock their opinions and sentiments ... The epithet unconstitutional as applied to conduct of a sovereign, and as used with the meaning which is more special and definite, imports that the conduct in question conflicts with constitutional law.'

Having described the characterists of sovereignty Austin seeks the locus of sovereignty within the British constitution. After analysing the powers of the Crown, the peers, the Commons, and the electorate he concludes, 'Adopting the language of most of the writers who have treated of the British Constitution, I commonly suppose that the king and the lords, with the members of the commons' house, form a tripartite body which is sovereign or supreme. But, speaking accurately, the members of the commons' house are merely trustees for the body by which they are elected and appointed: and, consequently, the sovereignty always resides in the king and the peers, with the electoral body of the commons.'

With regard to sovereignty in a federal form of government Austin says that, 'the several united governments of the several united societies, together with a government common to those several societies, are jointly sovereign in each of those several societies, and also in the large society arising from the federal union.'

Civil law within Austin's scheme

At this point we may revert to a point concerning Austin's classification of laws strictly so called into: (a) laws set by men as political superiors to men as political inferiors; and, (b) laws set by men to men in pursuance of legal rights. Under the latter head Austin placed civil laws such as in the law of contract, of tort, and property. In the case of these branches of law the sanction took the form of an obligation in the shape of an order of the court, eg to pay damages or to restore property, coupled with the sanction of imprisonment if the obligation was disregarded.

A difficulty concerns the sanction for a law which requires the observance of a certain formality for a transaction to be valid; for example, the requirement of the Wills Act 1832 that a will must be signed by the testator and attested by two witnesses. There is no requirement that this formality must, on pain of imprisonment, be complied with. At most, the state decrees that if the provision is not complied with the transaction is void. But is nullity a sanction? Austin considered that it was.[4] He said, 'Laws are sometimes sanctioned by nullities. The legislature annexes rights to certain transactions; for example, to contracts, on condition that these transactions are accompanied by certain circumstances. If the condition be not

---

4 See C F H Tapper 'Austin on Sanctions' (1965) CLJ 271.

observed, the transaction is void, that is, no right arises, or the transaction is voidable, that is, a right arises, but the transaction is liable to be rescinded and the right annulled. Whether the transaction is void or voidable, the sanction may be applied either directly or indirectly. The transaction may either be rescinded on an application made to that effect, or the nullity may be opposed to a demand founded on the transaction.'

The 'command' theory of law

Let us now summarise Austin's concept of law. Law is a command, given by a determinate common superior to whom the bulk of a society is in the habit of obedience and who is not in the habit of obedience to a determinate human superior, enforced by a sanction. It is the element of command that is crucial to Austin's thinking, and the concept of law expressed by Austin is sometimes described as the 'command theory' (or the 'imperative theory') of law.

Austin was not the first to expound the command theory of law. In many of his ideas Austin followed those of Jeremy Bentham. For example, in *A Fragment on Government,* written in 1776, Bentham had said, 'When a number of persons (whom we may style subjects) are supposed to be in the habit of paying obedience to a person, or an assemblage of persons, of a known and certain description (whom we may call governor or governors) such persons altogether (subjects and governors) are said to be in a state of political society. …' And in *Of Laws in General*[5] he said, 'A law may be defined as an assemblage of signs declarative of a volition conceived or adopted by the sovereign in a state, concerning the conduct to be observed in a certain case by a certain person or class of persons, who in the case in question are or are supposed to be subject to his power: such volition trusting for its accomplishment to the expectation of certain events which it is intended such declaration should upon occasion be a means of bringing to pass, and the prospect of which it is intended should act as a motive upon those whose conduct is in question.'

Bentham's thinking is in respects more penetrating than that of Austin. Austin placed constitutional law under the heading of 'law strictly so called'. Bentham, recognising that such should be considered part of the general body of the law, seeks to reconcile

5   Ed H L A Hart (1970) p l.

the existence of a sovereign, who is subject to no law, with law to which the sovereign is subject. He says 'There yet remain a class of laws which stand upon a very different footing from any of those that have hitherto been brought to view. The laws of which we have hitherto been speaking have for their passible subjects, not the sovereign himself, but those who are considered as being in subjection to his power. But there are laws to which no other persons in quality of passible subjects can be assigned than the sovereign himself. The business of ordinary sort of laws is to prescribe to the people what they shall do: the business of this transcendent class of laws is to prescribe to the sovereign what he shall do: what mandates he may or may not address to them; and in general how he shall or may conduct himself towards them. ... It appears then that there are two distinct sorts of laws, very different from each other in their nature and effect: both originating indeed from the sovereign, (from whom mediately or immediately all ordinances in order to be legal must issue) but addressed to parties of different descriptions: the one addressed to the sovereign, imposing an obligation on the sovereign: the other addressed to the people, imposing an obligation on the people. ... Here it may naturally enough be asked what sense there is in a man's addressing a law to himself, and how it is a man can impose an obligation upon himself. ... But take into account an exterior force, and by the help of such a force it is as easy for a sovereign to bind himself as to bind another.' As to the nature of the exterior force, Bentham suggested that this might take the form of a 'religious sanction', or a 'moral sanction' exerted by the subjects of the state in question, or by foreign states.

The command theory had antecedents earlier than Bentham. Hobbes,[6] in *Leviathan* (published in 1651) wrote, 'Civill law [as opposed to international law] is to every Subject, those Rules, which the Common-wealth has Commanded him, by Word, Writing or other sufficient Sign of the Will, to make use of, for the Distinction of Right, and Wrong. That is to say, of what is contrary, and what is not contrary to the Rule. ... The Legislator in all Common-wealths, is only the Soveraign, be he one Man, as in a Monarchy, or one Assembly of men, as in a Democracy or Aristocracy. For the Legislator, is he that maketh the Law. And the Common-wealth only, praescribes, and commandeth the observation of those rules, which we call Law: Therefore the Common-wealth is the Legislator. But the Common-wealth is no Person, nor has capacity to doe any thing, but by the Representative, (that is, the Soveraign;) and therefore

6 Thomas Hobbes, 1588–1679.

the Soveraign is the sole Legislator. … The Soveraign of a Common-wealth, be it an Assembly, or one Man, is not Subject to the Civill Lawes. For having power to make, and repeale Lawes, he may when he pleaseth, free himselfe from that subjection, by repealing those Lawes that trouble him, and making of new; and consequently he was free before. For he is free, that can be free when he will: Nor is it possible for any person to be bound to himselfe; because he that he can bind, can release; and therefore he that is bound to himselfe onely, is not bound …'.

And before Hobbes, Bodin (in *Six Books of the Republic* (published in 1576)) had written, '… it is the distinguishing mark of the sovereign that he cannot in any way be subject to the commands of another, for it is he who makes law for the subject, abrogates law already made, and amends obsolete law. No one who is subject either to the law or to some other person can do this. That is why it is laid down in the civil law that the prince is above the law, for the word law in Latin implies the command of him who is invested with sovereign power … If the prince is not bound by the laws of his predecessors, still less can he be bound by his own laws. One may be subject to laws made by another, but it is impossible to bind oneself in any matter which is the subject of one's own free exercise of will … It follows of necessity that the king cannot be subject to his own laws.'[7]

The imperative theory of law, together with the notion of sovereignty and the illimitable nature of a sovereign's power can thus be traced back into the writings of the sixteenth and seventeenth centuries. But while Austin was not the first to put forward all the elements which made up his concept of law, and while Bentham's thinking on the imperative theory of law was in many respects more penetrating than that of Austin, it is nevertheless Austin who is generally credited with the first full formulation of the theory: it was Austin who both drew the elements together and presented them as a coherent whole, and who gave the theory a central place in his conception of law.

Positivism

We say 'a' central place, because there is another concept that shares with the command theory the central ground of Austin's thinking,

---

7   Translated M J Tooley, p 28.

the concept of 'positivism'. To understand the nature of positivism it is necessary to anticipate a subject that will be considered in more detail in a later chapter; the subject of natural law.

Since early Christian times it had been widely considered that a relationship existed between the validity of a law and its moral content. For example, in the middle ages the view took the form of a belief that if a man-made law conflicted with the law of God (as propounded by the Church) then the law was not a valid law. The doctrine that a man-made law is valid only if it does not conflict with a higher law – religious or secular – constitutes a key element of the doctrine of natural law. This notion Austin rejects. For Austin a law is a valid law if it is set by a sovereign. It is a valid law if it exists, regardless of its moral content. If it is commanded by the sovereign, if the law is decreed, placed in position, *posited*, then it is valid law. '... [E]very law properly so called is a positive law. For it is put or set by its individual or collective author, or it exists by the position or institution of its individual or collective author ... [T]he aggregate of the rules, established by political superiors, may ... be marked commodiously with the name positive law.' Hence the term 'positivist' is used to describe one who regards a law as being valid not by reference to some higher law or moral code, but by reason of no more than its existence. 'The existence of law is one thing', Austin says, 'its merit or demerit is another. Whether it be or be not [ie whether law exists or does not exist] is one enquiry; whether it be or be not conformible to an assumed standard, is a different enquiry.' Austin does not deny that it is possible for this 'different enquiry' to be carried out. ('When we say that a human law is good or bad, or is what it ought to be or what it ought not to be, we mean (unless we intimate our mere liking or aversion) that the law agrees with or differs from something to which we tacitly refer it as to a measure or test.') But his thrust is to distinguish between the question of what the law *ought* to be (and in this he has no objection to reference being made to a higher law) and the determination of what the law *is*. 'Is' and 'ought' must be kept separate. For Austin the fact that the law, according to some higher principle, is not what it ought to be is no reason for saying that it is not.[8]

The reason for the confusion of posited law and a higher law, the blurring of the distinction of what ought to be and what is, Austin explains, is that 'In consequence of the frequent coincidence of positive law and morality, and of positive law and the law of God, the true nature and fountain of positive law is often absurdly

8 See S E Stumpff (1960–61) 14 Vand LR 117.

mistaken by writers upon jurisprudence. Where positive law has been fashioned on positive morality, or where positive law has been fashioned on the law of God, they forget that the copy is the creature of the sovereign, and impute it to the author of the model.'

The need to distinguish between what something ought to be and what it is had been anticipated by David Hume. In *A Treatise of Human Nature* he wrote, 'I cannot forbear adding to these reasonings an observation, which may, perhaps, be found of some importance. In every system of morality, which I have hitherto met with, I have always remark'd, that the author proceeds for some time in the ordinary way of reasoning, and establishes the being of a God, or makes observations concerning human affairs; when of a sudden I am surpriz'd to find, that instead of the usual copulations of propositions, is and is not, I meet with no proposition that is not connected with an ought, or an ought not. This change is imperceptible; but is, however, of the last[9] consequence. For as this ought, or ought not, expresses some new relation or affirmation, 'tis necessary that it shou'd be observ'd and explain'd; and at the same time that a reason should be given, for what seems altogether inconceivable, how this new relation can be a deduction from others, which are entirely different from it. But as authors do not commonly use this precaution, I shall presume to recommend it to the readers; and am persuaded, that this small attention wou'd subvert all the vulgar systems of morality, and let us see, that the distinction of vice and virtue is not founded merely on the relations of objects, nor is perceiv'd by reason ...'

Austin postulated both the theory of positivism and the command theory. But it should not be thought that adherence to the former view necessarily entails adherence also to the latter. One may, like Professor H L A Hart, whose views are considered later,[10] be a positivist while not accepting the command theory as satisfactorily representing the nature of law.

---

9   In the sense of final, conclusive, utmost (OED).
10   Chapters 3 and 4.

Austin's analysis of laws

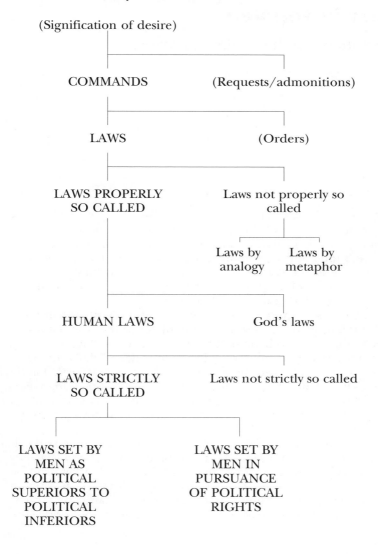

CHAPTER 3

Austin toppled
The attack on the command theory[1]

The Concept of Law by H L A Hart was published in 1961.[2] The book presented a new and illuminating view of law and dealt with a number of other jurisprudential topics, including the nature of justice, moral and legal obligation, and natural law. In the next chapter we shall consider the central theme of the book, Professor Hart's concept of law, a concept that, we shall see, extended to a new concept of what makes up a legal system.

Since it is his purpose to provide us with a positivist view that will stand in place of Austin's notion of law as the command of a sovereign, the early chapters of the book are devoted to explaining the shortcomings of this thesis. In order to demolish Austin, Hart begins by presenting Austin's theory in the strongest form that he can (as if, in order to prove the power of his armour-piercing shells, he first constructs a tank with the heaviest plating a tank can carry). This reinforcement of the command theory is undertaken in the second chapter of *The Concept of Law*.

The command (or *imperative*) theory of law (or, because it can be predicted that failure to observe a command will be followed by the imposition of a sanction, the *predictive* theory of law) can be represented at its simplest, Hart says, by a situation in which a command is given by a gunman to a bank clerk to hand over money. What elements must be added to this idea in order to produce the

---

1 J H Harris *Legal Philosophies* Chap 9; Davies and Holdcroft *Jurisprudence: Text and Commentary* Chap 3.
2 N MacCormick *H L A Hart* (1981); R N Miles *Definition and rule in legal theory: a re-assessment of H L A Hart and the positivist tradition* (1987); *Issues in contemporary legal philosophy: the influence of H L A Hart* ed R Gavison (1987).

predictive theory at its strongest? They are as follows: (i) the person giving the order must be internally supreme; (ii) the person giving the order must be externally independent; (iii) the orders must relate to a general type of conduct; (iv) the orders must be addressed to a group; (v) the orders must be of a standing nature (ie and not applying on only a single occasion); (vi) the orders must be generally obeyed; and (vii) there must be a general belief that the sanctions enforcing the orders are likely to be implemented in the event of disobedience.

The demolition of the command theory

The demolition of Austin is carried out in Chapters 3 and 4 of *The Concept of Law*. Hart's criticisms fall under three main heads.

1 Laws as we know them are not like orders backed by threats

There are three reasons why this is so.

(a) The content of law is not like a series of orders backed by a threat. Some laws, Hart concedes, do resemble orders backed by threats, for example criminal laws. But there are many types of law that do not resemble orders backed by threats, for example laws that prescribe the way in which valid contracts, wills or marriages are made do not compel people to behave in a certain way (as do laws that, for example, require the wearing of seat belts in a car). The function of such laws is different. They 'provide individuals with facilities for realising their wishes by conferring legal powers upon them to create, by certain specified procedures and subject to certain conditions, structures of rights and duties ...'[3] Again, laws of a public nature, in the field of constitutional and administrative law, and in the field of procedure, jurisdiction and the judicial process, are not comparable with orders backed by threats. Such laws are better regarded as power-conferring rules.

So, notwithstanding that '... the itch for uniformity in jurisprudence is strong' (and '... is ... by no means disreputable'),[4] the fact is that there is no head under which it is possible to bring

3 H L A Hart *The Concept of Law* p 27.
4 Ibid, p 32.

laws such as criminal laws (which do resemble orders backed by threats) and power-conferring rules (which do not).

If someone is going to contend that all laws are like orders backed by threats then they have got, Hart says, to argue that nullity (eg nullity resulting from failure to comply with the Wills Act) is a sanction. Hart confutes the notion. Nullity may well *not* be an 'evil' to the person who has failed to comply with some requirement (for example, as where a child who finds that a contract he has purported to enter into is not enforceable against him). And where a measure fails to become law because it is not passed by the requisite majority, this failure cannot meaningfully be thought of as a sanction.

(b)   The range of application of law is not the same as the range of application of an order backed by a threat. In Austin's scheme the law-maker is not himself bound by the command he gives: the order is directed to others, not to himself. It is true, Hart concedes, that in some systems of government this is what may occur. But in many systems of law legislation has a force that is binding on the body that makes it. So as a law-maker can be bound by his own law, the Austinian concept of sovereign – command – obedience – sanction cannot be of universal application and so fails. A supporter of Austin may attempt to overcome this objection by seeking to distinguish between the law-maker in his official capacity and the law-maker in his private capacity: in the first capacity he makes laws; in the second he, along with all the other citizens, is bound by them. Hart dismisses this view of the law-making process as failing to represent what actually occurs. What the legislator does, he says, is to exercise powers conferred by rules, within the ambit of which he himself may often fall. (As Hart's demolition of Austin proceeds, we note that it is Austin's failure to recognise the importance of rules that is a key weakness. This deficiency is one that Hart, in his own scheme, will make good.)

(c)   The mode of origin of law is different from the mode of origin of an order backed by a threat. An order backed by a threat originates from a deliberate act performed at a specific time. But not all laws can be said to have their origin in a deliberate datable act. For example those customs that are recognised as law within a particular society do not stem from any deliberate datable act.

Hart recognises the existence of an argument in support of the contention that custom does so originate; namely that a custom becomes law when it is recognised as representing the law and is enforced by a court: the sovereign, through the court, orders that the custom should have the force of law. Hart deals with this point saying that customs do not necessarily attain legal status only by application by a court. Just as a statute has legal force before it is (and irrespective of whether it ever is) applied by a court, so a custom can be accepted as having legal force before it is applied by a court. Thus a custom with legal force does not necessarily originate from a datable act.

Dealing further with the question of how custom attains legal status, Hart acknowledges that those who support the command theory of law could argue that custom acquires legal force as a result of a *tacit* order by the sovereign to his judges that a certain custom should henceforth be treated as law, and to his subjects to obey a judge's decision reached on the basis of a pre-existing custom. He illustrates the matter thus. 'A sergeant who himself regularly obeys his superiors, orders his men to do certain fatigues and punishes them when they disobey. The general, learning of this, allows things to go on, though if he had ordered the sergeant to stop the fatigues he would have been obeyed. In these circumstances the general may be considered tacitly to have expressed his will that the men should do the fatigues. His non-interference, when he could have interfered, is a silent substitute for the words he might have used in ordering the fatigues.'[5] So equally, when a sovereign learns that a custom is being enforced as law and does not intervene, then at that moment he tacitly orders that the custom should have the force of law. So the custom becomes law by a deliberate datable act – the decision not to interfere. So – if this is accepted – the way in which custom becomes law can be accommodated within the command theory. Hart will have none of this. The fault in the argument, he explains, lies in the fact that in any modern state it is in practice rarely possible to say at what point in time a sovereign, whether a supreme legislature or the electorate, learns of the application of a custom as law and decides not to interfere. So the tacit approval theory fails. Thus, since custom cannot be shown to become law by a deliberate datable act, and since the command theory requires the giving of a command, which can only be a deliberate datable act, the command theory, for this reason as well as those set out earlier, falls down.

2 The notion of the habit of obedience is deficient

To explain the ways in which he finds the notion of the habit of obedience to be deficient Hart tells a story. Suppose, he says, there is a country in which an absolute monarch has ruled for a long time.

5 Ibid, p 45.

The population has generally obeyed the orders of the king, Rex, and are likely to continue to do so. Rex dies leaving a son, Rex II. There is no knowing, on Rex II's accession, whether the people will obey the orders he begins to give when he succeeds to the throne. Only after we find that Rex II's orders have been obeyed for some time can we say that the people are in a habit of obedience to him. During the intervening time, since there is no sovereign to whom the bulk of society are in the habit of obedience, there can, according to Austin's definition, be no law. Only when we can see that the habit of obedience has become established can we say that an order by Rex II is a law. Yet, in practice, if Rex II was Rex I's legal successor we would regard Rex II's orders as laws from the start. So the notion of the habit of obedience fails to account for what our experience tells us in fact happens: it fails to account for the continuity to be seen in every normal legal system, when one ruler succeeds another. What is in fact found in any legal system is the existence of rules which secure the uninterrupted transition of power from one law-maker to the next. These rules 'regulate the succession *in advance*, naming or specifying in general terms the qualifications of and mode of determining the law-giver. In a modern democracy the qualifications are highly complex and relate to the composition of a legislature with a frequently changing membership, but the essence of the rules required for continuity can be seen in the simpler forms appropriate to our imaginary monarchy. If the rule provides for the succession of the eldest son, then Rex II has a *title* to succeed his father. He will have the *right* to make law on his father's death, and when his first orders are issued we may have good reason for saying that they are already law, before any relationship of habitual obedience between him personally and his subjects has had time to establish itself. Indeed such a relationship may never be established. Yet his word may be law; for Rex II may himself die immediately after issuing his first orders; he will not have lived to receive obedience, yet he may have had the *right* to make law and his orders may be law.

'In explaining the continuity of law-making power through a changing succession of individual legislators, it is natural to use the expressions "rule of succession", "title", "right to succeed", and "right to make law". It is plain, however, that with these expressions we have introduced a new set of elements, of which no account can be given in terms of habits of obedience to general orders.'[6] So in this further respect the command theory is proved to be inadequate.

6   Ibid, p 53.

Not only does the habit of obedience fail to account for the continuity of law when Rex II succeeds Rex I, it fails to account for the persistence of the legal force of Rex I's orders after his death. Yet, unless and until Rex II countermands an order by Rex I, the orders of Rex I will, we know from what happens, continue to be regarded as law. If it is contended that the persistence of the legal force of Rex I's orders is to be accounted for by Rex II having, on his accession, tacitly ordered that Rex I's orders should continue to be law, then the same objections to this notion can be made here as were made when the notion was sought to be used earlier to deal with the question as to how customs acquire legal force.

The answer to the problem of why Rex I's orders are still law after his death is, Hart says, in principle the same as the answer to the earlier problem, Why are Rex II's orders law before the populace have acquired the habit of obedience? The answer to both problems 'involves the substitution, for the too simple notion of habits of obedience to a sovereign person, of the notion of currently accepted fundamental rules specifying a class or line of persons whose word is to constitute a standard of behaviour for the society, ie who have the *right* to legislate. Such a rule, though it must exist now, may in a sense be timeless in its reference: it may not only look forward and refer to the legislative operation of a future legislator but it may also look back and refer to the operations of a past one.'[7] So here again the command theory fails to explain what we know happens in any actual legal system.

3 Austin's notion of sovereignty is deficient

In Austin's theory of law, while there may be political limits on a sovereign's power (eg regard for popular opinion), there can be no legal limits on a sovereign's powers, since, if he is sovereign, he does not obey any other legislator. Thus, according to Austin, if law exists within a state, there must exist a sovereign with unlimited power. But when we examine states in which no one would deny that law exists we find supreme legislatures the powers of which are far from unlimited. For example, the competence of a legislature may be limited by a written constitution under which certain matters are excluded from the scope of its competence to legislate upon. Yet no one would suggest that a legislative act by such a legislature did not create valid law. We cannot say that such restrictions are merely conventions or have merely moral force. If the restrictions are

7 Ibid, p 61.

overstepped the law purported to have been made will be declared invalid by the courts. So the restrictions have legal force. Thus '... the conception of the legally unlimited sovereign misrepresents the character of law in many modern states'.[8] To understand the true nature of a legal system and how law comes into existence we need to think in terms, not of a sovereign with unlimited powers, but in terms of rules, rules that confer authority on a legislature to legislate, rules used by the courts 'as a criterion of the validity of purported legislative enactments coming before them':[9] to show that a law is valid '... we have to show that it was made by a legislator who was qualified to legislate under an existing rule'.[10]

If, in the face of this argument, someone still clings to Austin's view of law as the command of a sovereign it is necessary for them to show that even if, as they may concede, the powers of the supreme legislator may be limited, a sovereign does nevertheless exist, a sovereign 'behind the legislature', a sovereign who (or which) makes the rules which determine the legislature's competence. If such a sovereign can be found one hole in the bottom of Austin's bucket is plugged.

Those who seek such a sovereign may contend that ultimate sovereignty rests with the electorate. But if it is in the electorate that sovereignty rests then when we apply this idea to Austin's concept of law as the commands of a sovereign to whom the bulk of the populace is in the habit of obedience, we find ourselves saying that the populace (or that part that constitutes the electorate) is in the habit of obedience to itself. 'Thus the original clear image of a society divided into two segments: the sovereign free from legal limitation who gives orders, and the subjects who habitually obey, has given place to the blurred image of a society in which the majority obey orders given by the majority or by all. Surely we have here neither "orders" in the original sense (expression of intention that *others* shall behave in certain ways) or "obedience".'[11]

In order to meet this criticism, Hart explains, 'a distinction may be made between the members of the society in their private capacity as individuals and the same persons in their official capacity as electors or legislators. Such a distinction is perfectly intelligible; indeed many legal and political phenomena are most naturally presented in such terms; but it cannot rescue the theory of

8   Ibid, p 67.
9   Ibid, p 68.
10   Ibid, p 69.
11   Ibid, p 74.

sovereignty even if we are prepared to take the further step of saying that the individuals in their official capacity constitute *another person* who is habitually obeyed. For if we ask what is meant by saying of a group of persons that in electing a representative or in issuing an order, they have acted not "as individuals" but "in their official capacity", the answer can only be given in terms of their qualifications under certain rules and their compliance with other rules, which define what is to be done by them to make a valid election or a law. It is only by reference to such rules that we can identify something as an election or a law made by this body of persons.'[12] And since such rules define 'what the members of the society must do to function as an electorate (and so for the purposes of the theory as a sovereign) they cannot themselves have the status of orders issued by the sovereign, for nothing can count as orders issued by the sovereign unless the rules already exist and have been followed.'[13]

These arguments against the notion of a sovereign with legally unlimited powers, Hart concludes, like those put forward earlier, 'are fundamental in the sense that they amount to the contention that the theory is not merely mistaken in detail, but that the simple idea of orders, habits, and obedience, cannot be adequate for the analysis of law. What is required instead is the notion of a rule conferring powers, which may be limited or unlimited, on persons qualified in certain ways to legislate by complying with a certain procedure.'[14]

Conclusion

We have dealt in some detail with Hart's attack on the Austinian theory of law for three reasons. First, because it constitutes probably the most rigorous and comprehensive analysis of the command theory so far undertaken. Secondly, because Hart's very criticisms throw light on the nature of law: at the end of the attack Austin may lie in ruins, but we feel that we have obtained insights that we should not otherwise have gained. Thirdly, because, by showing a principal weakness of Austin to have been his failure to take account of the part played by rules in any legal system, Hart paves the way for the presentation of his own concept. How rules fit into Hart's scheme of thinking we learn in Chapter 4 of his book.

12   Ibid.
13   Ibid, p 74.
14   Ibid, p 75.

Before leaving Hart's treatment of Austin a final point needs to be made. In one respect they share common ground, that of their approach to jurisprudence. Both set out to determine the nature of law by the process of analysis: they are both members of the analytical school of jurists, jurists who seek to strip the flesh from the skeleton to find the structure beneath. It is from Austin's conclusions that Hart dissents, not from his method and approach.[15]

---

15   On the widening scope of the analytical school, see R Summers (1966) 41 New York Univ L R 861. For a survey of analytical jurisprudence see Davies and Holcroft *Jurisprudence: Texts and Commentary* Part I.

CHAPTER 4

A matter of rules

Professor Hart's concept of a legal system

There are in any society, Professor H L A Hart tells us in *The Concept of Law*, certain matters that influence human behaviour. These can be divided into two categories, social habits and social rules.[1] (There is a diagram on p 53.)

Social habits

An example of a social habit might be the habit of a group to go to the cinema on Saturday evenings. Habits are not rules. If some people in the group do not go to the cinema on Saturday evenings, this will not be regarded as a fault, nor render them liable to criticism. When a group have a particular habit, although this may be observable by an outsider, no member of the group may be conscious of the habit – either that he is in the habit of going to the cinema on Saturday evening, or that others in the group do so. Certainly, members of the group do not in any way consciously strive to see that the habit is maintained.

An example of a social rule might be a rule that a man should take his hat off in church. If someone breaks the rule, this is regarded as a fault, and renders the offender liable to criticism. Such criticism is generally regarded as warranted, not only by those who make it but also by the person who is criticised. Further, for a social rule to exist, at least some members of the group must be aware of

---

1   H L A Hart *The Concept of Law* pp 54–55.

the existence of the rule, and must strive to see that it is followed, as a standard, by the group as a whole.

The internal and external aspects of rules[2]

This awareness of, and support for, a social rule Hart calls the *internal aspect* of a rule.

The fact that something is a social rule will be observable by anyone looking at the group from outside. The fact that the rule can be observed to exist by an outsider Hart refers to as the *external aspect* of the rule.

A statement about a rule made by an outside observer may be said to be made from an external *point of view*; a statement made by a member of the group who accepts and uses the rules as a guide to conduct may be said to be made from an internal *point of view*. Suppose that an observer watches the behaviour of a certain group, for example suppose that he watches traffic approaching traffic lights, and records everything that happens. After a while, although he does not know the highway code, he observes that when the lights turn red, the traffic stops. So he is able to predict that there is a high possibility that when the lights turn red, the traffic will stop. He treats the lights turning red *as a sign that* the traffic will stop. But this way of looking at the matter is very different from that of the people in the cars approaching the lights. For them, the light turning red is a *signal to them* to stop; for them what matters is the rule that if the light turns red, they ought to stop. The observer was looking at the rule from an external point of view: a person in a car looks at the rule from an internal point of view. Since social *habits* are observable by an outsider, but the group is not aware of them, they have an external aspect, but not an internal one. Social *rules* have both an external and internal aspect.

Social rules[3]

If something is a social rule, then we would find that such words as 'ought', 'must', 'should' are used in connection with it. Social rules are of two kinds:

(a) Those which are no more than social conventions, for example rules of etiquette or rules of correct speech. These are more than

2   Ibid, p 55.
3   Ibid, p 83.

habits, as a group strives to see that the rules are observed, and those who break them are criticised.

(b) Rules which constitute obligations. A rule falls into this second category when there is an insistent demand that members of the group conform, and when there is great pressure brought to bear on those who break the rule, or threaten to do so.

Rules of this second kind are regarded as important because they are believed to be necessary to maintain the very life of the society, or some highly prized aspect of it. Examples are rules which restrict violence or which require promises to be kept.

Rules of this kind often involve some sacrifice on the part of the person who has to comply with the rule – a sacrifice for the benefit of the others in the society.[4]

Obligations

Rules which constitute obligations may be sub-divided into two categories:[5]

(i) Rules which form part of the moral code of the society concerned: these rules are therefore moral obligations. Such obligations may be wholly customary in origin. There may be no central body responsible for punishing breaches of such rules, the only form of pressure for conformity being a hostile reaction (stopping short of physical action) towards a person who breaks the rule. The pressure for conformity may take the form of words of disapproval, or to appeals to the individual's respect for the rule broken. The pressure may rely heavily on inducing feelings of shame, remorse or guilt in the offender.

(ii) Rules which take the form of law – even if a rudimentary or primitive kind of law. A rule will come into this category if the pressure for conformity includes physical sanctions against a person who breaks the rule – even if the sanctions are applied, not by officials, but by the community at large.

In the case of both (i) and (ii), there is *serious* social pressure to conform to the rule, and it is this which makes the rule an obligation (as opposed to a mere social convention, or even a habit).

4 Ibid, p 85.
5 Ibid, pp 84, 85.

Primary and secondary rules

Legal rules are of two kinds, 'primary' rules and 'secondary' rules. Primary rules are ones which tell people to do things, or not to do things. They lay down duties. These primary rules are to do with physical matters.[6]

Secondary rules are ones which let people, by doing certain things, introduce new rules of the first kind, or alter them. They give people (private individuals or public bodies) *power* to introduce or vary the first kind of rule.[7]

The function of secondary rules[8]

It is possible to imagine a society which does not have a legislature, courts or officials of any kind. Many societies of this kind have in fact existed, and have been described in detail. In this kind of society, the only means of social control is the attitude of the group towards behaviour that it will accept as permissible. Such a society is one that lives by primary rules of obligation alone. For such a society to exist, certain conditions must be satisfied. They are as follows:

(1) In view of human nature, the primary rules must include rules which contain restrictions on violence, theft and deception.
(2) Although there may be a minority who reject the rules, the majority must accept them.
(3) The society must be a small one, with close ties of kinship, common sentiments and beliefs.
(4) The society must live in a stable environment.

If either of the last two conditions were not satisfied, the society could not continue to exist by means of such a simple system of social control. The following defects would show themselves.[9]

(1) If doubts arose as to what the primary rules were, there would be no means of resolving the uncertainty. There would be no procedure for determining what the rules were (eg by referring to some authoritative text, or asking guidance from an official whose function it was to decide such matters).
(2) There would be no means of altering the rules according to changing circumstances. The rules would be static.

---

6   Ibid, p 78.
7   Ibid, p 79.
8   Ibid, p 89.
9   Ibid, p 90.

(3) There would be no means of settling a dispute as to whether a rule has been broken. (This is the most serious defect of all.)

(4) There would be no one with authority to impose punishments for breaches of the rules. Conformity with the rules would only be secured by diffuse social pressure, or by punishments meted out by individuals or by the group as a whole. This would be an inefficient way of ensuring that the rules were observed. Unorganised efforts by the group to catch and punish offenders would waste time: punishment inflicted by individuals might lead to vendettas.

All these defects can be rectified by supplementing the primary rules by other rules of a different kind, rules already referred to as secondary rules.[10]

Secondary rules have something in common with primary rules and are connected with them. Primary rules are concerned with what people must do or must not do: secondary rules are concerned with the primary rules in that they lay down the ways in which primary rules may be introduced, varied and abandoned; the way in which primary rules may be ascertained; and the way in which it can be decided whether a primary rule has been broken.

Secondary rules can provide remedies for the defects listed above.

1. The defect of uncertainty as to what the primary rules are can be remedied by having secondary rules which provide a way of knowing whether a suggested rule is or is not in fact a rule of the group. There are many ways in which this can be achieved. For example it may become accepted that the rules are as written in some text (eg a statute, or Moses's tablets of stone). Or the secondary rule may be that a primary rule is to become a rule of the group if it is enacted by a certain body (eg Parliament) or it is decreed by a judge.

There may be more than one way of deciding what are the primary rules. And if there is more than one way, there may be a means of resolving possible conflicts by having an order of superiority (eg statutes override judicial decisions). A secondary rule which enables one to know what the primary rules are Hart terms a 'rule of recognition'. If a society has a 'rule of recognition' then it has a way of determining whether a law is valid.

10 See supra.

2. The defect (in a society having primary rules only) that the rules are static can be remedied by having secondary rules that provide for ways in which the primary rules can be changed. Secondary rules of this kind, 'rules of change', may specify the persons who are to have power to alter the law, and lay down the procedure to be followed in order to do so.

There will be a close connection between rules of recognition and rules of change. For example it may be a rule of change that the King can change the law. It may be a rule of recognition that what is enacted by the King *is* the law.

Rules of change are not concerned solely with changes in the general law of any society. They are also concerned with the way in which a private individual can change his own legal position. (It is worth repeating here what was said earlier about the nature of secondary rules: secondary rules are ones that let people, by doing certain things, produce new rules of first kind, or alter them. They give people (private individuals or public bodies) *power* to introduce or vary the first kind of rule.) For example if A makes no will, by law his property will pass to those entitled under his intestacy. If he makes a will, he alters this position, so that his property will pass to, say, B. So the law relating to the making of wills, since it gives power to a person to alter what had been the previous position, is a secondary rule. Similarly, if A enters into a contract with B, he alters the previous legal position (ie in which no contract existed). So the laws relating to the making of contracts are secondary rules also. For the same reason the laws relating to the transfer of property are secondary rules. Thus a law which authorises Parliament to enact a law, and a law which enables A to make a will are each examples of secondary rules: each enables the previous legal position to be altered.

3. The defect which we set out under (3) above, can be remedied by having secondary rules which enable any individual to find out whether or not a primary rule has been broken. Such rules can lay down who is to decide this (eg a judge) and any procedure which must be followed. These rules will be concerned with judges, courts, jurisdiction and judgments. These are 'rules of adjudication'.

A rule of adjudication, such as a rule conferring power on a judge to try certain issues, will be also a rule of recognition, as the fact that the judge is empowered to try an issue provides us with a means of determining what the law is – judges' decisions here being one source of law.

4. The defect which we set out under (4) above can be remedied by having secondary rules which prohibit individuals from taking

into their own hands the punishment of others for breaches of primary rules, and instead provide for an official system of penalties, with maximum penalties, administered by officials (eg judges). These rules provide the sanctions of the system.

The structure made up of the combination of primary rules and secondary rules of recognition, change and adjudication, and sanction imposing rules make up the heart of a legal system.

Rules of recognition

Wherever there is a rule of recognition, Hart says,[11] people have a way of finding out what the primary rules are. In modern societies there may be various sources of law. These may include, for example, a written constitution, legislation, and judges' decisions. These may be placed in an order of superiority; for example, legislation may be able to override judges' decisions. In the British system, judicial precedent is subject to legislation. Judicial precedent is, however, a separate source of law: it does not derive its authority as a source of law from legislation. Thus precedent is subordinate to legislation, but independent of it as a source of law.

In any society is there one rule of recognition, or may there be more than one? From one point of view there may be several – the constitution, legislation and judicial decisions, each of these can provide authority for establishing the validity of a law. From another point of view, the better view, there can be only one rule of recogition in any one legal system, that which establishes the supreme source of authority for legal validity, a rule that may have subsidiary rules but which lays down the order of priority between them.

A rule of recognition (ie one enabling people to know what is and what is not law) is seldom in practice expressed as an actual law, though occasionally the courts may make some statement about how the rule works, eg when they say that Acts of Parliament override other sources of law.

When people say that something or other is the law 'because Parliament has said so' they show that they accept this as a rule of recognition; they are looking at the rule from an internal point of view. Someone looking at the rules of recognition from an external

---

11   Hart *The Concept of Law* p 98.

point of view, someone who is an outsider who does not accept the British rules of recognition, would say 'In Britain, they accept as law whatever the Queen in Parliament enacts'.

When we say that a rule is 'valid' within any particular system, we mean that it complies with the rules of recognition of that system.[12] The validity of a rule does not depend on the fact that the rule is obeyed more often than it is not obeyed. There may, however, be a rule of recognition that provides that if a rule is not obeyed over a long period, it should cease to be a rule: there may be some kind of 'rule of obsolescence'. But nevertheless, the validity of a rule, and the question of whether it is obeyed, are two separate matters.

The fact that there are various rules of recognition, with one of them supreme – a hierarchy of rules of recognition, with one of them at the top – should not be thought of as meaning that in any legal system there is one supreme, sovereign, legislative power which is legally unlimited. Just because a particular rule of recognition is supreme, this does not mean that any legislative body necessarily has unlimited power. For example, in the United States there are rules of recognition but there is no legislator with unlimited powers.

Now, to introduce a further idea, Hart asks[13] us to suppose that someone questions whether a purported bye-law of the Oxfordshire County Council is valid. It is found that it is valid because it was made in exercise of powers conferred by a statutory order made by the Minister of Health. (So the bye-law satisfies this 'rule of recognition'.) The validity of the statutory order made by the Minister is questioned. It is found that it is valid because it was made according to the provisions of a statute empowering the Minister to make such an order. Next, the validity of the statute is questioned. We find that the statute is valid because it was passed by Parliament and signed by the Queen. At this point we have to stop, since, according to our notions in this country, what the Queen in Parliament enacts is law. The rule that what the Queen in Parliament enacts is law is a rule of recognition. In this it is like the other rules of recognition we have mentioned. But it is unlike the others in that there is no rule of recognition to test the validity of this rule: there is no rule of recognition to test the validity of the rule that what the Queen in Parliament enacts is law. So this rule of recognition is the ultimate rule of recognition.

12 Ibid, p 100.
13 Ibid, p 104.

A statement that a statute is valid because it complies with the rule that what the Queen in Parliament enacts is law, is made from an internal point of view.[14] It is internal because it looks at the matter from the viewpoint of people inside the legal system: they *accept* that what the Queen in Parliament enacts is law. If we say that in England the rule that what the Queen in Parliament enacts is law is used by the courts and citizens as the ultimate rule of recognition, we are making the statement from an external point of view.

We usually only talk of a rule being valid *within* a legal system. We say that the law is valid because it complies with the rule of recognition of that system. But, Hart explains,[15] no question can arise as to the validity of the rule of recognition itself: it can neither be valid nor invalid – it is simply accepted within the system as being appropriate for deciding what is and what is not a valid rule. To express this simple fact (of acceptance of the rule of recognition as being appropriate) by saying darkly that its validity is 'assumed but cannot be demonstrated' (as Kelsen does[16]) is like saying that we assume, but can never demonstrate that the standard metre bar in Paris (which is accepted as the correct length of a metre) is itself correct.

In a legal system which had only primary rules, because of the absence of any rule of recognition (a secondary rule) any statement that a certain rule existed could only be made as a statement of fact, such as might be made (and verified by observation) by an outside observer. On the other hand, where there is a mature system of law, with primary and secondary rules, including a rule of recognition, then a statement that a rule 'exists' can be made, not only from an external point of view, as a statement of fact, but also from an internal point of view. In the latter case, the statement that the rule 'exists' carries with it the implication that the rule complies with the system's rule of recognition and is thus valid according to the system's test of validity.[17]

A rule of recognition does not fit into any of the conventional categories used in classifying laws in a legal system. For example, a rule of recognition does not fit in to either of Dicey's two categories of constitutional arrangements – laws strictly so called (eg statutes,

---

14   See supra.
15   Hart *The Concept of Law* p 106.
16   See Chap 11.
17   Hart *The Concept of Law* p 107.

etc) and conventions (eg that the Queen does not refuse to assent to a bill passed by Parliament).[18]

Distinct from the problem of how to classify a rule of recognition, there is the problem of knowing how to show that a rule of recognition, which underlies the constitution and the whole legal system, and which surely must be law, *is* law. Some people would answer this question by saying that at the base of any legal system there is something which is 'not law', which is 'pre-legal' or 'meta-legal'. Others would say that this something which underlies the legal system is merely 'political fact'. The truth is that a rule of recognition is both law and a fact: we cannot convey the idea of a rule of recognition adequately if we think we must label it either 'law' or 'fact'. The best way of understanding the nature of a rule of recognition is to regard it as being capable of being looked at from two points of view – from an external point of view (that of an outside observer who notes that, as a matter of fact, the rule exists in the actual practice of the system) and from an internal point of view (that of someone inside the system who accepts the rule as the correct one for determining what is the law).

Hard positivism and soft positivism

Hart refers to a rule of recognition as that which constitutes 'the criteria for the identification of the laws which courts have to apply'.[19] What can these criteria include? For some – those referred to as 'hard positivistists – the criteria must be precisely identifiable, for example from sources that are written down, such as legislation. For others, 'soft positivists', sources of law can be found from a wider area and can include reference to principles or moral values. In the Postscript to the second edition of *Concept*, Hart, partly in response to criticsm of the book by Ronald Dworkin (of whom more anon[20]), adopts the soft positivist position, at any rate to the extent of recognising that where a judge is required to make a decision in a penumbral area in which no settled law exists, he may look outside the criteria recognised by the hard positivist (for example, earlier decisions) and take into account moral values and social practices as a valid source of legal authority, as for example in the decision in *Donoghue v Stephenson*, when the court looked outside the precedents laid down in earlier cases to establish the 'neighbour' principle as part of the law of negligence.

18   Ibid, p 108.
19   Ibid, p 246.
20   Chaps 8, 9 and 10.

What do we mean when we say that a legal system 'exists'?

The statement that a legal system exists in a given country or a given group expresses, in a summary form, a number of different social facts. These facts are obscured by the standard form of legal and political terminology. When we drop this terminology and look at the facts, we find that a legal system, like a human being, can go through various stages of development:

(i)　first it may be unborn;
(ii)　then it may be born but dependent on its mother;
(iii)　then it may have a healthy, independent existence;
(iv)　then it may decay; and
(v)　finally it may die.

So when we say that a legal system 'exists', this over-simplifies matters. The statement that a legal system 'exists' may be taken to refer to the stage when the legal system has a healthy independent existence. But the statement takes no account of the fact that other stages exist.

For a society to have a legal system certain conditions must be satisfied. One is that laws which are valid according to the system's rules of recognition are in practice obeyed by the bulk of the population. Secondly, the relationship of the officials to the secondary rules must be one of acceptance. It is not enough for the officials merely to obey these secondary rules, nor is it enough for them to 'respect' the rules, or even to 'follow', 'comply with', or 'conform to' them: the essential condition, Hart says,[21] is that the officials should collectively accept the secondary rules. The reason why it is not sufficient for the attitude of the officials to the secondary rules to be one of obedience is that a person who obeys a rule does not necessarily have to think that in obeying the rule he is doing the right thing, for himself or for others. He can obey a rule without necessarily accepting the rule as being a correct one (though he may of course in fact accept that it is correct). He can obey the rule out of laziness or out of fear. He can obey the rule without thinking about whether the rule is correct or not. But in the case of the officials, for a legal system to exist their relationship to the secondary rules, in particular the rules of recognition, must be one of *acceptance*. They must regard the rules of recognition as a common

---

21　Hart, *The Concept of Law*, p 112.

standard for making judicial decisions. Without this common standard there would be conflicting judicial decisions and orders, and ultimately there would be chaos.[22]

So we can say that for a legal system to exist two conditions must be satisified. They are:

(1) The rules which are valid according to the system's ultimate rule of recognition must be generally obeyed.
(2) The system's secondary rules (of recognition, change and adjudication) must be accepted as common public standards by the officials.

It will be seen that, for these conditions to be satisfied, private citizens need only *obey*: officials, as officials, must both obey and *accept*. Normally, the majority of private citizens will not only obey but will also accept, but it is not necessary for a legal system to exist that they should do so. If they do not accept, the society concerned might be deplorably sheepish and the sheep might end in the slaughterhouse, but this would not mean that a legal system did not exist.[23]

Breakdown of a legal system

Hart has explained that for a legal system to exist the secondary rules must be accepted by the officials, and the primary rules must be obeyed by the majority of the citizens. Sometimes, however, he says, it may happen that although the officials still accept the secondary rules, the citizens cease to obey the primary ones. This position may be reached in a variety of ways. One is by means of revolution (though a revolution may involve a takeover by a new set of officials without there being any change in the legal system). Another is where an enemy power occupies the country concerned. Another is where anarchy or banditry leads to breakdown of legal control.

In each of these cases (revolution, enemy occupation or general breakdown) there may be a half-way stage in which the courts continue to function, using the rules of recognition of the old regime, but their orders are not obeyed. It is not possible to say at precisely what moment the previous legal system ceases to exist, or even whether at any moment it has ceased to exist – for example,

22 Ibid, p 113.
23 Ibid, p 114.

there may be a chance that the old regime will be restored, or an outbreak of lawlessness may be merely temporary.

Difficult questions may arise when, for example, a country is occupied for a while by an enemy power, and then the enemy is driven out and the former government is re-established. Questions may then arise as to what was and what was not 'law' in the territory concerned while the enemy was in occupation. One way of answering such questions would be for the restored government to make a retrospective law which provided that whatever had been treated as being law while the enemy was in occupation was valid law.

Emergence of a legal system[24]

Having spoken of the breakdown of a legal system, Hart examines the emergence of a legal system. Consider, he says, the way in which new legal systems have emerged within the British Commonwealth. At the beginning there may be a colony with a local legislature, judiciary, and executive. The structure has been set up by a statute of the United Kingdom, the UK government retaining full power to legislate for the colony. At this stage the legal system is clearly a subordinate part of the wider legal system of which the ultimate rule of recognition is that what the Queen in Parliament enacts is law. At the end of the period of development, when the colony has achieved independence, we find that the ultimate rule of recognition of the legal system is no longer that what the Queen in Parliament enacts is law. The legal system now has its own, independent, locally-based, ultimate rule of recognition. The structure of the government – the legislature, the courts, etc – may still be in the same form as that laid down in the original UK statute, but the enactments of the legislature in what has now become a new state are valid not because of the former ultimate rule of recognition (that whatever the Queen in Parliament enacts is law) but because of the new local ultimate rule of recognition, that whatever the local legislature enacts is law.

This development from dependent colony to independent state may be achieved by the gradual retirement of parent legislature, followed by a final renunciation of legislative power over the colony, or it may be achieved by violence. But in either case, at the end of the road, there will be two independent legal systems.

24 Ibid, p 116.

There is another possibility: the colony may have in fact achieved independence, but the parent country may not recognise this fact.[25] In this case while there will in fact be two legal systems, the parent country will insist that there is only one. Only from the viewpoint of the parent country will the latter view be legally correct.

Conclusion

In the Postscript that Hart added to the second edition of *The Concept of Law*, he tells us that his aim in writing the book was to provide a theory of law that was both general and descriptive. 'It is general in the sense that it is not tied to any particular legal system or legal culture, but seeks to give an explanatory and clarifying account of law as a complex social and political institution with a rule governed ... aspect. This institution, in spite of many variations in different cultures and in different times, has taken the same general form and structure ...' The account is descriptive in that it is morally neutral and has no justificatory aims: it does not 'seek to justify or commend on moral or other grounds the forms and structures which appear in my general account of law ...'

The remainder of the Postscript is devoted to replying to criticisms of the book, in particular by Ronald Dworkin. Dworkin's work is considered in two later chapters, and the clash of opinion between him and Hart will be considered at the end of the second of those chapters, when the nature of Dworkin's own ideas will have been explored.

---

25   Ibid, p 118.

The components of Hart's scheme

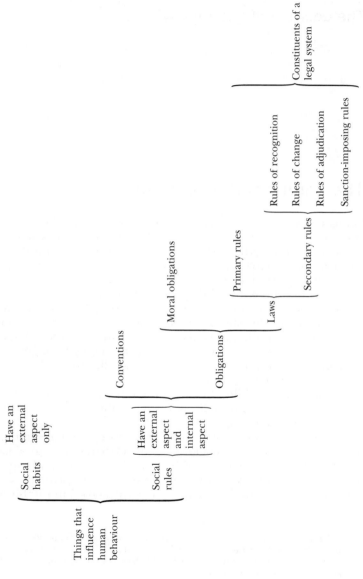

CHAPTER 5

It stands to reason ...

The doctrine of natural law[1]

The nature of the doctrine

Let us suppose that a fair-haired child returns from school one day and says to its father 'Mr Smith [the Headmaster of the school] has made a new rule. No children with fair hair are to get arithmetic lessons. They are to do extra woodwork instead. I think it's stupid,' the child says. 'After all, we're at school to learn aren't we? How can I do what I'm there for if I don't get arithmetic?'

'Well', says the father, 'it seems unfortunate, I agree. But Mr Smith is the Headmaster. He makes the rules. What he says goes.'

'But surely', replies the child, 'he can't make a rule like that? I mean, it goes against what the school is *for*. The school governors wouldn't allow it. It can't really *be* a rule at all, can it?'

'Um,' the father replies.

'Well', says the child, 'I don't think it is a rule. It can't be.'

'And do you intend to disobey it?' asks the father.

'Um,' says the child.

The views expressed by the child bear a degree of resemblance to those held by one who believes in the doctrine of natural law.

The adherent of natural law believes that beyond, and superior to, the laws made by man are certain higher principles, the principles of natural law. These principles are immutable and

---

1 A short bibliography would cover more pages than in this chapter. A useful introduction is A P d'Entreves *Natural Law* (2nd edn, 1970). See also J W Harris *Legal Philosophies* (2nd edn, 1997) Chap 2; Davies and Holdcroft *Jurisprudence: Texts and Commentary* Chap 6.

eternal. Man-made laws may vary from one community to another with respect to matters of everyday importance – the side of the road on which citizens are required to drive – but with regard to the highest matters, man-made law should be in accord with the principles of natural law. And to the extent that man-made law conflicts with natural law, it lacks validity: it is not a valid, binding law at all. Natural law is 'the theory that there are certain principles of human conduct, awaiting discovery by human reason, with which man-made law must conform if it is to be valid'.[2]

The notion of natural law is likely to strike at least some chord in many readers. If a citizen, after travelling for many years in far-off parts, returns to his own country to find that in his absence the government has enacted that returning travellers are to have the fingers of their left hand struck off by customs officers to indicate that they have been abroad, his reaction may well be 'This *cannot* be.' Even as the customs officer's machete is raised, he will think 'I cannot accept that such a law as this is a valid law of this country.' And, if learning of the law before entering the customs shed, he turns aside and makes a dash for it across the railway sidings, he will think as he runs 'I do not regard myself as breaking the law, as this is not the law.'

Far fetched? Perhaps. But think of this. The government, in order to reduce population growth, secures the passage of legislation that legalises the abortion of an unborn child at any time up until the time when it would be born. By many this would be regarded as the taking of life, and contrary to the will of God. Indeed, such would be the opinion of the Catholic Church – in whose view abortion at any stage of pregnancy constitutes (subject to certain exceptions) the taking of life and is therefore contrary to the will of God.

We do not need to look to the church for examples of an appeal to a higher code. Those who oppose the hunting of wild animals for pleasure, or who oppose the use of live animals for the purpose of research into the safety of consumer products such as cosmetics, these people base their case on an appeal to conscience, to a code that stands above man-made law, to a higher morality, to standards that have universal validity and applicability. People who have these kinds of views will find nothing surprising in the notion of natural law – indeed some may feel that, unknowingly, they had been subscribers to this doctrine all the while. Animal rights activists who break into laboratories to free rabbits that are held rigid by their heads being fastened through frames, to enable researchers to test

2 H L A Hart *Concept of Law* p 182.

liquids for toxicity by putting drops of the product in the animals' eyes, may well feel 'We have no qualms about what we do: a law as evil as one that allows the infliction of pain on animals for the purpose of augmenting commercial profit has no validity to us. We are not breaking the law. This for us is not the law.'

Those, who (whether they call themselves adherents of natural law, or not) look to a law, a code, a set of principles, a morality, that stands above the laws of men, by which the validity of man-made law is to be judged, can include both those who have belief in a God (a God from whom the code is perhaps in some way derived) and those who may have no religious faith; the ranks of natural lawyers include both the atheist and believer.

The doctrine of natural law has a long history; almost as long as the history of European civilisation. Notions that foreshadow the doctrine are found amongst the ideas of the philosophers of the golden age of Greece, in the fifth century before Christ. The doctrine reached a form that we can recognise in the writings of the Stoic school of philosophers in the early centuries of the Roman Empire. The doctrine, like much of the thought of the ancient world, passed into the thinking of the Church and took on a religious apparel. The doctrine underlay much of the thinking of secular philosophers in the sixteenth century, contributing in the seventeenth and eighteenth centuries to a parallel doctrine of natural rights. It remained a key element of the Catholic Church throughout post-reformation history, and remains such at our own day. Among the ranks of its adherents stand not only the Pope, but perhaps also the 'right to life' campaigner, the animal rights activist, and, in its own way, the child who opened our chapter.

'Natural' law

But why *natural* law? What is natural about it? Surely, if anything, 'unnatural law' would seem an apter term? In dealing with this matter we must explain first that 'natural law' is not to be understood as meaning the same as the law of nature – in the sense of laws that govern the physical world. (Also distinct must be kept the notion of a 'state of nature', indicating the condition in which man lived, or is by some philosophers supposed to have lived, before the birth of ordered society.)

The word 'natural' in natural law refers to an idea that provides the foundation of natural law – namely the reason why natural law ought to be obeyed. The idea is this. Man is part of nature. Within nature, man has a nature. His nature inclines him towards certain ends – to procreate children, to protect his family, to ensure his survival. To seek such ends is natural to him. Those things which assist the achieving of such ends assist the purposes of nature. Thus laws that further the achievement by man of his natural ends assist the achievement of the purposes of nature. Such laws, laws that are in accord with the ultimate purposes of man, constitute natural law. Natural law is thus that which furthers the attainment by men of the ends that nature has made it man's nature to seek to achieve. At once a difficulty in explaining the nature of natural law becomes apparent: we have had to use the word 'nature' in two senses, one indicating nature in the sense of 'the world of nature', the created universe, and the other bearing a meaning similar to 'character', or 'tendency'. But 'nature' as in 'it is the nature of a horse to eat grass' is a better word for what we mean than 'character' or 'tendency', and we should stick to it.

A further difficulty in explaining the idea of natural law is that in some places the two meanings of the word nature that we have described overlap: when we said above 'To seek such ends is natural to him', we intended to impart that the ends concerned are sought by man because of his nature, a nature that is his because of the sort of creature he is within the world of nature.

Sometimes it is easier to comprehend the negative of a concept than the positive. So we can say this. Those things which impede man attaining his natural ends are contrary to natural law. Thus if a man-made law obstructs the achievement by man of what has been decreed by nature as his ends, then the law is contrary to natural law.

What does natural law consist of? What are its precepts? Natural law ordains that society should be ordered in such a way as to assist man in fulfilling his purpose. Since violence will impede this fulfilment, violence is contrary to natural law. Since peace assists this fulfilment, man should honour promises, since to dishonour a promise can lead to disharmony or even violence.

Since man's natural ends are the same for all mankind, and remain the same for all time, it is natural (yet another meaning of the word) that the principles of natural law are constant. Thus natural law comprises a body of permanent, eternal truths, truths embodying precepts of universal applicability, part of the immutable order of things, unaffected by changing human beliefs or attitudes.

Discoverable by reason

Yet despite these transcendent qualities, it is a characteristic of natural law that the truths that it embodies are not made known to man by some Great Architect beyond the skies. We do not find that the heavens open and a hand comes through clouds, passing down to mankind a tablet of stone on which the truths of natural law are inscribed: the truths of natural law are not revealed truths. The truths of natural law are ascertainable by man though the exercise of the reason with which he is by nature endowed. The truths of natural law are determined by observation followed by reflection: What are man's natural ends? What ordering of society best enables these ends to be achieved? Despite its transcendence, man discovers the content of natural law for himself. God does not tell him – having given man reason, He does not need to.

Distinction between natural law and man-made law

This brings us to the final characteristic of natural law thinking: the distinction between natural law and man-made law. The natural lawyer recognises the existence of (and the need for) man-made law but regards this as inferior to natural law. Further, if man-made law conflicts with natural law, man-made law is deemed to lack validity.

This, then, is the doctrine of natural law. We have sought to describe the doctrine in its fullest form. And we have described the doctrine in the abstract – at no time in the history of European thought has any philosopher or theologian proposed a view of natural law entirely in the form here expressed. Our description of the doctrine has been a composite one putting ideas that in practice formed part of various thinker's philosophies. But it has perhaps been useful to give at the outset an idea of the shape of the doctrine under consideration.

Development of natural law thinking

The ancient world – Greece

Two giants bestride the philosophy of the ancient world – indeed over philosophy to our own day: Plato and Aristotle.[3] Neither can

---

3   The works on each occupy whole libraries. W K C Guthrie *A History of Greek Philosophy* stands out among modern works. Also of value are the introductions to the Penguin editions of the two authors' works.

be described as natural lawyers. But in the philosophies of each we see strands that find a place in natural law thinking as it was later to develop.

To Plato[4] can be traced that strand of natural law thinking that regards values as having an eternal existence and an eternal veracity. Plato went further than this. What for us are abstractions – redness, squareness, roundness, sharpness, honour, courage, beauty, equality, each had a permanent and unvarying existence, an existence that is independent of the fact that certain things or actions in the world as we know it reflect the qualities themselves. This is Plato's doctrine of 'forms'. Plato's 'forms' are transcendental archetypes that exist independently of the physical world, independently of the human mind, independently of space or time. Thus there is a 'form' of beauty, of which things on earth which have the quality of beauty are mere manifestations. Qualities such as justice and truth exist in their own right. All men can do is to attempt to reproduce them. To reproduce these qualities men must seek knowledge of the eternal truths, a quest that is man's finest endeavour. So, also, just as distinct from the fact that the total of two sets of two bottles can be counted to four bottles, outside time, outside space, ouside human thought, two plus two equals four. (Is this not so?)

The school of thought that subscribes to such a view is termed idealism, referring to the notion that the *idea* of a thing has its own existence. The word will be met at various places in a study of jurisprudence. (Used in this sense it should, of course, be distinguished from the word used in the everyday sense of a striving for perfection.)

One does not have to believe in Plato's theory of forms (one does not have to be an idealist) to subscribe to the doctrine of natural law. Idealism nevertheless has played a key part in the doctrine's history.

The few sentences above can give no hint of the scale and the majesty of Plato's philosophy. The full impact of his work can be understood only by reading the work in which the theory of forms is principally set out, *The Republic*. Whether one can learn the truths that, for Plato, have their own eternal existence and, if so, how this is to be done, are questions that are discussed at various places in Plato's *Dialogues*.[5] Plato himself believed it was possible for man to attain knowledge of the external truths, for example, 'goodness', 'justice', 'courage'. One who so believes, it will be recalled, is termed in

4   c 427–348 BC.
5   Eg *The Meno.*

philosophy a 'cognativist'. A natural lawyer is a cognativist. (But not all cognativists necessarily subscribe to the doctrine of natural law.)

Since for Plato the forms of 'goodness', 'virtue', 'honesty' were eternal and immutable, they constituted moral principles of universal and timeless validity existing above and unaffected by changing human attitudes or beliefs, moral principles by reference to which all human actions and views must be judged.

Aristotle[6] did not subscribe to Plato's theory of forms. But there was an element in his thinking that contributed a further strand to what was to become part of natural law doctrine. Aristotle was concerned with the world as he saw it existing around him. He was a zoologist, in particular a marine zoologist, with an acute observation of the minutest details of organisms observable by the human eye. From his studies of the natural world he became conscious of the fact that natural phenomena were in a state of perpetual change – the child growing into an adult; the seed growing into a plant. There was always progress. The acorn developed into the oak tree. The oak tree was what it was the acorn's nature to develop into. The oak tree was the acorn's predetermined end. The oak tree was the fulfilment of the progression that the acorn had started. Throughout the living world, Aristotle saw that, in the birth and growth of animals and plants, the earlier stages always lead up to a final development. Yet we should not think of this end as a termination. The process is constant. There is always potential for further change: in everything there is a potentiality striving to reach a further stage of actuality.

Thus, for Aristotle the universe is dynamic, always engaged in the process of becoming, of moving towards an end immanent within itself from the start. The philosophy that everything that exists has a predetermined end is termed teleology (from the Greek *teleos*, end, and *logos*, rule or principle).

Aristotle's teleology extended beyond the individual phenomena of the natural world to the activities of creatures within it, including human beings. For Aristotle, the highest form of human society lay in the Greek city state (a *polis*). It was the *polis* that provided the society in which man could achieve his culminating fulfilment. Thus from the start of organised human society, from its most primitive forms, through the various stages of agricultural existence to the building of cities, and the creating of political societies such as that at Athens, mankind was progressing towards that which had been its end from the beginning. In his *Politics*,[7] Aristotle says, 'Because it is the

---

6   384–322 BC.
7   Book II, Chapter 4. Translated, Sir Ernest Barker.

completion of associations existing by nature, every polis exists by nature, having itself the same quality as the earlier associations from which it grew. It is the end to which those associations move and the 'nature' of things consists in their end or consummation; for what each thing is when its growth is completed we call the nature of that thing, whether it be a man or a horse or a family.'

It seems but a short step from Aristotle's teleological view of the world to the doctrine of natural law as it later emerged. Did Aristotle take this step? At one point he seems close to doing so. In Chapter 5 of the *Nichomachean Ethics*,[8] in which Aristotle discusses the nature of justice, he says: 'There are two sorts of political justice, one natural and the other legal. The natural is that which has the same validity everywhere and does not depend upon acceptance; the legal is that which in the first place can take one form or another indifferently, but which, once laid down, is decisive: eg that the ransom for a prisoner of war shall be one mina, or that a goat shall be sacrificed and not two sheep ... Some hold the view that all regulations are of this kind on the ground that whereas natural laws are immutable and have the same validity everywhere (as fire burns both here and in Persia), they can see that notions of justice are variable. But this contention is not true as stated, although it is true in a sense. Among the gods, indeed, justice presumably never changes at all; but in our world, although there is such a thing as natural law, everything is subject to change; but still some things are so by nature and some are not, and it is easy to see what sort of thing, among those that admit of being otherwise, is so by nature and what is not, but is legal and conventional ... Rules of justice established by convention and on the ground of expediency may be compared to standard measures; because the measures used in the wine and corn trades are not everywhere equal: they are larger in the wholesale and smaller in the retail trade. Similarly laws that are not natural but man-made are not the same everywhere, because forms of government are not the same either; but everywhere there is only one natural form of government, namely that which is best.'

In this passage Aristotle seems to be on the point of declaring a doctrine that we can recognise as one of natural law. The element of natural law thinking can readily be detected, but he stops short, or veers on to another track before reaching the point we (looking back, and knowing what was to come later) are waiting for.

In another place Aristotle says: 'If the written law tells against our case already we must appeal to the universal law, and insist on

8   Translated J A K Thomson, Penguin Classics edition.

a greater equity and justice.' Here also we have a hint of natural law thinking, although it has been suggested that he is here giving a tip to the practising advocate rather than expressing anything fundamental to his views. It seems that Aristotle accepted that there is a natural and universal right and wrong, apart from any human ordinance or convention. But nowhere does he dwell on the matter. If we were able to ask Aristotle 'Should man-made laws be of a kind that enable man to achieve his natural ends?' perhaps Aristotle would pause, puzzled by so time wasting a question, shrug and pass on to something of interest – why rain falls from clouds, why a centipede has so many legs.

Perhaps for the Greeks of his time the notion that higher laws existed than those of man needed no special mention. Were the Gods not higher than men? What dire results did not ensue if puny man pitted himself against the will of the Gods? In Sophocles's *Antigone*, Antigone said to Creon, of an edict made by him, that she did not 'deem your proclamations so mighty that you, a mortal, could overthrow the sure unwritten laws of the Gods'. In *Oedipus Tyrannus*, the Chorus speaks of 'laws ... appointed on high, brought to life in the clear air of heaven, whose father is Olympus alone, for no mortal man begot them, nor will forgetfulness ever put them to sleep.'

In Plato's idealism, in Aristotle's teleology, in the Greek notion of a law higher than that of men, we can see strands that were later, with other elements, to form the full doctrine of natural law.

The Stoics

The next steps in the history of the doctrine are to be found in the writings of certain of the authors who form what has come to be termed the Stoic school of philosophy. Stoicism held sway from the lifetime of its founder Zeno (during the third century before Christ) down to about the fourth century AD. It was thus the prevailing philosophy during the greater part of the Roman Republic and Empire. The contribution of the Stoic school of philosophy may be represented by the writings of Cicero[9] (who although not fully a Stoic was sympathetic to and reflected many Stoic views), Seneca,[10] and the Emperor Marcus Aurelius.[11]

In Cicero's work *On Duties* the following passages occur. 'Besides, the Stoics' ideal is to live consistently with nature. I suppose what

9   106–43 BC.
10   c 4 BC–AD 65.
11   Emperor, 161–180 AD.

they mean is this: throughout our lives we ought invariably to aim at morally right courses of action, ...'[12]

'Indeed this idea – that one must not injure anybody else for one's own profit – is not only natural law, an international valid principle: the same idea is also incorporated in the statutes which individual communities have framed for their national purposes. The whole point and intention of these statutes is that one citizen shall live safely with another.'[13]

'... the finest and noblest characters prefer a life of dedication to a life of self-indulgence; and one may conclude that such men conform with nature and are therefore incapable of doing harm to their fellow men.'[14]

'So everyone ought to have the same purpose to identify the interest of each with the interest of all. Once men grab for themselves, human society will completely collapse. But if nature prescribes (as she does) that every human being must help every other human being, whoever he is, just precisely because they are all human beings, then – by the same authority – all men have identical interests. Having identical interests means that we are all subject to one and the same law of nature: and, that being so, the very least that such a law enjoins is that we must not wrong one another.'[15]

'... neglect of the common interest is unnatural, because it is unjust ... nature's law promotes and coincides with the common interest.'[16]

'Not that we possess any clear-cut, tangible images to show us what true, authentic law and Justice really look like! We only have outline sketches. And the extent to which we allow ourselves to be guided even by these leaves a great deal to be desired. For at least they have the merit of derivation from the finest models – those which have been vouchsafed to us by nature and by truth.'[17]

'For there is an ideal of human goodness: nature itself has stored and wrapped this up inside our minds. Unfold this ideal, and you will straightaway identify the good man as the person who helps everybody he can, and, unless wrongfully provoked, harms none.'[18]

In his letters Seneca wrote: 'You ask what [is particularly man's]. It is spirit, and the perfection of his reason in that spirit. For man is

12 Part II. Translated M Grant, Penguin Classics edition.
13 Ibid, Part III.
14 Ibid.
15 Ibid, Part III.
16 Ibid, Part IV.
17 Ibid, Part VII.
18 Ibid, Part VIII.

a rational animal. Man's ideal state is realised when he has fulfilled the purpose for which he was born. And what is it that reason demands of him? Something very easy – that he live in accordance with his own nature. Yet this is turned into something difficult by the madness that is universal among men; we push one another into vices. And how can people be called back to spiritual well-being when no one is trying to hold them back and the crowd is urging them on?'[19]

'What has the philosopher investigated? What has the philosopher brought to light? In the first place, truth and nature (having, unlike the rest of the animal world, followed nature with more than just a pair of eyes, things slow to grasp divinity); and secondly, a rule of life, in which he has brought life into line with things universal.'[20]

In the work that has become known as his *Meditations*, Marcus Aurelius wrote: 'If the power of thought is universal among mankind, so likewise is the possession of reason, making us rational creatures. It follows, therefore, that this reason speaks no less universally to us all with its "thou shalt" or "thou shalt not". So then there is a world-law; which in turn means that we are all fellow-citizens and share a common citizenship, and that the world is a single city.'[21]

'The purpose behind each thing's creation determines its development; the development points to its final state; the final state gives the clue to its chief advantage and good; therefore the chief good of a rational being is fellowship with his neighbours – for it has been made clear long ago that fellowship is the purpose behind our creation.'[22]

'Injustice is a sin. Nature has constituted rational beings for their own mutual benefit, each to help his fellows according to their worth, and in no wise to do them hurt; and to contravene her will is plainly to sin against this eldest of all the deities. Untruthfulness, too, is a sin, and against the same goddess. For Nature is the nature of Existence itself; and existence connotes the kinship of all created beings. Truth is but another name for this Nature, the original creator of all true things.'[23]

'Nature always has an end in view; and this aim includes a thing's ending as much as its beginning or its duration.'[24]

---

19 Letter XLV. Translated R Campbell, Penguin Classics edition.
20 Letter XC.
21 *Meditations* Book 4, 4.
22 Ibid, Book 5, 16.
23 Ibid, Book 9.
24 Ibid, Book 8, 20.

'In what I do, I am to do it with reference to the service of mankind. In what befalls me, I am to accept it with reference to the gods, and to that universal source from which the whole close-linked chain of circumstance has its issue.'[25]

From these passages it will be seen that those who adhered to the Stoic school added flesh to the bones of natural law. Tolerance, forgiveness, compassion, fortitude, uprightness, sincerity, honesty – these were the qualities that the Stoics believed that natural law required of men. These were the qualities to which reason dictated that man should aspire in order that he might live in accordance with what nature had ordained.

If we were to single out Stoic thinking's principal contribution to the evolution of the doctrine of natural law, it would perhaps be its universality. Stoics saw mankind as one brotherhood. They looked outside the city state, outside the Empire and saw the whole of the human race as being bound and united by the brotherly love that the precepts of natural law enjoined.

Christianity

The parallels between the tenets of Stoicism and the teaching of Christ come readily to mind. But Christianity offered an advantage not made available by Stoicism or any of the other religions competing to fill the place left by the decline of the old state religion of Rome. Stoicism taught that men should love one another, since this was in accord with nature and thus was man's duty. Christianity taught – 'Love one another', and it added 'and if you do, there is a bonus – life everlasting.'

For the Stoic, death was the end. The only reward for living a good life was to be able to die in the knowledge that one had done one's duty. For the Christian the reward was Heaven, coupled with satisfaction of knowing that the sinner (among whom no doubt were numbered one's enemies) would suffer the eternal torments of Hell. Christianity offered a carrot.

The teaching of Christ provided a code of conduct, but not a comprehensive theology. The creation of the latter was the accomplishment of the Fathers of the early church, principally St Augustine, St Ambrose and St Gregory. Having been born into the Roman world it was natural that these men should reflect in their writings aspects of the philosophies of Greece and Rome that could be enlisted to give intellectual support to the teachings of the new church.

25 Ibid, Book 8, 23.

The incorporation of natural law into Christian theology was accomplished at a later period, but when St Augustine wrote 'If a law be unjust, it is no law at all', we can see foreshadowed what was to come later: the idea that if a man-made law conflicts with natural law, it is invalid.

It is understandable that natural law should be among the ideas of the pagan philosophies that became part of Christian teaching. The doctrine lent itself readily to adoption. Under the old ideas, natural law had, if not for Aristotle at any rate for some, been seen as being derived ultimately from the Gods, or from the spirit from which the earth and the universe were in some way derived. It needed no great adjustment for the doctrine to be incorporated into Christian theology. For was not the Christian god the architect of the universe and all that lay within it, the creator of the natural order from the nature of which man, by reason, might deduce those principles by which, in pursuance of God's will, he should conduct himself?

The central place attained by natural law by the time of the early Middle Ages is demonstrated in Gratian's *Concordantia Discordantium Canonum* (later referred to as Gratian's *Decretum*[26]), a collection of texts dealing with canon law, with a commentary designed to reconcile inconsistencies and contradictions that had accumulated during the previous centuries. The work became the principal text on canon law in the church and retained its importance down to the codification of 1917. In the *Decretum* natural law is treated as part of the immutable law of God. Not only was natural law anterior in time, and superior, to man-made law, but, as St Augustine had asserted, to the extent that man-made law ran counter to natural law, it was null and void.

St Thomas Aquinas

It was in the work of St Thomas Aquinas,[27] principally in the *Summa Theologica*, that the final and most complete synthesis of the classic doctrine of natural law and the doctrine of the Christian church was achieved. The writings of Aristotle had been lost to the western world from the fall of the Empire in the west and only became available to western Scholars in the twelfth century. It was the achievement of St Thomas to reconcile the philosophy in newly-discovered writings with the doctrines of Christianity and to do so in such a way as to strengthen mightily the intellectual basis on which Christianity rested.

---

26   1140.
27   The bibliography is extensive. Of particular assistance is *Aquinas: Selected Political Writings* (ed A P d'Entrèves). See also D J O'Connor *Aquinas and Natural Law*, H V Jaffa *Thomism and Aristotelianism*; A Kenny *Aquinas*.

The influence of Aristotle resulted in the re-emergence of teleology as a feature of natural law thinking. St Thomas's chain of thinking is this. God is the creator. The world, the universe, the cosmos is his creation. Everything, physical and intellectual, stems from Him. When God created man He enabled him to know truth. Truths are of three kinds. Divine truths are those made known to man by revelation. For example, it is revealed to man by the Holy Scriptures that Jesus Christ is the Son of God, who was sent into the world; that, by his death on the cross, a means of salvation should be offered to all those who confess their sins and acknowledge Christ as their Saviour; further that it is God's will that on six days should man labour, and on the seventh, rest; that Mary, the mother of Jesus, was a virgin, and that at her death she was taken up into Heaven.

Next came those truths that man can discover by exercise of speculation, by what St Thomas calls 'speculative reason'. For example, by reflection man can come to know that the three interior angles of a triangle equal two right angles. Truths in this category are concerned with 'necessary truths, which could not be otherwise than they are'. A conclusion derived from such a truth is as valid as the truth from which it is derived.

Third are truths which man discovers by the exercise of 'practical reason'. These are truths, Aquinas tells us, that are concerned with matters into which human actions enter. It is here that we see the teleological influence of Aristotle. Within everything is an 'inclination' to seek its own preservation. Man, as part of the created world, shares this inclination. The achievement of this inclination is furthered by man having other inclinations, ones that he shares with other animals. These inclinations are the instincts with which nature has imbued all animals, for example to copulate and to rear offspring. But, says Aquinas, man has certain inclinations peculiar to himself. He alone has an inclination to know the truth about God, and to live in society.

From the fact that man is inclined to these general ends, man is able to know, by the exercise of practical reason, that he should not, for example, give offence to those with whom he must associate, since offence would risk strife, and strife would disturb the peace necessary to man to live, as is his natural end, in society. Matters that man can discover by the exercise of practical reason Aquinas terms the eternal law.

For Aquinas, natural law consists of participation by man in the eternal law. It is not altogether clear, it must be said, how Aquinas distinguishes between eternal law and natural law. In places the two terms appear to be used indiscriminately. Perhaps we should understand him to mean that natural law is that which requires men to adhere to eternal law. But as his exposition unfolds it is natural law that he treats as containing the precepts that men should follow.

To discover how man's affairs should be regulated it is necessary, Aquinas said, to proceed, by the exercise of human reason, from the first principles of natural law, to other more particular dispositions.

The first principles of natural law are immutable, eternal, and binding on all mankind. But when we go from the general to the particular we may find that the conclusions reached do not necessarily have the same universal validity. For example, if we deduce from the principle that man should live at peace with his fellows, the principle that debts should be repaid, we find that: 'This conclusion holds in the majority of cases. But it could happen in some particular case that it would be injurious, and therefore irrational, to repay a debt; if, for instance, the money repaid were used to make war against one's own country. Such exceptions are all the more likely to occur the more we get down to particular cases. The more specialised the conditions applied, the greater is the possibility of an exception arising ...'

Since the nature of human activity may change, it may happen that 'in some particular case, or in a limited number of instances', natural law, in its more detailed workings out, may change. Thus things may be added to, or subtracted from, the body of the law. But with regard to first principles, 'it is wholly unchangeable'.

In a passage of crucial importance St Thomas explains the relationship between man-made law and natural law. He says,[28] 'St Augustine says "There is no law unless it be just".[29] So, the validity of law depends upon its justice. But in human affairs a thing is said to be just when it accords aright with the rule of reason: and, as we have already seen, the first rule of reason is the natural law. Thus all humanly enacted laws are in accord with reason to the extent that they derive from the natural law. And if a human law is at variance in any particular with the natural law, it is no longer legal, but rather a corruption of law.'

This raises the question, if a human law conflicts with natural law, and thus 'is no longer legal' (or as we might express the matter today, it lacks validity) does this mean that a citizen may in good conscience disobey it? Can he say, 'For me, this is *not* law'? In answering this question, St Thomas explains that law may be unjust, by which he means in conflict with natural law, in one of two ways. First, 'by being contrary to human good, through being opposed to the things mentioned above – either in respect of the end, as when

28   Qu 92 Art 2. Translated J G Dawson.
29   1 *De Lib Arbitrio* 5.

an authority imposes on his subjects burdensome laws, conducive, not to the common good, but rather to his own cupidity or vainglory; or in respect of the author, as when a man makes a law that goes beyond the power committed to him. The like are acts of violence rather than laws, because, as Augustine says, "A law that is not just, seems to be no law at all." Wherefore such laws do not bind in conscience, except perhaps in order to avoid scandal or disturbance, for which cause a man should even yield his right ...

'Secondly, laws may be unjust through being opposed to the divine good: such are the laws of tyrants inducing to idolatry or to anything else contrary to the divine law; and laws of this kind must nowise be observed because, as stated in Acts v 29, "we ought to obey God rather than men".'

So if a ruler makes a law that conflicts with natural law, for example a law that people's legal rights and economic entitlements should vary according to the colour of their skin, then notwithstanding the law's injustice, the law should not be disobeyed, since of greater import than the validity or invalidity of the law is the need to avoid disturbance. For the sake of avoiding disturbance, the citizen should 'yield his right'. In modern parlance, law and order take precedence over matters of justice.

On the other hand, if the state makes a law that 'is opposed to the divine law' – the content of which it is the Church's function to decree – then man is freed from the obligation to obey. (Whether or not a man-made law conflicts with divine law is a question for the Church to determine.)

Thus if the state makes a law that the citizen regards as unjust he should obey it. If the state makes a law that the Church ordains to be unjust, he should not. (The value of this conclusion for the Church in conflicts with state will be appreciated.)

St Thomas's contribution was to provide a synthesis between the Judeo-Christian understanding of law and justice, with its view of law as derived from revelation of God's intention for the world, and the Greco-Roman view of law as being interdependent with reason.

St Thomas's integration of Aristotle's philosophy into the structures of Christian theology gained official acceptance in 1270. His view of natural law has continued to provide the foundation of the thinking of the Catholic Church until our own day.[30]

---

30 For one of the most concise, complete and confident statements of the doctrine in recent times, see J Maritain *Man and the State* pp 90–91. See also J M Finnis 'Natural Law in Humanae Vitae' (1968) 84 LQR 467.

The seventeenth century

Although it has been within the theology of the Catholic Church that the doctrine of natural law has found its fullest expression, the seeds of the doctrine, as we have seen, were sown before the Christian era. It was politic for Christianity to absorb the doctrine. But the doctrine was not (and is not) dependent on Christianity. This being so, did the doctrine continue in its original non-Christian form? During the Dark and Middle Ages, to the European it was not conceivable that the world was other than the creation of God. But by the seventeenth century there came to be a realisation that natural law, as a system from which rules of conduct could be deduced, was not logically dependent on the existence of a superior being. The most famous assertion of this view is that by Grotius[31] who, in 1625, in *De Jure Belli ac Pacis*,[32] after a dissertation on various aspects of natural law, wrote: 'And what we have said would still have great weight, even if we were to grant, what we cannot grant without great wickedness, that there is no God.' By the inclusion of the words '... what we cannot grant without great wickedness', Grotius protected himself against the charge of heresy. But, because of his eminence, the seed of a secular natural law doctrine was resown. Natural law *could* provide the foundation of a system of ethics, a reason why men should behave in a certain way, that was independent of the fact that God's will, revealed in the Scriptures, directed men to act in the same manner. The atheist, observing the world, the nature of man, and the things towards which man strived, could deduce the first principles of natural law equally as well (and would come to the same conclusion as to the content of natural law), as the devoutest and most orthodox of Catholic theologians.

It remains to be said that during the seventeenth and eighteenth centuries there grew up a doctrine that had affinities with, and shared certain of the foundations with, the doctrine of natural law: the doctrine of natural rights. This doctrine is discussed in a later chapter.

Conclusion

If this chapter was intended as a history of the doctrine more would have been said at various stages of our account,[33] and consideration

31 1583–1645.
32 *Proleg* 11; bk i, 10(6).
33 Eg concerning the Roman concept of the *ius gentium*, the principles that in practice were regarded as forming a common substratum of law among peoples of all states, and nations, and concerning the place of natural law in the thought of great Roman jurists such as Ulpian, and in the *Institutes* of Justinian.

would have had to be given to the importance of the doctrine as an influence on philosophy,[34] on the development of law, and on the conduct of affairs of state.[35] But the purpose here has been more limited: to explain the nature of the doctrine, in particular the various strands of thought that became woven together to make up one cord with which the history of the doctrine has been compared. Of these strands, not all run continuously throughout the cord's whole length. The elements that make up the cord vary with the passage of time. But nevertheless the cord remains a single one, a line of thinking, a doctrine with a clearly recognisable identity that has formed an element of crucial importance in European thought for nearly 2,000 years.

But enough. To say more would be to labour the point. It stands to reason, surely, that there are some principles of conduct so basic as to be of constant and universal application. It stands to reason (it stands to *reason*) that from what man can observe of his condition he can deduce how he ought to behave. Is this not so?

---

34 Eg on Pufendorf (1632–1694), Thomas Hobbes (1588–1679), John Locke (1632–1704).
35 Eg as the foundation of Grotius' structure of international law in *De Jure Belli ac Pacis*.

CHAPTER 6

Of big fish and little fish

The attack on natural law

The unacceptable jump

Is this not so? Well, there are, we know,[1] two persons who did not agree, John Austin and, before him, David Hume. It will be recalled[2] that the nub of the objection made by these two was that inherent in the doctrine of natural law was a logical inconsistency: that half way through the doctrine's exposition came a switch from 'is' (ie what man's nature is) to 'ought' (ie how man ought to behave). They did not object to chains of reasoning based on 'is' (fire is hot; it is the tendency of heat to burn; a burn is painful); nor chains of reasoning based on 'oughts' (man ought to love his fellows; an individual ought to show forgiveness; if A offends B, B ought to forgive him). But they protested that natural law entailed a jump – because man's nature *is* such and such, he *ought* to behave in such and such a way.

Kelsen, in a valuable article attacking natural law,[3] agrees. Natural law, he says, obliterates the essential difference between the scientific laws of nature, the rules by which the science of nature describes its objects, and the rules of ethics, or morality. We may describe certain behaviour that is in conformity with a pre-existing standard as good, right, or correct; and behaviour that is not in conformity with the norm as wrong, bad, or incorrect. But these are

---

1 See Chap 2.
2 Page 28 supra.
3 'Natural Law Doctrine and Science' in Hans Kelsen *What Is Justice?* See also A Ross *On Law and Justice* Chap 2.

value judgments. Such value judgments may be expressed by saying that a person ought or ought not to behave as he does. But, and this is the crux of Kelsen's attack, 'value is not immanent in natural reality. Hence value cannot be deduced from reality. It does not follow from the fact that something is, that it ought to be or to be done, or that it ought not to be or not to be done. The fact that in reality big fish swallow small fish does not imply that the behaviour of the fish is good, nor yet that it is bad. There is no logical inference from the "is" to the "ought", from natural reality to moral or legal value.'[4]

The content of human laws, Kelsen explains, depends on the purpose of the laws, what the laws are designed to achieve. And what they are designed to achieve depends on the kind of society that the law-making authority wishes to see exist. A decision about this entails a value judgment. Values here may conflict – for example between personal freedom and social security. On such an issue a decision has to be made: which of the two is to be preferred. This question cannot be answered in the same way as the question whether iron is heavier than water, or water heavier than wood. The question as to which of two conflicting values is to be preferred can only be decided emotionally, according to the feelings or wishes of whoever makes the decision.

This is why, Kelsen says, we find that laws and systems of government supposedly all derived from natural law vary from place to place and from age to age, there being no unanimity between philosophers as to the conclusions to be deduced from natural law. For example, with regard to the ideal form of government, for Hobbes natural law taught that the civil government should have absolute authority; for Locke and Rousseau, under natural law democracy is the ideal. For Sir Robert Filmer democracy is contrary to natural law: 'God did always govern his own people by monarchy alone.' With regard to private property, Kelsen demonstrates that while natural law has been called in aid by such writers as Grotius, Cumberland and Locke to defend the rights to private property, natural law can equally be used to form the basis of an argument against private property (as in *Code of Nature or the True Spirit of the Law*, by Morrelly, published in 1755). Thus, as Ross[5] observed, 'like a harlot, natural law is at the disposal of everyone'. That this is so can be seen by the way that down the centuries slavery was justified within the Christian natural law tradition.

4 Ibid, p 140.
5 Ibid, p 261.

What actually happens, Kelsen contends, is that natural lawyers do not deduce natural law from man's nature, but to presuppose natural law principles and then deduce from these the characteristics of an ideal man – they say what principles ought to rule supreme, and then from these say how men ought to behave. Kelsen challenges a natural lawyer's choice to have sole access to what principles ought to rule supreme; he denies the natural lawyer's claim to infallibility. Kelsen accepts the logic that deduces an 'ought' from an 'ought'. It is the natural lawyers' insistence that their 'ought' is derived from an 'is' – that 'value is in immanent in reality'[6] – that he will not accept.

Superfluity

In a second prong of his attack on natural law, Kelsen points out that 'if it is possible – as the natural law doctrine asserts – to find the rules of natural law by an analysis of nature; if, as some writers assert, the law of nature is even self-evident, then the positive law is quite superfluous. Faced by the existence of a just ordering of society, intelligible in nature, the activity of positive-law makers is tantamount to a foolish effort to supply artificial illumination in bright sunshine. This is another consequence of the natural-law doctrine. But none of the followers of this doctrine had the courage to be consistent. None of them has declared that the existence of natural law makes the establishment of positive law superfluous. On the contrary. All of them insist upon the necessity of positive law.'[7]

Good/bad contradiction

This leads Kelsen to a further flaw in natural law doctrine. Natural lawyers justify positive law (and a state with coercive machinery to enforce it) on the ground that these are needed because of man's badness. At the same time their doctrine requires an assumption that man is good, because it is from human nature that the principles of natural law are to be deduced. Thus natural lawyers entangle themselves in a contradiction.[8]

6   *Kelsen*, supra, p 141.
7   Ibid, p 142.
8   Ibid, p 143.

Insincerity

Next Kelsen criticises natural lawyers on the ground of their insincerity: they fail to carry their doctrine to its logical conclusion. According to their doctrine, if a positive law conflicts with natural law, it is void. But do they, Kelsen asks, abide by the consequences of this test? Where a law of the state conflicts with natural law do natural lawyers in fact say that a citizen should (or even that they may) disobey it? Kelsen examines what certain natural law writers have said on the matter. He considers Pufendorf. This writer concedes that 'a civil law could, of course be passed which is opposed to natural laws'. But he believes that 'none but an insane man, and one who had in mind the destruction of the state, would wish to pass legislation of this kind'. And 'in all commonwealths most features of the law of nature, at all events such as those without which peace in the society itself cannot stand, have the force of civil law. . .'. This is to be the presumption. And it is not open to an individual to challenge the presumption since 'the presumption of justice stands always on the side of the prince'. Thus the citizen must obey the civil law. Any judgment by him that the civil law conflicts with natural law is irrelevant.

For Locke resistance to the civil law is justified only if force is used against the citizen 'unjustly and unlawfully'; 'unjustly' meaning contrary to natural law, 'unlawfully' meaning contrary to civil law. But since whether force has been so used is a matter not for the individual but for the authorities to decide, justifiable resistance is in practice ruled out.[9]

Another line of argument by natural lawyers in support of unprotesting acceptance of the civil law consists in the thesis that since the position of the civil government derives its authority from natural law, opposition to the civil powers cannot be justified. Thus Grotius '... if unjust treatment be inflicted upon us, we ought to endure it rather than resist by force', and Pufendorf 'the lesser injuries of princes should be overlooked out of consideration for the nobility of their position and other benefits, and indeed for the sake of our fellow citizens and the entire state ...' Kelsen concludes that an analysis of the thinking of the classical natural law writers shows the function of natural law being treated, not as a basis for criticism of, let alone for challenging, the civil law but as a means of strengthening the authority of the civil law and the civil authorities, the doctrine thus having a strictly conservative character.[10]

9   Ibid, p 150.
10 Ibid, p 150.

From his examination of the logical flaws inherent in, and practical shortcomings of, the doctrine, Kelsen's conclusion would therefore accord with that of Austin, that natural law is 'nothing but a phrase'.

The pull of natural law

Why is it that the natural law doctrine, despite its flaws and inconsistencies, has had such an influence in the history of European thought? Kelsen's answer is that natural law 'satisfies a deeply-rooted need of the human mind, the need for justification. To justify the subjective value judgments which emerge from the emotional element of his consciousness, man tries to present them as objective principles by transferring to them the dignity of truth, to make them propositions of the same order as statements about reality. Hence he pretends to deduce them from reality, which implies that value is immanent in reality.'[11] This has a comforting corollary: belief in natural law enables a person to obey a civil law, not because he is compelled to do so by the civil power, but because of the law's intrinsic value. But, as we have learned, at the heart of Kelsen's argument lies the contention that value is *not* immanent in reality. Natural law nevertheless strikes a chord with a long-lasting and deep-seated need felt by mankind – the need for certainty, for the existence of truths that are absolute and unchanging.

Absolute values and relative values

The debate over whether certain values (in particular over questions of right and wrong) are absolute, or whether values are relative, varying with civilisations, religions, and different periods of time, is as old as European philosophy. That ethical judgments and values are relative was the tenet of philosophers known as the Sophists, active in the fifth century, in the life time of Plato. For the Sophists there can be belief, but not knowledge, in the sense of knowledge of absolute truth. All knowledge is relative to the person seeking it. Sophists pointed out that customs and standards of behaviour earlier accepted as absolute and universal, and of divine institution, were, in fact, local and relative. Habits abhorrent to the Greeks, for

11 Ibid, p 159.

example marriage between brother and sister, might be accepted as normal elsewhere. The customs of other races collected and described by Heroditus, and the contacts between Greeks and barbarians, confirmed that values were relative – to particular people, in particular places at particular times. The Sophists were sceptics, believing that certainty is unattainable. Their view was reflected by Democritus: '... we know nothing, for truth is in the depths, and either truth does not exist or it is hidden from us.' The notion of 'truth' and 'knowledge' are thus illusions. What *seems* to each man, *is* as far as he is concerned. For Protagorus, the Sophist, nothing exists save what each of us perceives. Reality exists only in relation to our own feelings and convictions. No man is in a position to call another mistaken. One of Euripides's characters asks 'What action is shameful if it seems not so to the actor?' Kelsen expressed the relativist view in our own century: '... there are, as a matter of fact, very different systems of morality and very different systems of law, whereas there is only one system of nature. What according to one system of morality is good may, under another system of morality, be bad; and what under one legal order is a crime may be under another legal order perfectly right. This means that the values which consist in conformity or non-conformity with an existing moral or legal order are relative values.'[12]

It was against the Sophists that Plato's writings are directed. Because of his artistry, his wit, his shrewdness, his humanity, his enthusiasm, it is with Plato that our sympathies lie when, albeit in translation, we read the *Dialogues*. And because in the *Dialogues* it is Socrates who scores the points, we feel that it is Plato who comes out best. But, looking back over the intervening two millennia we must admit that it is the Sophist attitude that comes closest to the views that most generally prevail today. We know that over a myriad of matters opinions as to right and wrong differ not only from one community to another but within one community – over pornography, homosexuality, the use of drugs, divorce, contraception, the freezing of human embryos, human fertilisation, the cloning of human genes (and other issues concerning genetic engineering on which the Human Fertilisation and Embryology Authority is asked to make recommendations), surrogate motherhood, the use of animals for research, whether it is sinful to eat pork, the appropriateness of various forms of punishment, the distribution of wealth, responsibility by society for the care of individuals – judgments over all these things, as to what is right and what is wrong, differ. Not many people today believe, with Plato, in a

12 Ibid, p 141.

'form' of goodness, an absolute and ideal standard by reference to which we can determine universal, absolute, ethical values. The Sophists, to most present day ways of thinking, were correct.

So when Japanese soldiers entered villages in Malaysia in the Second World War and for sport threw babies and young children into the air catching them as they fell on the end of their bayonets they committed nothing that can be regarded as absolute wrong: when two teenagers broke into the flat of a partly blind widow of 92 and beat and raped her and gouged out one eye, these actions were wrong merely according to the particular code of our own time. Absolute certainty as to the wrongness of any act can never be laid down. All values are merely relative. Is this not so, dear reader, is this not so?

CHAPTER 7

And yet, and yet ...

The revival of natural law and the 'Hart–Fuller debate'

A revival? Since natural law thinking has continued as a living doctrine at the heart of the thinking of the largest of the Christian churches down to our own day it seems inappropriate to speak of a revival of natural law. And it is true that reassertions and reformulations of the traditional doctrine have continued to be made down to our own time, a particular resurgence in interest occurring in France and Italy in the early years of the century.[1] In the second half of the century there has been an emergence of fresh ideas that have such strong affinities with traditional natural law thinking that they can be regarded as new strands in the cord with which the history of natural law can, as we saw in chapter 5, by analogy be compared. At the heart of this new thinking lies the idea that, despite the force of the arguments levelled against natural law, despite their logic and seeming unanswerability, surely it must be the case that if some matter is so terrible, or so contrary to the basics of rationality, as to be beyond human acceptance, and the law upholds this matter, then the law must be so flawed as to be incapable of properly being regarded as 'law', whatever meaning one may choose to attach to the word.

Whether this idea can be justified was the subject of a debate between Professor H L A Hart and Professor L H Fuller. (This is the 'Hart–Fuller debate' – a debate, be it noted, that is distinct, and very different in its content, from the 'Hart–Devlin debate', over the enforcement of morality, considered in a later chapter.[2])

---

1 G Haines *Revival of Natural Law Concepts* (1930).
2 Chapter 13.

The debate was sparked by an article written in the Harvard Law Review by Professor Hart in 1958.[3] Professor Fuller responded in an article in the same journal.[4] Hart replied in a chapter in *The Concept of Law* in 1961. Fuller responded in a chapter in his *The Morality of Law* in 1963. Hart replied in an article in 1967. For simplicity we shall consolidate the arguments of the two protagonists, stating first the views put forward by Professor Fuller.

The pivot, or at least the common starting-point, in the debate was the attitude taken by Gustav Radbruch to the legality of laws passed during the Nazi era in Germany. Radbruch had originally been a positivist, holding that resistance to law was a matter for personal conscience, the validity of a law depending in no way on its content. However, the atrocities of the Nazi regime compelled him to think again. He noted the way in which obedience to posited law by the legal profession had assisted the perpetration of the horrors of the Nazi regime, and reached the conclusion that no law could be regarded as valid if it contravened certain basic principles of morality.

After the war it was this thinking that was followed in the trials of those responsible for war crimes, or who had acted as informers for the former regime. In 1949 a woman was prosecuted in a West German court for an offence under the German Criminal Code of 1871, that of depriving a person illegally of his freedom, the offence having been committed, it was claimed, by her having denounced her husband to the war-time Nazi authorities as having made insulting remarks about Hitler, while on leave from the army. (The husband was found guilty and sentenced to death, but not executed, and sent to the eastern front.) The woman, in defence, claimed that her action had not been illegal since her husband's conduct had contravened a law prohibiting the making of statements detrimental to the government – a law that, having been made according to the constitution in place at the time, was valid. The court found that the Nazi statute, being 'contrary to the sound conscience and sense of justice of all decent human beings', did not have a legality that could support the woman's defence, and she was found guilty. The case thus illustrated a conflict between positivism and natural law, the latter triumphing. The principle adopted in the decision was followed in many later cases.

3   (1958) 71 HLR 593.
4   (1958) 71 HLR 630.

Professor Fuller's case

Professor Fuller (unlike, as we shall see, Professor Hart) believes that the German courts were correct in their approach. In the article[5] that expresses this view, Fuller introduces us to the notion of 'fidelity to law'. At first it seems that Fuller is saying that 'fidelity to law' is something that exists. We may find this puzzling in view of the evidence that some people, ranging from petty criminals to revolutionaries, do not *have* feelings of fidelity to law. It transpires, however, that Fuller is using the notion as a lead-in to mentioning that a legal system must have certain characteristics if it is to command the fidelity of a right-thinking person. Foremost among these characteristics is respect for what Fuller calls the 'inner morality of law'. By this Fuller refers to the essential requirement of a legal system that it should provide coherence, logic, order. These characteristics were lacking in the system of government instituted by the Nazis, as Fuller illustrates by reference to the retroactive decree by which the murder of 70 people in the Roehm purge of 1934 was validated, an event 'demonstrating the general debasement and perversion of all forms of social order that occurred under the Nazi rule'.[6]

Professor Fuller proposes that a system of government that lacks what he terms the 'inner morality of law' cannot constitute a legal system, the system lacking the very characteristic – order – that is a sine qua non of a legal system (just as a structure designed so as to stay stationary cannot be a 'vehicle').

In his book, *Morality of Law*, published in 1963, Fuller turns from the negative to the positive and explains what characteristics a system must show in order to be capable of constituting a legal system. He begins his explanation with an allegory about 'the unhappy reign of a monarch who bore the convenient, but not very imaginative and not very regal sounding name of Rex'.[7] Rex was determined to reform his country's legal system, in which procedures were cumbersome, remedies expensive, the language of the law archaic and the judges sometimes corrupt.

His first step was to repeal all existing laws and to set about replacing these with a new code. But, inexperienced in such matters, he found himself incapable of formulating the general principles necessary to cover specific problems and, disheartened, gave up the attempt.

---

5 (1958) 71 HLR 630.
6 Ibid, at 646.
7 *Morality of Law* p 33.

Instead he announced that in future he would decide all disputes that arose himself. He accordingly heard numerous cases but it became clear that no pattern was to be discerned running through the judgments that he handed down. The confusion that ensued caused the fiasco to be abandoned.

Seeking to learn from his mistakes, Rex undertook a course of study on making generalisations. Having completed the course he resumed the task of providing a code and after much labour produced a lengthy document, and announced that in future he would be governed by its principles in deciding cases. But, he decreed, the code was to remain a state secret known only to himself and his scrivener. The resentment of his subjects was such that the plan had to be abandoned.

Next, Rex resolved that reform should be achieved by his deciding at the beginning of each year all the cases that had arisen during the preceding year. This method would enable him to act with the benefit of hindsight. His rulings would be accompanied by his reasons for making them. But, since his object was to act with the benefit of hindsight, it was to be understood that reasons given for deciding previous cases were not to be regarded as necessarily applying to future cases.

After his subjects had explained that they needed to know *in advance* the principles according to which decisions would be made, Rex realised that he had no choice but to publish a code setting out the rules by which future disputes would be determined and after further labours a new code was published. But when the code was finally published, Rex's subjects were dismayed to find that its obscurity was such that no part could be understood either by laymen or lawyers.

To overcome this defect Rex ordered a team of experts to revise the code so as to leave the substance intact but clarify the wording so that the meaning was clear to all. However, when this was accomplished it became evident that the code was a mass of contradictions, each provision being nullified by some other.

Undeterred by this latest failure, Rex ordered that the code should be revised to remove the previous contradictions, and that at the same time the penalties for criminal offences should be increased, and the list of offences enlarged. This was done, and it was made, for example, a crime punishable by ten years' imprisonment to cough, sneeze, hiccup, faint or fall down in the presence of the king. Failure to understand, believe in, and correctly profess the doctrine of evolutionary, democratic redemption was made treason.

The near revolution that resulted when the code was published caused Rex to order its withdrawal. Once again a revision was undertaken. The new code was a masterpiece of draftsmanship. It was consistent, clear, required nothing that could not reasonably be complied with, and was distributed free. However, by the time that the new code came into operation its provisions had been overtaken by events. To bring the code into line with current needs, amendments had to be issued daily.

With time the number of amendments began to diminish and public discontent to ease. But before this had happened Rex announced that he was resuming the sole judicial role in the country: all cases would be tried by himself. At first all went well. His decisions indicated the principles that had guided him, and those by which future issues would be determined. At last a coherent body of law seemed to be appearing. But with time, as the volumes of Rex's judgments were published, it became clear that there was no link between Rex's decisions and the provisions of the code.

Leading citizens met to discuss what should be done but before any decision was reached Rex died, 'old before his time and deeply disillusioned with his subjects'.[8]

The 'inner morality of law'

Corresponding to the eight defects illustrated by Rex's mistakes Fuller lists eight qualities of excellence. In a legal system the laws must be: 1. general (not made ad hoc); 2. published; 3. prospective, not retroactive; 4. intelligible; 5. consistent; 6. capable of being complied with; 7. endure without undue changes; 8. applied in the administration of the society. These qualities make up the 'inner morality of law'. The word 'morality' is misleading. The word carries ethical connotations, yet none are intended. What Fuller refers to is the inner character of a legal system, the characteristics without which a system cannot properly be regarded *as* a legal system. The phrase also used by Fuller, 'fidelity to law', reflects the notion that a citizen can owe a duty to obey only where the features that make up the inner morality of law are present.

Does Fuller's view that a system of government that lacks the 'inner morality of law' can command no allegiance from a citizen mean that Fuller is to be regarded as a natural lawyer? In one sense Fuller stands outside the natural law camp. Imagine a law that required all children of ten who were left-handed to be executed. To a natural lawyer the law would, being in conflict with a code higher than man-made decrees, be void. Yet the law would not conflict with any of the Fuller requirements: the law would display the inner morality of law. So for Fuller the law would, we must presume, be valid. In this sense Fuller stands as a positivist. And yet the flavour of natural law hangs about him. Consider this passage: 'To me there is nothing shocking in saying that a dictator-ship which clothes itself with a tinsel of legal form can so far depart from the morality of order, from the inner morality of law itself, that it ceases to be a legal system. When a system calling itself law is predicated upon a general disregard by judges of the terms of the laws they purport to enforce, when this system habitually cures its legal irregularities, even the grossest, by retroactive statutes, when it has only to resort to forays of terror in the streets, which no one dares challenge, in order to escape even those scant restraints imposed by the pretence of legality – when all these things have become true of a dictatorship, it is not hard for me, at least, to deny to it the name of law.'[9] Here and elsewhere in his writing we gain the impression that it is not so much the failure to observe the inner morality of law that sticks in Fuller's throat as the evil that in practice results from this failure. Be that as it may, what we can say is this: under mainstream natural law thinking a law is not a valid law if it conflicts with a higher moral code. For Fuller a law is not valid if it forms part of a purported legal system that fails to comply with a higher code, the code in Fuller's case, however, being one based not on ethical values, but on values stemming from rationality. In this sense, in that he judges a law's validity by reference to an outside standard, Fuller's thinking can fairly be regarded as forming a strand in the natural law tradition.

Professor Hart's case

Professor Hart's point of divergence from Fuller is over the Radbruch issue. Hart, the positivist, rejects the notion that because of the circumstances in which it was made, a Nazi law should be deemed invalid. Is Hart, by so doing, in effect endorsing the legality of what may be wholly evil? No, Hart explains, he is not. People who claim that a posited law is not valid because it fails to meet certain external criteria muddy the water. The positivist approach makes people face up to the real issue. The positivist confronts people with the question – 'That law *is* the law. Is it so evil that you intend to

9   (1958) 71 HLR 630 at 660.

disobey and suffer the consequences?' 'This' Hart says 'is a moral [question] which everyone can understand and it makes a immediate and obvious claim to moral attention. If, on the other hand, we formulate our objection as an assertion that these evil things are not law, here is an assertion which many people do not believe, and if they are disposed to consider it at all, it would seem to raise a whole host of philosophical issues before it can be accepted.'[10] The natural lawyer blurs the issue. If we are going to criticise institutions or laws we ought to do so by speaking plainly and facing reality, not basing our criticisms on 'propositions of a disputable philosophy'.[11]

In *The Concept of Law* Hart, in a powerful plea, restates this point, 'So long as human beings can gain sufficient co-operation from some to enable them to dominate others, they will use the forms of law as one of their instruments. Wicked men will enact wicked rules which others will enforce. What surely is most needed in order to make men clear sighted in confronting the official abuse of power, is that they should preserve the sense that the certification of something as legally valid is not conclusive of the question of obedience, and that, however great the aura of majesty or authority which the official system may have, its demands must in the end be submitted to a moral scrutiny. This sense, that there is something outside the official system, by reference to which in the last resort the individual must solve his problems of obedience, is surely more likely to be kept alive among those who are accustomed to think that rules of law may be iniquitous, than among those who think that nothing iniquitous can anywhere have the status of law.'[12]

It is an irony of the Hart–Fuller debate that in deciding how, after the war, cases such as those concerning 'grudge informer' cases should have been dealt with,[13] both Hart and Fuller believe that (as also had Gustav Radbruch) retrospective legislation should have been the answer. But Fuller's reasons differed from those of Hart. 'But as an actual solution for the informer cases, I,' Fuller wrote, 'like Professors Hart and Radbruch, would have preferred a retroactive statute. My reason for this preference is not that this is the most nearly lawful way of making unlawful what was once law. Rather I would see such a statute as a way of symbolising a sharp

---

10 (1958) 71 HLR 593 at 620.
11 Ibid, at 621.
12 *The Concept of Law* pp 205–206.
13 Various solutions are discussed by L H Fuller in the Appendix to *The Morality of Law*. See also H O Pappe (1960) 23 MLR 260.

break with the past, as a means of isolating a kind of clean-up operation from the normal functioning of the judicial process. By this isolation it would become possible for the judiciary to return more rapidly to a condition in which the demands of legal morality could be given proper respect.'[14]

The most wide-ranging and closely-argued reassertion of natural law thinking in recent times has been that made by J M Finnis. The importance of Professor Finnis's work demands treatment in a separate, later, chapter.[15]

14   (1958) 71 HLR 630 at 661.
15   Chap 12.

CHAPTER 8

There all the time?

Ronald Dworkin[1]

Professor Dworkin's principal contributions to legal theory are contained in two books, *Taking Rights Seriously*, published in 1977 (and in a revised edition in 1978) and *Law's Empire*, in 1986. The first book presents ideas that had been foreshadowed in materials published earlier.[2]

In Chapter 2 of *Taking Rights Seriously* Professor Dworkin explains that his purpose will be to criticise what he calls, because of its influence and popularity, 'The ruling theory of law'. This theory, he explains, has two parts. The first is the theory that law consists of rules decreed by certain specific institutions. The second is the theory that finds the answer to the question 'What purpose should law serve?' to be that law should serve the general welfare of the community – the answer of the utilitarians.

The 'ruling theory' has been opposed, Dworkin says, by thinkers on the political left, to whom it seems that the formalism inherent in positivism compels the courts to enforce justice of a procedural

---

1 J W Harris *Legal Philosophies* (2nd edn, 1997) Chap 14; Davies and Holdcroft *Jurisprudence: Text and Commentary* Chaps 4, 10; N E Simmonds *Central Issues in Jurisprudence* Chap 6; D Lyons *Ethics and the Rule of Law* Chap 3; G Marshall 'Positivism, Adjudication and Democracy' in *Law, Morality and Society*; E P Soper (1977) 75 Mich LR 473; D Lyons (1977) LJ 415; D N MacCormick (1978) Phil LR 585; W J Waluchow (1985) 5 OJLS 187; J Raz (1986) 74 Cal LR 1103; E P Soper (1987) 100 HLR 1166.

2 'The Model of Rules' in *Law and Philosophy* (ed E A Kent, 1967); (1967) 35 Univ of Chicago LR 14; (1972) 81 YLJ 855; (1975) 88 HLR 1057; 'Is Law a System of Rules?' in *The Philosophy of Law* (ed R M Dworkin, 1977). *A Matter of Principle* (1985) brings together a number of articles by Dworkin since the first publication of *Taking Rights Seriously*.

character, preventing them from administering a richer, substantive, justice. Critics of the ruling theory on the political right follow the view of Edmund Burke that law consists not simply of the rules that are ordained, but also of the diffuse customary morality of a community. These critics on the right believe also that the optimism of the utilitarians (that society can be improved by the passing of laws that promote the greatest good of the greatest number) is ill-founded. They believe, with Burke, that the rules best suited to promote the welfare of a community will emerge only from the experience of that community, so that more trust should be put in the established social culture than in the social engineering of the utilitarians (who suppose that they know better than history).[3]

But neither of the two sets of critics, on the left or the right, base their opposition on the view that the ruling theory is defective because it has no place for the idea that individuals can have rights against the state that are prior to the rights created by explicit legislation.[4] This idea – that individuals can have rights that are prior to rights conferred by legislation (the notion of natural rights) is rejected also by adherents of the ruling theory. The positivist part of the ruling theory rejects the idea on the ground that the only law, including individual legal rights, that can exist is that decreed by the relevant authority. The utilitarian part of the ruling theory rejects the idea of natural rights on the ground that it is the general welfare of a community (not the protection of individual rights) that must serve as the overriding goal.

At this point[5] Dworkin lets it be known that his theory of rights will be concerned with *individual* rights. It will be the purpose of *Taking Rights Seriously* to explain the nature of these rights, and their place in a legal system. His theory of rights will not necessarily indicate what rights people actually have in a particular situation. But neither will his notion of individual rights be one that is purely abstract and in this respect his theory will emerge as one that is markedly different from the old, traditional theory of natural rights.

In Chapter 2 of *Taking Rights Seriously*, after setting out the essential elements of positivism, the version of positivism proposed by Austin, and the scheme proposed by Hart, Dworkin begins to explain his theory. Cases arise before the courts, he tells us, in which there is a larger than normal degree of uncertainty as to the outcome, owing to the fact that there is no pre-existing rule governing the relevant

---

3   R M Dworkin *Taking Rights Seriously* p x.
4   Ibid, p xi.
5   Ibid, p xi.

situation, or in which a pre-existing rule appears likely to produce a result that will not seem satisfactory. In cases such as these there are likely to be factors that pull judges in different directions. Such cases Dworkin terms 'hard cases'. (It should be understood that Dworkin uses this term in his own way. He is not using the term as it might be used in common parlance, eg to refer to cases that are difficult to understand, or to cases in which the outcome might seem hard, ie bad luck verging on unfairness, on one of the parties. 'Hard cases' are ones in which it is hard for the judge to decide which of two conflicting principles should prevail.)

Dworkin cites here the US case of *Riggs v Palmer*.[6] A grandson, who was a beneficiary under his grandfather's will, murdered his grandfather in order to inherit his property. Since the will was validly executed under the existing law, there was no bar to the grandson benefiting under the will. But the court held that because of the legal principle that no one should be permitted to profit from his own fraud or to take advantage of his own wrong, the grandson was disbarred from the inheritance.

Dworkin gives *Henningsen v Bloomfield*[7] as another example of a 'hard case'. H bought a car under a contract that contained an exemption clause which provided that the manufacturer's liability was limited to making good defective parts. As a result of a fault in the car there was an accident and H was injured. He claimed that he ought to be able to recover from the manufacturer notwithstanding the exemption clause. The court held in his favour. Dworkin shows that in reaching its decision the court was influenced by a variety of intersecting principles and policies which together provided authority for a new rule respecting a manufacturer's liability for automobile defects.

Thus law is concerned not only with established, posited, rules but also with principles. Positivism, Dworkin claims, being a system of rules, misses the importance of these principles – principles that do not, like rules, act in an 'all or nothing fashion', but act as guidelines that judges must take into account if they are relevant in reaching a conclusion.

It is a feature of principles, Dworkin says, that, unlike rules, they have the dimension of weight, or importance. When two principles lead to different conclusions, the judge must take into account the relative weight, the persuasive pull, of each. Rules do not have this quality: if two rules conflict, then only one can be valid. (Which one

---

6   115 NY 506, 22 NE 188 (1889).
7   (1960) 32 NJ 358.

is valid will have to be decided by some further rule, eg that a rule laid down by a higher court prevails over one laid down by a lower court, or that a later rule supersedes an earlier one.) But once we 'identify legal principles as separate sorts of standards, different from legal rules, we are suddenly aware of them all around us. Law teachers teach them, lawbooks cite them, legal historians celebrate them. But they seem most energetically at work ... in difficult lawsuits such as *Riggs* and *Henningsen.*' In cases like these, principles play an essential part in arguments supporting judgments about particular legal rights and obligations. After the judgment has been given we may say that the decision establishes a new rule (eg that a murderer is not entitled to take under the will of the person murdered). 'But the rule does not exist before the case is decided; the court cites principles as its justification for adopting and applying a new rule. In *Riggs* the court cited the principle that no man may profit from his own wrong as a background standard against which to read the Statute of Wills and in this way justified a new interpretation of that statute. In *Henningsen,* the court cited a variety of intersecting principles and policies as authority for a new rule respecting manufacturers' liability for automobile defects.'[8]

Positivists recognise that rules may not always be sufficient to enable judges to reach a decision. They hold that where a case cannot be decided by the application of a clear rule a judge must decide it by the exercise of his discretion, and that when this happens the judge creates new law. Hart, for example, accepts that where rules run out the law is open-ended, that the rules of law, at their fringes, have an 'open texture'. This notion is defective, Dworkin maintains, since it fails to recognise that where rules run out, judges, in reaching their decisions, are guided by principles.

There is a flaw, Dworkin contends, in another aspect of Hart's concept, that concerning the rule of recognition – the idea that in each legal system there is an ultimate test for determining the validity of a particular law. This idea is defective, he says, because it provides no place for establishing the validity of principles – principles cannot be traced back to any rule of recognition. 'The origin of legal principles (such as those in *Riggs* and *Henningsen*) lies not in a particular decision of some legislature or court, but in a sense of appropriateness developed in the profession and the public over time. Their continued power depends upon this sense of appropriateness being sustained. If it no longer seemed unfair to allow people to profit by their wrongs, or fair to place special burdens upon oligopolies that

8   R M Dworkin *Taking Rights Seriously* pp 28, 29.

manufacture potentially dangerous machines, these principles would no longer play much of a role in new cases, even if they had never been overruled or repealed. (Indeed, it hardly makes sense to speak of principles like these as being "overruled" or "repealed". When they decline they are eroded, not torpedoed.)

'True, if we were challenged to back up our claim that some principle is a principle of law, we would mention any prior cases in which that principle was cited, or figured in the argument. We would also mention any statute that seemed to exemplify that principle ...

'Yet we could not devise any formula for testing how much and what kind of institutional support is necessary to make a principle a legal principle, still less to fix its weight at a particular order of magnitude. We argue for a particular principle by grappling with a whole set of shifting, developing and interacting standards (themselves principles rather than rules) about institutional responsibility, statutory interpretation, the persuasive force of various sorts of precedent, the relation of all these to contemporary moral practices, and hosts of other such standards. We could not bolt all of these together into a single "rule", even a complex one, and if we could the result would bear little relation to Hart's picture of a rule of recognition, which is the picture of a fairly stable master rule specifying "some feature or features possession of which by a suggested rule is taken as a conclusive affirmative indication that it is a rule...".'[9]

Having shown the importance of legal principles (and the deficiency of positivism as set out by Hart, ie because this has no place for principles) Dworkin proceeds, in Chapter 4 of *Taking Rights Seriously*, to propound the theory that he will erect in place of the 'ruling theory'. The starting point is the distinction between two types of argument that are employed to justify a legislature to enact a law or a judge to reach a particular decision. One type Dworkin terms arguments of policy,[10] the other arguments of principle. 'Arguments of policy justify a political decision by showing that the decision advances or protects some collective goal of the *community as a whole*. The arguments in favour of a subsidy for aircraft manufacturers, that the subsidy will protect national defense, is an argument of policy. Argument of principle justify a political decision by showing that the decision respects or secures some *individual or group right*. The argument in favour of anti-discrimination statutes, that a minority has a right to equal respect and concern, is an argument of principle.'

9   Ibid, p 36.
10   See J D Bell *Policy Arguments in Judicial Decisions* (1983).

But when a case arises in which no settled rule dictates a decision either way, then it might seem that the judge could reach a conclusion on the basis of policy or of principle. He asks us here to consider the case of *Spartan Steel and Alloys Ltd v Martin & Co.*[11] The defendants' employee broke an electric cable belonging to a power company that supplied power to the plaintiff. As a result, the plaintiff's factory was shut down and, through loss of production, suffered financial loss. The court had to decide whether the plaintiffs were able to recover for this loss. The court might, Dworkin says, have reached its conclusion by asking whether a firm in the position of the plaintiff had a right to a recovery, which is a matter of principle, or whether it would be economically wise to distribute liability for accidents in the way the plaintiff suggested, which is a matter of policy.

In Dworkin's view, and this is a crucial element in his theory, the decisions of judges in cases such as *Spartan Steel*, should be, and in fact are, reached on grounds of principle not on grounds of policy. By this he means that a judge will find in favour of a plaintiff if the latter is able to show that he has a *right* to recover damages. Thus 'judicial decisions enforce existing political rights'.

Existing? How can they be existing if we do not know that such and such a right exists until a judge has found in one party's favour, thus showing that he has the right he needs to win the case? Dworkin proceeds to tell us. These 'political rights' are creatures of both history and morality: 'what an individual is entitled to have, in civil society, depends upon both the practice and the justice of its political institutions'.

Such as? What rights do men and women actually have? It is not the purpose of Dworkin's theory to tell us what such rights are. Rather his theory will 'provide a guide for discovering which rights a particular political theory supposes mean and women to have.' This is the nub of the matter. The rights that Dworkin focuses on are inherent in the political system.

These rights may be of an abstract nature, rights that emanate from abstract principles. In the case of an abstract principle there is no way of testing how important the principle is in relation to other principles with which it may conflict. Political principles which are the basis of rights such as speech or dignity or equality ('the grand rights of political rhetoric') are of this kind. Politicians speak of these without attempting to suggest how they can be given effect to in particular situations. To be contrasted with abstract rights are concrete rights. These are more

11   [1973] QB 27.

precisely defined, and their definition expresses the weight they have in relation to other concrete rights in particular situations. Thus a right of free speech is an example of an abstract right. A right of a newspaper to publish defence plans classified as secret provided that this publication will not create immediate physical damage to troops would fall into the category of concrete rights.

How is a judge to decide what are the principles inherent in the legal system within which he operates, and the purposes of statutes operative within it? In order to show what factors a judge would take into account in reaching his conclusions, Dworkin invents 'a lawyer of superhuman skill, learning, patience and acumen' who is a judge in a representative American court. This judge Dworkin calls Hercules. Hercules accepts the main, uncontroversial, constitutive and regulative rules of law in his jurisdiction. He accepts, that is, that statutes have the general power to create and extinguish legal rights, and that judges have the general duty to follow earlier decisions of their court or higher courts whose rationale, as lawyers say, extends to the case at bar.

Dworkin then considers how Hercules would reach a decision in the case of various types of problem that might arise before him.[12] He asks us to suppose that in Hercules' state there is a written constitution which provides that no law shall be valid if it establishes religion. The legislature passes a law purporting to grant free busing to children in church schools. A child at such a school seeks a declaration that he had a right to free busing. Whether or not the right exists depends on whether or not the enacted law is void as being contrary to the constitutional provision against the establishment of religion. (Dworkin then sets out the various questions that Hercules should ask in order to be in a position to decide whether the child who appears before him has a right to free busing.) Another of the problems that Dworkin proposes for Hercules' consideration is whether a statute that makes it a crime to unlawfully seize, confine, inveigle, abduct, or carry away by any means whatsoever any person, makes a criminal of a man who persuaded a young girl that it was her religious duty to run away with him, in violation of a court order, to consummate a 'celestial marriage'.

In making a decision on one of the problems that Dworkin poses for him, Hercules is not, as the views of some positivists suggest, breaking new ground; he is not operating in an area of what Hart termed 'open texture'; he is not exercising his discretion as to a just

---

12   See G Marshall 'Positivism, Adjudication, and Democracy', in *Law, Morality and Society* (eds P M S Hacker and J Raz, 1977).

outcome. He is looking at the totality of the objectives on which his society is based, and deducing from these, from the theory of society that he constructs, the principles immanent within that society. Having done this, having elucidated these inherent principles, he will be able to see what rights citizens have. And when he knows what rights people have, he can decide the outcome of cases that come before him. Thus Hercules is deciding cases in the light of what already exists. The law is already there – not, it is true, in an express form, but in a form that can be elucidated from the warp and weft of the fabric of the society within which Hercules lives. Where no statute or previous decision points to the proper outcome, the proper outcome nevertheless exists before the case arose.

This is an important idea. Our understanding is assisted by considering an analogy that Dworkin uses, that of a game of chess. In a game between the Russian Grandmaster Tal and the American Fischer, Dworkin tells us, Tal continually smiled at Fischer, causing him annoyance and putting him off his game. Suppose that the rules observed at the championship, although making elaborate provision for a wide range of eventualities (whether players might leave the table, the length of time allowed for each move, and so on) contained nothing about smiling. Fischer objects to the referee and claims that Tal should forfeit the match. The positivist who accepts Hart's concept would say that here, as no rule existed that covered the point, the referee had discretion as to the outcome; and that his decision (assuming that the doctrine of precedent operated in the field of the rules of championship chess) created a new rule. According to Dworkin, on the other hand, the correct decision *did* already exist. Whether or not Fischer had a right not to be smiled at by Tal was something that the referee could determine by examining the history, the nature, the objects and the existing rules of chess. The referee should consider the very character, the chessness of chess. He might come to the conclusion that the game was one of intellect, requiring concentration; that the object was to test which player had the greater capacity for assessing the consequences of a permutation of possible moves, that the exercise of the intellectual skills involved required concentration, that behaviour which disturbed a player's con-centration was something that hindered a true test of the competing skills. And, from all these factors, and perhaps others, he might deduce that inherent within the nature of chess was the principle that a player had a right not to be distracted by the deliberate conduct of the other. (By way of comparison one can imagine that the referee of a football match might decide that there was no principle inherent within the essence of the game of football that gave a goalkeeper a right not to be smiled at by an advancing forward.)

As in a game, so in society. The judge, in reaching a decision in a 'hard case', must look at the totality of laws, institutions, moral standards, and goals of the society. He must breathe the very atmosphere of the society in order to determine the principles on which the whole edifice rests. 'Judges do not decide hard cases in two stages, first checking to see where the institutional constraints end, and then setting the books aside to stride off on their own. The institutional constraints they sense are pervasive and endure to the decision itself ...'

Thus for Dworkin the law, at any rate the Anglo-American system of law, is a seamless web of principles within which are manifested the legal entitlements of a citizen in any piece of litigation. Thus, if an issue has not arisen previously before the courts, a judge does not (exercising Hartian 'discretion'), acting as a 'deputy legislator',[13] create new law. He gives effect to what is already implicit in the society within which the legal system operates. Judges do not make law, they find it.

In Dworkin's view, not only is this the way that judges *ought* to reach conclusions, it is the way they *do* reach decisions. They may not be conscious of this. They may think that, exercising Hartian discretion and operating in an untilled field, they are creating new law. But they are not. The law, the existing law of a society, contains the pointer to the decision that must be made. And when the decision is reached, the law it lays down will not be a new law so much as the crystallisation of what is already inherent in the society within which the legal system operates. The principle that a chess contestant has a right not to be smiled at, once enunciated, can be seen as having been implicit in the chessness of chess all along.

In this account of Dworkin's theory we have sought to present the theory as it unfolds, page by page, in *Taking Rights Seriously*. Looking back over this account it will be seen that at some stages Dworkin concentrates on principles, at others on rights. The two concepts at times do not appear always to be clearly distinguished. It seems, however, that Dworkin intends to give primacy (notwithstanding that the discussion commences with principles) to rights. The sequence is this:

(1) the society in which the legal system operates;
(2) the rights accorded by the society to the individuals within it;
(3) the principles inherent in the judges' decisions that give effect to these rights.

13 See E P Soper (1977) 75 Mich LR 475 at 476.

Although rights and principles are clearly linked in Dworkin's thinking, it may be that it is appropriate to think of the two notions as performing different rôles. In stressing the significance of principles Dworkin is criticising Hart's concept by demonstrating its incompleteness and asserting that any valid concept of law must find a place for principles as well as rules. In asserting the existence of rights, he is giving expression to the notion that judges find the law, not create it.

CHAPTER 9

How judges decide cases[1]

Law's Empire

In *Law's Empire* Dworkin leaves intact the essentials of his thesis about rights set out in *Taking Rights Seriously* and carries forward certain of the earlier ideas, in particular regarding adjudication.

Hard cases

In dealing with adjudication in *Law's Empire*, Dworkin's focus continues to be on 'hard cases'. These, it will be recalled from the last chapter, are cases in which there is no pre-exiting rule that governs the situation on which a judge is called upon to adjudicate, or where a pre-existing rule would produce a result that seems manifestly unsatisfactory. In such cases there will commonly be factors that pull a judge in different directions. In Dworkin's usage, the phrase 'hard cases' does not (as mentioned in the last chapter) refer to cases that require mental effort to understand, nor to cases in which the outcome might appear to be hard, in the sense of bad luck, on one of the parties. Nor does the phrase indicate that a judge necessarily finds it hard to decide the outcome. A hard case may come before a judge in which he may have no difficulty in quickly concluding what should be the outcome. Indeed, it may be that a non-hard case can cause a deal more heart searching for a judge than a hard one, for example where a judge has to decide whether

---

1 H Davies and H Holcroft, *Jurisprudence: Text and Commentary*, Chap 12; MDA Freeman, *Lloyd's Introduction to Jurisprudence* (6th edn) Chap 15; AG Guest *Ronald Dworkin*; J M Miller (1986) 9 Campell LR 203; P Soper (1987) 100 HLR 1166.

such and such an act did or did not amount to negligence, whether such and such an act was or was not properly to be regarded as being within a person's 'course of employment', or whether it was witness A or witness B who was telling the truth. No, hard cases are ones in which existing rules of law provide no answer, one way or the other, or in which existing rules pull in different directions, or (and here we add a third category) where a rule exists but a case arises in which the rule provides no answer as to whether a particular circumstance falls within its ambit. Dworkin gives an example. A statute provides that it shall be an offence for vehicles to enter a public park. Somebody who runs through the park clearly commits no offence. A person who drives a car through the park clearly does commit an offence. But what about a person who goes through the park on a skateboard? These have wheels; they are a means of locomotion. So is an offence committed or is it not?

Discretion at the edges

How do judges decide hard cases? One view, Dworkin says, is that of those who subscribe to the form of positivism exemplified by Hart in his *Concept of Law*, the view that where a rule exists, for example in the form of unambiguous provision of statute, a judge applies the rule concerned. But where rules conflict, or where a rule exists but it is fuzzy at the edges – that is, where the rule has a penumbra of uncertainty, where after a certain point the law 'runs out', where the law 'simply cannot be read off'[2] – judges exercise their discretion as to the outcome, thus creating new law, and so in this respect acting as legislators (or at any rate deputy legislators). Thus if a judge decided that a skateboard constitutes a 'vehicle' for the purpose of the statute, he would be creating new law for the future – that it is an offence to use a skateboard in the park.

Dworkin terms this view of how adjudication works 'strong positivism',[3] or 'conventionalism'

Pragmatism

Another view of how decisions are reached, Dworkin says, is that of pragmatism. According to this view, held for example by those within

2   Guest, supra, p 169.
3   As opposed to what Dworkin terms 'weak positivism' under which judges have discretion but the discretion is hedged with constraints such as analogies with similar situations.

the school of American realism, judges decide cases according to what will best achieve social goals. ('Pragmatism: The determination of matters solely according to their practical consequences and bearing on human interests', OED). Supporters of the pragmatic view of adjudication may recognise that consistency with past decisions can usefully be claimed for strategic reasons, but maintain that it has 'no intrinsic value in deciding what is best for a community's future'.[4]

We know from what was said in the last chapter that Dworkin must reject pragmatism since this view of adjudication has no place for rights: according to the pragmatist's view, a litigant asks the court to decide in his favour, not on the ground of pre-existing rights, but because a finding in his favour will accord with the betterment of society. Judges may give the impression that they are deciding a case on the ground of pre-existing rights but do so in fact on pragmatic grounds. Dworkin call this practice the *noble lie*.

Thus Dworkin rejects both conventionalism and pragmatism as satisfactory explanations of the judicial process. His greatest attention, however, is given to the attack on conventionalism. (Indeed, *Law's Empire* might well have been subtitled 'Why Hart's *Concept of Law* is wrong'.)

Retrospection

A defect in the conventionalist view of law, Dworkin believes, is that if in hard cases judges have discretion to decide the outcome, thus making new law, the new law would operate retrospectively. The unsuccessful party would find himself bound by law that did not exist before he brought the case. We shall see as this chapter progresses that Dworkin's view of how hard cases are to be decided avoids this alleged drawback.

The semantic sting

One reason for Dworkin's objection to conventionalism is that it has the shortcoming of all theories that adopt a semantic approach; that is, seeking the nature of something by means of describing the thing's most obvious features and then identifying which of those features are the most essential in explaining how the word is used.[5] For Dworkin the method is flawed, not only because the decision as to what is 'essential' may be a matter of opinion, but also because the use of the method assumes agreement over the meaning of the

4   AC Hutchinson.
5   P Soper.

words used in the formulation of the definition. Thus the semantic method begs the question. (To 'beg the question' means, not (as many journalists and broadcasters imagine) to 'raise the question', but to 'take for granted without warrant'.[6] Thus the query, 'Wherein lies a citizen's obligation to obey the law?' begs the question, since it assumes as fact the truth of something that has not been shown, namely that an obligation to obey the law exists.)

Dworkin's term for what he considers to be this defect in conventionalism is the *semantic sting.*

The proper role – Interpretation

Dworkin's principal objection to conventionalism rests, however, on the fact that (in saying that judges have discretion to decide the outcome in hard cases) conventionalism differs from what Dworkin believes to be the way that judges, at any rate ideally, decide hard cases. A judge's proper function is to be seen, he maintains, not in filling gaps by the exercise of his discretion, but in undertaking a process that Dworkin terms 'interpretation'. *Interpretation* – this is a key theme of *Law's Empire.*

The chain novel

In order to illustrate what he means by interpretation Dworkin speaks of the way in which a chain novel is written. 'Suppose,' he says, 'that a group of novelists is engaged for a particular project and that they draw lots to determine the order of play. The lowest number writes the opening chapter of a novel which he or she then sends to the next number who adds a chapter, with the understanding that he is adding a chapter to that novel rather than beginning a new one, and then sends the two chapters to the next number, and so on. Now every novelist but the first has the dual responsibilities of interpreting and creating, because each must read all that has gone before in order to establish … what the novel so far created is. He or she must decide what the characters are 'really' like; what motives in fact guide them; what the point or theme of the developing novel is; how far some literary device of figure, consciously or unconsciously used, contributes to these, and whether it should be extended or refined or trimmed or dropped in order to send the novel further in one direction or another …

6 Oxford English Dictionary.

'... in my imaginary exercise the novelists are expected ... to create, as far as they can, a single, unified novel rather than, for example, a series of independent short stories with characters bearing the same names.'[7]

As one reads this passage the analogy with the evolution of the common law cannot but spring immediately to mind. Judges *are* at the end of a long chain. It makes sense when Dworkin says 'Each judge must regard himself, in deciding the new case before him, as a partner in complex chain enterprise of which [the] innumerable decisions, structures, conventions and practices are history. He must interpret what has gone before because he has a responsibility to advance the enterprise in hand rather than strike out in some new direction of his own. So he must determine, according to his own judgment, what the earlier decisions come to, what the point or theme of the practice so far, taken as a whole, really is.'

Fit

So a judge's responsibility is to ensure that his judgment fits what has gone before - his interpretation must fit. *Fit* – this is another key theme of *Law's Empire*. '"Fit" is something people understand. The reason is simply the brute rational pull of bare consistency.'[8] Indeed, 'consistency' is a word that Dworkin might well have used instead of fit – though 'fit', it is true, has the advantage of punch.

'Fit' is not the only matter to which a judge must have regard if he is properly to fulfil his judicial role. There are other requirements. One is that his judgments must rest on principles, not on the furtherance of policies.

Principles

In employing the word 'principle' in *Law's Empire*, Dworkin does not use the word with the sense it carries in the phrase 'as a matter of principle', ie to act in compliance with a standard regardless of the consequences. He uses the word in his own sense of meaning 'propositions that describe rights'.[9]

A 'policy' (for the furtherance of which, as stated above, a judge is not to direct his decision) 'sets out a goal to be reached, generally an improvement in some economic, political, or social feature of the community'.[10]

---

7 *Law's Empire* p 540.
8 Guest, *Ronald Dworkin* p 52.
9 *Law's Empire*, p 438.
10 Ibid.

So a decision in a hard case must both fit, and must be directed to upholding what the judge finds to be the rights of the parties (rights embodied in principles); not to the attainment of goals – objectives intended to benefit a community generally.

It may be noted here that in *Taking Rights Seriously* Dworkin uses the word 'principles' to refer to those standards or guidelines of which the law consists in addition to rules; in *Law's Empire* he uses the word, in contradistinction to goals, in connection with rights.

Fairness

What are these rights? One is the right of an individual to be treated with *fairness* – another important word. Fairness relates to equality of control over the legislative process in any society: 'We all believe in political fairness: we accept that each person or group in the community should have a roughly equal share of control over decisions made in parliament or congress or the state legislature.' Fairness is a matter 'not just of enforcing the will of the numerical majority, as if its views were unanimous, but of trades and compromises so that each body of opinion is represented, to a degree that matches it numbers, in the final result'.

Checkerboard solutions

But is this enough? Dworkin believes not. The reason, he says, is that fairness alone would permit what he terms 'checkerboard solutions'. Use of this phrase assumes the existence of a dispute over whether it is best for a certain board to be black, or for it to be white. The parties are equally divided. A compromise under which squares are alternately black and white, as on a chess board, satisfies neither side to the dispute, but it is not unfair, as each side to the dispute obtains what it wants in proportion to its voting power. A checkerboard solution is arbitrary in the same way that Solomon's decision, to which Dworkin refers, in the case of the dispute between two women over a baby, was arbitrary. (Split the baby down the middle.[11])

Where a dispute involves a matter of merely practical convenience (for example over how parking should be restricted in a certain road) a checkerboard solution may be acceptable (permit parking on one side on even dates and on the other on odd dates). But where moral claims compete, for example over whether

11   1 Kings 3, v 16–28 (the judgment was, of course, a means of eliciting the truth).

abortion should be permitted, a checkerboard solution (for example, making abortion a criminal offence every other year) fails to satisfy. But why? Dworkin asks. The solution taken overall is not unfair since, assuming that the society is evenly divided on the issue, each side in the dispute gets half of what it wants, an outcome reflecting the equal division of opinion.

Does the deficiency of a checkerboard solution lie in its failure to achieve justice? Dworkin argues that this cannot be the case since rejection of a checkerboard solution may produces greater injustice than its acceptance. 'Suppose we can rescue only some prisoners of tyranny; justice hardly requires rescuing none even when only luck, not any principle, will decide whom we save and whom we leave to torture.'

The missing factor

Dworkin's conclusion, therefore, is that we cannot explain our hostility to compromise (to checkerboard solutions) by appeal to principles either of fairness or of justice. So why do we reject them? What is the missing factor? Here we come to the heart of Dworkin's book. He writes,[12] 'Astronomers postulated Neptune before they discovered it. They knew that only another planet, whose orbit lay beyond those already recognised, could explain the behaviour of the nearer planets. Our instincts … suggest another … ideal standing beside justice and fairness. Integrity is our Neptune.'

'Integrity is our Neptune' – from this Dworkin derives the phrase 'Law as integrity'.

Law as integrity

'Law as integrity' has so major a part to play in Dworkin's scheme that the book could well have been given this title rather than *Law's Empire*. It is therefore a matter of some regret, and frustration, that in no place does Dworkin spell out exactly what he means by 'Law as integrity'. We are told that 'Law as integrity asks…'[13] 'Law as integrity requires…', 'Law as integrity insists …', 'Law as integrity demands … '.

What happens is that we meet the phrase 'Law as integrity' so frequently that we forget that nowhere have we been told what the phrase means. The shape of the planet stays hidden. This is unfortunate, as the phrase 'integrity' is the keystone of the arch on

12 *Law's Empire* p 184.
13 Ibid, p 238.

which the book's thesis rest and nowhere are we told what shape the stone is.[14]

The result is that the reader is left on his own to decide what Dworkin means. If 'integrity' is used in the same sense as honesty or uprightness, the phrase is meaningless. Law as honesty? *As* honesty? What does 'as' mean? Does it mean playing the part of? – as in, 'Kate Winslet as Juliet', 'Donald Sinden as Widow Twankie"?

Equality of treatment

In our search for the meaning of 'Law as integrity' we begin to get warmer when we realise that the phrase can carry different meanings in different contexts. In the context under consideration (why our rejection of checkerboard solutions cannot be attributed solely to reasons of justice or fairness), 'Law as integrity' – the missing factor – refers to a requirement that the state should accept the moral rightness of treating all people as equals. Equality of treatment – this is another key theme of *Law's Empire*, one of the building blocks that goes to the making up of Law as integrity. The nature of the equality that should be sought is a subject to which Dworkin gives close attention. By equality Dworkin means more than merely an entitlement to have the law treat like cases alike (though this is part of the picture). Equality includes also equality of resources, not in the sense of the redistribution of wealth but, as far as practicable, in placing people on an equal footing in such non-material resources as freedom from racial discrimination. Thus in the case of those who are disadvantaged by racial prejudice, Law as integrity, wearing its equality hat, would require 'redistribution of a kind such that they are placed in the position they would have been had there been no prejudice'.[15]

Law as integrity 'demands ...'

This, though, is only one aspect of Law as integrity. It is clear that the phrase has a wider meaning than this. In our search for the wider meaning we get closer still if we regard 'Law as integrity' as a phrase employed by Dworkin to express the requirement that a judge must comply with if he is to operate in the manner that Dworkin thinks judges ought to operate in the kind of society that Dworkin thinks ought to exist. So when we meet such beginnings

---

14 'It is difficult to give a general characterisation of Dworkin's thought', Guest, p 14.
15 Guest, p 283.

as 'Law as integrity requires...', 'Law as integrity assumes...', 'Law as integrity demands...', we realise that what Dworkin means is 'Judges ought to...'.

Law as an integrated whole

But what is the over-arching requirement? A clue is to be found in another meaning, in fact the primary meaning, of 'integrity' – the meaning from which integrity in the sense of honesty is derived. This meaning, as given by the Oxford English Dictionary, is – 'The condition of having no part or element wanting; unbroken state; material wholeness, completeness, entirety'.

Seen in the light of this definition we can perhaps make sense of what Dworkin means by Law as integrity by understanding the phrase to represent a requirement that, in deciding hard cases, judges should look at the law and the society of which it forms a part as being in a 'condition having no part or element missing'; as being in a state of wholeness, completeness. In this light, 'integrity' means, not honesty, but 'integratedness'.

It is in fact, we learn as the book progresses, towards the attainment of this state of what we have termed integratedness that judges must strive in reaching their judgments – it is this, the attainment of integratedness that is the object of the process of interpretation that we saw earlier it is the duty of judges to undertake. So 'fit' refers not merely to consistency with statutes and previous decisions in the field of law immediately concerned. Fit must be directed to the far greater objective of ensuring that each decision forms part of a coherent whole,[16] so that the *whole* of the law itself forms a coherent system, each part fitting with the rest, each part, by the way it dovetails in, providing greater coherence, greater logical strength, to the total structure.

Thus when a hard case comes before a judge he is not to think of himself as deciding merely the point of law before him. The task is infinitely greater: he must test his conclusion 'by asking whether it could form part of a coherent theory justifying the network as a whole'.[17]

The uniquely correct answer

This notion of the law as an integrated whole carries forward the idea, noted in the last chapter, of the law as a seamless web,[19] in

---

16 *Law's Empire* p 251.
17 Ibid, p 251.
18 Ibid.
19 Lloyd, p 1270.

which the answers are already there, not in an express form, but derivable through, we learn in *Law's Empire,* the process inter-pretation. So that in every hard case there is a uniquely correct answer. Dworkin concedes that, judges being human, the right answer may not always be that given, and that judges may not always agree; and, further, that there may be instances when two different conclusions are equally good as interpretations of the law – that there may be 'ties'.

Ties

Where such a tie exists it is necessary for the judge to determine which of the two competing outcomes is best. It might seem that here we find an Achilles heel. If a judge in such a case has to decide which of two outcomes is best, is he not here exercising the kind of discretion that is the subject of Dworkin's attack on Hart? Dworkin makes no such concession. Dworkin's position is defended and explained by Guest.[20]

Guest asks us to consider this illustration.[21] 'A company runs a competition to advertise its breakfast cereal. A number of questions are set, matching heads to bodies of famous rock stars. There is also a "tie-breaker" question which does not admit of a demonstrable right answer as, obviously, the questions about the pop stars do, which asks competitors to say in a jingle of a set number of words what the virtues of the particular brand of cereal are.

'Five competitors obtain right answers to the head and body matching and, unlike some competitors who have also obtained right answers here, have written their jingles within the word limit. The task is then left to the competition judge to decide between them, on the basis of the tiebreak, which one should receive the prize on the basis of the jingle.

'In other words the judge has to decide which of the five entries is the "best" one. There are no precedents, nothing. Yet, would it seem right if the judge was random in his selection? We expect some judgment. Would it seem right if he exercised some sort of aesthetic judgment and came to the view that the two tied? Imagine that he does this and asks the sponsor to award two prizes or split the prize but the sponsor refuses. What does the judge do?

'The answer in Dworkin's terms is that a proper understanding of the competition is that the best entry must win and that the judge must go back to the entries and decide which one is the best. There

---

20   Guest, pp146-147.
21   Ibid, p 146.

is no more to it than that. The best entry is that which, according to the best understanding of the competition, is the best.

'… It is not as if there are no criteria other than the judge's feeling or transient taste. Rival interpretations [of which is best] could be: the most 'catchy', the most literate, the one with most advertising appeal, and so on. Test the different possible interpretations. What if the judge decided on the basis that a jingle pointing out the dangers to the environment of the sponsor's factory was the best entry? Or the one that made a political statement in favour of apartheid? Or one that made a plea for nuclear disarmament?

'The point is that the cornflakes judge does not operate, even with this sparse set of rules, as if there were no right answer.'

Thus 'judgments of an interpretative and argumentative nature are perfectly conceivable …' in order to reach a decision as to the best conclusion.

So, returning to the process of adjudication, it transpires that the one right answer will not always the *only* answer, but it will always be the one *best* answer. The task of finding it is, of course, of Herculean proportions and it is for this reason that in *Law's Empire* Hercules appears again, ready to show us the process of reasoning through which adjudication in the form of interpretation is exercised[22] (the process consisting of the elimination, one by one, of conclusions that fail to fit).

Decisions not retrospective after all

We are now in a position to understand Dworkin's answer to the unsuccessful litigant who complains that he is bound by law that operates retrospectively. The law he finds himself, by the judge's decision, bound by is not new law. The decision gives effect to the answer that was there all the time, ready to be found by anyone who sought it in the proper way. (Whether the unsuccessful litigant accepts this answer as satisfactory, is not our business here.)

Rights still central

There is another idea, in addition to that of the uniquely right answer, that is carried forward from *Taking Rights Seriously* – that of rights. The one correct answer, the answer that judges will find if they carry out the process of interpretation correctly, is one framed in terms of

---

22 Hercules is asked to act as if he had been the judge in *McLouglin v O'Brian*.

individual rights, rights derived from principles, principles that must always take priority over social goals.

But why?

Having reached this far in the journey through the realms of *Law's Empire*, it will be appreciated, looking back, how far we have travelled from what may now seem the simplistic idea that when the law 'runs out' judges have discretion – discretion to decide what the law is, to make new law, to act as deputy legislators.

But why? Why must the judicial process, carried out through interpretation, create law as an integrated whole? Why must principles prevail over goals? *Why*? The answer concerns justification for state coercion. What moral justification is there for the state to impose its will on inhabitants by the use of force? Dworkin looks at this question from what he terms the insider's point of view – the view of a citizen who requires justification for the exercise by the state of coercion over him. (The outsider is not concerned with justification – the outside observer is interested merely to note that coercion exists and the circumstances when it is exercised.)

Justification

Coercion by the state, Dworkin believes, is justified only where principles that give effect to individual rights and elucidated through the process of interpretation as forming part of the law's seamless web, prevail and are *accepted* by the citizens of the community. '... [M]embers of a genuine political community ... accept that they are governed by common principles, not just rules hammered out in political compromise.' It follows that 'Politics ... is a theatre of debate about which principles the community should adopt as a system ... so each member accepts that others have rights and that he has duties flowing from that scheme, even though these have never been formally identified or declared'. Thus 'each accepts political integrity as a distinct political ideal and treats the general acceptance of that ideal ... as constitutive of political community'.[23]

Fraternity

Thus '[l]aw as integrity is the organic bond as a political association that goes beyond bare similarity of interest and aspires to fraternal status'.[24] *Fraternity*, this is another key word, the word that describes

23   *Law's Empire* p 211.
24   AC Hutchinson.

the nature of the society in *Law's Empire's* realm, that in which people are bound together by reciprocity of interest.[25]

Coercion by the state is, in short, only justified[26] if the principles inherent in Law as integrity prevail, Law as integrity being (as, looking back, we can now recognise) a phrase that incorporates the notions of fit, integratedness, findability (because it is always there), and the supremacy of principles (giving effect to right of all citizens to be treated as equals).

The cake

Law as integrity is thus like a fruitcake. It is a composite of ingredients – flour, eggs, butter, milk, fruit, baking powder. Without any of the components, the thing is not a fruitcake. With all of them, it becomes a new entity distinct from its component parts, a cake – a cake, to carry the analogy one stage further, with a function, to provide food; the function of Law as integrity, for its part, being, we have seen, to provide justification for the exercise of coercion by the state over its citizens.

Is Dworkin a positivist or a natural lawyer?

We know that Dworkin is not a positivist in the narrow sense of one who considers that when the law runs out a judge makes new law, the sense that Dworkin terms conventionalism. On the contrary, we know that the central thrust of Dworkin's thesis in *Law's Empire* is an attack on this conception of the law.

But as between the positivist in the sense of one who maintains that the law is one thing and its morality is another, and the natural lawyer who believes that the validity of law depends on its accordance with higher principles, where does Dworkin stand?

Since Dworkin believes that the law, and adjudication as its central function, ought to comply with certain standards – those embodied in the phrase Law as integrity – it might seem that he stands in the school of the natural lawyers rather than that of the positivists. Yet nowhere does Dworkin appeal to higher principles above and outside the law. True, he adopts such concepts as fairness and justice. But in so doing he is not appealing to justice as a concept with a higher existence outside the legal system he proposes. He

25 *Law's Empire* p 198.
26 Ibid, p 151.

believes that justice has a part to play because he thinks that justice has merit in its own right. Thus when Dworkin says that adjudication ought to operate in such and such a way, the ought is one that refers to compliance with the standard, not of eternal principles in the sky, but of what Dworkin thinks is right. Thus what Dworkin is telling us about is the kind of society that he thinks is a good society. Seen in this light *Law's Empire* represents Dworkin view of a just society. In Rawlsian terms, we can regard Dworkin as saying that the kind of adjudication that he describes is that which people in the original position would choose (at any rate if they were people of Dworkian good sense).

But nowhere does Dworkin suggest that if a legal system fails to comply with his scheme, its laws lack validity. He speaks of morality, it is true, but when he does so it is to indicate what he thinks is right. Nowhere does he link morality with validity after the manner of a natural lawyer. Validity is not a concern of his.

If Dworkin is not a natural lawyer, is he to be ranked with the positivists? Hardly. The positivists – Hume, Austin, Kelsen, Hart – tell us what exists. They observe, and then tell us what they see. Not for them any idea of expounding on what ought to be. What ought to be, they assert, is for politicians, sociologists, reformers, not the jurist at his proper task.

Dworkin is ...

So Dworkin does not fall comfortably into either camp. This need cause no unease. Why should any object fall into one or other of the categories that certain things may be capable of being divided into? Dworkin is a jurist who explores the nature of, and proposes an ideal form for, the process of adjudication. And that is the end of it.

CHAPTER 10

Talking past ...

The Hart v Dworkin debate

In Chapter 1 remark was made on the difficulty for a student confronted by the multiplication of comments that result from commentators commenting on each other's comments on a particular writer. It has to be conceded, however, that just as when two rocks are banged together sparks can fly, sparks that may illuminate the shape of the rocks concerned, so the collision between the views of Professor Hart and Professor Dworkin throws light on the nature of the thesis of each of them.

The sequence of the debate has been:

1. Hart's *Concept of Law*, published in 1961.
2. Dworkin's criticism of Hart's thesis, principally in *Law's Empire*, published in 1986.
3. Hart's response, contained in the Postscript to the second edition of the *Concept of Law* published in 1994.

The principal difference between the two writers, it will be recalled, is that whereas for Hart, at the point where the law is incomplete in that it provides no answer to a question at issue (the point where the law 'runs out') judges exercise their discretion in reaching a solution that fills the gap, thereby creating new law; for Dworkin, on the other hand, the law never runs out, the answer is always there to be found, just as, in the cornflake competition,[1] if the judge applied his mind to the matter properly, the winner could be found. On this issue the jury is still out.

As for the wider question as to whether Hart's concept of a legal system withstands Dworkin's attack, we can be on surer ground.

---

1 See p 106 supra.

Hart's concept is not affected by Dworkin's criticisms since he and Hart have different notions of the proper task of jurisprudence. For Hart, while a jurist may have things to say about a wide range of matters, the central task is to pinpoint the nature of a legal system – anywhere, at any time in history. Even if Hart were to concede that judges in hard cases 'find' law, not create it, this would not affect his construction. Hart does not evaluate, or justify: his purpose is to analyse and describe.

For Dworkin the central task of legal theory 'consists in the identification of the principles which both best fit or cohere with the settled law and legal practices of a legal system and also provide the best moral justification for them [ie justification for coercion], thus showing the law "in its best light"'.[2] In his earlier writing Dworkin maintained that general descriptions of the kind that Hart provides serve no useful purpose, useful theories being ones that are 'interpretative of a particular stage of historically developing practice' – in Dworkin's case that of the United States at the time that he wrote. Although he later conceded that descriptive jurisprudence does have its place, he remained critical of key elements of Hart's thesis.

Dworkin's principal criticisms (as set out in the Postscript to the second edition of *Concept*) are given below, followed in each case by Hart's response, concluding with the main point of disagreement – What happens when the law 'runs out'?

1. Any meaningful legal theory must take account of the viewpoint of the participant of the legal system considered. Hart's descriptive approach fails to do this.

Hart replies, '... there is in fact nothing in my book to preclude a non-participant external observer from describing the ways in which participants view the law from such an internal point of view ... I explained ... that participants manifest their internal point of view in accepting the law as providing guides to their conduct and standards of criticism. Of course a descriptive legal theorist does not as such himself share the participants' acceptance of the law in these ways, but he can and should describe such acceptance, as indeed I have attempted to do ... It is true that for this purpose the descriptive legal theorist must understand what it is to adopt the internal point of view and in that limited sense he must be able to put himself in the place of an insider; but this is not to accept the law or share or

2   HLA Hart, *Concept of Law* (2nd edn) p 241.

endorse the insider's internal point of view or in any other way to surrender his descriptive stance.'[3]

2. Hart's thesis is defective in that the criteria according to which the rule of recognition identifies what is law is confined to 'plain facts', of an historically established 'pedigree', ie that Hart is what in Chapter 4 we learned is termed a 'hard positivist'. (It will be recalled that for the 'hard positivist', the criteria must be precisely identifiable, for example from sources that are written down, such as legislation. For the 'soft positivist', sources of law can be found from a wider area and can include reference to principles or moral values.)

Hart rejects the charge. In attributing to him a doctrine of 'plain-fact positivism', Dworkin 'has mistakenly treated my theory as not only requiring (as it does) that the existence and authority of the rule of recognition should depend on the fact of its acceptance by the courts, but also as requiring (as it does not) that the criteria of legal validity ... should consist exclusively of the specific kind of plain fact which he calls 'pedigree' matters and which concern the manner and form of law-creation or adoption. This is doubly mistaken. First, it ignores my explicit acknowledgement that the rule of recognition may incorporate as criteria of legal validity conformity with moral principles or substantive values; so my doctrine is what has been called 'soft positivism' and not as in Dworkin's version of it 'plain-fact' positivism. Secondly, there is nothing in my book to suggest that the plain fact criteria provided by the rule of recognition must be solely matters of pedigree: they may instead be substantive constraints on the content of legislation such as the Sixteenth or Nineteenth Amendments to the United States Constitution respecting the establishment of religion or abridgements of the right to vote.'[4]

3. Hart's scheme fails to accommodate the fact that the purpose of a jurisprudential system is to justify coercion.

Hart dismisses the charge: '...whereas Dworkin's interpretative legal theory ... rests on the presupposition that the point or purpose of law and legal practice is to justify coercion, it certainly is not and never has been my view that law has this as its point or purpose. Like other forms of positivism my theory makes no claim to identify the point or purpose of law ... In fact I think it quite

3 Ibid, p 242.
4 Ibid, p 250.

vain to seek anymore specific purpose which law ... serves beyond providing guides to human conduct and standards of criticism of such conduct'.[5]

4. Hart cannot have it both ways. He cannot present a positivist picture of a legal system that provides 'reliable public standards of conduct which can be identified with certainty on matters of plain fact without dependence on controversial moral arguments, and at the same time adopt the position of a soft positivist. (Hart cannot, we can imagine Dworkin asserting, be sharp and fuzzy at the same time.)

Hart responds: The criticism exaggerates 'both the degree of certainty which a consistent positivist must attribute to a body of legal standards and the uncertainty which will result if the criteria of legal validity include conformity with specific moral principles or values. It is of course true that an important function of the rule of recognition is to promote the certainty with which the law may be ascertained. This it would fail to do if the tests which it introduced for law not only raise controversial issues in some cases but raise them in all or most cases. But the exclusion of all uncertainty at whatever ... is not a goal which I have ever envisaged for the rule of recognition. This is made plain, or so I had hoped, both by my explicit statement in this book that the rule of recognition itself as well as particular rules of law identified by reference to it may have a debatable 'penumbra' of uncertainty. ... A margin of uncertainty should be tolerated, and indeed welcomed in the case of many legal rules, so that an informed judicial decision can be made when the composition of an unforeseen case is known and the issues at stake in its decision can be identified and so rationally settled. Only if the certainty-providing function of the rule of recognition is treated as paramount and overriding could the form of soft positivism that includes among the criteria of law conformity with moral principles or values which may be controversial be regarded as inconsistent. The underlying question here concerns the degree or extent of uncertainty which a legal system can tolerate if it is to make any significant advance from a decentralized regime of custom-type rules [towards a system that provides] generally reliable and determinate guides to conduct identifiable in advance.'[6]

5. Hart's treatment of social rules is defective. Hart accepted the thrust of these criticisms and made modifications to his account. It

5   Ibid, p 249.
6   Ibid, p 251.

is this modified account that appears in the treatment of this topic in Chapter 4.

6. In representing law as consisting of fixed rules, Hart's picture is defective in that it ignores the existence and significance of another form of legal standard, namely principles.

On this Hart comments, 'Some critics who have found this defect in my work have conceived of it as a more or less isolated fault which I could repair simply by including legal principles along with legal rules as components of a legal system, and they have thought that I could do this without abandoning or seriously modifying any of the main themes of the book. But Dworkin, who was the first to press this line of criticism, has insisted that legal principles could only be included in my theory of law at the cost of surrender of its central doctrines. If I were to admit that law consists in part of principles I could not, according to him, consistently maintain, as I have done, that the law of a system is identified by criteria provided by a rule of recognition accepted in the practice of the courts, or that the courts exercise a genuine though interstitial law-making power ... in those cases where the existing explicit law fails to dictate a decision, or that there is no ... necessary or conceptual connection between law and morality. These doctrines are not only central to my theory of law but are often taken to constitute the core of modern legal positivism; so their abandonment would be a matter of some moment'.[7]

Before answering the charge Hart sets out the features that distinguish principles from rules.

(a) Compared with rules, principles are broad, general and un-specific. A number of rules could be cited that are instances of the application of a single principle.

(b) Principles, because they refer more or less explicitly to some purpose, goal, entitlement or value, are regarded from some points of view as desirable to maintain and so not only as providing an explanation or rationale of the rules which exemplify them, but as at least contributing to their justification.

These two features Hart accepts as valid distinctions.

A third distinction, according to Dworkin, is that:

(c) Rules 'function ...in an "all-or-nothing" manner in the sense that if a rule is valid and applicable ... to a given case then it ...

---

7 Ibid, p 259.

conclusively determines the legal result or outcome' (as in the case of a law prescribing a maximum speed limit, or the number of witnesses required for a will to be valid). Legal principles, on the other hand, according to Dworkin, differ from such all-or-nothing rules in that while they may point or count in favour of a decision, they do not necessarily and invariably determine the outcome.[8] This feature of principles Hart refers to as their 'non-conclusive' character.

Dworkin's charge is, therefore, that Hart's concept of a legal system made up of rules is defective in that it fails to take account of the existence and importance of principles, and that this omission is fatal to his thesis.

Hart replies[9] that he sees no reason to accept a sharp distinction between legal rules and legal principles, or the view that if a valid rule is applicable to a given case it must, unlike a principle, always determine the outcome. The difference is a matter of degree'.

Non-conclusive principles are, Hart acknowledges, an important feature of adjudication and legal reasoning, and it was not his intention that his use of the word 'rule' should give the impression that legal systems comprise only 'all-or-nothing' rules. On the contrary, although not using the term 'principles', in *Concept* he had drawn attention to 'variable legal standards' which specified factors to be taken into account and weighed against others in reaching a decision.

Thus Hart rejects Dworkin's contention that *Concept* failed to find a place for principles. He maintains that his thesis therefore stands unshaken, with no question arising of a fault needing to be corrected. He does, however, concede that it is a defect of *Concept* 'that principles are touched upon only in passing'.

7. The next bone of contention concerns the rule of recognition. Since it is an essential feature of Hart's thesis that not only must there be rules but also that these must be capable of being identified by a rule of recognition; and since, so Dworkin's argument goes, a legal system comprises principles as well as rules, and since principles are not capable of being identified by a rule of recognition, the doctrine of a rule of recognition must be abandoned.

Principles are capable of being recognised, Dworkin asserts, not by a mechanically applied rule of recognition but through the

8   Ibid, p 261.
9   Ibid, p 261.

process of constructive interpretation, under which principles are identified as being 'members of the unique set of principles which both best fits and best justifies the whole institutional history of the settled law of a legal system'.[10]

In response to this charge, Hart relies on a notion that Dworkin had himself introduced, namely that of principles having 'pedigree'. Dworkin is wrong, Hart says, to dismiss pedigree as a means by which principles can be identified (Dworkin maintaining that principles can only be identified only by 'constructive interpretation'). Pedigree (ie authority being traced upwards to an ultimate source) can, Hart says, provide the means by which principles can be identified. For example, various principles of the common law can be traced up to the principle that a person should not be allowed to profit from his own wrong, a principle given authority by its approval by the courts. So, Hart concludes, 'there is nothing incompatible such as Dworkin claims between the admission of principles as part of the law and the doctrine of a rule of recognition'.

In Hart's view, Dworkins's 'interpretative' test for establishing the validly of principles in no more than the specific form that is taken in some legal systems by a conventional rule of recognition whose existence and authority rests on its acceptance by the courts. He recognises, though, that Dworkin would utterly reject this view as misrepresenting and demeaning Dworkin's notion of a 'constructive interpretation' designed to show the law in the best moral light.[11]

8. The next issue concerns the relationship between law and morality, in particular with regard to rights and duties. For Hart, who as a positivist treats law and morality as being separate, there can be legal rights and duties that have no moral justification whatsoever. Dworkin, on the other hand, holds the view (ultimately derived from his own interpretative theory of law) that there must be at least prima facie moral grounds for assertion of the existence of legal rights and duties.

9. The matter of law and morality brings us to the next difference between the two. Can something be the law notwithstanding that it is morally iniquitous? Can provisions that puts in place procedures for the genocide of a minority population be valid law? Hart answers, yes, they can.

10 Ibid, p 263.
11 Ibid, p 267.

Dworkin is here in difficulty. His initial position is described by Hart thus: '... every proposition of law stating what the law on some subject is necessarily involves a moral judgement since according to his holistic interpretative theory propositions of law are true only if with other premises they follow from that set of principles which both best fit all the settled law identified by reference to the social sources of the law and provide the best moral justification for it'. So, says Hart, where the 'social sources' of the law sanction iniquity, the principles derived from these may be iniquitous and lack any moral justifying force. Thus, Dworkin's scheme can lead to the same result as that of a positivist – that law may be identified without reference to morality.

How does Dworkin deal with the position where a legal system is so evil that no morally acceptable interpretation of its laws is possible? The positivist holds that if the system operates, if its rules are accepted and enforced by officials, then the rules are law. Dworkin concedes that this is so but only in what he terms (in a distinction introduced in *Law's Empire*) a 'pre-interpretative' sense.

10. Hart portrays the law as being incomplete, with gaps, when they appear, being filled by judges exercising a discretion to create new law. This picture is defective in that it misrepresents both the nature of law and the function performed by judges. The law is not incomplete – there are no gaps to be filled, so there is no question of judges creating new law to fill gaps.

This because, in addition to the law that is laid down explicitly, there are, implicitly, principles that guide a judge to what the law properly is when the explicit law fails to give the answer.

That this is so, Dworkin says, is demonstrated by three things. The first concerns the language used by practitioners in the courts. In hard cases, advocates do not invite the judge to create new law in their client's favour: they submit that the law *is* such and such, and invite the judge to agree that their submission is correct. The judge does not say that he has decided to create new law to fill a gap. He says that he 'finds' that the law is such and such – he *finds*. If he finds, he must find something that is already there.

Hart dismisses this as no more than the 'familiar rhetoric of the judicial process'. It is, he says, 'important to distinguish the ritual language used by judges and lawyers in deciding cases in their courts from their more reflective general statements about the judicial process'[12] and it is significant that judges of great distinction in the

---

12 Ibid, p 274.

United States and England have insisted that there are cases in which no settled law applies, cases which could be decided either way and in which the judge therefore performs the task of law-making.

It is true, Hart recognises, that in cases in which no pre-existing law determines the outcome, judges proceed by analogy 'so as to ensure that the new law they make, though it *is* new law, is in accordance with principles or underpinning reasons recognized as already having a footing in the existing law ... when particular statutes or precedents prove indeterminate, or when the explicit law is silent, judges do not just push away their law books and start to legislate without further guidance from the law. Very often, in deciding cases, they cite some principle or some general aim or purpose ... which points towards a[n] ... answer ...'.

But although judges in hard cases may proceed by analogy, and will take account of any relevant law that has a bearing on the case, this does not 'eliminate the moment for judicial law-making, since in any hard case different principles supporting competing analogies may present themselves and a judge will often have to chose between them, relying, like a conscious legislator, on his sense of what is best and not on any already established order of priorities prescribed for him by law. Only if for all such cases there was always to be found in the existing law some unique set of higher-order principles assigning relative weights or priorities to such competing lower-order principles, would the moment for judicial law-making be ... eliminated'[13]. But there is no such scheme for determining a hierarchy of principles. Judges have to *choose* between competing principles, and thus do, Hart is adamant, create new law.

Second, Hart's thesis, if correct would, Dworkin asserts, endorse a form of law-making that is undemocratic and unjust, in that in a democracy only elected representatives, not officials (ie judges) appointed by the government, have the power to make law.

Hart's answer is that for judges to 'be entrusted with law-making powers to deal with disputes which the law fails to regulate may be regarded as a necessary price to pay for avoiding the inconvenience of alternative methods of regulating them such as reference to the legislature; and the price may seem small if judges are constrained in the exercise of these powers and cannot fashion codes or wide reforms but only rules to deal with the specific issues thrown up by particular cases';[14] and since ultimate control will, in any case, normally lie with a legislature than can repeal or amend a judge's decision.

---

13 Ibid, p 275.
14 Ibid, p 275.

Third, the way in which Hart maintains that judges decide hard cases would, if correct, be unjust in that it would entail law being made retrospectively. A just system requires that litigants should be able to assume that the legal consequences of their acts will be decided according to the law as it exists at the time that the acts are committed, not ex post facto, at a later date.

Hart dismisses the charge as being irrelevant since, by definition, hard cases are ones in which the state of the law is not known, so there is no law on which litigants can rest expectations.

Postscript – the jig-saw

In order to understand Dworkin's concept of adjudication we can perhaps imagine a judge saying to himself 'This person in front of me for trial is going to suffer if I find against him. He may go to prison. He may have to pay a fine. He may have to pay compensation. My exercise of the power conferred on me by the state, the power to coerce this person, can only be justified if I get things right. There is no settled law on the matter. Principles have been advanced before me that pull in opposite directions. So what is the law? What would an ordinary American, if there was such a person, decide? What would be his instant gut reaction? What would he decide if he took into account everything that goes to make up this society – its history, its multifarious religions and racial origins, its traditions, its form of economy, its constitution, its notions of justice, and the whole mass of law that already exists. What decision would make sense in the light of all this? What decision would fit in with everything else? What decision, by its good sense, would add cohesion to the rest of the law?

'Think of a jigsaw puzzle. This ordinary American has got to find the right piece to fit the hole in the picture. If he finds the right piece, it will assist our comprehension of what the picture is of. ("I see, that's someone's foot.") It will also actually, physically, strengthen the puzzle on the board, since as the puzzle gets completed it gets stronger until, when finished, it will be so strong that if you pull the thing one way or the other it will stay together.

'Of course there's only one piece that will do. The way to find it is to look at the pieces already in place around it, so that you can see the shape of the hole, and the surrounding picture.

'So it is with the decision that I have got to make: it has got to fit in with everything else, by being right in the light of everything else. Then it will make sense itself and consolidate the good sense of everything else. Unless I can find the right decision I am not justified – the state of which I am the instrument – is not justified, in penalising the man in front of me (and, in a civil case, penalising the plaintiff if I find the defendant not liable). This ordinary American is outside the courthouse now. He knows the facts of the case. He knows the answer – it's obvious to him. Bearing in mind everything else, *everything* else, to him the answer stands out a mile. If I asked him, he'd throw down his cigarette and say, "Ye'ar, of course the guy's liable," and wander off. But I can't ask him. I have got to make my own mind up as to what his answer would be. I've got to find the right piece of the puzzle, the one that fits the shape of the hole. It's not my job to go out to the shed and cut a piece any shape I choose. If I did, even if I forced it in, it wouldn't fit the picture, and it would weaken not strengthen the whole thing. No, I've got to find the piece. One thing I'm sure of, is that it exists *now*, on the table. It's *there*, in front of me. All I've got to do is find it.'

Dworkin's purpose is to tell us how, if coercion is to be justified, judges ought to decide hard cases, and how in fact, in his own society the best of them, consciously or unconsciously, do try to decide such cases. His defect (apart from the obscurity[15] of his language) lies in his failure to provide a satisfactory answer to the question whether the duty of constructive interpretation applies irrespective of the evil of the regime of which judges find themselves a part.

Hart's defect lies in his assertion that in all legal systems, at all times in history in which legal systems have existed, hard cases are decided by judges having the discretion that he ascribes to them. Even if at the present time in the United Kingdom hard cases are decided by judges acting with Hartian discretion, this is not the position in all societies. Judges may decide hard cases by a variety of means. In some societies hard cases may be decided by the toss of a coin (or of a flat stone); or by the parties drawing straws; or by the judge having a Hartian discretion to decide what the law should be; or by a judge making his decision in the light of orders received from the King, or his local party chief.

Who wins the debate? Neither, since they are talking past each other. Dworkin is saying what *ought* to be if coercion is to be justified and what, at its best, actually happens in his own society. Hart is telling us what, in any legal system, *is*; but, in one particular respect (hard cases in all cases being decided by judicial discretion), getting it wrong.

15 Ibid, p 257.

A final thought: How, at the present time, in Britain, do judges regard themselves as deciding hard cases? With Hartian discretion, or by Dworkinian interpretation? (As we say in Derbyshire, "Think on't".)

CHAPTER 11

The great pyramid

Hans Kelsen[1]

> Treason doth never prosper; what's the reason?
> For if it prosper, none dare call it treason.
>
> *Sir John Harrington (1561–1612)*

Hans Kelsen began thinking about the nature of law during the course of examining the Austrian Constitution before the First World War. The first full formulation of his theory appeared in 1918. The first presentation of the theory in English was in 1934[2] after Kelsen had gone to the United States. In 1945 he published *General Theory of Law and State* and, after various articles,[3] a second, revised, edition in 1967. A complete presentation of the theory was made in 1964.[4]

Kelsen called his theory (which he modified over the course of his life) the 'pure theory of law', his object being to identify the very essence of law, the one thing that makes something *law*, as opposed to the other forms of direction that can exist in any society. He wanted to find the common characteristic of law whether one is looking at 'a negro tribe under the leadership of a despotic chieftain' or 'the constitution of the Swiss Republic'.[5] His theory was a reaction to the theories that had been current earlier in the century in which law was regarded as being comprehensible only if seen as a branch of sociology, or an aspect of politics, or as part of

1 J W Harris *Legal Philosophies* (2nd edn, 1997) Chap 6; Davies and Holdcroft *Jurisprudence: Texts and Commentary* Chap 5.
2 (1934) 50 LQR 474, (1935) 51 LQR 517.
3 In particular 'What is the Pure Theory of Law?' 34 Tulane LR 269.
4 'The Function of a Constitution' (trans I Stewart) (1980) Jur Rev 149, 214.
5 J M Finnis *Natural Law and Natural Rights*.

a nation's historical tradition. Kelsen wanted to rid (and succeeded in ridding) his theory of all such, for him, extraneous elements. He wanted, and has given us, a *pure* theory of law. (Kelsen was not the first to seek such a theory. Grotius, in 1625 in the Prolegomena to *De Iure Belli ac Pacis* had written: 'With all truthfulness I aver, just as mathematicians treat their figures as abstracted from bodies, so in treating law I have withdrawn my mind from every particular fact.')

Kelsen's pure theory of law forms a system with a number of component parts, each linked like links in a chain, the chain forming a circle.

Directions to officials

Let us begin, since we must break into the chain somewhere, with the component that consists of the proposition that law is made up of statements that take the form that if A happens, then X should follow: *If* so and so, *then* so and so. How this relates to law is apparent when we understand that statements in this form (subject to what is said later) are directed to officials who form part of a state's apparatus, in particular to officials concerned with the administration of the law. An example might be a direction to a judge, 'If a person is prosecuted for an alleged crime, then try him and, if he is found guilty, sentence him.' Another example might be a direction to a bailiff, 'If a judge orders you to take a specified person's goods (and sell them in order to obtain money to satisfy a debt), then do so.'

Seen in this light a law that makes it an offence to drive above 70 mph on a motorway is not a direction to motorists 'Do not drive above 70 mph'. It is a direction to officials, in the first place to the police, 'If you believe a person to have driven above 70 mph, arrest him'. It is a direction to a judge, 'If a person is brought before your court accused of driving above 70 mph, try him and sentence him if he is found guilty'; to a prison governor, 'If a person is sentenced to a term in prison, arrange for his imprisonment'; and finally to the jailer, '… close the door and turn the key'.

The idea that law is a command of the sovereign has had a long ancestry and we saw that it lay at the heart of Austin's concept of law. But previously the command of the sovereign had been conceived as an order to citizens (to use our example), 'Do not drive above 70 mph', the command creating a rule that people should not drive above this speed. Kelsen recognised that, in practice, from a direction to officials a rule could be deduced. From a direction to a judge to hang murderers could be deduced a rule prohibiting murder. But for Kelsen the rule was secondary: what mattered was the direction to officials.

This was a startlingly new conception of the nature of law.

Does the idea work? Does the idea fit, say, the law of negligence? Does it work if we try to apply it to the law of trusts? In the few examples that he gives Kelsen uses criminal law by way of illustration. It is submitted, though, that in a wide range of law Kelsen's theory does hold good. Take the requirement of the Wills Act 1831 that a will must be attested by two witnesses. Can this be seen as an order to officials? Surely failure to comply merely results in invalidity? Perhaps so, but the consequences of invalidity will be enforced by officials to whom orders are directed in the form of, 'If ..., then do ...' For example, suppose that a will fails to comply with the Act. A judge is, by the law, ordered, 'If you find that a will fails to comply with the Act, make an order to this effect.' Suppose that a person named as a beneficiary, defying the court's judgment, seizes property left to him in the will; the next of kin proceed against him; the beneficiary defies an order from the court to hand over the property to the next of kin; the court finds him in contempt and sends him to prison. At the end of the road we have the direction, '... close the door and turn the key'.

In this light what might appear to be provisions having no more than regulative effect are seen to be backed by 'teeth that bite'.[6] At virtually whatever field of law one looks (consider, for example, the law governing elections to Parliament), refusal to abide by the provisions of the law leads eventually, at the very end of the road, to the imposition of a sanction. And this applies equally to the law of tort and of contract. (It is unfortunate that Kelsen did not give more examples. He had plenty of time since he indulges in much repetition.)

That law consists, in essence, primarily of directions to officials was recognised by Hart as being a 'formidable and interesting theory'.[7] But did it accurately represent reality? Hart thought not. 'The principal functions of the law as means of social control are not to be seen in private litigation or prosecutions, which represent vital but still ancillary provision for the failures of the system. It is to be seen in the diverse ways in which the law is used to control, to guide, and to plan life out of court.'[8] The response from a disciple of Kelsen would be that such a view is 'impure', in that it fails to stick to the task of elucidating the essence of law and blurs the line between law and sociological observation. However, we can at this point note that in his later writings Kelsen did show increasing acceptance of the significance of law as a guide to citizens, of law

6 E A Hoebel *The Law of Primitive Man* (1954) p 285.
7 *Concept of Law* p 36.
8 Ibid, p 39.

being capable of being validly seen, at least to some extent, in, as it were, a secondary capacity, as consisting of rules.[9]

'... then X ought to ...'

Here we must explain two matters that can be a source of confusion in seeking to understand the pure theory. The first is that Kelsen's view that law is composed of 'If ..., then ... should follow' directions was, when the first translation of Kelsen's work appeared in English, translated from the German as 'If ... then ... *ought* to follow', the law thus consisting of a series of 'ought' statements.[10] This was, and has remained, unfortunate because of the overtones of ethics that inseparably associate themselves with the word 'ought', it being primarily with regard to moral obligations that the word is most commonly used – one *ought* not to tell lies. But Kelsen intends no flavour of morality – very much the reverse. So when, in the English translations we read that Kelsen thought of the law in terms of, 'If A does x, then B ought to do y', we must understand that what is intended is that 'If A does x, then B is required to do y'; that it is part of the intended system that B should do y; or even, that B must do y. The word 'ought' as it appears in the English translations therefore connotes action in order to comply with a prescribed requirement. The word indicates an expression of intention.

Norms

The second source of misunderstanding is the fact that in the English translations we read that each of the 'ought' statements that make up the law constitutes a norm; so that the law consists of a series of norms (arranged in a way that we shall shortly see).

But what is a norm? The word is redolent of sociology – 'Among his peer group it was the norm for boys of 11 to make a practice of ...' The word indicates behaviour that is standard within a certain category of people. This is not what Kelsen means by a norm. Far from it. Why, then, is the word used? The answer is that Kelsen, writing in German, used the German word *norm*. So it was natural that what seemed the closest English word, that with the same spelling, should be used. But in German *norm* can have various meanings, of which what has become the most usual English meaning is only one. The principal meaning of *norm* in German is 'standard'. This meaning makes sense when the

---

9   The change can be seen in *Pure Theory of Law* p 5.
10   On the word 'ought' in Kelsen's work, see A Wilson (1981) 44 MLR 270; W Ebenstein (1971) Calif LR 617, 628.

derivation of the word is noted: it comes from the Latin *norma*, a carpenter's square. So a norm, viewed in the light of the word's derivation, is something that is fixed, so as to provide a standard against which other things are judged; a norm is thus something to be conformed to. *This* is the sense that the word norm carries in Kelsen's theory of law. (If, when Kelsen's work was first translated into English, instead of 'ought', the word 'should' had been used, and if, instead of 'norm', the word 'requirement' had been used, Kelsen's theory would have been more readily intelligible and acceptable.)

What makes an act a legal act?

Now we turn to the next link in the circular chain of the theory. We can explain it like this. People may close and lock a door for a variety of reasons, for example to secure their home against thieves; to prevent members of the public gaining access to a private part of a National Trust stately home. But when a jailer closes a cell door and turns the key he is performing an act with legal significance. People may raise their hands for a host of reasons, for example to cast a vote at the annual meeting of a club, to indicate at a conference that they wish to ask a question, to indicate (at school) that they wish to go to the lavatory. When members of a legislative assembly raise their hands this may constitute the assent that, if a majority so vote, converts a proposal into a legal enactment. In the last case the act of raising the hand has legal significance: it is a legal act. People may post a letter for a myriad of reasons, but in certain circumstances allowing the letter to drop inside the box constitutes a legal act, since the posting of the letter in the circumstances concerned creates a contract. So out of all the acts that people may perform, some have legal significance, some are legal acts. What makes a particular act a legal act, Kelsen says, is the existence of a legal norm in respect of which the act is carried out. What makes the jailer's turning the key a legal act, is the existence of the norm that ends with, '… then the jailer ought to turn the key'.

Kelsen uses as an example an order by one person to hand over money to another. The order may be by a gangster or by a tax official. Both have what Kelsen calls the same 'subjective meaning' (ie as to what actually happens, an order is made to hand over money). But if the tax official's order is made in accordance with a valid norm, then the order has what Kelsen calls an 'objective' meaning (ie a legal significance). So it is the existence of the legal norm that distinguishes the order of the official from that of the gangster.

Note that Kelsen says that it is the existence of a *legal* norm that has this effect. Kelsen recognises that non-legal norms exist, norms that confer a special, but non-legal, significance on a particular act. For example the laying of two hands on a person's head may, by a church's constitution and beliefs, constitute the ordination of a priest; the signing of a piece of paper may, by the rules of an examining board, constitute confirmation that a person has passed an examination. But in Kelsen's usage a norm is an expression of intention: one individual (or entity) wills that in specified circumstances another should act in a certain way.

What about a law that gives power to a subordinate body to make law, for example a law that confers power on a certain tier of local government to make bye-laws (eg making it an offence to ride a horse on a public footpath)? Kelsen realised that his notion of norms as 'ought' statements was not able satisfactorily to encompass a law of this kind – one that delegated law-making powers. To take account of this difficulty he said that norms could, in addition to requiring certain acts, authorise, or permit, specified acts. In what way a norm should be expressed in the 'ought' form where the norm relates to the conferment of delegated law-making powers, is a matter for speculation. (Kelsen gave no illustration.)

Validity

The next link in the chain of Kelsen's theory concerns validity. Consider a norm that ends, '… then the jailer ought to turn the key'. The validity of the norm depends on the validity of the norm under which the judge had passed sentence, the norm that ended '… then the judge ought to pass sentence on the prisoner'. The validity of this norm, the norm that made the judge's act a *legal* act (since anyone can say 'I sentence you to six months in prison') depends on the validity of the norm under which the law that the accused person had broken was made (and the norm under which the judge was appointed). So the validity of every norm depends on the validity of another norm, the whole series forming, as it were, an ascending hierarchy.

The grundnorm[11]

But what is at the top? Whether a statute is valid will depend on whether it was made according to the requirements of the constitution, eg being passed by a stipulated majority in two houses of a legislature. But what of the validity of the constitution? The

---

11 See G Hughes 'Validity and the Basic Norm' (1970) Calif LR 695.

constitution may have been introduced under a law passed under an earlier constitution (perhaps one in which the legislature consisted of only one house). So the validity of the present constitution will rest on the validity of the earlier constitution from which it was born. In this way validity could be traced back, perhaps, to the validity of the orders of a monarch who first decreed that laws should be made by a legislative assembly. At the end of the road, however, we come to a point beyond which it is not possible to go. For example, the validity of the king's order might depend on his being the heir to his father's throne. But his father might have been a usurper who had assassinated the previous king. What claim to validity could the usurper make for his decrees?

Consider the case of the jailer in the United States turning the key of a cell door. The validity of the norm under which he had performed the act can be traced back to the validity of the constitution established by the fathers of the constitution after the War of Independence, when British suzerainty over the American colonies was overthrown. On what does the validity of this original constitution rest? Kelsen says that the very first norm in the American legal system, the norm on which all the others rest (that the constitution established by the founding fathers ought to be obeyed) is not traceable to any other norm. Since the validity of the norm is not disputed, the conclusion must be that the validity of the norm is *presumed*.

Thus in any legal system it is only by presuming the validity of the original, basic norm (which Kelsen calls the 'grundnorm'), that the norms that descend from it can be counted as valid. (In this aspect of his theory Kelsen showed the influence of Kant, for whom, in any branch of knowledge, some things must be presupposed. Kant believed that it was a task of the philosopher to search for the universal elements of knowledge that have to be presupposed in order that sense can be made of all the rest.)

What Kelsen says holds water. When today a jailer in South Carolina turns the key, the validity of his action *does* rest on the assumption that the constitution established in 1782 ought to be observed. Without this assumption, no act in the United States is capable of being counted as a legal act. So we can see what Harris[12] means when he says that for Kelsen 'The grundnorm is the hypothesis which closes up the arch of legal logic' – the grundnorm is the keystone at the top that locks, and holds, the arch in place. Remove this and the whole edifice of legal validity collapses.

---

12 'When and Why does the Grundnorm Change?' [1971] CLJ 103.

In the United Kingdom the validity of a bye-law that makes it an offence to ride a horse on a public footpath rests, ultimately, on the grundnorm of the British legal system. Every British statute is prefaced by the words: 'Be it enacted by the Queen's most Excellent Majesty, by and with the advice and consent of the Lords spiritual and Temporal, and Commons, in the present Parliament assembled, and by the authority of the same, as follows – ...' In Kelsenian terms this can be interpreted as representing the norm: 'The following law, being made according to the British constitution, ought to be obeyed'. This particular ought rests on the unstated norm that exists, as it were in invisible ink, at the head of every statute, 'All laws made according to the existing constitution ought to be obeyed.' The validity of this norm in turn depends on the norm on the basis of which the present constitution is accepted as being valid. And so on back until the grundnorm is reached.

How far back in history the grundnorm of the British legal system lies is a matter for speculation and debate. But it must rest somewhere. If it is not found at a later time (eg 1660), then certainly it is traceable to no earlier than 1066, when William I overthrew the rule of the Saxon kings. If this is where the grundnorm of British law rests, then the grundnorm of a bye-law that prohibits the riding of horses on public footpaths is that the decrees of William I ought to be observed.

The validity of the grundnorm is assumed. But *why?* Or rather, how do we tell whether in any legal system the validity of the grundnorm is to be assumed? Kelsen's answer is that we look to see what happens. If the judge does, as the norm requires, pass sentence, and the jailer does, as the norm requires, turn the key – if the norms of the system are observed, then we have no option but to accept that the validity of the grundnorm is presupposed.

That this is so can be seen by imagining a country in which the constitution provides that whatever the king decrees is law. There is an insurrection. The king is ousted and a usurper installs his own regime, under which whatever he decrees is law. The usurper's writ runs throughout the land. In such circumstances we cannot but assume that the validity of the norms established by the usurper's decrees, since to do otherwise would be non-sensical: it would be nonsensical to continue to assume the validity of the decrees of the exiled king (living on mackerel in a wooden shack on some far distant island) when we can *see* that his decrees are no longer observed.

The moral validity of the usurper's regime is another matter. It might, according to some moral codes, have been unethical for the usurper to oust the king and seize his throne. But Kelsen is not concerned with morals, or moral validity. He is concerned solely with the law, and *legal* validity.

Thus we assume the validity of the grundnorm if the norms that descend from it are observed, if the 'oughts' are implemented. So we can say that with regard to the individual norms of a system, validity depends on another 'higher' norm. With regard to the grundnorm, validity depends on efficacy. With this in mind we are in a position to understand what Kelsen means when he defines law as 'A system of coercion imposing norms which are laid down by human acts in accordance with a constitution the validity of which is pre-supposed if it is on the whole efficacious.'[13] So, in establishing whether the grundnorm is valid we look to the implementation of the individual norms, ie we look to see whether the directions to officials are carried out, the subject with which we began our discussion, thus completing the circle and coming back to our starting point.

Concretisation

If the system of norms is visualised as being shaped in the form of a pyramid, with the grundnorm at the apex, it will be appreciated that from the apex downwards the norms become increasingly less general and more specific: the move is from the general to the particular. The higher norms will be concerned with how law, eg statute law, is created; then at the next tier with the administration of justice; and finally with a norm that decrees certain action in a specific case. The process by which norms get more and more specific, Kelsen calls 'concretisation'.

The test of efficacy

If the test of the validity of the grundnorm is efficacy, what is the test of efficacy? When can we say that efficacy exists? Efficacy is to be judged, Kelsen says, by two criteria. The first test is to see whether the rules that can be deduced from legal norms are obeyed, for example whether the rule 'Do not drive over 70 mph' (the ruled deduced from the norm 'If X drives over 70 mph, then Y (a police-man) ought to ...') is obeyed. Secondly, if the rule is not obeyed, whether the primary norm, that directed to officials to take specified action, is complied with. The addition of this second test, and for Kelsen this is the test that has primacy, throws new light on the

13 *General Theory of Law and State* p 11.

notion of efficacy. (Austin's 'habit of obedience' took account only of the first test.) If there is an uprising, people defy the law, take to the streets and fire at the king's soldiers over barricades, then if the soldiers fire back, seize insurgents and drag them before judges who order their execution, we can say that the legal system is efficacious. But when the soldiers cease to fire, or the judges, panicking, decline to order execution, then the law ceases to be efficacious: the orders directed to officials are no longer obeyed, the 'oughts' no longer complied with.

What happens then? What actually *happens* to the law in the event of a revolution?

Revolutions[14]

What happens, Kelsen says, is that after a successful revolution the grundnorm changes.[15] Once an existing regime, A, has been replaced by a new one, B, and the laws of regime B are observed, then the grundnorm of the new regime becomes, 'The constitution established by regime B, and the laws made under it, ought to be observed.' It is only on this assumption that the validity of the laws of the new regime *can* rest. A moment's thought shows that no other conclusion can rationally be held. If today a bill is passed in Britain by the two Houses of Parliament and assented to by the Queen, then no one doubts that a valid law has been created. The assumption rests, we have seen, on the grundnorm that (if we ignore the intervening usurpations, assassinations and revolutions) the laws instituted by William I ought to be obeyed. It would be nonsensical to maintain that a law passed at the present day lacked validity because the Conqueror overthrew what had hitherto been the established regime. No one would maintain that 'after a successful revolution the old constitution and the laws based thereupon remain in force, on the ground that they have not been nullified in a manner anticipated by the old order itself'.[16]

This is all very well for the disinterested observer. But revolutions may present a dilemma for officials of a regime that is overthrown, in particular for the judges. 'All my life,' a judge may think, 'I have administered the laws duly made under the constitution of regime A. Now I find that the president of the regime

14 J M Finnis 'Revolutions and Continuity of Law' in *Oxford Essays in Jurisprudence* (2nd series, ed Simpson).
15 Of great value here is J W Harris, 'When and Why does the Grundnorm Change?' [1971] CLJ 103.
16 *General Theory of Law and State* p 118.

has fled the country and an insurgent has established himself as a dictator who has decreed that anyone who drives a car above 50 mph is to be executed. And here is someone up for trial before me whom the jury has found guilty of doing just that. Is this new law a valid law, with the result that I, who all my life have respected the concept of validity, must sentence this man to death? I know all about Kelsen and validity resting on efficacy,' thinks the judge (who studied jurisprudence for his law degree), 'but if I sentence this man to death, not only do I offend my conscience and show disloyalty to the regime that appointed me, I shall also be helping to produce efficacy, particularly as my act will have a knock-on effect with the judges in the lower courts and with the officials who administer the law. The man who has proclaimed himself ruler is in the Presidential Palace, his tanks patrol the streets and his propaganda pours from radio and television. Yet I hear gunfire in the distance. Resistance in the capital is not crushed, and I do not know what is happening in the provinces. *Are* the laws of the new regime efficacious? If I refuse to sentence this man to death, my example may spark a resistance within the judiciary that may tip the balance against the new regime consolidating its power and lead to the restoration of the regime to which I took my oath of loyalty. On the other hand, I may be shot.' The decision that the judge takes is likely to turn on such factors as his assessment of the military situation and the degree to which his character is cast in the heroic mould. It may be that the judge finds that he has a bad cold and retires to his house in the country to await the outcome of events.

Our judge, at home in the country (no hero, it transpires), will want to know whether the revolution has succeeded. If it has failed, he will be able to return to the city, clutching his (bought) doctor's note, and take his place in his old court. If it succeeds, then he will have to decide whether to return to court or to resign.

But at what point can it be said that a revolution has succeeded? Resistance in the outlying suburbs may continue for weeks, resistance in the provinces may not be overcome for months. At what point can it be said that the laws of a rebel regime are efficacious?

This is a matter of political and military reality, not a matter of jurisprudence. All that can be said is that at *some* point it will be possible to say conclusively that the efficacy of the new regime's laws is no longer in doubt. The fact that this point is reached imperceptibly does no more negate the fact that the point has been reached than the fact that although we may be unable to pinpoint the exact moment when autumn gives way to winter, nevertheless when snow covers Bradwell Edge and farmers take hay out to sheep on the hills, we can say without question that winter has come.

A shrewd test for assessing whether the grundnorm has changed has been suggested by Harris[17] – it has changed when a person who proposed to write a law textbook presenting the law of the former regime would be considered as fulfilling no juristically useful purpose.

In dealing with revolutions we have spoken of a change in the grundnorm, the key stone in the arch of logic of legal validity. But because the keystone is changed, this does not mean that all the laws of the previous regime, laws whose validity was traced to the previous grundnorm, have changed. Changed they may be, as where a left wing group overthrows a right wing government, or vice versa. But it is equally possible that all, or virtually all, the laws of the country remain unchanged. For example after a palace coup when one individual or group seizes power from another, in matters of both criminal and civil law there may be complete continuity. Such a circumstance does not, though, mean that no change in the grundnorm has taken place. The grundnorm has changed: it becomes this – all laws that the new government decrees together with all laws that the new government has not, by refraining from annulling, impliedly decreed should remain in force, ought to be obeyed.

The question faced by the judge in our example has been faced by judges and officials on many occasions after revolutions during this century. It was faced, for example, by the judges who had been appointed by the British Crown in Rhodesia after the government led by Ian Smith declared the independence of the country from British overlordship in 1965. (In *R v Ndhlorn*[18] the appellate division of the Rhodesian High Court held that the revolution (for such the secession of the country constituted) had been successful and that the laws of the new regime, being efficacious, had validity within the country.[19])

It should not be thought that a judge who decides to continue in office after a successful revolution is incapable of advancing any argument in support of his decision. 'I am,' he can point out, 'a judge. I am a technician with a particular craft – that of interpreting the law. I apply the law of the state that pays me. I am not concerned with the content of that law any more than a train driver is concerned with the moral character of his passengers. Just as it is the train driver's job to drive the train, so it is my job to administer

17   [1971] CLJ 103.
18   (1968) 4 SA 515.
19   For the implications, see J M Eekelaar 'Principles of Revolutionary Legality' in *Oxford Essays in Jurisprudence* (2nd series, ed Simpson).

the law. (I didn't like some of the laws passed by the last regime but that didn't stop me from doing my best to interpret and apply them.) It is my assessment, based on what I see with my own eyes, that the grundnorm has changed. So be it. I will continue to perform my function as judge in the best way that I am able.'

Whether a judge follows this line of thinking or resigns will depend on matters of loyalty, conscience, and judgment as to the moral value of the new regime. (A judge may find a new regime more to his personal liking than the previous one.) Kelsen would not dispute that ethical considerations of this kind are in practice taken into account in making such decisions. But such matters are for him of no relevance in pursuing the task of propounding a pure theory of law.

Kelsen as positivist

From what has gone before, it should perhaps hardly need saying that Kelsen stands squarely in the line of the positivist tradition running from Hume, through Bentham, Austin, down to our own day. The moral value of a legal system or of an individual law is one thing, its validity as law is another. Thus validity is in no way concerned with content. A law (in the shape, for Kelsen, of a norm) is valid because it is created in a certain way. It is for this reason that Kelsen has been said to be 'doubly pure' – pure in that he excluded alien elements such as sociology from his theory, and in that he excluded morality from the question of legal validity.

CHAPTER 12

The point of it all?
John Mitchell Finnis[1]

'If the Deity does not exist, only the ill-disposed can be said to reason, the good are without sense.'

J-J Rousseau

Introduction

A recent major work concerning natural law is *Natural Law and Natural Rights* by John Finnis. This is not a history of natural law, nor an exposition of current natural law thinking, nor a criticism of this thinking. It is a restatement of natural law, but expressed in fresh terms.

At the heart lie two assertions. These are the leitmotiv that runs through the whole work. They appear in the very first sentence. The first is this, 'There are human goods that can be secured only through the institution of human law ...'[2] Well, this seems all right. 'Human goods' might seem a bit strange, but presumably it means that there are things that are good for human existence, such as an ordered society, freedom from tyranny, and so on. And it is true that certain of such 'human goods' can only be secured through the existence of law. (What kind of matters are included within 'human goods' are explained in Chapters III and IV of Professor Finnis's book).

1 See J W Harris *Legal Philosophies* (2nd edn, 1997) pp 14–19; Davies and Holdcroft *Jurisprudence: Texts and Commentary* pp 186–204.
2 *Natural Law and Natural Rights* p 1.

The second of the assertions is that there are 'requirements of practical reasonableness that only those institutions [ie of human law] can satisfy.'[3] Finnis defines 'the requirements of practical reasonableness' (a phrase that occurs throughout the book) as 'a set of basic methodological requirements ... which distinguish sound from unsound practical thinking and which provide criteria for distinguishing between acts that ... are reasonable ... and acts that are unreasonable ...'[4] So it seems at first sight that practical reasonableness indicates the use of reason, of common sense, in choosing courses of action. The phrase does contain this meaning, but a lot more is meant than this and in Chapter V we learn the full meaning. But first, what are the 'human goods'?

The human goods

In some places Finnis speaks of 'human goods', in others, referring to the same thing, he speaks of 'forms of human flourishing'. The word 'flourishing' is helpful. We know what it means for a plant to 'flourish' – to have achieved (or to be on its way towards achieving) its fullest potential. And we know that certain conditions are necessary for flourishing to occur. Finnis regards certain things as being basic to human flourishing: those matters without which the achievement by humans of their fullest potential is not possible. There are, we are told, seven of these 'basic values of human existence', 'forms of good that ... are irreducibly basic'.[5] They are as follows.

1 Knowledge

The meaning here is knowledge sought for its own sake (as distinguished from knowledge sought for some objective, 'such as survival, power, popularity, or a money-saving cup of coffee'; knowledge of *truth*; knowledge sought out of 'the pure desire to know, to find out the truth about [any matter, in any field of knowledge] simply out of an interest in or a concern for truth and a desire to avoid error or ignorance ...'[6]

The 'good', the 'basic value', is not the knowledge of truth obtained, it is the pursuit of knowledge of truth that is the good –

3 Ibid.
4 Ibid, p 23.
5 Ibid, p 59.
6 Ibid, p 60.

'the activity of trying to find out, to understand, to judge matters correctly':[7] it is the quest that matters, and behind the quest, the motivation – curiosity. 'What did the authors of the Fourteenth Amendment care for economic equality? What happened on the night of the murder … ? Does e=mc²? How does this clock work? *It would be good to find out.*'[8]

The good of curiosity does not relate solely to curiosity about 'the intellectual cathedrals of science, mathematics and philosophy'.[9] It finds its response and satisfaction in detective stories, daily gossip[10] – in whatever form of knowledge-gathering people choose to interest themselves. (What is going to happen next in the play on television? What's on the other channel? Is there anyone going down the street? A person who wants to cease to know is the person who takes his own life.)

Thus it is a basic principle that 'knowledge is a good to be pursued and ignorance is to be avoided', it is 'an aspect of authentic human flourishing'.[11] Further, the good of knowledge is 'self-evident, obvious. It cannot be demonstrated but equally it needs no demonstration.' 'It is obvious that a man who is well informed, etc, simply *is* better-off (other things being equal) than a man who is muddled, deluded, and ignorant, that the state of the one is better than the state of the other …'[12] So the 'principle that truth is worth pursuing is … an underived principle. Neither its intelligibility nor its force rests on any further principle …[13] For in every field there is and there must be, at some point … an end to derivation and inference. At that point we find ourselves in face of the self-evident, which makes impossible all further inferences in that field.'[14]

2 Life

The term life 'here signifies every aspect of the vitality … which puts a human in good shape for self-determination'.[15] So life here includes physical (including mental) health, and freedom from pain and injury. The quality corresponds to the drive for self-preservation coupled with the drive to preserve the species by procreation, and

7   Ibid.
8   Ibid, p 66.
9   Ibid, p 84.
10   Ibid, p 85.
11   Ibid, p 64.
12   Ibid, p 72.
13   Ibid, p 69.
14   Ibid, p 70.
15   Ibid, p 86.

so includes the urge to bear a child. (The urge to copulate, Finnis suggests, is related to the good of life and also to the further goods set out under 3 and 5 below.)

3 Play

Each one of us 'can see the point of engaging in performances which have no point beyond the performance itself, enjoyed for its own sake'.[16] (We shall see that play as a good has a fundamental place in Finnis's concluding observations.)

4 Aesthetic experience

The experience relates to beauty, whether natural or man-made, and whether experienced by the creator or the spectator.

5 Social ability, or friendship

This further component of human flourishing 'is realised by a minimum of peace and harmony amongst men, and ... ranges through the forms of human community to its strongest form in the flowering of full friendship.' The good of friendship 'involves acting for the sake of one's friend's purposes, one's friend's well-being'.[17]

6 Practical reasonableness

This is the basic good 'of being able to to bring one's own intelligence to bear effectively ... on the problems of choosing one's actions and life-style and shaping one's own character'.[18] The value is 'complex, involving freedom, and reason, integrity and authenticity'.[19]

7 Religion

Finnis recognises that some people might have doubts about the inclusion of 'religion' in the list of human goods, but he makes it clear that what he means by religion is the good of determining for oneself whether the universal order of things has any origin beyond that known to natural science – even if the answer is negative or agnostic. For if there is such a transcendental origin then 'one's life and actions are in fundamental disorder if they are not brought, as

16   Ibid, p 87.
17   Ibid, p 88.
18   Ibid.
19   Ibid.

best they can, into some sort of harmony with whatever can be known or surmised about that transcendental other ...'[20]

There are other forms of good besides the seven proposed above, but any other forms of good will, Finnis says, be found on analysis to be ways of, or combinations of ways of, pursuing one of the seven basic forms of good. Human characteristics such as generosity, moderation, courage, are not basic values but form ways of pursuing these.

The basic goods are not to be thought of as being deduced from human inclinations, which can include such urges as the inclination to take more than one's share or gratuitously to inflict cruelty. '[S]elfishness, cruelty, and the like, simply do not stand to something self-evidently good as the urge to self-preservation stands to the self- evident good of human life. Selfishness, cruelty, etc, stand in need of some explanation, in the way that curiosity, friendliness, etc, do not.'[21]

All the basic goods, life, knowledge, etc, are equally fundamental. None is merely an aspect of any of the others, and each one can, when focused on, be regarded as the most important. Together they constitute a 'common good for all human beings' and embody 'everything one could reasonably want to do, to have, to be.'[22]

The requirements of practical reasonableness

'Practical reasonableness' has a dual role in Finnis's scheme. Wearing one hat 'practical reasonableness' is, as seen above, one of the human goods. Wearing its other hat 'practical reasonableness' means the reasoning process that 'distinguish[es] sound from unsound practical thinking and which, when brought to bear, provides the criteria for distinguishing between acts that ... are reasonable-all-things-considered (and not merely relative-to-a-particular-purpose) and acts that are unreasonable-all-things-considered ...'[23] So in essence practical reasonableness is reasonableness with regard to making practical decisions, decisions, for example, relating to the achievement of the human goods. (It

20   Ibid, p 90.
21   Ibid, p 91.
22   Ibid, p 155.
23   Ibid, p 23.

is important to remember that 'practical reasonableness' is used in these two ways – as a target, and as means to attaining targets, and to decide which meaning is intended at any one time.)

The requirements of practical reasonableness consist of a 'set of basic methodological requirements'.[24]

1. The first is that one should have a 'harmonious set of purposes and orientations, not as the "plans" or "blueprints" of a pipe dream, but as effective commitments'. We should have, says Finnis, adopting the words of Rawls, 'a rational plan of life'.[25]

2. In committing ourselves to a coherent plan of life we must pay equal regard to all the basic goods, not discounting some, exaggerating others. This does not mean that we must pursue all the goods equally – a scholar may incline towards the pursuit of knowledge rather than pleasure or friendship. But he must recognise the equal validity of all the basic goods. Thus there must be no arbitrary preferences between values.

3. There should be no arbitrary preferential treatment among those who partake of the human goods. The principle here finds expression in such dicta as '"Do to (or for) others what you would have them do (or for) you". Put yourself in your neighbour's shoes. Do not prevent others from getting what you are trying to get for yourself. These are requirements of reason, because to ignore them is to be arbitrary as between individuals'[26] and there must be 'no arbitrary preferences among persons'.[27]

4. 'In order to be sufficiently open to all the basic forms of good in all the changing circumstances of a lifetime … one must have a certain detachment from all the specific and limited projects that one undertakes.'[28] So the fourth requirement is detachment.

5. The requirement here is that 'having made one's general commitments one must not abandon them lightly'.[29] There must be fidelity to one's objectives, requiring 'a balance between fanaticism and

24 Ibid.
25 Ibid, p 105.
26 Ibid, p 108.
27 Ibid, p 106.
28 Ibid, p 110.
29 Ibid.

dropping out, apathy, unreasonable failure or refusal to "get in-volved" with anything'.[30]

6. This is 'the requirement that one bring about good in the world (in one's own life and in others) by actions that are efficient for their ... purpose(s). One must not waste one's opportunities by using inefficient methods.'[31]

7. The seventh requirement is that one should not do any act which *of itself* does nothing but damage, notwithstanding that the reason for doing the act was that the beneficial consequences of doing the act were judged to outweigh the damage done by the act itself. Thus the end does not justify the means; 'evil may not be done that good might follow therefrom'.[32] The requirement rests on the principle that there must be respect for every basic good in every act performed.

8. 'We can label this the requirement of favouring and fostering one's own communities.'[33]

9. This is the requirement that 'one should not do what one judges or thinks or "feels" all-in-all should not be done. That is to say one must act "in accordance with one's own conscience".'[34]

These are the nine requirements of practical reasonableness. Together they form a set of guidelines for behaviour, a 'mechanism for producing correct judgments'; each plays its part in reaching reasonable decisions. In seeking to pin down the meaning of 'requirements of practical reasonableness', (a meaning that tends to slip through one's fingers just as a grasp was thought to have been got) we should perhaps attend to the word *practical.* The requirements relate to how we should *act* in seeking to have regard to the basic human goods (of which, it must be remembered, practical reasonableness, seen from the angle of conditions necessary for human flourishing, is itself one).

As we progress through Finnis's book, we come to realise the way in which the requirements of practical reasonableness, natural

---

30 Ibid.
31 Ibid, p 111.
32 Ibid, p 122.
33 Ibid, p 125.
34 Ibid.

law and morality are intertwined. The requirements of practical reasonableness form the content of natural law; and they constitute what Finnis understands by morality; they form the 'reasons why ... there are things that morally ought [and ought not] to be done'.[35] Each of the requirements is 'a mode of moral obligation'.[36]

Natural law and man-made law

According to the Thomist tradition, man has certain ends, and human affairs, including man-made laws, should be so ordered as to enable these ends to be achieved. Where a man-made law implements a requirement of natural law (as where a law that makes murder an offence implements the natural law requirement of respect for life) then the man-made law derives part of its authority from natural law. Finnis's thinking runs on a parallel, if more elaborately worked out, pattern: there are certain goods and certain principles observance of which facilitates human flourishing. Man-made laws should be applications of the universally valid requirements of reasonableness. (Although 'the effort to integrate these ... into [man-made law] will require of judge and legislator countless elaborations ...')[37]

What of unjust laws? What if a man-made law conflicts with natural law? According to the Thomist tradition, *lex injustia non est lex*, an unjust law is no law, with the proviso that Aquinas stated.[38] Finnis considers that a theory of natural law need not have as its primary concern the affirmation of the view that unjust laws are not law. The principal concern, he believes, is 'to trace the way in which sound laws are to be derived ... from unchanging principles that have their force from reasonableness, not from any originating acts or circumstances'.[39] However, although Finnis does not consider the question whether an unjust law lacks validity as being important, he does deal with a question that is closely related, and of more significance in practice. Given that a legal system is by and large just, does a particular unjust law impose on a citizen any moral obligation to conform to it? – does an unjust law create a moral obligation in the way that a just law of itself does? Finnis concludes that since a

---

35 Ibid, p 103.
36 Ibid, p 126.
37 Ibid, p 289.
38 See p 69 supra.
39 *Natural Law and Natural Rights* p 351.

ruler's authority to give directions and make laws rests on the needs of the common good, if he uses his authority against the common good (or against any of the principles of practical reasonableness) then his directions or laws lack the authority that they would otherwise have and therefore create no obligation to obey them. But to this an important proviso is added. If a citizen disobeys or disregards an unjust law, his being seen to do so by other citizens may weaken the general respect of other citizens for the authority of a generally desirable ruler or constitution and so render ineffective the just parts of the legal system. So there may be an obligation to comply with an unjust law to the extent that such compliance is necessary to avoid bringing the law as a whole into contempt. (The correspondence of this view with that of St Thomas will not pass unnoticed.) The ruler remains under an obligation to repeal the unjust law, and in this sense the ruler has no right that the law should be complied with. 'But the citizen, or official, may meanwhile have the diminished, collateral, and in an important sense extra-legal, obligation to obey it.'[40]

Rights

Finnis treats natural rights as being synonymous with human rights: to the extent that humans have rights, these are the rights that are derived from natural law. Chapter VIII of the book examines recent analyses of rights, in particular that of Hohfeld, concluding that 'On the one hand, we should not say that human rights are subject to the common good; for the maintenance of human rights is a fundamental component of the common good. On the other hand, we can appropriately say that most human rights are subject to or limited by each other and by other *aspects* of the common good, aspects which could probably be subsumed under a broad conception of human rights ... indicated ... by such expressions as "public morality", "public health", "public order".'

Eternality and universality of natural law

For writers down the ages it has been a quality of natural law that it is eternal and universal. Finnis believes that the principles of natural

40 Ibid, p 362.

law hold good, as principles, however extensively they may be overlooked, misapplied or defied and however little they may be recognised.[41] They 'would "hold good" just as the mathematical principles of accounting "hold good" even where, as in the medieval banking community, they are unknown or misunderstood'.[42]

Does Finnis derive an 'ought' from an 'is'?

It will be recalled that from Hume onwards, it has been a mainstay of the criticism of natural law that the thinking entails an illogical jump from the 'is' of the facts of human existence to the 'ought' of moral obligation. Finnis rebuts any suggestion that he is guilty of making any such jump.[43] Indeed it is his contention that the jump from 'is' to 'ought' is one that natural lawyers have never in fact made. 'They have not, nor do they need to, nor did the classical exponents of the theory dream of attempting any such derivation.' For Finnis the principles of natural law are the principles of practical reasonableness, and reasonableness does not stem from the facts of human existence. Reasonableness pre-exists the human situation. True, it is in relation to the human goods that practical reasonableness operates. And the goods of human existence are evident from the 'is' of human existence – for example that for mankind 'play' is a 'good'. So if the human situation was different, if human nature was different, for example if 'friendship' was abhorrent, then the moral code produced by the requirements of practical reasonableness would be different. But the code would not be the product of the 'is' of (inter alia) the abhorrence of friendship, it would be the product of the application of the principles of practical reasonableness. The reasoning is therefore this: if a human good, A, can in certain circumstances be best advanced by doing the act X, then as a matter of practical reasonableness X ought to be done. The logical necessity that X ought to be done stems from *reasonableness*, not from the fact that the good happened to be A. (This, Finnis claims, forms the underlay of the doctrine as propounded by St Thomas.)

---

41 Ibid, p 24.
42 Ibid.
43 Ibid, p 17.

The purpose of the book

'This is a book', Finnis says,[44] 'about natural law. It expounds or sets out a theory of natural law, but is not *about* that theory. Nor is it about other theories. It refers to other theories only to illuminate the theory expounded [in the book], or to explain why some truths about natural law have at various times and in various ways been overlooked or obscured. The book does not enter into discussions about whether natural law doctrines have exerted a conservative or radical influence on Western politics, or about the supposed psychological ... origins of such doctrines, or about the claim that ... specific natural law doctrines are asserted ... as a disguise or vehicle for expressions of ecclesiastical faith. For none of these discussions has any real bearing on the question whether there is a natural law and, if so, what its content is.'[45] The book thus presents us with what is, to borrow a phrase from Kelsen, a 'pure' theory of natural law.

The function of natural law, Finnis believes, is to provide us with a rational foundation for moral judgment.[46] It is a crucial feature of his presentation of the theory in that it does not rest its foundations on religious belief – the theory is presented 'without needing to advert to the question of God's existence or nature or will':[47] it is a theory that is wholly secular in form. Yet, though the theory stands or falls on the facts of logic, Finnis does not leave things here. Beyond the theory, he has something further to say.

The ultimate question – Why?

'What', Chapter XIII begins, 'further explanations are required?' The basic forms of human flourishing are obvious to anyone acquainted with human opportunities. The requirements of practical reasonableness are as obvious as the first principles of logic. The implications of practical reasonableness as they affect such matters as authority and justice, can be worked out. But further questions do remain. When we think about the lives and deaths of countless people, countless communities down the ages, when 'we notice the succession of human persons (and of their communities), evidently separated beyond all contact with another by time and

44   Ibid, p 25.
45   Ibid.
46   Ibid.
47   Ibid, p 49.

distance ... the question arises whether my good (and the well-being of my communities) has any further *point*, ie whether it relates to any more comprehensive participation in good.'[48] Further, when the requirements of practical reasonableness require self-sacrifice, action for the good of the community, one may reasonably enquire whether there is any *point* to the benefit that accrues to the community, which will itself sooner or later come to an end. Further again, 'each of us is an item not only in the succession of persons (and their communities) but also in a universe, indefinitely extended in space and time, of entities and states of affairs, many of which have intelligible patterns of flourishing and decay. Of each, and of the ensemble, it is possible to ask whether it too has a good, a point, a value – and, in any case, how that entity or state of affairs, or ensemble of entities and of states of affairs, relates to anybody's good, not to mention my good and my community's.'[49] What, in short, is the point of the totality of human experience? Does self-cultivation, moral athleticism (corresponding to an athlete's cultivation of his body for its own sake) provide a meaningful point for human existence?

As a step towards an answer Professor Finnis proceeds to elaborate a theory of first causes. We cannot here trace the steps in his reasoning and must content ourselves with saying that he concludes that when the causes of all things, of all circumstances and sets of circumstances are traced back, it is possible to postulate the existence of a state of affairs that has no cause, a state of affairs that causes others but is uncaused itself, a state of affairs that he calls an 'uncaused causing', and refers to as D, representing a state of affairs that exists by being what it is. The postulation of D affirms nothing about the state of affairs 'other than that it has what it takes to make all other states of affairs to exist'.

Beyond this, Finnis says, the argument will not take us. But it is nevertheless possible, he believes, to speculate that in causing all caused states of affairs, D 'determines between contingent possibilities' (ie makes choices as to which way things are to go) and in so doing in some respects acts in a way analogous to that of a human being exercising free choice. If this analogy holds good, it would seem that D can be thought of as having knowledge of the alternatives available in deciding which way to set things going. This 'speculation suggests that D *acts* and *knows*' and that D's existing is conceivable on the model of *personal* life.[50] Further, speculation

48   Ibid, p 372.
49   Ibid, p 373.
50   Ibid, p 392.

'suggests that some sort of communication from, or self-disclosure of, D might occur'. Whether this does occur 'is a matter of fact, of experience and history' (and, we might be inclined to add, of faith).

It must not be overlooked, Finnis points out, that originators of natural law thinking (the early Greek philosophers, in particular Plato and Aristotle), who did not suppose that god has revealed himself to man, believed nonetheless that men can, through philosophic meditation 'gain access to the transcendental source of being, goodness and knowledge ...'[51]

Indeed. But what we want to know is whether, according to Finnis's thinking, any link exists between human rationality and the entity postulated as D. For unless some link is established, unless the precepts of natural law can be reckoned to be founded on something more than reasonableness, we leave unanswered, *wholly* unanswered, the ultimate question of ethics – *why* should I act in a way that is good rather than bad? – *why* should I observe the requirements of practical reasonableness? – why, that is, apart from my own self-interest (for example, to enjoy the satisfaction of being thought good, to secure advancement by compliance with a society's moral code, to avoid punishment or ostracism, to build up goodwill among others in the hope of gaining a return for my investment in the future, to obtain, through admission to Heaven, eternal life)? *Why?* Where does the obligation, if there is one, come from? What, for example, and specifically, is the good, the good to me, involved in self-sacrifice? What 'is the *point* of living according to the principles and requirements of practical reasonableness'?[52]

In seeking to give an answer Finnis speculates that if it is accepted that it is possible that D, the uncaused cause, exists in a way something like personal human life, and that D's causing is to some extent analogous to decision-taking by humans, then this way of thinking about D allows the further speculation that D might disclose itself to human understanding and that the entity so disclosed might reveal itself to be lovable and to favour the well-being of everyone. If these speculations and hopes were confirmed, then an answer to the question, 'Why should I favour the common good above my own interests?', would be reached, namely because of 'love and friendship for the personal being ... who not only makes possible whatever well-being of persons there can be and actually is, but also positively favours (though in ways often unintelligible to us) that common good'.[53]

51   Ibid.
52   Ibid, p 405.
53   Ibid, p 406.

Sacrifice of oneself for others for their own sake would have meaning, since others could be regarded as 'persons whose good is favoured also by one whose own goodness is unrestricted and whose love is no way blind but rather is given knowing fully the true worth and all-explaining point of everything, of the existence of every person, and of the history of every community'.[54]

We do not, at the end of Finnis's exploration, find that we learn the source of moral obligation in the sense of a binding authority. If we simply say that we act for the sake of God, we would suggest that God somehow needs us, needs creation, the success of creation, the achieving of the creative purpose. But D needs and lacks nothing. Finnis does, though, give us a slant that is perhaps as close as we are likely to come to resolution of the eternal problem. There may not be a *reason* for favouring others before ourselves, for having regard for the common good, for observing the requirements of practical reasonableness, but there may be a *point* in so doing. 'The requirements of practical reasonableness (which generate our obligations) have a "point" beyond themselves. That point is the *game* of co-operating with God. Being *play*, this co-operation has no point beyond itself the sharing, in a limited way, in the divine play.

'Practical reasonableness, therefore, need not be regarded as ultimately a form of self-perfection. That is not its final significance. Nor, on the other hand, are its requirements sheer categorical imperatives; they gain practical force from the most basic explanation that can be provided for them – that they are what is needed to participate in the game of God.

'Play, too, can now be more adequately understood. It is to be contrasted with business, with responsibilities, with the serious things of life. But, in the last analysis, there is a play that is the *only* really serious matter. In such a "final analysis", in which we seek an understanding going beyond our feelings, the "serious things of life", even atrocious miseries, are really serious only to the extent that they contribute to or are caught up into a good play of the game of the God who creates and favours human good.'[55]

Whether we find this conclusion satisfactory is a matter for each to determine. At the end of the road Professor Finnis's conclusion rests on the existence of God, however remote, and however conceived. If we reject any notion of an entity beyond human existence, we are left on our own to decide whether any such thing as moral obligation exists and, if we think it does, where it comes from.

54 Ibid.
55 Ibid, pp 409–410.

CHAPTER 13

Pleasures and pains

Utilitarianism

Utilitarianism is one of a number of bridges between jurisprudence and philosophy. Since jurisprudence can be regarded as a branch of philosophy, it is to be expected that such bridges exist. That part of philosophy in which utilitarianism lies is Ethics.

Ethics is defined[1] the 'science of moral in human conduct', science here being used in the sense of 'organised body of knowledge on a subject'. Ethics has as its purpose, first, to determine whether absolute standards of right and wrong exist; if they do, whether it is possible to know what they are; and, if so, *how* we are to know what they are; and, second, if such standards do exist, and we can know them, what, specifically, they are.

The first branch of the subject, which is termed metaethics, thus deals with the nature and knowability of ethical standards. It considers what we mean when we say that one thing is good and another is bad. It considers whether such statements have any meaning at all. This branch of ethics is concerned with whether rules or standards of human conduct are prescribed and, if so, by what means.

The second aspect of ethics is termed normative ethics. It is concerned (assuming that moral standards exist and can be known) with what constitutes good conduct; with the principles that should govern and direct the conduct of individual humans, and of human affairs.

During the twentieth century a third branch of ethics emerged – the examination of how ethical principles that have general acceptance are to be applied in such real life situations as where a

1 OED.

doctor is faced with the decision whether to facilitate the death of a grossly malformed baby; or with a patient in the terminal stages of cancer who requests that his life should be brought to an end. Here the layman turns to the philosopher and says, 'You are the expert. You know about ethics. What's the answer? What is the right thing to do?' The philosopher replies, 'Let me refer you to a book of mine on the subject'. Many such books have appeared – on medical ethics, legal ethics, environmental ethics, the ethics of war, the ethics of discrimination. This third aspect of ethics, ethics in relation to current issues, is not here our concern. The first two aspects, if we are to understand utilitarianism's place in the development of thinking, are.

Metaethics

Is there such a thing as goodness? Are there absolute standards of right and wrong? The question has been asked for two and a half thousand years. From Chapter 5 we know that Plato answered, 'Yes. There is a "form" of goodness, of which it is possible for humans to gain a glimpse'. We know too from Chapter 5 that the Sophists held the opposite view: standards are relative. What is right in the eyes of Athenians might be abhorrent elsewhere.

The debate has reverberated down the centuries.

For some the question of absolutes and their knowability presents no problem. We know what is good because God (or the Gods) tells us. For Jews, Moses brought down the Ten Commandments from the mountain. Christians look to the Ten Commandments coupled with the precepts of Jesus in the Sermon on the Mount. So good is that which God approves of.

But those who maintain that moral values are of divine origin are faced with a problem. If goodness is what God approves of, and God approved of the ill treatment of children, then the ill treatment of children would be good. Unless we accept that what God approves of and disapproves of is purely arbitrary, we must accept that in deciding what to approve of (and to ordain to humans accordingly), God must decide what to approve of according to some pre-existing, supra-God, criteria. What are the criteria God adopts in making His decisions as to whether acts are good or bad?

The believer may reply 'I do not know the answer to this question, but for me it is sufficient that it is only through divine intervention that good can be known. God tells us what is good and what is bad.'

If the believer is asked 'And which faith correctly interprets the divine intervention of God? – which priests have got the message down as God intended?' and he replies, 'My own', his answer takes us no closer to establishing the existence of absolute values of good and evil.

During the centuries in which the Christian churches of east and west held unthreatened sway, the question of absolute values was not one that was considered as requiring attention. Christianity continued to adhere to the Jewish position that goodness was to be known from what God had ordained; in the case of Christianity, from the scriptures of the Old and New Testaments, and from Revelation, as interpreted by the Church.

Not until the twelfth century did questions of an ethical nature again begin to be considered, as when the French priest and theologian Peter Abelard proposed that it was not an illicit sexual act that was sinful, nor the desire to commit the act, but the mental decision to give way to that desire, thus introducing the factor of intention into considerations of right and wrong.

The first major advance since Roman times came with the writings of Thomas Aquinas. In Chapter 5 we saw that it was the achievement of St Thomas to reconcile the teaching of the Church with the wisdom of the ancient world, in particular by harnessing the teleology of Aristotle with the theology of Christianity so that thereafter guidance as to how men should behave was to be learned not only from God's revelation but also by the employment of God's gift to men of reason.

After the Renaissance and the Reformation it began to be to reason alone, unyoked from religion, that philosophers looked for answers to questions concerning absolute values, thereafter theologians and moral philosophers following separate paths, and loosing sight of each other until, much later, the revival of natural law thinking described in Chapter 5.

How, then, have those who hold that absolute values exist proposed that they are to be known? For some, the truths of good and evil are to be discovered by a kind of rational intuition, by 'an immediate apprehension of ethical truth'.[2] Just as the truths of mathematics are self-evident, so too can the truths of moral values, by the application of reason, be ascertained. This view came to be termed *intuitionism*.[3]

Others have held that we know of the distinction between good and evil as a result of an inborn inclination towards benevolence, towards such qualities as sympathy, honesty, friendship, gratitude. Members of this school,[4] the *moral sense* school, recognise that

---

2 Encyclopaedia Britannica.
3 Ralph Cudworth (1617–1688), Henry More (1614–1687), Samuel Clarke (1675–1729).
4 The 3rd Earl of Shaftsbury (1671–1713), Francis Hutchinson (1694–1746), David Hume (1711–1776).

contrary desires exist but believe that the better side of human nature is that which prevails since the pleasures of benevolence are greater than those of opposite qualities, moral values thus being buttressed by enlightened self-interest. Reason, though, they reject as a source, since reason can on occasions direct a man towards evil conduct (if such conduct benefits him and he fears no detection).

It was during the seventeenth century that the debate between the intuitionists and the moral sense school was at its height, although the echoes of the debate have continued in various guises down to the present century. In which camp did Hume rest? As a rationalist it might be thought that he would side with the intuitionists, who held that moral values could be observed as self evident truths, in the same way that mathematics could be seen to be true. But to have sided with the intuitionists would have meant accepting that moral values could be derived from factual observation, a departure from his observation that no 'ought' can be derived from an 'is'. So Hume was with the moral sense school of thinking, values were no more than feelings.

Normative ethics

By the middle of the eighteenth century the debate over the nature of moral values (whether they are subjective or objective, and if the latter, what is their source) had been played out and philosophers' attention turned to what today we term normative ethics – according to what criterion are we to judge what actions are right and which are wrong? And if we can agree upon a criterion, what is good conduct? What is bad? What are the *norms* of conduct that human should observe?

It was as much with this question, as much as the questions posed by what we term metaethics, that the ancients were occupied. Indeed it was the purpose of the major work on ethics in the golden age of Greece, Aristotle's *Nichomachean Ethics* to provide a code by which the right thinking man should conduct his life. Succeeding philosophers and philosophical schools – the Stoics, the Epicureans – added their own views. With the coming of Christianity, discussion as to right and wrong conduct ceased to be meaningful – it went without saying that man should conduct himself and his affairs as God had, through the Scriptures and the guidance of the Church, ordained.

For those who find the Christian answer deficient, or who seek an independent buttress for the Christian view, or who reject the Christian answer and seek an answer in purely secular terms, is there no touchstone by which an action can be judged to be right or wrong?

It was one of the many contributions of Jeremy Bentham (1784 – 1832) to philosophy and political thought, building on ideas put forward by earlier writers, to propose, in his *An Introduction to Principles of Morality and Legislation,* published in 1789, an answer that has retained a sway over thinking down to our present day.

Jeremy Bentham

To the question, by reference to what criterion do we judge whether an act is good or bad? Bentham answers, by reference to its *consequences.*

Consequences with regard to what? With regard, Bentham answers, to the effect that the act has on subsequent human pleasure and pain. 'Nature,' he said. 'has placed mankind under the governance of two sovereign masters, pain and pleasure ... They govern us in all we do, in all we say, in all we think ... [M]an may pretend to abjure their empire: but in reality he will remain subject to [their governance] all the while.'

Thus, for Bentham, we are to approve or disapprove of any action 'according to the tendency which it appears to have to augment or diminish the happiness of the party whose interest is in question: or what is the same thing in other words, to promote or oppose that happiness.' This is the benchmark against which all acts are to be judged, private acts, and 'of every measure of government'.

Pleasures and pains

Bentham undertakes an elaborate analysis of pleasures and pains. Pleasures are of the following kinds.

1. Pleasures of sense (taste and the satisfaction of hunger and thirst; intoxication; smell; touch; hearing; seeing; sex; health; gratification of curiosity).
2. Pleasures of wealth (the pleasure of acquisition and of possession).
3. Pleasures of skill.
4. Pleasures of amity (being on good terms with others).
5. Pleasures of having a good name.
6. Pleasures of power.
7. Pleasures of piety.
8. Pleasures of benevolence (pleasures resulting from the sympathy or benevolence of others).
9. Pleasures of malevolence (pleasures resulting from the view of pain suffered by others who may become the objects of our malevolence (including the pleasures of the 'irascible appetite')).

10. Pleasures of the memory.
11. Pleasures of the imagination.
12. Pleasures of expectation.
13. Pleasures 'depending on association' with other pleasurable things.
14. Pleasures of relief, eg from pain.

Bentham then proceeds to list the various categories of pain.

1. Pains of privation (the pains that result from the thought of not possessing any of the pleasures).
2. Pains of desire (ie unfulfilled desire).
3. Pains of disappointment.
4. Pains of regret (at not expecting to enjoy a pleasure again, or at not having enjoyed a pleasure as much as was expected).
5. Pains of the senses (these are the reverse of the pleasures of senses and so include, eg hunger thirst, bad tastes, bad smells, un-pleasant sounds, disagreeable sights, excessive heat or cold, disease. Bentham does not mention the reverse of the pleasures of sex – presumably the pains of frustration).
6. Pains of awkwardness (Bentham may have had in mind his own extreme shyness).
7. Pains of enmity (from being on bad terms with people).
8. Pains of having an ill name.
9. Pains of piety (from believing that one is 'obnoxious ... to the Supreme Being').
10. Pains of benevolence (from the knowledge of the sufferings of others).
11. Pains of malevolence (from the knowledge that those one does not like are having pleasures).
12. Pains of expectation (from apprehensiveness).

Bentham is nothing if not thorough.

The notion of utility

Since in judging the merits of any act we are to look to its effects, Bentham's ethics are classified as '*consequentionalist*'. What is the consequence of the act with regard to the promotion or the hindering of happiness? What in this respect is its 'use'? The word 'use', meaning usefulness for a purpose, provides a key to understanding what Bentham means when he says that it is the notion of *utility* on which his scheme rests. He explains, 'By utility is meant that property in any object, whereby it tends to produce benefit, advantage, pleasure, good or happiness, (all this in the present case comes to the same thing) or (what comes again to the same thing) to prevent the happening of mischief, pain, evil, or unhappiness to the party whose interest is considered.'

In speaking of the effects of an act, he distinguishes between the effects on the interests of an individual and on the interests of the community. With regard to individuals 'a thing is said to promote the interest ... of an individual, when it tends to add to the sum total of his pleasures: or what comes to the same thing, to diminish the sum total of his pains'. And in the case of communities, correspondingly, ' An action may be said to be conformable to the principle of utility ... with respect to the community at large ... when the tendency it has to augment the happiness of the community is greater than it has to diminish it'. A 'community is a fictitious body, composed of the individual persons who are considered as constituting as it were its members. The interest of the community then is, what? – the sum total of the several members who compose it.'

It is with the rightness or wrongness of government action (including the legislature) that Bentham perhaps most clearly envisages his principle as playing its part. He applies the principle of utility specifically to government action, 'A measure of government (which is but a particular kind of action, performed by a particular person or persons) may be said to be conformable to or dictated by the principle of utility, when ... the tendency it has to augment the happiness of the community is greater than any which it has to diminish it'.

It is understandable that Bentham's concern should be with government action since what motivated him was his interest in reform, in particular the reform of parliament and of criminal law and the penal system. Having rejected natural law (which, it will be recalled, he dismissed as 'nonsense on stilts') and theories based on a social contract, he needed another calculus by which to show the merits or demerits of the matters under his scrutiny. (The pertinence of 'utility' in attacking archaic laws and inhuman practices will be appreciated.)

The calculus

Since 'Pleasures ... and the avoidance of pains, are the ends which the legislator has in view [,] it behoves him ...' Bentham says, 'to understand their *value*'. But how is a legislator to measure the 'value', ie the *degree*, of happiness produced by an act? He needs some means to measure happiness because an act may result in happiness (free medical treatment) to some and pain (eg increased taxes) to others. Further, some acts may produce a large measure of happiness or of pain, others a trifling amount. So what is needed, we can imagine, is a pair of scales. On one side is put the weight of the happiness that an act will result in, on the other side the weight of pain that will result, and then one sees whether the value, the 'weight', of the happiness exceeds the weight of the pain. If it does, the act satisfies the test of utility.

In the case of an individual person the value of a pleasure or pain, Bentham explains, will be greater or less according to the following circumstances:

- intensity;
- duration;
- certainty or uncertainty; and
- propinquity or remoteness.

Where it is the pleasure or pain of a group that is to be measured, then to the above factors there must be added the number of persons that will be affected by the act.

Bentham explains how, in the case of a community the assessment is to be carried out. We must begin with any one person of those whose interests seem most likely to be affected and take account of the immediate happiness produced for him by the act (the value of the happiness being assessed according to the four factors above), and then the longer-term happiness. Then we must do the same thing with regard to pain (again the immediate and long-term effects). Then we 'sum up all the values of all the pleasures on the one side, and all the pains on the other. The balance, if it be on the side of pleasure will give a good tendency of the act …with respect to the interests of that individual person; if on the side of pain, the bad tendency of it upon the whole.' Then we repeat the process in the case of each individual in the community, and total all the goodness and the pain values. This is what Bentham calls the *felicific calculus.* Here is a crude example.

Individual	Value of goodness (+)	Value of badness (-)
A	27	5
B	2	4
C	6	8
D	1	8
E	3	15
F	2	7
G	18	4
H	19	5
I	4	10
Total	82	66

The result here is that the proposed act satisfies the test of utility since the units of good exceed those of bad. It will be noted that this result ensues notwithstanding that the number of people who would vote against the proposed action exceeds those in favour. This is because of the strength of the benefits to be enjoyed, albeit by a minority, exceeds the weight of the drawbacks suffered by the majority. From this it will be appreciated that the formulation of Bentham's thesis as being that an act is good if it promotes 'greatest good of the greatest number', unless properly understood, over-simplifies and misrepresents what he proposes.

Bentham does not expect the process to be carried out with the kind of exactitude set out above on every occasion that a matter arises for decision. But even if the test of utility cannot in reality be applied before every decision, the fact remains that the test is, Bentham says, nothing 'but what the practice of mankind, where-soever they have a clear view of their own interest, is perfectly conformable to' – it is what *happens*. Is this not so? Consider an appeal against a refusal by a local planning authority to grant planning permission for a new development. Does not the inspector, even if subconsciously, consider who will be affected, in what way they will be affected, the degree to which each will be affected, and then apply Bentham's felicific calculus? Where an injunction is sought to prevent the continuation of a public or private nuisance, does not the judge adopt the same balancing of interests? (Indeed, the cases and the textbooks on tort spell out the factors that a court should take into account in reaching a decision.) Are not proposals for new road schemes determined by the balancing of pains and pleasures – current moves away from building new roads being a result of the reassessment of the weight of the pains involved? Bentham is right. Consciously or not, the felicific calculus is a guide to decisions every day.

In putting forward the test of utility Bentham makes no claim to originality. It is not, he recognises, a 'novel theory' and he expressly recognises his debt to earlier writers, in particular Francis Hutchinson.[5]

Private morality

Speaking of Bentham's felicific calculus in the context of public affairs should not cause us to forget that his system of ethics applies as much to individual morality as to that of governments.

---

5   1660–1739. Other influences were those of Bishop Richard Cumberland (1631–1718) and William Paley (1743–1805).

'Morality'? How does 'morality' relate to 'ethics'? The two words are closely related, in times past being virtually interchangeable, for example the phrase 'ethical judgements' carrying no different a meaning from 'moral judgements'. Indeed, the study of ethics came under the head of moral philosophy – moral philosophers being those who made ethics the subject of their study. More recently, the word morality has come to be used in a narrower sense, to refer to individual behaviour, for example with regard to sexuality; ethics being used (in addition to its use for the subject as a whole) to refer to the conduct of groups, as in references to medical ethics, or legal ethics, or business ethics; or to particular issues, as, for example, ones affecting the environment.

It is with regard to private morality that the revolutionary character of Bentham's criterion for judging right and wrong can be appreciated. No longer is an act to be judged according to religious precepts or conventional mores handed down from previous generations. An act that is right or wrong, not because of any intrinsic rightness or wrongness, but solely with regard to its consequences.

However, if we remember that many acts proscribed by religious authority or social convention have been so prescribed because of their likely consequences, the effect of Bentham's test might not in practice always produce a judgement that differed from a society's existing code. Conventional morality and utilitarianism may, although running on separate tracks, and eyeing each other distrustfully, nevertheless reach the same destination.

It was, though, the substitution of a test independent of religion or convention, and one well capable of producing a result different from the existing moral norms that was revolutionary and, for some, subversive.

In considering the acts of an individual, we should note that Bentham includes the actor among those affected by an act. So if A contemplates an act that will affect B, C, and D, he is to count his own pleasures and pains in the calculus. It follows that if A's score for benefit is, let us say, 97 and the pain score for B, C and D is 52, A is justified in performing the act – notwithstanding that the consequences for others is wholly adverse.

Characteristics

We said above that Bentham's thesis is *consequentialist* in nature. Another characteristic is its *universality*. It is applicable at any place in any period. But his utilitarianism is not universal in the sense that it prescribes whether each individual *kind* of act is right or wrong.

It does not say that taking another person's life is wrong. It says that the taking of another's life is to be judged right or wrong according to the consequences of the taking of that act. Thus utilitarianism is not *prescriptive* in nature.

Utilitarianism is not, however, universal in the sense of producing the same result at different times. If the likely consequences of an act change, so may how it is judged by the principle of utility. In some earlier times, for a girl, sex outside marriage could result in disaster. With the introduction of contraception, the situation is no longer the same. The act of sex outside marriage is no different whether it occurs in 1798 or 1998, but the result of the application of the test of utility may be different.

This fact demonstrates the continuing gulf between those for whom, because of religious principle or for some other reason (eg intuition) an act is intrinsically wrong (wrong in itself, regardless of its consequences or other factors), and those who accept the test of utility.

Bentham's ethics are *hedonistic,* hedonism being the view that the pursuit of pleasure (however conceived) is the proper objective for all action.

Is his scheme *altruistic*? The answer is that it is altruistic in part. The interests of others must be considered, but as noted above, the interests of others are not conclusive. (But, as Mill observed, 'As between his own happiness and that of others, utilitarianism requires him to be as strictly impartial as a disinterested and benevolent spectator'.)

Since the interests of all those affected are to count, not exclusively those of the actor, utilitarianism is not *egotistic* (egoism being the view that man should pursue his own self interest to the exclusion of the interests of others).

In judging the rightness or wrongness of any act, utilitarianism takes no account of the *motive* for the performance of the act. Thus an act may be right notwithstanding that the motive was bad.

It is another characteristic of Bentham's thesis that it is *anti-rationalistic,* in the sense that it rejects reason as the source of moral values: ('How can we say that moral values are founded on reason when there would be nothing wholly unreasonable for me to prefer the destruction of the whole world to a scratch on my finger?')

It is sometimes said that utilitarianism is *teleological* in nature since it is concerned with ends. This is to misconstrue the word teleological. Teleology is concerned with the ends that is something's nature to grow towards, as it is the end of an acorn to grow into an oak tree; and, for the catholic theologians, it is man's end to grow towards a knowledge and a love of God. In natural law thinking, we judge an act by whether it furthers or impedes man's progress towards his natural end. Natural law unrepentantly obtains an 'ought' from an 'is'. To the extent that he is concerned with ends, Bentham looks towards the ends that an act will result in. He is concerned with consequences, which are very different from the notion of ends as they have a place in natural law thinking. The natural lawyer thinks of ends in the sense of final culminations; Bentham thinks of 'starts', and what ends will *follow* from these.

Criticisms

Critics of utilitarianism have fallen into two categories: those who reject the thesis in its entirety, and those who, while not rejecting the thesis as a whole, point to deficiencies and, in some cases, suggest modifications.

Rejection

In the first category lie those who deny the meaningfulness of any talk of moral values being true or false. Those in the school of logical positivists, in particular A J Ayer, maintain that moral judgements are no more than statements of fact coupled with an indication of disapproval. If I say that stealing money is wrong, all I am saying is that I disapprove of people taking things that do not belong to them. Rightness and wrongness do not enter into the matter. This view is termed *emotivism*.

Also in the first category lie those who uphold the sovereignty of natural law, either in its traditional form or in a modern guise, such as that of John Finnis.[6]

Among the critics of utilitarianism are also found those whose view of ethics is shaped by the Darwinian theory of evolution, according to which in the natural world each species displays hierarchies whose existence is antipathetic to values being determined by reference to consequences. Those of this persuasion form in effect a secular version of natural law. Darwinism shows that inequality in any animal society is natural. Whether among rabbits, wolves, chimpanzees or humans, it is natural, at any rate for males, to climb to a place higher up the hierarchy; it is a creature's 'end' to be top dog. According to

6 See Chapter 12.

the Darwinian perspective, the rightness or wrongness of any act is determined not by the felicific calculus but by whether the act assists towards reaching this end.

Another criticism concerns the lack of sufficient certainty in the application of the calculus. Thus, first, it is never possible to predict the consequences of an act with sufficient certainty for the calculus to be a satisfactory guide. (To which Bentham would no doubt reply (a) no act should be performed without an attempted assessment of its consequences; (b) we do assess consequences all the time.)

Secondly, it is impossible to assess the weight that should be attributed to the pleasures and pains that will result from an act. There would be no agreement over for example, the pleasures (to shareholders and workers) and the pains (to visitors and residents) resulting from a new quarry in a National Park. (To which Bentham would no doubt reply: There is no question of disagreement. The assessment is to be made by one person, he who contemplates the act; and, as in the first matter, in practice consequences are being assessed all the time.)

It is another line of attack to assert that Bentham falls into the trap of obtaining an 'ought' – how individuals and government sought to conduct themselves – from an 'is' – the fact that mankind seeks pleasure over pain. He rejects this assertion as follows: 'Is it [the validity of the felicific calculus] susceptible of any direct proof? It should seem not; for that which is used to prove everything else, cannot itself be proved: a chain of proofs must have their commencement somewhere. To give such a proof is as impossible as it is needless'.

Modification

Among those who built on the foundation that Bentham con-structed, pride of place must be accorded to John Stuart Mill whose presentation of the matter provides utilitarianism with one of its strongest statements. (Mill believed that it was he who first brought the word 'utilitarian' into use[7]). He states the principle thus: 'The creed which accepts as the foundation of moral, Utility, or the Greatest happiness Principle, holds that actions are right in pro-portion as they tend to produce happiness, wrong as they tend to produce the reverse of happiness. By happiness is intended pleasure, and the absence of pain; by unhappiness, pain and the privation of pleasure.'

---

7   Having adopted it, he says, from 'a passing expression in Mr Galt's Annals of the Parish'. *Utilitarianism*, Chap II.

The greater part of Mill's *Utilitarianism* is occupied by responses to criticisms that had been levelled at Bentham's thesis. In the course of this, Mill augments the notion of utility in a number of directions. Thus he extends Bentham's list of pleasures to include pleasures of an intellectual nature, such as 'pleasures of the imagination' and 'of the gratification of the higher emotions'. Further, he rejects Bentham's position that all pleasures carry the same 'weight', Mill according intellectual pleasures a higher place than purely 'pleasures of the moment'. ('It is quite compatible with the principle of utility to recognise the fact, that some kinds of pleasure are more desirable and more valuable than others. It would be absurd that … pleasures should be supposed to depend on quantity alone'.)

It was in dealing with the objection that there is no time to employ the calculus each time an action is contemplated that Mill makes a substantial departure from Bentham's thesis. There is no need, he says, for us to test each individual action directly by the test of utility. This is because past experience has shown that certain principles pass the test utility and so can guide our actions without our needing to apply the test directly on every occasion. He illustrates the point by reference to navigation at sea. It would be possible for a sailor, if he had the skill and the time, to calculate the mathematical co-ordinates necessary to pinpoint his position each time he wanted to know this. But he has no need to do this because he can look up the figures in the Nautical Almanac. The Almanac has passed the relevant test, that of accuracy for determining position at sea, and so the sailor can rely on it for the information he needs. Thus for Mill there is an intermediate level between the principle of utility and our deciding whether an action is right, namely rules of conduct (Mill speaks of 'intermediate generalisations' and 'subordinate principles') that the past experience of mankind has shown to pass the test of utility and so are there to guide us without the need to apply the test on every occasion that a decision arises.

For example, instead of asking whether making this man who has broken a contract pay compensation has consequences that pass the test of utility, we should ask whether a rule that those who break contracts should pay compensation passes the test. If it does, the rule should be adopted.

Mill's form of utilitarianism came to be termed '*rule utilitarianism*' (and Bentham's thereafter, by way of distinction, *act utilitarianism,* for Bentham the calculus being used to test specific acts, not rules governing classes of act). The attraction of rule utilitarianism for those wishing to impose a moral code will be appreciated. Act utilitarianism could permit many acts that rule utilitarianism would prohibit, as, for example, euthanasia, the use of cannabis, and, in earlier times, sex outside marriage. Act utilitarianism opens the way (subject to the test being satisfied) to individual freedom of choice. Rule utilitarianism puts on a break.

Bentham did not, in *Principles of Morality and Legislation,* move beyond act utilitarianism. He did, though, as an advocate of reform, apply the test of utility to existing laws and social institutions and practices and rules. But the fact that he asked whether the consequences of such and such a rule passes the test of utility does not make him a rule utilitarian in the sense that that term later came to carry.

Other forms of utilitarianism

Another form of utilitarianism proposed has (particularly among economists) been *preference utilitarianism* under which the place of pleasure in Bentham's scheme is taken by anything that appears as an object of (rational or informed) desire.[8] Under another variant, *negative utilitarianism,* greater weight is attached to preventing pains (or other disadvantages) than to promoting pleasures (or other benefits), proponents holding that the reduction of suffering is more important than, and should therefore take precedence over, the increase in the happiness of those already happy.

Utilitarianism and jurisprudence

In this chapter utilitarianism has been placed within the framework of ethics. And this is where it belongs; it *is* a branch of ethics. In what way, then, is utilitarianism the concern of jurisprudence? There are various reasons.

In dealing with the notion of justice we noted the views of such writers as John Rawls. By providing a different approach, utilitarianism throws into relief, and helps us consider afresh, the views of those, such as Rawls, who have written on justice. Conversely, Rawls's notion of the original position[9] and what people would choose in it prompts us reappraise utilitarianism

---

8   Encyclopaedia Britannica.
9   See Chap 15.

and its assumptions. Thus the utilitarian approach and that of others who have explored the meaning of justice illuminate each other. Similarly, by providing its own answer, utilitarianism throws new light on the subject of rights – What rights should exist? Those that pass the test of utility. How does this view stand up against other views on the subject, such as those of Dworkin?

For various writers, for example Rawls, Dworkin and Nozick, it has been what they considered the defects in utilitarianism that has provided the motivation[10] for the exposition of their own views. These views cannot properly be followed without a knowledge of what it was that they considered defective.

Utilitarianism has formed the other side of the coin of legal positivism. The positivist, it will be recalled, holds that a legal system and its law are what they are, and that what they ought to be is of no concern of a jurist whose seeks to pinpoint the essence of law. But having once analysed the nature of law and then turned to the separate question of what laws should exist – having turned from the analytical to the normative – positivists such as Bentham and Austin held that utilitarianism was the method by which the value of laws should be judged. All through, in fact, legal positivism and utilitarianism have walked hand in hand.

Important though utilitarianism has been for the study of jurisprudence, its importance for the law generally, the law in practice, the actual content of the law, has been of even greater significance, in that it was the test of utility, summed up in the phrase 'What *use* is it?' that provided nineteenth century reformers with their most potent argument for change.

The final question

If there is to be one criticism of utilitarianism to which no reply has been given, it is no more than the criticism to which no system of ethics has provided a satisfactory answer. Even if we are able to agree that, whatever their source, ethical standards exist, ie that some forms of conduct are good and some are bad, and that we can determine what the standards are (by whatever means, from religion, or utilitarianism or intuition), why should we observe them? *Why* should we be good? Why should a person desist from an act because, for example in the case of utilitarianism, the calculus

---

10 Davies and Holdcroft, p 205.

shows that the consequences produce greater pains than pleasures? Why, if it is not in a person's interests to be good (if he has no wish to please God and has no fear of Hell, if he has no fear of detection, if he has no expectation that he will suffer from a guilty conscience, if he has no fear that he will suffer because others will do the same – if he sees no down side to himself resulting from his act) why should he refrain from an act that morality – any scheme of morality – decrees is bad? Philosophers have given no answer, no answer since as far back as, in Plato's *The Republic,* Socrates is asked, 'Suppose that a person holds the ring of Gyges [a ring with the magical quality of making the holder invisible], would that person have any reason to act in a good way?'[11]

But the question begs the question. The question assumes that a person should be good. Whether we reject it or not, one answer to the question, 'Why should a person be good?' is, 'Unless it is in a person's own interests to be good, there is no reason why he should be.' We may recoil. But to recoil is no answer.

Be that as it may, notwithstanding that no proof is available to show the validity of utilitarianism, the concept has not only continued to be a major influence in ethics, but has been adopted as a structure for assessing values in a wide range of fields outside moral philosophy. Thus statisticians, evolutionary biologists, environmentalists, economists, mathematicians, sociologists, politicians, and reformers of a multitude of persuasions, have all at some time employed for their own purposes forms of the utilitarian calculus of which Bentham provided the first major exposition.

11   And the reader may recall the quotation at the head of Chap 12.

CHAPTER 14

On stilts?

Rights[1]

The child, with whom we opened the chapter on natural law, said: 'In fact, it can't be a rule at all, can it?' In this he showed himself perhaps at heart to be a natural lawyer. His protest at not receiving lessons in arithmetic might, however, have been couched in a different form. He might have said, 'I have a right to receive arithmetic lessons.'

At the present day, people claim many rights, either for themselves or for others, – prisoners' rights, the rights of the unemployed, women's rights, the rights of the unborn child, the rights of the homeless, rights of the starving, coloured people's rights, the rights of religious or ethnic minorities. Claims such as these may take the form of a claim to have a right to something – the right to receive medical treatment, the right to a good education, the right to free speech, the right to receive legal advice. The rights claimed for a certain group, and a claim to a particular thing may often be, of course, merely two sides of the same coin: the right of religious minorities is the right not to be discriminated against on religious grounds, the right of the starving is the right to eat, the right of the homeless is the right to a roof over one's head.

The questions that arise for discussion are these. First, if someone claims, for humanity or for a particular group, a right to X (or when he proclaims the rights of the X-less) on what basis is it alleged that the rights exist? Where is it supposed that the right comes from? And, secondly, of what does a right per se consist? What do we mean by a 'right'?

---

1 Davies and Holdcroft *Jurisprudence: Texts and Commentary* Chap 8.

Development of the concept of human rights

It is not until the sixteenth and seventeenth centuries that we find more than incidental treatment of the nature of rights. The notion of a right was barely perceived in Roman law, and formed an element of little significance in that system. For the medieval philosopher, natural law, to whose wagon the notion of rights would later be attached, was concerned primarily with good conduct, - obligations, duties, not rights. (Indeed, systems of thought that accepted the validity of serfdom and slavery could have no place for what were later to be regarded as among the most fundamental of human rights.) Thus although the nature of rights was the subject of discussion among certain of the late schoolmen, the subject was never central to the main stream of medieval thought.

It was with the rise of the nation state that discussion began as to the nature of the relationship between a citizen and the state, and concerning the question as to what rights, if any, an individual had, or should have, against the state, in particular against a government that acted tyrannically towards its citizens ('... absolutism [having] prompted men to claim rights precisely because it denied them'[2]). Surely, if, under natural law, rulers were under a duty to rule justly, must it not follow that if rulers were in breach of this obligation, citizens had rights against them?

By no means all agreed. For some, the power of the state, for example in the shape of a monarch, was absolute. The royalists of the seventeenth century based their belief in the supreme authority of the King on the theory of the Divine Right of Kings, the view that a monarch's powers had been conferred by God. It was the purpose of John Locke, in the first of his Two Treatises of Government, to refute this theory,[3] and to construct a system within which citizens had rights, rights that could with moral justification be asserted against the state.

Locke's Second Treatise gives us his explanation of the basis of government. His view of this matter has come to be termed the contract theory of the state – citizens, in a state of nature, contract with each other to give up certain of their rights to one of their body or to a group in order to achieve the advantages with regard to peace and security that such an arrangement brings.

---

2   M Cranston, quoted in Encyclopaedia Britannica, *Human Rights*.
3   Specifically, as put forward in *Patriarcha* by Sir Robert Filmer.

Locke's was not the first formulation of the theory that the basis of a civil right rested on a contract.[4] For Thomas Hobbes (1588–1679), by the social contract the governed signed away their natural rights to a sovereign who thus acquired unfettered powers. Grotius wrote: '... the Mother of Civil Laws is obligation by mutual compact';[5] '[the] many, individually feeble, fearing to be oppressed by those who were stronger, combined to establish judicial authorities, and to uphold them by their common strength; that those they could not resist singly, they might, united, control';[6] 'Civil rights were derived from ... mutual compact.'[7] The first fully developed formulation of the theory is ascribed to Marsilius of Padua (1270–1343), but the theory has roots almost as old as European philosophy being foreshadowed by Plato in The Republic[8] and in Crito.[9]

Locke's theory did not form a direct continuation of the history of natural law thinking. Locke and the natural lawyer both share a common starting point in the notion of an original state of nature. But where the two go from there differs. The natural lawyer sees man having certain inclinations, and the chain of reasoning ends with the conclusion that it is fitting that men should behave in a certain way; natural law is concerned with what men ought to do. Locke, when he looks back to the original state of nature, sees men having certain rights; and his chain of reasoning ends with the conclusion that, in the last resort, the citizen has a right to reject the authority of his government. So, while both theories share similar ground at the start (and both, we may add, hold that it is by man's reason that the truth is reached), the theories are essentially different. The fact that the rights of a citizen under Locke's theory may be referred to as 'natural rights' should not be allowed to blur this difference. By the seventeenth century the attention had shifted from duties to rights.

Locke's Second Treatise and later Rousseau's Social Contract, were profoundly to influence the course of European affairs. The two works between them constituted important ideological support for two revolutions: the secession of the American colonies and the overthrow of the French monarchy.

---

4 For a full survey, see R Tuck *Natural Rights Theories: Their Origin and Development* (1979).
5 Proleg 16.
6 Ibid, 19.
7 Ibid, 15.
8 Book II, 159.
9 Pages 51–52.

'Rights' in practice

We shall have occasion to return to the subject of the United States later in this chapter, but at this point let us consider the subject of rights, not from a philosophical, but from a practical point of view.

Earlier we mentioned various rights that may be alleged to exist – the right to work; the right to a good education; the right to enough food to sustain a reasonable existence, the right to eat. What is the factual content of the statement that a starving person has a right to eat?

If a man is sitting on the ground starving, to say that he has a right to eat achieves nothing, means nothing.[10] If we ask him 'Do you have a right to eat?' whether he nods or shakes his head is immaterial. Indeed the futility of the assertion that any person has a right to something is shown if we imagine that the starving man has died and a passer-by observes 'He had a right to eat.' Even if he did, it did him no good.

What we can say, though, is that we believe that a starving man wants to eat. To assert that people have wants is to make an assertion that is empirically verifiable. We can state that people who are physically ill want medical treatment; that women want equal treatment with men; that children want not to be ill treated. That people want certain things can be ascertained as fact. The world is filled with 5 billion people wanting things.

If we rephrase the matter and instead of saying that the starving man has a right to food, we say that he ought to have food, then the move takes us to no firmer ground. To say that people ought to have such and such is mere window-dressing. If one can persuade others that the 'ought' carries some kind of moral weight then the 'ought' may be useful in seeking support in obtaining the thing sought from those who have power to confer it. But the 'ought' in itself adds nothing. If we rephrase the matter again and say 'I believe that in a just society a starving man has a right to food', we barely improve matters. Even if 'just' is accepted as having an ascertainable meaning, the statement remains merely one of belief, and when we enter the sphere of beliefs we slip further from the sphere of verifiable fact.

That talk of rights which are devoid of means of enforcement is meaningless was forcibly expressed by Bentham. 'Rights,' he wrote, 'is the child of law; from real law come real rights; but from imaginary laws, from "law of nature," come imaginary rights…. Natural rights

---

10   The view that the notion of a right is empty unless the right is backed by law was proposed by Jeremy Bentham.

is simple nonsense; natural and imprescriptible rights (an American phrase), rhetorical nonsense, nonsense upon stilts.' (Bentham's objection was not based on a view that people should not have rights, but because the advocacy of rights in the abstract distracted attention from taking the practical steps necessary for securing the changes in society that he sought.)

Hume, before him, had also considered natural law and natural rights to be unreal metaphysical phenomena.

Thus talk of natural rights of the kind we have mentioned is empty of meaning. On the other hand, if someone says that, for example, young people want to have work, then a meaningful response can be made – to agree, or to disagree and challenge the person making the statement to produce evidence for his assertion. If someone says that in a just society young people would be able to get a job, then it is a meaningful response to enquire what is meant by a just society. And, if someone says 'I intend to campaign to secure action that will ensure that young people have a job', then here too a meaningful response can be made – 'I will support you', or, 'I will oppose you.' But if someone says that young people have a right to a job then, as far as the jurist is concerned the appropriate response is a shrug.

Or is it? Is there nothing more to be said? Look at the matter this way. When the sceptic turns away with a shrug the person who believes in the existence of basic human rights might call after him, 'I note that you contribute to a charity that works to relieve poverty in the Third World. Why do you do this?'

'Because I believe that it is morally wrong that people should starve when action can be taken to prevent this,' the sceptic replies.

'And where does this moral wrongness come from?' the believer asks.

'I don't know what you mean,' the sceptic answers.

'Does it come from religious belief?'

'No.'

'Well, where does it come from?'

'It's just a feeling I have that it is wrong that people should suffer unnecessarily.'

'"Just a feeling." Precisely. You cannot provide a rational basis for your view. So why should you question my belief that men have certain rights? Is not my belief in a human being's right to life no more than an expression in different terms of your view that it is morally wrong that people should starve when this can be avoided?'

'Um,' says the sceptic, and the two part.

A few moments later the sceptic turns and calls, 'There is a difference. I recognise that my view is no more than an opinion, a hunch, an application of my own moral code, a code for which I claim no infallibility. You claim the existence of human rights as fact. It is your presentation of rights as fact that I dispute.'

But by this time the believer is out of hearing.

Belief in a right

Whether or not the view that human rights exist can be sustained, the notion of rights assumes undoubted significance in terms of practicalities when, even if no right in the sense of a legally enforceable entitlement exists, there is a belief that a particular right exists. For example, there is a widespread view that the uncultivated and uninhabited moors and fells of upland Britain should be open to those who wish to walk there. If permission has not been granted by the landowner and no access order or agreement has been concluded under the provisions of Part V of the National Parks and Access to the Countryside Act 1949, no entitlement exists to enter what in law is private property. But what cannot be disregarded is the fact of the existence of the belief that in a densely-populated island of over 55 million people, where walking is the most popular outdoor recreation, it can no longer be regarded as acceptable that a small handful of landowners should be entitled to preserve for their exclusive use the six million acres of British uplands.

The fact that, although a right does not exist, a belief in the right does exist, may be relevant in two ways. First, the strength of feeling over a particular issue may be a major factor in a campaign for the introduction of legislation that confers as a legal right the entitlement that was believed to have existed. Secondly, strength of feeling over an issue may be one among various factors (considered in a later chapter[11]) that tilts a person towards taking action that contravenes the law.

An example of such strength of feeling was the outrage expressed in 1989 by many people at the prospect that the privatisation of the public water authorities, proposed in the Water Bill then before Parliament, would lead to the closure of moorlands that had for generations been open for the enjoyment of walkers. The issue was given expression when a group of over 2,000 individuals present at Rivington in Lancashire on 7 May 1989, made the following pledge:

'We PLEDGE our lifelong intent to regard ourselves at liberty, in exercise of the simple human freedoms which we rightly claim, to walk with our families and friends for recreation of body and mind wherever public access to open country is presently allowed by the

11 Chapter 22.

water authorities. We shall cause no damage, break no criminal law, neither threaten nor commit any violence nor intrude upon any-body's privacy. But if free access to these lands is at any time denied we now declare that the threat of legal action for trespass, which is not a criminal offence, shall not deter us from exercising our traditional right of access to the hills.'

If we pass from belief in a specific right, such as that illustrated above, to rights generally, we pass, at the highest level, into the domain of what are referred to as human rights. 'It is', states the Encyclopaedia Britannica,[12] 'a common observation that human beings everywhere demand the realisation of diverse values to ensure their individual and collective well-being. It also is a common observation that these demands are often painfully frustrated by social as well as natural forces, resulting in exploitation, oppression, persecution, and other forms of deprivation. Deeply rooted in these twin observations are the beginnings of what today are called "human rights" and the legal processes, national and international, associated with them.' More will be said about the nature of human rights and their status in jurisprudence later in this chapter.

What does belief in a right mean?

If X says that he believes that there should be, say, a right to freedom of speech, what does he mean? If X says that there ought to be freedom of speech, this gets us no further since, as was seen in Chapter 1 (at any rate by those who did not make the mistake of not reading that chapter) the word 'ought' implies compliance with some standard. But by what standard? By reference, X may reply, to justice.

In this case, X's statement can be recast in Rawlsian[13] terms as a statement that in the original position people would opt for a society in which freedom of speech was guaranteed. Even in these terms, though, it is only X's view that people would so opt.

We have reached the stage at which it can be seen that a claim that a right exists rests on the is/ought fallacy exposed by Hume. A statement that the starving man ought – by the standards of justice – to have bread jumps to the statement that it is the right of the man to have bread. With a quickness that can deceive the eye the conjurer has converted the expression of an opinion into the postulation of an absolute.

12 *Human Rights.*
13 See Chapter 15.

Criticisms

But surely everyone would agree that in the original position people would opt for a legal system that guaranteed what are today commonly thought of as basic human rights? Does it not go without saying that such rights are, in common parlance, a good thing? This in fact is far from being the case. The notion of human rights has been criticised as strongly as its validity has been defended.

One criticism rests on the assertion that the postulation of any right is at once undermined by the fact that no sooner is the existence of a right postulated than it is seen that another's right is infringed. Your right to smoke tobacco where you wish infringes my right to breathe smoke free air. My right to drive my car into Bakewell conflicts with your right not to have an attractive town despoiled by traffic. A's right to freedom of speech conflicts with B's right not to have his religious sensibilities outraged by blasphemy. A's right to possess hand guns (upheld in the United States) runs counter to B's right to live free of being shot (a right sought to be upheld by legislation in the United Kingdom).

Thus while liberty can validly be regarded as a prerequisite for (to use Finnis's term) human flourishing, one person's liberty results in the reduction in the liberty of another: 'My freedom to do what I want conflicts with your freedom to do what you want'.[14]

'Freedom'? The meaning of freedom? If after only seven pages into a chapter on rights we find ourselves in the maelstrom that whirls round the word 'freedom', what chance can there be of making progress towards elucidating, from the perspective of jurisprudence, the nature and significance of the concept of a right. Suffice to say that throughout much of this chapter the subject of rights coincides in significant respects with the perennial debate over the meaning of freedom (as also does a later chapter,[15] on the enforcement of morality, when the question of freedom is taken further, in particular when examining the views of John Stuart Mill).

With regard to the matter of conflicting rights, mentioned above, we may note that such conflicts may exist not only between individuals but also between an individual and the state (as between a right claimed by a journalist, asserting a right to freedom of speech, to publish what he finds, and the right claimed by the

14   Kellman.
15   Chapter 21.

state to prevent the publication of information that would endanger national security); or between one group of citizens and another (as where a right claimed by parents to have their children educated in classes of not more than twenty pupils would, if implemented, by diverting additional money to schools, adversely affect those who claim a right to treatment in hospital within three months of referral by their doctor (and the allocation of resources necessary for this to be achieved).

Seen against the background of competing claims, the assertion of a right is exposed as no more than the pressing of an interest – rights being no more than interests dressed up in fancy clothes.

True? In many cases, perhaps yes. The conflict between the claimed right to walk over uncultivated mountain, moor and heath, and the right of private landowners to prevent this, is clearly a conflict between competing interests, a conflict that lies in the arena of politics (where promises by the Labour party when in opposition to introduce a legal right to walk over such land were abandoned once the party came to power). Such conflicts are settled by one side winning because it has the support of government. Political muscle, not reasoned debate, is, at the end of the road, the deciding factor.

Instances do occur, however, where there is less validity in seeing a conflict in political terms, instances where a conclusion is sought, not by political power but, in a neutral fashion, by reasoned debate. But in such instances the difficulty arises that reasoned debate can be hamstrung by the absence of criteria with which to assess competing claims. By what criteria is the 'right' of a foetus to life to be balanced against the 'right' of a woman to abort? By what criteria is one to balance the 'right' of a woman to receive at her own expense fertility treatment to enable her to bear a child irrespective of her age against the 'right' of a child to have a mother of an age that will enable the child to be tended until maturity?

In the United States the outcome of such conflicts are, in the last resort, decided by the Supreme Court in proceedings that take the form of seeking interpretation of the constitution (of which more will be said shortly). In some societies referendums may be employed to learn the prevailing national view. In the United Kingdom such conflicts, if not settled by legislation, fall to be determined by the courts, usually in an application for judicial review of an administrative decision. In performing this function the courts, by defining where rights lie, are creating new law. (For some, this departure from the judiciary's traditional role of interpreting the law is undesirable, the proper place for new law to be created being Parliament. Others point out that the evolution of the common law shows that judges have always in effect made new law and that if the legislature wishes to define rights then it is open to it to do so.)

And yet even if to proclaim a right is no more than to mouth an ought, or to press an interest, the power of the word is not to be gainsaid. Advances by the disadvantaged in the twentieth century have been made under banners proclaiming rights. In spheres such a race, employment, public health, education, disablement and gender, changes in the law have been rights driven – driven by the imbalance between the rights that people believe ought to obtain and the rights that in fact exist in law. Indeed, much of the social history of the century consists of pressure on governments to bring the latter into line with the former.

Discussion within philosophy followed a parallel path, with the abandonment of the quest for the holy grail of an ideally balanced utilitarian solution (one that achieves the greatest good of the greatest number while at the same time protecting valid interests of a minority) and instead sights being set on establishing what rights should be conferred for the attainment of what a particular writer believed to be a just society (Hart speaks of 'the rough seas which the philosophy of political morality is presently crossing between the old faith in utilitarianism and the new faith in rights').[16]

Despite the word's undeniable power, it cannot but be recognized that so often has the banner been taken out of the cupboard that its edges are at risk of becoming frayed. From overuse and from misuse (as a label for what is patently an interest) the word's emotive power has been diminished. The word's strength can, for example, be dragged down by parasitical claims. Thus few would disagree that in a just society prisoners have a right to humane treatment; that this includes a right not to be sexually abused by warders; also that prisoners should have a right to have access to a lawyer; and to have sufficient food to sustain their health. But then we may find under the same head of humane treatment asserted a right to not to be locked in a cell for 24 hours a day; a right to reasonable exercise; a right to receive visitors; a right to receive education that will facilitate rehabilitation; a right for this purpose to have a radio; a right to have a radio for general information; a right to have a television; a right to have colour television; a right to have multi-channel colour television. Thus, by being highjacked, what starts as a notion with moral force, that prisoners have a valid claim to certain basic rights, ends tarnished.

---

16 *Between Utility and Rights*, from *The Idea of Freedom* ed A Ryan, p 98. (Quoted, Lloyd, *Jurisprudence*, p 454.)

Rights in twentieth-century jurisprudence

For some writers the subject of rights has been incidental to their main theme, the word 'right' being used in a way that indicates that the writer assumes that the concept of a right per se needs no scrutiny. For example, Dworkin, in *Taking Rights Seriously*, sees rights as entitlements accorded by a society to the individuals within it. Where rights form part of a writer's scheme (as in the case of Dworkin, and Hart in *The Concept of Law*), it is clear that rights are thought of not as abstract entities, but as entitlements that have the backing of law. For Hart, for example, Rex II has a right to make law on his father's death because of the existence of a legal rule to this effect.

Hohfeld

Others have made it their business to analyse the meaning of the word 'right'. A writer who, early in the twentieth century, made a significant contribution was WH Hohfeld.[17] For Hohfeld, one reason for misunderstandings and confusion that can exist in seeking to understand the nature of a right is the failure to appreciate that right is used with reference to four distinct legal concepts. When we speak of a right this may, he said, refer to:

- A right in the sense of a right to claim something, as where X, a landowner, has the right to recover his land from Y, a squatter (or to obtain an order ejecting Z, a trespasser). This, Hohfeld terms a *right* (or a 'claim').
- A right in the sense of a right to the enjoyment of something, as where X enjoys the right to go onto his own land. This Hohfeld terms a *privilege*.
- A right in the sense of a right to effect a legal transaction, as where X has a right to sell his land to Y. This Hohfeld terms a *power*.
- A right in the sense of a right not being subject to some disadvantage, as where X, a bankrupt, has the right not to have his clothes (and certain other possessions) seized (and sold) by an officer of the court levying execution. This Hohfeld terms an *immunity*.

From the first sense of 'right' it will be seen that Hohfeld uses the word 'right' both as a genus, to cover all rights generally, and as a

---

17 *Fundamental Legal Conceptions as Applied in Judicial Reasoning* (1923) Essays 1 and 2.

species, to refer the first of his four species of right. So we can say that rights in the general sense are either rights in the narrow sense, or privileges, or powers, or immunities.

For each of these four, Hohfeld says that there is 'correlative', by which he means the other side to a legal relationship. Thus in the case of X's right to recover his land from S, the correlative is S's duty (if he is to abide by the law) to give up the land to X. The correlative of right Hohfeld therefore terms a *duty*.

The correlative of privilege, Hohfeld terms a *no-right*. This is because if X, as landowner, has the 'privilege' of going on to his own land, and he is therefore the only person entitled to go on to the land, the other side of the matter must be that everyone else has no right to stop A entering, so any other person has a '"no-right" that X shall not enter'.[18]

The correlative of power is *liability*. Hohfeld gives this example from the law of contract. A makes an offer to B. B has the power to bring a contract into being between them by accepting A's terms. Thus, during the period that it is open to B to accept A's terms – during the period that B has power to bind A – A is liable to become bound by the contract, so in this respect A is under a liability.

The correlative of immunity is *disability*. Thus where X, a bankrupt, is immune from having his clothes seized by an officer of the court levying execution, the officer is 'disabled' from seizing them.

Hohfeld proposes that each of the four heads of right, privilege, power and immunity have not only correlatives, but also what he terms 'opposites'. In setting out the opposites of right, etc what Hohfeld is doing is telling us in each case what cannot be the position at the same time: if a piece of paper is white it cannot at the same time be black. Thus if A has a right to exclude B from his land, A cannot at the same time have no right to do so. The opposite of right Hohfeld therefore terms a *no-right*. If A has the privilege of going onto his own land, he cannot at the same time be under a duty in the same regard. (He cannot be under the same kind of duty that X is to abide by A's right to sole possession of his land.) So the opposite of privilege is *duty*. If A has a power, for example to transfer the title of his land to B, he cannot at the same time be under a disability that prevents him from doing so. So the opposite of power is *disability*. If A is immune from having his clothes seized by a court officer, he cannot at the same time be liable to have them seized. So the opposite of immunity is *liability*.

18   Ibid, p 50.

Hohfeld's scheme is therefore as follows:

Form of right	Correlative	Opposite
Right	Duty	No right
Privilege	No right	Duty
Power	Liability	Disability
Immunity	Disability	Liability

Later writers[19] have suggested amendments to Hohfeld's scheme and proposed diagrams in various forms to show the oppositions and reciprocities between the terms that Hohfeld employs.

Criticisms

Among various criticisms of Hohfeld's scheme are the following.

1. Some of the terms he employs are misleading. For example, the meaning of Hohfeld's term 'Privilege' is better conveyed by 'Liberty'. (A is at liberty to go onto his own land.)
2. While the scheme can be applied to aspects of civil law, it fails to meet situations found in criminal law and public law where duties exist but in respect of which no Hohfeldian correlative is to be found.
3. Hohfeld fails to tell us the common feature shared by right, privilege, power and immunity that makes them rights in the general sense: he does not tell us what a right is.
4. Hohfeld's scheme, even if it is accepted as being in isolation logically coherent, does not provide the categories necessary to accommodate the kind of relationships that exist: the innumerable square pegs that exist in practice cannot be fitted into Hohfeld's eight round holes. Consider the position where a testator, T, by will appoints A as his executor and with regard to his shares in Z plc confers on B and C a power of appointment to appoint between his nieces D, E and F living at his death, with a gift over in default of appointment to G, or if G is not living at his death to H and I on trust for such charitable purposes within the village of Tideswell as they should decide. H and I commence proceedings to establish the validity of the gift over and the

19 See JW Harris *Legal Philosophies* (2nd edn, 1997).

Attorney-General is made a party to the proceedings. T's widow challenges the validity of the will on the grounds that one person who signed as a witness to the will was not present at the time of T's signature. How would the relationships between the eleven parties involved here be accommodated within Hohfeld's scheme?

To criticise Hohfeld's scheme is not to question the significance of his contribution to the quest for a satisfactory analysis of legal concepts: sixty years on he still makes us stop and think. Nor is it to underestimate the difficulty of achieving Hohfeld's object of providing a scheme that is valid with regard to law generally, not merely with regard to the legal system of one jurisdiction. Nor is it to dispute that reciprocities do exist within the law: where trustees are under a duty to act in a certain way, eg to provide information, then beneficiaries under the trust can certainly be validly regarded as having a reciprocal right to obtain the information. But is the undoubted existence of relationships such as these sufficient to support the sandcastle that Hohfeld constructed? Or, when we scrutinise in the light of the real world each of the relationships that Hohfeld proposes (for example that between the correlatives 'privilege' and 'no-right'; and that between the opposites 'right' and 'no-right'), do we see the sandcastle crumble, to be washed away, by the incoming tide?

What do rights protect? Choice? Interests?

Instead of seeking to determine the essential nature of that which is represented by the word right, others have sought to clarify, and establish, what, if a right exists, it exists for: they seek to determine what it is that rights protect. Some, prominently Hart,[20] maintain that what a right protects is the ability of a person to choose whether to do something. For example the rights attaching to ownership of land enables a person to choose whether to take action against a squatter, whether to lease the land, whether to mortgage it. If a person is injured by the negligence of another, his right is to choose whether to sue for damages. If a statute is passed that prohibits the mortgaging of land of under a quarter of hectare, a landowner no longer has a choice whether to mortgage land of under this area. If a statute bars actions for negligence after three years from the date

20   HLA Hart *Essays on Bentham* Chap 7.

of the injury, after this date the injured person no longer has a choice as to whether or not to sue. Proponents of this view see will, in the sense of wish, as the key to the matter. If a person wishes to blow his nose in the park, but a bye-law prohibits this, then his wish to blow his nose, no longer being protected by the right of a person to so what is not prohibited, cannot (legally) be satisfied.

It is in the context of reciprocal rights and duties that proponents of the will theory see their theory as most effectively portrayed. If D is under a duty not to injure P, and he nevertheless causes him injury, P has a choice as to whether he sues D or waives his entitlement to do so.

Opponents of the will theory maintain that what a right protects is not choice, but some interest of the person who holds the right: a landowner's right of ownership protects his interest in the land. One among several of the weaknesses of the will theory, they point out, is that the theory fails to cover situations where a person has a right, but they have no choice with regard to whether action should be taken to protect the interest. For example, beneficiaries under a trust have an interest but it is the trustees, who have no beneficial interest, who have the choice as to whether action should be taken in respect of the trust property. Infants have interests, but decisions regarding the protection of these are taken not by the infant but by the infant's parents or guardian. Thus the will theory fails to draw the necessary distinction between what is protected and the ability to take steps to protect it. Adoption of the interest theory concentrates attention on what is in fact protected and, its supporters contend, meets all situations – regardless whether the right holder is or is not the person who has a choice as to whether steps should be taken to enforce the right.

Individual rights and communitarian rights

A debate in recent years has been that between those who consider that, if rights are to be conferred by law, priority should be accorded to rights that protect the interests of the individual against society, and those (including those in the utilitarian camp)who contend that rights should be directed towards achieving the goal of the betterment of the community, notwithstanding that thereby along the way the interests of individuals may be adversely affected.

Those in the former group therefore conceive rights as properly being concerned with such matters as the protection of privacy, the right to inherit wealth and, generally, freedom from interference by the state. (In Chapter 15, on Justice, we shall see that R Nozick is a prominent member of this camp.) Those in the second group – those who hold a 'communitarian' view, see rights as properly being more positive in nature, rights as 'rights to' rather than 'rights against'. They see rights as capable of existing only by the positive action of the state (the championship of individual liberties having proved ineffective against unregulated capitalism and the inequalities and injustices that followed in its wake). The communitarian view does not dispute the need for individual rights (such as a right to freedom of thought, conscience and religion, a right to privacy) but always balances these against the public interest. Thus individual rights are conferred, but with a proviso – that in the event of conflict, the public interest should prevail. The European Convention on Human Rights and Freedoms, which follows a communitarian pattern, provides an example. Article 9a states 'Everyone has a right to freedom of thought conscience and religion'. The proviso follows in Article 9b: 'Freedom to manifest one's religion or beliefs shall be subject to such limitations as are prescribed by law and are necessary in a democratic society in the interests of public safety, for the protection of public order, health or morals, or for the protection of the rights and freedoms of others'. Thus individual rights can be trumped by public interests.

The two sides are thus divided on the lines of liberty versus equality, individualism versus collectivism. It might seem that the angels are on the side of those who place the welfare of the community above the selfishness of the individual, altruism above egotism. But those of an anti-communitarian persuasion are not without arguments that command attention.

Edmund Burke, watching the outbreak of the French Revolution, predicted that as the rights of certain groups were increased so would the power of the state to enforce them, resulting in increased state control with a consequent threat to the liberties of individual citizens.

It has been against the conferring of rights on certain groups that criticism has, in fact, been especially directed. For example, in 1995 Roger Scrutton wrote,[21] '... the problem lies less with the concept of a right, than with the unprincipled application of it, in the service of massive social experiments. This is how we should understand the idea of "group rights", used to grant privileges to some people and remove them from others, solely on the basis of their social groups. The idea is alien to English law. But pro-

---

21   *The Times*, 21 December.

grammes of "affirmative action" in America and judgments in the European Court have both taken it for granted.

'… certain groups, it is argued – women, homosexuals, blacks, "Native American" – have suffered unjust disadvantages. To rectify the situation, we must therefore tip the balance the other way …It does not require much intellectual acumen to recognise that this practice ex-emplifies the very injustice complained of: the injustice of favouring one person and penalising another on account of a wholly irrelevant characteristic. If it was unjust to offer privileges to a white person and to withhold them from a black on account of the colour of their skin, it is equally unjust to reverse the imbalance and favour blacks against the whites.

'Although that is obvious, it does not stop the concept of group rights from penetrating [British politics]. "Women only" lists of prospective candidates are rightly condemned by the men who are excluded from them …'

But where are we? We have propounded in this chapter the futility,[22] and the illogicality[23] of asserting the existence, in the abstract, of a right. But in the passage above, and in the criticism by Burke, it is not rights in the abstract that are being dealt with. Scrutton deals with rights that do have meaning because they do have legal force. What is criticised is the fact that the rights concerned have been conferred: what is criticised is the political decision to confer legal rights on a group, on the ground of the anomalies and injustices that it is contended follow from this practice. Thus our discussion has jumped from jurisprudence into politics. That this is something that time and again happens when the nature of a right is being discussed is no justification.

Legal rights and their nature

When we turn from the notion of a right as an abstraction to the word as used to confer a specific legally enforceable entitlement, we find that a right in this sense may take a positive form, as where a statute confers on an arrested person a right to have advice from a solicitor within a certain period from his arrest. Another form of positive right exists where the law provides a remedy for a wrong. Thus where the law provides a remedy to a landowner against

---

22 The starving man point; and that rights conflict.
23 Ie is/ought.

someone who interferes with the quiet enjoyment of his land (eg in the shape of an action in tort for nuisance) the landowner can be regarded as having a legal right to the quiet enjoyment of his land. Similarly, where the law provides a remedy to a person who is wrongfully imprisoned (in the shape of the writ of habeas corpus, or an action in tort for false imprisonment) we can say that a citizen has a right not to be imprisoned without due cause.

Some legal rights exist in a negative form: where no legal means exists of preventing a person from doing something, he can be regarded as having a legal right to do that thing. For example, a person, A, would be entitled to claim that he has a legal right to blow his nose in the park, if he wishes to do so. By this, A means that (a) no law (eg a local authority bye-law) prohibits him from blowing his nose in the park; (b) the law gives no right of action to any other person, eg B, to restrain him, A, from blowing his nose; (c) the law will give him, A, a right of action against B if B, objecting to A's nose-blowing, takes steps to stop A from blowing his nose.

It is, in fact, in a negative form that legal rights in English law exist: 'the starting point of our domestic law is that every citizen has a right to do what he likes, unless restrained by the common law or by Statute'.[24] In English law rights are by tradition inferred, not conferred.

That rights do not sit easily in English law is illustrated by the distinction between the manner in which a right is introduced in English law and in jurisdictions that lie under the influence of Roman law. Consider the Harassment Act 1997. Section 2, which applies to England and Wales, provides[25] that it shall be an *offence* to harass another person. Section 8, which applies to Scotland, a country which, by reason of 'the auld alliance' with France, is influenced by Roman law, provides[26] that 'Every individual has a *right* to be free from harassment ...'.

The word 'right', with its connotation of absoluteness, and certainty and invariability, does not sit easily with matters that might be considered to be legal rights in English law. For example, suppose that P lends D £100, repayable in a month's time. At the end of the month, we might say that P has a legal right to the £100. But what do we really mean? We mean that the law entitles P to bring an action against D; that if P succeeds in satisfying the court of his claim, judgment will be entered in his favour and D served with the court's decision; that if D fails to pay the sum due, P can bring further

24   Lord Donaldson M R, *A-G v Guardian Newspapers (No 2)* [1990] AC 109.
25   Italics added.
26   Italics added.

proceedings against him; that if the court is satisfied as to the validity of P's claim, it can order D's goods to be taken in execution; that if D has property and if £100 is realised when this is seized and put up for sale, then P will obtain the £100 he is owed. But all this amounts to something less than might be gathered from the original statement that P has a legal right to the £100. It is therefore perhaps wise for English law to speak not so much in terms of rights as in terms of causes of action. When P seeks to recover his £100, it is more realistic, and better advice, to tell him, not that he has a legal right to the money but that the law makes available a cause of action. His right, to the extent that he has a right, is to bring legal proceedings (if he can afford to do so).

Consider another example. Section 130 of the Highways Act 1980 imposes a duty on the highway authorities (usually the county council) to 'assert and protect the rights of the public to the use and enjoyment of any highway for which they are the highway authority, including any roadside waste which forms part of it.' A landowner moves the fence bordering his land so as to encroach on the roadside verge. From the imposition of a duty, it would seem that a right exists to require the authority to fulfil its duty by taking proceedings to securing the removal of the illegal encroachment. But if the authority declines to act, the law provides no means by which it can be compelled to act. (The nature of a legal right is examined by the Scandinavian realist Hagerstrom. See Chapter 17.)

If the word right does not fit easily into the thinking of English law, the word must surely have a greater significance where a legal system confers on citizens what the law expressly terms a 'right'? Where rights are referred to expressly, it is commonly in a country's constitution that the rights concerned are set out. A prime example is provided by the Constitution of the United States of America.

Rights under the constitution of the United States

The thirteen British colonies founded on the eastern seaboard of the north American continent during the seventeenth and early eighteenth centuries were subject to taxation imposed by the English Crown. But the inhabitants had no representation at Westminster. This anomaly became focal to a series of other (mainly economic) matters over which the colonists felt themselves unfairly treated. In 1776 representatives from the 13 colonies declared independence from the English Crown. This independence was achieved when the

British were defeated in the War of American Independence (termed, in the United States, the American Revolution). Here is the text of the Declaration by which the colonies declared their independence. In reading the Declaration the influence of Locke's doctrine of natural rights will be seen throughout.

'IN CONGRESS, July 4 1776

THE UNANIMOUS DECLARATION of the thirteen united STATES OF AMERICA[27]

When, in the course of human events, it becomes necessary for one people to dissolve the political bands which have connected them with another, and to assume, among the powers of the earth, the separate and equal station to which the laws of nature and of nature's God entitle them, a decent respect to the opinions of mankind requires that they should declare the causes which impel them to the separation.

We hold these truths to be self-evident, that all men are created equal; that they are endowed by their Creator with certain unalienable rights; that among these are life, liberty and the pursuit of happiness.

That to secure these rights, governments are instituted among men, deriving their just powers from the consent of the governed; that, whenever any form of government becomes destructive of these ends, it is the right of the people to alter or abolish it, and to institute a new government, laying its foundation on such principles, and organising its powers in such form, as to them shall seem most likely to effect their safety and happiness.

Prudence, indeed, will dictate that governments long established should not be challenged for light and transient causes; and, accordingly, all experience hath shown, that mankind are more disposed to suffer, while evils are sufferable, than to right themselves by abolishing the forms to which they are accustomed.

But, when a long train of abuses and usurpations, pursuing invariably the same object, evinces a design to reduce them

27 It will be noted that the word 'United' in the name of the country appeared first merely as an adjective, describing the States of America by which the declaration was made. (The wording and capitalisation are as set out on the original document.)

under absolute despotism, it is their right, it is their duty, to throw off such government, and to provide new guards for their future security.

Such has been the patient sufferance of these colonies, and such is now the necessity which constrains them to alter their former systems of government. The history of the present King of Great Britain is a history of repeated injuries and usurpation, all having in direct object, the establishment of an absolute tyranny over these States.

To prove this, let facts be submitted to a candid world:

He has refused his assent to laws the most wholesome and necessary for the public good.

He has forbidden his governors to pass laws of immediate and pressing importance, unless suspended in their operation till his assent should be attained; and, when so suspended, he has utterly neglected to attend to them.

He has refused to pass other laws for the accommodation of large districts of people, unless those people would relinquish the right of representation in the legislature: a right inestimable to them, and formidable to tyrants only ...'

Before the war ended the colonies – the states as they now regarded themselves – considered the form of government that should exist when the war was won. Should the thirteen states remain separate, form one state, or become grouped in some way? In 1787, a convention adopted a constitution under which was established a central, federal government to which the thirteen states gave up certain of their powers. The Constitution, which remains that of the United States, contained eight articles, providing for the establishment of a legislature, and setting out its powers, an executive vested in a President, a judiciary, for the amendment of the Constitution, and for the ratification of the Constitution by the separate states. But it was soon felt that while the Constitution dealt carefully with the rights of states as against the federal government, sufficient protection had not been afforded to what were regarded as being the rights of citizens. Amendments were therefore made which established certain rights under the Constitution. For example, the First Amendment decreed that no law made by Congress should, inter alia, abridge 'the right of the people peaceably to assemble'. The Fourth Amendment laid down that 'the right of the people to be secure in their persons, homes, papers, and effects against unreasonable searches and seizures, shall not be violated...' The Fifth

188 *Chapter 14 On stilts?*

Amendment provided that no person should be deprived of life, liberty, or property without due process of law. The Sixth conferred a right to jury trial in criminal cases. The Eighth prohibited 'cruel and unusual punishments'. The Thirteenth (made in 1865) outlawed slavery. The Fourteenth Amendment decreed that no state should deny to any person the equal protection of the laws. The first eight Amendments together make up what is termed the Bill of Rights.

So here, set down in black and white, enshrined in the Constitution, were a series of legal rights. (Some, it will be noted, were included to deal with specific grievances under the former British rule, for example the Fourth Amendment; others were general, partaking of the nature of 'natural' rights.)

Much time has been devoted by the American courts to considering the meaning of the rights set out in the Constitution, and the ways in which it is appropriate that the various rights conferred in the Amendments should be applied in a multitude of different circumstances. A central issue has concerned the question whether the rights conferred in the Amendments are to be applied literally, narrowly, according to the words originally used, or in a wider manner, according to what should be taken to have been their intention, their spirit. The trend has been for the latter attitude to prevail. The 'specific guarantees ... have penumbras, formed by emanations from those guarantees that helped to give them life and substance.' Thus, although not referred to in the Amendments, the Supreme Court has held that the Constitution confers a right to educate one's children as one chooses, to study a particular language at a private school, the right to distribute, receive and read the printed word. Implicit in the First Amendment is a right to a zone of privacy protected from governmental intrusion. (It was for this reason that the Supreme Court declared unconstitutional, and so void, a law passed by the state of Connecticut that forbade the use of contraceptives.) The prohibition of the deprivation of 'liberty' without due process of law as contained in the Fourteenth Amendment is not confined, the Supreme Court has held, to the specific liberties mentioned in the Bill of Rights: it protects all those 'personal rights that are fundamental'. That the framers of the Constitution intended this interpretation was shown, it has been said, by the language and history of the Ninth Amendment: 'The enumeration in the Constitution, of certain rights, shall not be construed to deny or disparage others retained by the people.' This revealed, the claim is, that the framers believed that there are additional fundamental rights, protected from governmental infringement which exist alongside those fundamental rights specifically mentioned in the first eight constitutional amendments. In determining what rights are fundamental judges should 'look to the traditions ... of our people' to determine whether a principle is 'so rooted [there] ... as to be ranked as fundamental'. The enquiry is whether a right involved 'is of such a character that it cannot be denied without violating those "fundamental principles of liberty and justice which lie at the base of all our civil and political institutions"'. Laws enacted by states that infringe those fundamental principles of justice are unconstitutional and so void.

Void? Void as infringing certain higher principles not set out in any man-enacted law? The reader will see at once the influence of natural law. There is a strong strand of this thinking running through the history of American constitutional law. That the principles to which the court should appeal lie beyond even the emanations of the constitution's Amendments was asserted by Douglas J in *Griswold v Connecticut*.[28] The case concerned a law made by the state of Connecticut prohibiting the use of contraceptives. The validity of the law was challenged on the ground that it infringed the freedoms guaranteed by the First Amendment. In his judgment Douglas J said: 'We deal with a right of privacy older than the Bill of Rights – older than our political parties, older than our school system.'

This view of the interpretation of the Constitution has not been without strong challenge. The Constitution should be read literally, it has been argued. To do otherwise means that judges create new rights, thus amending the Constitution – a function of the legislature not of the judiciary. A judge's view as to the character of a law is irrelevant. If the law ought to be repealed it is up to the legislature to decide that that should be done. An important champion of this, the positivist view, was Black J. In *Griswold v Connecticut*[29] he said: '... the scientific miracles of this age have not yet produced a gadget which the Court can use to determine what traditions are rooted in the "collective conscience" of our people ... I cannot rely on ... any mysterious and uncertain natural law concept as a reason for striking down this state law ... So far as I am concerned Connecticut's law as applied here is not forbidden by any provision of the Federal Constitution as that Constitution was written, and I [therefore uphold it].' In *Adamson v California*[30] Black J said: 'I cannot consider the Bill of Rights to be an outworn 18th Century "strait jacket". Its provisions may be thought outdated abstractions by some. And it is

28 (1965) 381 US 479.
29 Ibid.
30 (1946) 332 US 46 L ed 1903.

true that they were designed to meet ancient evils. But they are the same kind of human evils that have emerged from century to century wherever excessive power is sought by the few at the expense of the many. ... I fear to see the consequences of the Court's practice of substituting its own concepts of decency and fundamental justice for the language of the Bill of Rights as its point of departure in interpreting and enforcing that Bill of Rights.' And in *Harper v Virginia State Board of Education*[31] the same judge said: 'I have in no way departed from the view I expressed in *Adamson v California*,[32] that the "natural-law-due-process formula" under which courts make the Constitution mean what they think it should at a given time "has been used in the past, and can be used in the future, to license this court, in considering regulatory legislation, to roam at large in the broad expanses of policy and morals and to trespass, all too freely, on the legislative domain of the States as well as the Federal Government. ... The Court's justification for consulting its own notions rather than following the original meaning of the Constitution, as I would, apparently is based on the belief of the majority of the Court that for this Court to be bound by the original meaning of the Constitution is an intolerable and debilitating evil; that our Constitution should be "shackled to the political theory of a particular era," and that to save the country from the original Constitution the Court must have constant power to renew it and keep it abreast of this Court's more enlightened theories of what is best for our society. It seems to me that this is an attack not only on the great value of our Constitution itself but also on the concept of a written constitution which is to survive through the years as originally written unless changed through the amendment process which the Framers wisely provided. Moreover, when a "political theory" embodied in our Constitution becomes outdated, it seems to me that a majority of the nine members of this Court are not only without constitutional power but are far less qualified to choose a new constitutional political theory than the people of this country proceeding in the manner provided by Article V' (which laid down the procedure for the amendment of the constitution).

Despite, however, such trenchant pronouncements as these, positivists in the Supreme Court have most often been in the minority: the wider, more liberal, moving-with-times, natural law-influenced, view has been that which has most frequently prevailed.

31   (1966) 383 US 663, 16 L ed 2d 169.
32   (1946) 332 US 46 L ed 1903.

Rights in English and Welsh law

If the notion of rights has not had the same place in English law as in that of other countries, why has this been? One reason is that English common law developed, through the forms of action, by the gradual accretions of remedies for specific wrongs. The Englishman did not ask 'Have I a right to recover my land from X?' He asked 'Do I have a remedy – is there a form of action – obtainable from the Royal courts against X?'

Another reason is that rights are brandished by those who seek to overthrow tyranny. Rights are the sustenance of revolutionaries, as in America in 1776 and in France in 1789. But England has had no revolution since 1688 (and then only a revolution in the constitutional sense - no barricades). So England has not provided the same seedbed for the germination of the notion of rights as have other countries. The landed aristocracy that governed Britain until the twentieth century had no need for the notion. The remedies made available by the common law gave them adequate means for settling any disputes that came their way. ('Rights' smelled of subversion, of troublemakers, people who wanted to change things.) Certain specific rights were acceptable as part of the normal order, for example the right of a landlord to evict a tenant for non-payment of rent; the right of the Scottish lairds to clear the highlands of crofters. But 'Rights', in the abstract, smelled foreign, suspect.)

Thus it has come about that English common law is rarely couched in terms of rights. Where the word right does appear it is often as a result of its use in newspaper headlines. Thus a report of the failure of an action for damages for the tort of nuisance brought by residents against a developer whose new high-rise building interfered with television reception was headlined 'Viewers have no right to watch TV'. A decision that an illegal immigrant, who was dying of Aids, should not be removed to his country of origin was headlined 'Aids victim has right to stay'. A decision that there was nothing in section 15 of the Adoption Act 1976 to preclude a single person applying to adopt a child even if in a homosexual relationship at the time was headlined 'Lesbian couple have right to adopt child'.

The use of the word right in such instances may be convenient in providing a shorthand description of the effect of the decision, but such usage is nevertheless misleading, since the word right carries connotations of permanence and universality, qualities that a right expressed to arise in such circumstances does not have. What a judge decides today may, even if not reversed on appeal, be overruled in a later decision. Even rights that arise from statute fall far short of the kind of rights that come to mind when we speak of the universal rights of man, since what is enacted by the legislature today may be repealed tomorrow: '... a woman's right to abortion is only as secure as the majority in Parliament that will vote to keep it in place, and the rights for gays and lesbians to live according to their own sexual preferences rests on the same fragile foundations'.[33]

Declarations

We have, so far, treated rights as being in two categories, abstract and legal. There is, though, what some might consider a third category: that which exists where some body of recognised authority declares that something is to be a right. The prime example of such a body is the United Nations.

In 1945 the *Charter of the United Nations* affirmed 'a faith in fundamental human rights, in the dignity and worth of the human person, in the equal rights of men and woman and of nations large and small'. The purposes of the United Nations were stated in its Charter to include the achievement of 'international co-operation ... in promoting and encouraging respect for human rights and for fundamental freedoms for all without distinction as to race, sex, language or religion'.

In 1948, the General Assembly of the United Nations adopted the *Universal Declaration of Human Rights*. The purpose of the Declaration was to proclaim 'a common standard of achievement for all peoples and all nations'. The rights declared were wide ranging and included not only rights to individual freedoms such as the right to respect for private life, freedom of expression, freedom of assembly and association, the right to own property, and the right to freedom of thought, conscience and religion, but also rights in the economic and social field such as the right to work and the right to join trade unions.

In 1966 the United Nations opened for signature the International Covenant on Civil and Political Rights. In adding its signature a state undertook to respect the rights set out in the Covenant. These overlapped[34] those set out in the Universal Declaration. A parallel Covenant dealt with economic, social and cultural rights.

---

33 F Raphael, *The Times*, 18 May 1994.
34 But did not replicate.

For the United Nations to make a declaration on the rights of prisoners does not of itself turn off the electrodes in the interrogation room of the police headquarters. But if the United Nations makes a declaration on prisoners' rights, and the state concerned is a signatory to the relevant Convention, does this not have more significance than if Mrs Z of Hay-on-Wye says to her friend, 'Prisoners have a right not to be tortured'? Not a lot, surely, for the man in the chair, but something more, perhaps – if only in the setting of a standard against which the conduct of a state can be measured and its actions made the subject of comment.

Where we can be more certain a declaration has practical effect is where formal machinery is established for the purpose of ensuring that rights, for example those set out in a convention, are respected.

In 1950 the Council of Europe adopted the European Convention for the Protection of Human Rights and Fundamental Freedoms. The Convention embodied certain of the rights proclaimed in the United Nations International Covenant on Civil and Political Rights[35] (but is narrower in that it omits rights that relate to equality (as in the field of employment).) For the purposes of administration and adjudication, the Convention established two bodies, the European Commission of Human Rights and the European Court of Human Rights.

Although one of the first to subscribe its signature to the Convention, it was not until 1966 that the United Kingdom government accepted the jurisdiction of the European Court of Human Rights. But from that time on, where it was claimed that a breach of a right contained in the European Convention had been infringed, a citizen was able to appeal above the courts of the United Kingdom to the European Court of Human Rights, in Strasbourg.

35 The rights in the European Convention comprise:
- The right to life.
- Freedom from torture and degrading treatment.
- Freedom from slavery and forced labour.
- The right to private and family life.
- Freedom of thought and religion.
- Freedom of expression.
- The right to peaceful assembly and to belong to a trade union.
- The right to marry and to have children.
- The right to education; The right to free, fair and regular elections.
- The right to leave one's own country.
- Freedom from expulsion from one's own country.
- The prohibition on the collective expulsion of immigrants.

Express conferment of rights in British law

It was for long argued[36] that the UK Parliament should enact a statute that would place on a statutory basis what are generally accepted as the basic civil rights and liberties of British subjects. Only by this means, it was contended, could adequate protection be afforded against the threats to freedom from actions by governments that, although democratically elected, had increasingly come to be seen by many as being, in practice, elected dictatorships. Those who opposed the enactment of such a statute maintained that rights were already adequately protected by the multitude of remedies afforded by existing common law and statute. If further rights were thought to be needed, these were, it was argued, more effectively provided by the passage of legislation that conferred in specific terms the rights required, rather than by the passage of legislation, of necessity in general terms, from which, as in the case of the American constitution, rights would have, after much uncertainty and legal wrangling, to be deduced.

With the passage of time, however, the flaws in the contention of John Major when Prime Minister, that 'We have no need for a Bill of Rights because we have freedom' came increasingly to be recognised and the balance of public opinion swung towards the view that a more definite place had to be found for the notion of rights. This view was given weight by the consequences following from the UK government's acceptance of the jurisdiction of the European Court of Human Rights, in particular in the light of a long and embarrassing series of cases in which the British government was held by the Court to be in breach of the Convention (with regard to the rights of, inter alia, the mentally ill, refugees, homosexuals and suspected Irish terrorists). Despite the pull of tradition and the advantage of flexibility, an unwritten constitution came increasingly to be regarded as no longer an adequate safeguard against abuses of power.

Some who wished to see human rights and freedoms given express protection by British law argued the case for a statutory 'Bill of Rights' (so-called after the Bill of Rights of 1688). In the event this course

36   The debate can be dated from the publication, in 1968, of a pamphlet by Antony Lester (later Lord Lester), *Democracy and Individual Rights*. The call in 1974 by Lord Justice Scarman (as he then was) in the Hamlyn Lectures for a Bill of Rights provided powerful impetus, but opposition from other senior judges at the time, in particular Lord Denning, then Master of the Rolls, remained strong. The first attempt in Britain to introduce human rights legislation was the Private Member's Bill promoted by Lord Lester in 1975.

was not followed. Instead, in 1998, the Human Rights Act provided for the incorporation into British law of the rights and liberties set out in the European Convention on Human Rights. The Act has two key components. First, the Act requires all legislation to be interpreted in a way that is compatible with the Convention. If that cannot be done, judges have power to declare the law to be incompatible and it will then be open to Parliament, through a fast-track procedure provided by the Act, to change the law. Second, the Act makes it unlawful for any public body to act in a way that is incompatible with the Convention, eg by infringing a right conferred by the Convention. Of particular importance here is the fact that a breach of the rights conferred by the Convention becomes actionable at the suit of a private individual before the British courts (and not merely, as previously, by taking the slow and tortuous path to a hearing before the European Court of Human Rights, in Strasbourg).

The significance of the Human Rights Act 1998, in particular with regard to the effects of the Act with regard to state sovereignty, and its impact on the existing procedure for judicial review of administrative decisions, on judicial scrutiny of legislation, on judicial interpretation of statutes, on the relationship between the legislature and the judiciary and the balance of power between the executive, the legislature and the judiciary – the significance of these matters, although of major importance for the constitution and the working of the legal system, lies outside the province of this book. It can, though, be remarked that the Act marks a further step in the 'transformation of English public law from a sovereign system of rules to a more rights-based constitutionalism'.[37]

---

37 M Hunt, *Using Human Rights Law in English Courts.*

CHAPTER 15

Banging on the table?

The idea of justice

Introduction

'But that's not *fair!*' How often has the cry gone up? – in the playground, in the school-room, in the home, on the beach. 'Why,' says Cheryl, 'should Sharon [her twin sister] get a bigger piece than me?' 'If you'd let me, I could've *told* you why I was late.' 'You weren't cross with Sharon when *she* did that.' 'It's *my* turn, Sharon had first go last time.'

An appreciation of unfairness develops early.[1] A child of five, perhaps younger, is likely to know the meaning of unfairness. Or, at any rate he or she could give examples of treatment that he or she regarded as being unfair. And a child of a slightly older age might be conscious of the unfairness of the situation in which half the children in the world go hungry. What any child might have more difficulty in doing is to give expression to the converse notion, the idea of fairness. Unfairness shouts out. Fairness goes unremarked.

The position is similar in the case of justice, a concept that has affinities with fairness. The absence of justice, injustice, proclaims itself. But what is *justice*? What *is* this quality the absence of which produces outcry? For writers in the ancient world the word that we translate as justice was a virtue, in some schemes of thinking the highest virtue, the supreme good, of which other virtues were aspects. Today the word is used in a less indefinite sense. So surely it should be possible to arrive at some definition that expresses the characteristics that we readily sense but find difficult to pin down?

---

1 A Ross *On Law and Justice* p 269.

C H Perelman[2] points out that for logicians a definition can be the replacement of a collection of symbols by a new symbol. Thus rooms for living in + walls + roof = house; to employ friction for the purpose of slowing a moving object = to brake. When a definition in the form of a new symbol is created there is no difficulty: the definition comprises the sum of the component parts. Where difficulty arises is where we attempt to define an existing word, a difficulty that is particularly acute where the word carries a pre-existing value content that refers to a quality that all agree is desirable (or undesirable, as the case may be).

Such is the case with the notion of justice. Justice is a quality considered to be desirable. Everyone claims to want justice, and people know what they want. The result is that there is a likelihood that in seeking to define justice people attach the label, justice, to the ends that they desire. So 'justice' becomes no more than a rallying cry. As Perelman says,[3] 'One has only to remind oneself that for thousands of years protagonists, in public and private conflicts, in wars, in revolutions, in lawsuits, in clashes of interest, have always done their best to prove that justice is on their side.' 'Justice' is the word pinned to the flag of the ends we seek, each defining justice according to his own scale of value, according to the conception of justice that puts himself in the right and his opponent in the wrong. In so doing the conviction may be sincere, but then it is 'easy to believe in the illusions which excite the emotions by stimulating the suprarenal glands'.[4]

At the end of the road are we to conclude no more than that to 'invoke justice is like banging on the table'?[5] Is 'justice' a word, like 'liberty', that can mean all things to all men? ('Liberty! Freedom! Justice!' roar the mob, when what they mean is 'Bread!')

So is the search fruitless, the goal as elusive as the end of the rainbow? Are the emotive, value-laden overtones ineradicable, the word so burdened by preconceptions that a dispassionate analysis is impossible? Can we find no common thread running through all the myriad interpretations of the word? At the start of the chapter a child complained of unfairness. If it had been older, it might have used the word injustice. Is there, to limit our search, any common thread running through the four instances of which complaint was made? One factor that comes to mind is lack of equality of treatment. It was the fact that Sharon's piece of cake was larger that produced the outcry.

---

2 *The Idea of Justice and the Problem of Argument* (1963) p 2.
3 Ibid, p 6.
4 A Ross *On Law and Justice* p 275.
5 Ibid, p 274.

Equality of treatment is certainly a constituent of justice, and the existence of a relationship between the two concepts has long been recognised, in the view of some writers (eg those in the school of Pythagoras) the two being treated as one and the same. But equality cannot be the sole ingredient of justice. There must be more, since if little six-year-old Cheryl's big 18-year-old weight-lifting brother Tom had been given a bigger piece of cake than she had received she might have felt no cause to demur, no sense of injustice. And in our own society the fact that men are not all treated equally – all receiving the same wage, all being awarded the same decoration in the New Year's Honours list – produces no complaint of injustice. So equality is only part of the picture. There must be some further element to be found.

Perelman

In the search for this an important step was taken by C H Perelman in *De la Justice* in 1945[6] in which he pointed out that there are various criteria by reference to which different people consider that justice is, with regard to the distribution of the benefits and burdens of life, attained. Each of these criteria, and Perelman enumerated six, he termed instances of 'concrete justice'. Thus,

1. From one standpoint justice is done if what people receive is determined according to what contribution they make, whether in the local sphere, as at the workplace, or in the wider social sphere. The principle here is that people should be rewarded by reference to what they do, a principle expressed by Perelman as: 'To each according to his works'. It is on this concept of justice that piecework systems of payment, and examinations are based. It provides the basis also of the philosophy of a free enterprise, entrepreneurial society.

2. For some people justice is served if what people receive is determined according to their needs – needs measured according to varying degrees of health or ill-health, varying degrees of incapacity, varying degrees of financial or social (eg housing) need. Perelman referred to this instance of concrete justice as: 'To each

---

6   Reprinted in C H Perelman *The Idea of Justice and the Problem of Argument* (1963) Chap 1.

according to his needs'. It is on this concept of justice that the welfare state is based (and it was because Cheryl was viewing justice from this standpoint that she saw no injustice in her elder brother Tom getting a bigger piece of cake than she did).

3. For some justice means that benefits and burdens are distributed according to personal merit ascertained according to some ethical code, the good receiving the benefits and the bad the burdens of life. The principle here is: To each according to his merit. On this view of justice rests the Christian view that it is just that the good should go to Heaven and the wicked to Hell.

The three instances of concrete justice mentioned so far are not necessarily incompatible. It is possible that a situation could exist in which all three concepts of justice produced the same result, as where a morally virtuous hardworking and productive man had large needs. But generally in practice the concepts are likely to conflict, the first two rarely being reconcilable. According to the first (to each according to his works) a person who is intentionally unemployed should receive nothing; according to the second (to each according to his needs) justice may be served by providing him with a large house and sufficient income to support his 11 children.

Having set out instances of 'concrete justice', varying concepts of the criteria by reference to which justice is to be attained, Perelman seeks to determine whether there is anything that the advocates of the different concepts would find that they had in common. He finds that there is such a common link. We can explain the matter like this. In order that any one of the instances of concrete justice should operate, and let us take 'to each according to works' as our example, it will be necessary, in order that the benefits and burdens of life should be distributed according to this criterion, to divide people into categories according to how extensive or minimal their works are, ranging from (and the examples here are ours, not Perelman's) 'extremely industrious and productive', which we can imagine as Category A, all the way down to Category Z, 'bone idle and achieves nothing'.

The categories into which people are divided for the purpose of applying any one of the instances of concrete justice Perelman terms (a little confusingly) 'essential categories'. We can imagine the essential categories in the case of concrete justice in the form of 'to each according to his needs' ranging from Essential Category A, 'destitute and desperate', down to Category Z, 'wants for nothing'. In practice, where in any society certain matters are allocated according to need, the essential categories are likely to be divided into need with regard to a whole range of matters – housing need, medical need, educational need, need for legal advice, and so on, and in the case of each there will be essential categories going, as we have imagined it, from Category A down to Category Z. The 'points' system used by local authorities to determine priorities in allocating housing, points being counted for such matters as whether the applicant is married, how many children he has, and their ages, is an example of essential categories being determined in the case of concrete justice in the form of 'to each according to his housing need', all the people with the same number of points forming one 'essential category'.

The thing which Perelman says that everyone would agree on, and this is the common thread that we are looking for, is that irrespective of the form of concrete justice applied, once a form of concrete justice has been selected, *all the people in any one essential category should be treated in the same way.*

The idea that equality lay at the heart of justice was, we have noted, appreciated in early times. Also recognised, as an application of this, was the principle that like cases should be treated alike. Perelman's contribution was to give added meaning to this principle. He showed like cases of *what* must be treated alike, ie that all the people in any one essential category in any one scheme of concrete justice must be treated alike; eg that all the people in the 'bone idle' category under the 'to each according to works' form of concrete justice should be treated in the same way.

This common denominator, 'the principle of action in accordance with which beings of one and the same essential category must be treated in the same way' Perelman[7] terms 'formal justice'.[8]

Having explained the nature of Perelman's theory we can complete the picture by mentioning the other three examples of concrete justice that he cites.

4. To each according to his rank – the higher the rank, the greater the advantages. Rank can be measured in various ways, for example, by social rank, ranging from the monarch through dukes, marquises, earls, viscounts, barons, down to commoners (and, in earlier times, serfs, or slaves), or rank determined according to age (older children being allowed to go to bed later than younger ones), or military rank, or rank according to the colour of one's skin, or religion, caste, language or ethnic group.

7 Ibid, p 16.
8 See D Lloyd *The Idea of Law* Chap 6.

5. To each according to his legal entitlement. For example, a legal system might lay down degrees of privilege for prisoners according to certain standards of good behaviour, the essential categories here being the various grades of good behaviour, or that all those charged with a criminal offence punishable by imprisonment should have access to a solicitor within one hour of their arrest, and those charged with an offence punishable by a fine, access to a solicitor within two hours, the essential categories here being merely two in number. At the time when he wrote Perelman was no doubt thinking of legal entitlement in terms of the entitlement conferred by the sovereign state within which a person lives. Since that time legal entitlement has come to be capable of carrying a wider meaning, as for example where the entitlement arises under the terms of the Convention for the Protection of Human Rights and Fundamental Freedoms, under the jurisdiction of the European Court of Human Rights.

6. Finally, of the forms of concrete justice listed by Perelman there is: to each the same thing. This certainly can be regarded as a form of concrete justice, but it stands apart from the other forms in that in the case of the other forms we can see that there will be various essential categories, eg different levels of work, of need, and so on. But in the case of 'to each the same thing' there is only one category, that into which everybody is put.

A form of concrete justice not referred to by Perelman but worth mentioning because of its relevance at the present day is: to each according to his ability to pay – the essential categories here being various levels of wealth. It is this concept of the proper form of concrete justice, coupled with that which provides 'to each according to his works', that tends to be upheld by those on the right of the political spectrum, while those towards the left attach importance to that which says 'to each according to his needs'. Therefore it will be appreciated that the argument between those who believe that it is right that people should have the right to use their own money to buy medical treatment and those who consider that money should not enable people to jump the queue for medical treatment is an argument between those who believe that the proper form of concrete justice is 'to each according to his ability to pay', and those who adhere to the form of concrete justice that provides 'to each according to his needs'.

From what has been said it will be realised that if someone proclaims that a certain act is unjust, his statement can, using Perelman's analysis, have two meanings. First, it can mean that the speaker rejects the form of concrete justice that society applies, as for example where someone says that it is unjust that the rich can get a hospital bed without having to wait many months until one becomes available under the National Health Service. Or it can mean that the speaker maintains that within an essential category all cases have not been treated alike, as where Cheryl complained that her twin sister Sharon had been given a larger piece of cake than she had received. Here the complaint is that formal justice has not been done. (Formal justice consists in sticking to the rules of the game, once the game to be played has been decided. Disagreements over concrete justice are disagreements over the game that ought to be played.)

Can, Perelman asks, justice conflict with the law? He answers that the law, assuming that it is properly administered, cannot conflict with formal justice, since formal justice consists in treating like cases alike within an essential category. If the law sees that this is done, then justice, formal justice, is done.

With regard to concrete justice, a conflict may well exist between the form of concrete justice followed in a particular society in respect of a particular matter and the form of concrete justice that a person believes ought to be followed, but in saying this we are saying no more than that the moral values of a citizen may differ from the values of the society, or at any rate the government of the country, in which he lives – that opinions as to what constitutes justice may differ. Seen in this light it might seem that Perelman takes us no further forward in the search for what lies at the heart of the notion of justice. Perelman did, though, make a significant contribution to the continuing debate by his analysis of justice into formal justice and concrete justice, with the latter's hierarchy of essential categories. He showed us what we *mean* when we say that justice is achieved by treating like cases alike.

Perelman was content to leave it that justice was formal justice. This may seem an arid, bloodless, conclusion and not what we feel must lie, if we could find it, at the end of the rainbow. But just as Kelsen posited a 'pure' theory of law, so Perelman posits a pure theory of justice. What he says may not satisfy us completely, but, as far as it goes, it holds water.

How, though, would justice as the word is used with reference to legal proceedings be fitted into Perelman's scheme? If we say, 'The murderer was hanged and so justice was done', or, 'The injured man received compensation from the person whose negligence caused him injury, and so justice was done', or, 'The court's refusal to grant the plaintiff a remedy meant that justice was denied', in what sense is the word 'justice' used in each of these instances? If justice consists of treating like cases alike, what, as between the

parties involved in legal proceedings, are the 'like' cases? – what is
the essential category?

If, seeking to apply Perelman's notion we say the 'like cases' in
the first example are 'all murderers', and that justice is done if all
murderers are treated alike, we would probably feel that Perelman's
notion of justice failed to match our understanding of the word if,
under a particular system, all murderers were treated alike by being
given a free pardon. (Yet *formal* justice would have been done.)
Perhaps Perelman's essential category regarding merit, 'to each
according to his merits', comes closer to meeting the point, all
murderers being accorded due punishment. But even this way of
thinking about justice does not cover the point that, in the examples
above, the reason why justice was (or was not) done was concerned
with the relationship between two parties, the murderer and his
victim, the plaintiffs and the defendants. So while Perelman's
scheme seems to hold good when we think in terms of the distribution of benefits and burdens within a society, it fails to meet
our notion of justice as we think of it done as between one individual
and another. It is here that H L A Hart throws light.

H L A Hart

In Chapter 8 of *The Concept of Law*, after following the theme that
justice consists of treating like cases alike (and differing in no
material respect from the approach of Perelman) Professor Hart
recognises that he has so far applied the 'like cases alike' theory of
justice to laws which distribute things among individuals, whether
tangible or intangible. But how does this notion of justice, he asks,[9]
stand up when we are speaking of the compensation which ought
to be given to a person who has received injury? Here we could speak
of just compensation or unjust compensation (ie too little or too
much). But what are the 'like cases' and how are they to be treated
alike? It might seem that the 'treat like cases alike' notion of justice
does not adequately explain what is meant by justice in the context
of compensation. But, Hart maintains, there is in fact a connection.
Suppose that a system of law failed to provide any remedy to a person
who had been physically injured by another. It would generally be
agreed here that the law (ie the system of law as a whole) was unjust.
But why? The law is treating all cases (ie all citizens) alike (ie none

9 *The Concept of Law* p 159.

has a remedy). Does this mean that this notion of justice has failed to provide a means of explaining injustice of this kind? No, Hart says, even here the kind of injustice instanced can be explained by means of the notion that justice consists of treating like cases alike. To understand how this may be done it has first to be recognised that the morality of every social group includes a belief that those within the group have a right to be protected against certain kinds of harmful conduct. This belief will be given effect to by the existence of a structure of reciprocal rights and obligations (eg a right not to be harmed, an obligation not to harm others) which will proscribe those forms of harm which the society is not prepared to countenance being inflicted. The effect of the existence of this structure of rights and obligations will be to prevent one citizen from robbing or attacking another – something which he would have been able to do if no law proscribing these forms of conduct existed. In this way the strong or cunning citizen is prevented from making use of his strength or cunning to injure another weaker or less cunning citizen. Thus the effect of the law is to place the strong and cunning on a level with the weaker and less cunning ones. The law thus creates among individuals an equality which would not be present if the law did not exist.[10]

The moral basis of such a law is that it is regarded as being morally right that the strong should not be able to use their strength to the detriment of the weak; that the strong and the weak should be placed in an equal position. Thus if a strong man injures a weak one the equilibrium which the moral code considers correct has been disturbed; and, in order to restore the equilibrium, the wrongdoer is required to compensate the person he has injured. How can this be related to the thesis that justice consists of treating like cases alike? By these steps: (i) When a wrongdoer injures another, the wrongdoer and his victim are no longer alike; the wrongdoer has benefited and his victim has suffered; (ii) When the law compels the wrongdoer to provide compensation, the wrongdoer and his victim are restored to their previous 'like' positions.

Seen in this light justice consists not only of treating like cases alike, but ensuring that, if like cases cease (as a result of the wrong-doer's act) to be alike, they are made like again (by compelling the wrongdoer to provide compensation). The law, by placing the victim and wrongdoer back on a footing of equality, restores 'likeness' (so bringing back to equilibrium the scales of justice). That this notion of justice holds good when we talk in terms of 'just compensation'

10   Ibid, p 161.

can be seen, Hart says, if we consider the position where the law does not provide a remedy for what is regarded as a certain type of wrong. For example suppose that A obtains some enrichment at the expense of B in a way which society regards as morally wrong. The law, let us suppose, provides no remedy to B, since A has not committed any tort and is not in breach of contract or quasi-contract. The fact that the law provides B with no remedy would be said to be unjust. The reason for this view would be that the society would consider that A had flouted part of the structure of obligations which the society believed should be protected. In the eyes of society A and B would be no longer 'alike', A having obtained a wrongful advantage over B. And the fact that the law failed to restore 'likeness' (by requiring A to give up his gain, or by requiring him to compensate B) would make the law unjust.

This view of the nature of justice, ie that justice consists of restoring likeness, of restoring a disturbed equilibrium (as well as treating like cases alike) depends, Hart recognises, on acceptance of the existence of a moral conviction by the society conerned that citizens should be subject to the reciprocal rights and obligations which place them, to the extent that these exist, on an equal footing.

Rawls[11]

In his *A Theory of Justice*, published in 1971, John Rawls says that justice is that which prevails in a just society. A just society is one that people would agree to be members of if they had the choice. At first sight this might seem to be no more than a variant of the contract theories of writers such as Locke and Rousseau. Rawls says that this is indeed his aim: 'My aim is to present a conception of justice which generalises and carries to higher level of abstraction the familiar theory of the social contract'. But Rawls's ideas constitute a major advance and there are significant differences between his theory and that of the earlier writers. They sought an explanation for the basis of existing society, their theories visualising people at

---

11 J W Harris *Legal Philosophies* p 263; Davies and Holdcroft *Jurisprudence: Texts and Commentary* Chap 9. N McCormick 'Justice according to Rawls' (1973) 89 LQR 393; T Scanlon, 'Rawls' Theory of Justice' (1973) Penn LR 1020; *Reading Rawls* (ed N Daniels, 1975); R P Wolff *Understanding Rawls* (1977); H G Blocker and E H Smith *John Rawls' Theory of Social Justice* (1980); N W Simmonds *Central Issues in Jurisprudence* Chap 2 (1986); J Feinberg 'Justice, Fairness and Rationality' 81 Yale LJ 1004; C Kukathas and P Pettitt *Rawls: A Theory of Justice and its Critics* (1990).

some (albeit hypothetical stage) as having entered into a contract. Rawls's theory is concerned with what people *would* agree to if they had the choice. Rawls does not envisage people as ever having actually made the choice.

Anyone who thinks about the kind of society he would agree to live in – the laws in force, the form of government, the protection afforded to private property, the assistance given to those who have fallen upon hard times – will consider the matter in the light of his own circumstances. The old, poor, sick person will want to live in a society that has regard to his needs. The healthy, rich, intelligent, educated young person will want to live in a society that respects private property and gives credit for individual initiative. In Perelman's terms, one will favour a form of concrete justice that accords 'to each according to his needs', the other will favour that which accords 'to each what he has been able to secure', by good fortune or his own talents.

The twist that Rawls gives to his theory is this. A just society, he says, is one which we would agree to if we did not know what our circumstances in that society were going to be.[12] So the rich, talented young man might be brought up with a start. 'What kind of society would I want if I was old, and poor, and sick?' he might think. And the sick old man might have second thoughts too. 'Suppose that I was a skilled surgeon, having undergone many years of training and passed numerous examinations, would I want to be paid little more than a drunken layabout who had never lifted a finger to help himself in his life? No I would not. I would want to be paid according to my qualifications and my skills.'

Rawls's theory of justice can be understood by considering the analogy of the rules that would be agreed upon by people who knew that they were going to be the members of the crew of a sailing ship, but who did not know the position that they were going to hold in the ship's company – whether they were going to be the captain or the boatswain or the sail maker or the carpenter or the cook or a deckhand, and not knowing either what their own personal circumstances were going to be – whether they were going to be young or old, or weak or strong, black or white, intelligent or slow-witted. A just set of rules for the ship's conduct is one which all members of the crew would agree to. 'Even if I am a deckhand', a person will think, 'it will be in my interests if the captain has his own cabin so that he can have undisturbed sleep and so not make the kind of mistake that would take the ship on to the rocks. It is in my interests that the cook should not have to keep watches, so that he can concentrate on cooking. I'm

12 John Rawls *A Theory of Justice* p 12.

not too keen on the captain having a power to flog malefactors, but if chaos is not to break out the captain must have some powers of discipline in cases of disobedience. And of course, I might be the captain, and I wouldn't want the responsibility of running the ship unless I had at least some sanctions to enforce my orders.'

The position is the same in the case of a complete society. Justice is that ordering of things that would be agreed to by a person if he had no knowledge of where he would stand in the society of which he was to be a part. In order for his choice of the laws that are to prevail to be wholly disinterested, he must have no knowledge of what his circumstances will be. So in making the choice he must not be permitted to know anything about the place that he will hold in the society – his class, his intelligence, his strength, his physical health, whether he stands to inherit a fortune or nothing, his age (*en ventre sa mère* or aged 102), his colour, his religion or moral convictions, nor even his psychological propensities, whether he will be an optimist or a pessimist, whether he will be the kind of person who is willing to take risks, or one who prefers to play safe. Nor does he know into what kind of society he will be born, neither its culture nor its time in history or prehistory. And, be it noted, lest it be thought to have been overlooked, he does not know whether he might not be a she.

The good

Finally, Rawls does not let the chooser know the things he will attach importance to in life, what things he will value. He does not know whether he will be preoccupied with gardening and domestic life, or golf or amateur dramatics or socialising, or solitary walks on high moors or debauchery or philosophy or train spotting. He will have no idea of what will be the best thing or things for him in life, no idea of what Rawls describes as being, for him, 'the good'.

The veil of ignorance

The choice of what laws are to prevail, what system of government, must be made, Rawls says, behind a 'veil of ignorance',[13] since only if people make the choice with no knowledge of where they will stand can they be counted on to decide on a system that is just for all. ('Thus there follows the very important consequence that the parties have no basis for bargaining in the usual sense. No one knows his situation in society, nor his natural talents, and therefore no one is in a position to tailor principles to his advantage.'[14])

13 Ibid, pp 12, 136.
14 Ibid, p 136.

Primary goods

But while they are not to be allowed to know of anything that could influence them in their decision, there are some things that it is necessary, if a rational choice is to be made, for them to know. Thus they know that if people are going to live, they have got to eat. They know that they want what Rawls terms 'primary goods'. These are all the things with more of which men can generally be assured of advancing their ends,[15] the things that are required for the execution of their rational plans,[16] the things that every rational man is presumed to want in order to pursue what for him is 'the good'.[17] Certain of the 'primary goods' are of a social nature, and of this kind Rawls mentions rights and liberties, powers and opportunities, income and wealth. These are the primary goods that are at the disposition of society. Other primary goods are of a natural character and of these Rawls mentions health and vigour, intelligence, imagination and self-respect. In making the choice men know that they would prefer more rather than fewer primary goods.[18] And they look to their own interests: they are 'mutually disinterested';[19] none is concerned with the interests of others.

Those making the choice are also permitted to understand about political affairs, for example voting systems, the principles of economic theory (eg market forces, economic planning) and of social organisation, and the laws of human psychology. There is no limit, in fact, to their knowledge of general principles and theories, since these are things that they need to know in order to be in a position to decide the social structure, the economic system and the legal framework that will constitute the society that are going to opt to live within. What they do not know, what is behind the veil of ignorance, is their own circumstances within that society: their hand of cards is face down on the table.

The original position[20]

People in this situation, people who understand the factors that influence rational choice (eg that it is better to have more primary goods than fewer) and the laws and principles that regulate human affairs, but who, as regards their own

15 Ibid, p 92.
16 Ibid, p 93.
17 Ibid, p 62.
18 Ibid, p 93.
19 Ibid, p 13.
20 Ibid, p 12.

circumstances, are behind the veil of ignorance, Rawls describes as being in the 'original position'.[21]

He emphasises that such a position is not to be thought of as ever actually having existed as an actual historical state of affairs.[22] The original position is purely a hypothesis[23] used to reach the answer to the question – what is justice? We have to imagine people in the original position and then consider what principles they would choose to govern their society. Because *this* is justice – the body of principles that a person in the original position would choose, since the person making the choice will make sure that the principles he chooses are fair however he finds himself placed when he picks up his cards from the table and sees what kind of hand fate has dealt him. This way of regarding justice, and it lies at the core of his thinking, Rawls terms 'justice as fairness'.

Justice as fairness, and its extrapolation

Justice as fairness begins, Rawls explains, 'with one of the most general of all choices which persons might make together, namely, with the choice of the first principles of a conception of justice which is to regulate all subsequent criticism and reform of institutions. Then, having chosen a conception of justice, we can suppose that they are to choose a constitution and a legislature to enact laws, and so on, all in accordance with the principles of justice initially agreed upon. Our social situation is just *if* it is such that by this sequence of hypothetical agreements we *would* have contracted into the general system of rules which defines it. Moreover, assuming that the original position does determine a set of principles (that is, that a particular conception of justice would be chosen), it will then be true that whenever social institutions satisfy these principles those engaged in them can say to one another that they are cooperating on terms to which they would agree if they were free and equal persons whose relations with respect to one another were fair. They could all view their arrangements as meeting the stipulations which they would acknowledge in an initial situation that embodies widely accepted and reasonable constraints on the choice of principles. The general recognition of this fact would provide the basis for a public acceptance of the corresponding principles of justice. No society can, of course, be a scheme of co-operation which men enter

---

21 Ibid, p 120.
22 Ibid, p 12.
23 *Reading Rawls* (ed N Daniels) Chap 1 (T Nagel); Chap 2 (R Dworkin).

voluntarily in a literal sense; each person finds himself placed at birth in some particular position in some particular society, and the nature of this position materially affects his life prospects. Yet a society satisfying the principles of justice as fairness comes as close as a society can to being a voluntary scheme, for it meets the principles which free and equal persons would assent to under circumstances that are fair'.[24]

What form of society is likely to result from the choices that people make, as they stand in the original position and hedge their bets? Rawls does not attempt to predict. But he does put forward certain general principles that he believes people in the original position would, as rational beings, conclude were in their interests to subscribe to.

The principle of reciprocity

One of these is that no one would acquiesce in a system that entailed an enduring loss for himself in order to bring about a greater net balance of satisfaction for society as a whole. Such a system would be 'inconsistent with the principle of reciprocity that is implicit in any well ordered society'.[25] Thus no one in the original position would, Rawls suggests, accept the principle that society should be so ordered as to produce the greatest good of the greatest number.[26] '"The greatest good of the greatest number" sounds fine', we can imagine someone in the original position saying, 'but a society in which 49% of the population were slaves serving a majority of 51% of slave owners would conform with the principle, and I might be a slave'.

The just savings principle

Another principle that Rawls believes must have a place among those selected is what he terms 'the just savings principle'.[27] Under this a level of conservation and savings is to be adopted sufficient to promote the best interests of the worst off members of future generations to the greatest degree acceptable to the worst off class of people of the existing generation. The way in which this principle is framed might not seem entirely satisfactory to conservationists of the present day, but nevertheless the inclusion by Rawls of the

---

24   John Rawls *A Theory of Justice* p 13.
25   Ibid, p 14.
26   See Chap 13 for the inappropriateness of this phrase as a summation of Bentham's utilitarianism.
27   John Rawls, *A Theory of Justice*, p 284.

principle does show prescience, when writing in 1971, of the importance that was going to be increasingly attached to the need to protect the workings of the planet's eco-systems.[28] The effect of the principle is that justice as fairness must operate not only between individuals in any given society, but also between members of one generation and those of generations that succeed it.

In addition to the above two principles, and lying deep in the core of Rawls's theory, are two fundamental principles of justice that Rawls believes people in the original position could not fail to adopt, two principles that are inescapable sine qua non if justice as fairness is to exist.

The first fundamental principle

The first of these is that 'Each person is to have an equal right to the most extensive total system of equal basic liberties compatible with a similar system of liberty for all.'[29] The basic liberties are to include the right to vote and to be eligible for public office; freedom of speech; freedom of assembly; liberty of conscience; freedom of thought; freedom of the person; the right to hold property; and freedom from arbitrary arrest and seizure, as defined by the rule of law.[30] It will be noted that the principle that Rawls here lays down corresponds closely with the basic tenet of John Stewart Mill in *On Liberty*.[31]

The second fundamental principle

The second principle is that 'Social and economic inequalities are to be arranged so that they are both':

(a) 'reasonably expected to be to everyone's advantage'; and
(b) 'attached to offices and positions open to all'.[32]

As a result of (a) the distribution of wealth does not have to be equal, provided that the unequal distribution is for everyone's advantage.[33] For example, it will be for the benefit of the poorest that doctors should be paid more than they, the poorest, receive so that an incentive exists for people to qualify, and remain in

---

28 '"Take what you want", says God. "Take it, and pay for it"', Spanish proverb.
29 Ibid, pp 302, 303. In *Political Liberalism*, see infra, this becomes 'a fully adequate scheme of equal basic liberties'.
30 Ibid, p 60.
31 See p 297 et seq.
32 John Rawls *A Theory of Justice* p 60.
33 Ibid, p 61.

practice, as doctors. Thus there is no injustice in greater benefits being earned by a few provided that the situation of persons not so benefited is thereby improved.

The difference principle

The principle that people should be treated differently only if this is to the advantage of those so treated Rawls terms 'the difference principle'.

The priority rule

To the above two fundamental principles we might perhaps respond with a nod. But on reflection the thought might occur that the application of the first and second principles could run counter to each other. For example, the principle that economic inequalities are to be arranged so that everyone benefits (which envisages at least some restriction on inequalities in the distribution of wealth) might conflict with the principle that protects the basic liberty concerning the right to hold property.

Rawls foresees this possibility and in order to resolve any such possible conflict, lays down an order of priority. Under this the first fundamental principle (protection of individual liberties) takes precedence over the second.

Thus the basic liberties are supreme. The only restrictions that Rawls will allow on one of these is either (a) where the curtailment of one liberty will result in greater liberty overall (for example, the restriction of freedom of the person constituted by the power of the police to arrest and hold a criminal confers on the populace the greater liberty of freedom from the fear of wholly uncontrolled crime); or (b) where a 'less than equal liberty' is 'acceptable to those citizens with the lesser liberties'. (It has been suggested that the latter exception might cover 'such cases as the granting of special privileges and immunities to members of the legislature in so far as these are justifiable as tending to protect and strengthen the political institutions and thus the overall liberties of all, on which ground they should be acceptable to the rest of society. Likewise immunities of witnesses, counsel and judges in litigation.')[34] So just as economic inequalities are acceptable where they result in a benefit for all, so restrictions on the basic liberties are acceptable where the overall result is a greater liberty for all.

The primacy afforded to the basic liberties means that these take precedence over the second fundamental principle, in particular over

---

34 N MacCormick (1973) 89 LQR 393 at 409.

that part of the principle that lays down that economic inequalities must be for the benefit of all, including the least well off. Rawls is explicit about the effect of this: 'This ordering means that a departure from the institutions of equal liberty required by the first principle cannot be justified, or compensated for, by greater social and economic advantages'.[35]

But, as has been observed,[36] 'To choose basic principles [including a priority rule] it to choose forms of society'. Between competing political ideologies, Rawls does not stand neutral. By excluding the entitlement of people to attach more importance to reducing the gap in a society between the rich and the poor than to protecting the libery of the rich to retain what they hold, by excluding the political left, Rawls places himself and his theory on the right. We can perhaps agree that human beings, in seeking to select a system of law and government that will safeguard their interests irrespective of the position in which they find themselves when the veil of ignorance is lifted, will adopt Rawls's two fundamental principles of justice. But it may be thought that Rawls presumes too much when he tells us that people in the original position cannot rationally do other than decide that the first should invariably take precedence over the second. By doing so Rawls breaks the rules of his own game. First he tells us that people in the original position are free to decide the nature of their society and the principles that govern it. Then he tells us what they will decide. Having left the decision to the jury, he lays down the parameters within which their decision must lie.

The precedence that Rawls says the first principle must take over the second brings to mind the age-old dialogue between the rich man and the starving peasant. The peasant says 'Justice demands that you give me bread.' The rich man replies, 'For me to be compelled to give you bread would entail an infringement of my liberty to decide what I do with my own property.' The peasant answers, 'For me bread matters more than liberty.' To which the rich man responds, turning away, 'Disgraceful!' (As has been pointed out, in the cry of the mob in the French Revolution, 'Liberty! Fraternity! Equality!' the middle word is empty of meaning, the other two are irreconcilable.)

Rawls is, though, not unaware of the difficulties that his imposition of the priority rule may produce. 'In more extreme and tangled instances', he concedes, at '... some point the priority rules

---

35 John Rawls *A Theory of Justice* p 61.
36 N MacCormick (1973) 89 LQR 393 at 412.

... will fail; and indeed, we may be able to find no satisfactory answer at all' – an honest, if disappointing, conclusion to a theory that has had such major influence.

Be that as it may, the fact is that an account of justice which begins by conveying an impression of majestic impartiality ends by revealing as much partiality as schemes that openly attach their wagons to the ideologies of the left or the right.

Rawls tells us by what principles people in the original position would elect to be guided in determining the nature of the society they would choose to live in. He does not take the further step of telling us the system of law and government that would be chosen. Indeed, in *A Theory of Justice*, Rawls does not intend us, when thinking about justice as he views it, to attempt to build in our minds a picture of utopia, covering every eventuality in a society's existence, as it would be constructed by people in the original position. Rather, he would have us consider when any *particular* issue arises how people in the original position, guided by the principles he prescribes, would decide that *that* issue should be dealt with.

Political Liberalism

This, at any rate, was how Rawls left matters in *A Theory of Justice*. In 1993, in his collection of essays, *Political Liberalism,* Rawls replies to criticism of the earlier work, clarifies certain matters, and in one respect takes his thinking a stage further. We now learn that he intends that the principles of justice set out in *A Theory of Justice,* although not a recipe for utopia, are nonetheless to provide a substructure for actual societies. 'Justice as fairness' is now given a political dimension, a political dimension in the real world. The question dealt with in the second book is *how?*

In the course of explaining what, in *A Theory of Justice,* he meant by the phrase 'justice as fairness'[37], Rawls now says that we can suppose that people, having chosen a conception of justice, will proceed 'to choose a constitution and a legislature to enact laws, and so on, all in accordance with the principles of justice initially agreed upon'. But how is agreement to be reached - reached in a way that is fair to all, acceptable to all? How, for example, and in particular, can agreement be reached in view of the fact that many western societies are multi-cultural, multi-faithed, with the consequence that it is inevitable that there will be wide variations in what is regarded as 'the good'? ('How is it possible that there may

37 See p 209 supra.

exist over time a stable and just society of free and equal citizens profoundly divide by reasonable though incompatible religious, philosophical, and moral doctrines? Put another way: How is it possible that deeply opposed though reasonable comprehensive doctrines may live together and all affirm the political conception of a constitutional regime?')

One approach, Rawls says, might be 'to look at the various comprehensive doctrines actually found in society and specify an index of [primary] goods so as to be near to those doctrines' center of gravity, so to speak; that is to find a kind of average of what those who affirmed those views would need by way of ... protection ... [ie, of their own values]'. This approach Rawls rejects. Instead he proposes that what a 'political conception of justice' (ie, 'justice as fairness' wearing its political hat) requires is an 'overlapping consensus' between the divergent elements within a pluralistic society: a sufficient area of common ground on which to establish a political structure that has room for the multifarious views that a pluralistic society contains.

'An overlapping consensus ... is not,' he explains, 'merely a consensus on accepting certain authorities, or on complying with certain institutional arrangements, founded on convergence of self- or group interests. All those who affirm the political conception start from within their own comprehensive view and draw on the religious, philosophical, and moral grounds it provides. The fact that people affirm the same political conception on those grounds does not make their affirming it any less religious, philosophical, or moral, as the case may be, since the grounds sincerely held determine the nature of their affirmation.' It follows that 'those who affirm the various views supporting the political conception will not withdraw their support of it should the relative strength of their view in society increase and eventually become dominant ...' Thus '...the political conception will still be supported regardless of shifts in the distribution of political power. Each view supports the political conception for its own sake, or on its own merits.'

Rawls recognises, however, that there may be elements within a society with views so unreasonable that they will be incapable of forming part of the consensus. This being so, a democratic society will be well-ordered only if two conditions are satisfied. First, 'citizens who affirm reasonable but opposing comprehensive doctrines belong to an overlapping consensus ...'. Secondly, 'unreasonable comprehensive doctrines do not gain enough currency to undermine society's essential justice'. (We may note, from the reference here to well-ordered societies that the scope of Rawls's scheme in *Political Liberalism* is no longer universal, as was the notion of justice in the earlier book, but confined to societies that are democratically constituted.)

In *Political Liberalism* Rawls does not disavow the notion of justice he proposed in *A Theory of Justice*, the notion built on the foundation of people envisaged in the original position. But the question arises as to whether, and if so to what extent, the principles in a *Theory of Justice* remain unaffected by ideas advanced in the later work. On this Professor Freeman points out, 'if overlapping consensus is reached because people in the real world want it, there seems no reason to construct justice [from the foundation of people in] the original position'.[38] If Rawls's reply to this was that the overlapping consensus is what people in the original position would chose, then he could not so hold '... without clothing the formerly naked participants so as to make them much like people who have experienced the real world',[39] so removing the foundation under the starting point of justice as propounded in the first work.

Nozick[40]

A view of justice markedly different from those considered so far was presented by Robert Nozick in 1974 in *Anarchy, State and Utopia*.

For Nozick a just society is one in which the rights of the individual are accorded the respect that is their due. Rights form such an integral part of Nozick's thinking that his views might well have been treated in Chapter 14, which dealt specifically with rights, and much that was said in that chapter will be relevant to what follows. But since Nozick's concern is as much with the kind of society that exists when rights are respected as with the nature of the rights themselves, his views are on balance better dealt with here, this treatment having also the advantage of providing an illuminating contrast with the views of Rawls.

The starting point of Nozick's thinking is the fact of the existence of each human being as an individual, separate and distinct from all others. At their origins, when in a state of nature (and here

---

38 Lloyd's *Introduction to Jurisprudence*, 6th edn, p 365.
39 Ibid.
40 J Harris *Legal Philosophies* (2nd edn, 1997) pp 269–271; Davies and Holdcroft *Jurisprudence: Texts and Commentary* Chap 11; M Teitelman (1977) 77 Col LR 495; H L A Hart (1979) 79 Col LR 828; P Pettit *Judging Justice* Pt III; J Paul *Reading Nozick*.

Nozick follows Locke's concept closely), individuals existed in a state of perfect freedom, subject only to the laws of nature. In the state of nature individuals could act as they thought fit without leave of any other person. The restraint that the law of nature imposes is that no one is permitted to act in ways that harm another's life, health, liberty or possessions.

The natural rights that are thus conferred consist of (a) a right to enjoy one's life, health, liberty and possessions without interference by others in the shape of violence, theft, or fraud (the last including breaches of contract); and (b) a right to be compensated by any person who causes injury by violating one's natural rights (the compensation levied being capable of including such sum as may serve to act as a restraint on future violations).

The right of an individual not to have his natural rights infringed thus imposes a restraint on the activities of other individuals. This restraint Nozick terms a 'moral side restraint'; each individual is entitled to the enjoyment of his own natural rights subject to a 'moral side restraint' in respect of the rights of others.

In a state of nature it is for each individual to protect his own rights. This could be unsatisfactory since each individual, in deciding whether his rights had been infringed and what reparation he was entitled to extract for their violation would, acting as a judge in his own case, tend to give himself the benefit of the doubt and over-estimate the harm he had suffered, seeking to exact excessive compensation. This would lead to retaliations and feuds and, there being no way of deciding disputes, neither party would be able to know when a matter was settled.

The anarchy that is as a consequence endemic in a state of nature will lead to the creation of the machinery of a state. The evolution of this follows certain stages.

1. First, small groups, perhaps consisting of a family and its friends, are formed for the purpose of self-protection. The groups so formed Nozick terms 'Mutual Protection Associations'. Each member acts in the defence of all the other of the Association's members.

2. The inconvenience of each member being liable to be called upon to assist in the defence of other members will lead to the appointment of some person or body to undertake the defence of the Association's members. The person so appointed Nozick terms the 'Protection Agency'. This Agency would be paid a fee for its services. It would take over not only the defence of the Association against outsiders, acting as 'retaliator', but would also deal with complaints by one member of the Association against

another, extracting compensation from an internal offender where this was found to be due.

3. With time, after conflicts between different Protection Associations within a certain area, one would emerge as dominant. Since not everyone would have chosen (and some might not have been able to afford to pay) to join a Mutual Protection Association, some individuals – 'Independents' – would remain outside the protection provided by the now dominant Protection Agency. These Independents would retain the right to protect themselves against all others; against them the Protection Agency would protect the members within its care, for example by punishing 'any one who uses on one of its clients a procedure that it finds unreliable and unfair'. At this stage, since the Protection Agency does not provide protection for all the individuals living within the area it covers, it falls short of having the characteristics of a fully-constituted state.

4. The final step is taken when the dominant Associations' Protection Agency assumes control over all the individuals within its area, the former Independents being compensated for the loss of their autonomy by the extension to them of the protection afforded by the Agency. At this stage a state comes into existence.

The essential characteristic of the emergence of the state is that its development is spontaneous, unplanned and unintended, those involved perhaps not noticing the evolution that is occurring. This process Nozick terms the 'invisible hand process' – the invisible hand being the forces of rational self-interest that determine at each stage what is to follow.

At its full development the function of the state remains that of the first Protection Agency – the protection of the natural rights that are central in Nozick's scheme of things. Of particular significance among these is the right to possessions. An individual has a natural right to whatever he holds, provided that the way he came to hold each part of his property was justified. A person is entitled to hold property (Nozick speaks of 'justice in holdings' being satisfied) if either:

(i) the property, when acquired, was not the property of anyone else – if it was 'unheld'. Entitlement under this head Nozick terms 'justice in acquisition'; or
(ii) the property was transferred to the present holder by a valid means, such as gift or sale (and not, eg, as a result of fraud or theft). This form of entitlement Nozick terms 'justice in transfer'. In addition to transferring property to another, a person may

divest himself of it, thereby returning it to an 'unheld' state and so making the item available to be acquired by another person.

Since the role of the state is not to extend beyond protecting the rights of the inhabitants against infringements in such forms as the use of force, theft, fraud, or breach of contract, its function is confined to acting as 'nightwatchman' – to see that nothing wrong is done and, in the absence of wrongdoing, to do nothing. Its functions are minimal; it is a 'minimal state'.

The functions that may legitimately be undertaken by a minimal state are twofold. It must obtain compensation for a person whose rights have been infringed from the person who has done the damage and, in order to prevent possible future damage, it may prohibit certain forms of potentially dangerous conduct. Nozick gives as an example here a restriction on the right of an epileptic to drive a motor car. But since such a prohibition restricts a person's right to conduct his affairs as he chooses, the prohibition can only be justified if the person on whom the restriction is placed receives compensation for the loss of his freedom of action in the sphere concerned. (In the case of the epileptic, Nozick suggests that the compensation could take the form of free public transport.) There will, however, be a check on the extent to which the state imposes prohibitions. This is because, if the restriction constitutes such a degree of interference that the sum payable as compensation would be higher than the value to the community of the increase in security obtained, members of the state would be unwilling, or unable, to pay the price, and so no restriction would be imposed.

Perhaps the most important factor determining what for Nozick is a just society is the principle that, although a person's natural rights include a right to life and health, this does not include a right to the things needed for the realisation of these rights, for example food or medicine. A person without food cannot have a right to require a person with food to share it with him since this would violate the natural right of the person with food to decide for himself what he does with his possessions. 'No one has a right to something whose realisation requires certain uses of things and activities that other people have rights and entitlements over.'[41] Thus a right to life consists, not of a right to the means necessary to live, but a right not to be killed or injured by others. By the same reasoning there can be no right to equal opportunities.

Since an individual's natural rights do not include a right to be assisted by others, there can be no question of the state using its

41 *Anarchy, State and Utopia* p 238.

coercive powers to compel one group of citizens to aid others, as by the imposition of taxation for purposes of social welfare. Any measure that had the effect of redistributing wealth would infringe the natural right of those who held property to retain it. 'Taxation of earnings from labour is on a par with forced labour ... taking the earnings of "n" hours labour is like taking "n" hours from the person; it is like forcing the person to work "n" hours for another's purpose ... The fact that others intentionally intervene to threaten force – (to ensure payment of taxes) – makes the taxation system one of forced labour.'[42]

Any attempt to justify the redistribution of property on social grounds (or to reduce the degree of inequality of the distribution of property) within a state is ill-founded since it looks at entitlements from the viewpoint of how things stand at the time of the proposed redistribution (ie and says 'the present distribution is unjust'). This viewpoint is defective since the proper perspective is historical: the present distribution is just if it came about in a just manner, ie if the present holders (both the haves and the have-nots) acquired whatever they hold in a just manner, that is to say in accordance with the principles of 'justice in holdings'. '... the holdings of a person are just if he is entitled to them by the principles of justice in acquisition and transfer ...'[43]

Nozick recognises that transfers can, and do, take place that are not in accordance with the principle of justice in acquisition (as where a person takes what is not 'unheld', being already possessed by another) or justice in transfer (as where a person acquires property as a result of fraud). Where this has happened the injustice ought to be rectified. The execution of this rectification Nozick treats as a third aspect of 'justice in holdings'. The scheme is therefore this:

$$
\text{Natural rights} \begin{cases} \text{Life} \\ \text{Health} \\ \text{Liberty} \\ \text{Possessions – Justice in holdings} \end{cases} \begin{cases} \text{Justice in acquisition} \\ \text{Justice in transfer} \\ \text{Justice in rectification} \end{cases}
$$

Where the failure to observe justice in acquisition or justice in transfer was that of the present holder of property (eg as where A defrauds B of property and A still holds the property concerned) then the injustice is capable of being, and should be, rectified (ie in our example, by requiring A to restore the property to B). Where the

42   Ibid, p 169.
43   Ibid, p 153.

injustice occurred at an earlier stage, before the present holder acquired the property, then the question arises, Nozick recognises, as to whether the present holder, who has acquired possession by legitimate means, owes a duty to restore the property to the person, or the descendants of the person, who was wrongfully deprived. A further question, Nozick realises, is whether a present holder owes a duty to restore property (on the ground that a predecessor in title of his had acquired the property wrongfully) if the person originally wronged had himself acquired the property wrongfully. Nozick concedes,[44] 'I do not know of a thorough or theoretically sophisticated treatment of such issues.'[45] He suggests that what should be done is for the best estimate possible to be made as to what would have happened if the illegality had not occurred and for present holdings to be brought into line with this.

In the absence, however, of any defects in the way that property has been acquired (either by original acquisition or subsequent transfer) then the existing distribution of property within a society is just: 'If each person's holdings are just, then the total set of holdings is just.'[46]

These, then, are the views that Nozick puts forward. At the end of the road, whether Nozick's concept of justice represents a fairy-tale for the fireside, or a presentation of justice according to a Perelmanian essential category in the form 'to each according to what he has legitimately obtained', or a fanciful dream (good or bad according to the state of one's bank account) or a juris-prudentially neutral analysis, or a political manifesto, is for the reader to decide.

---

44 Ibid, p 153.
45 A 'thorough and sophisticated', though not necessarily just or perfect, treatment is provided in English law by the application of the principle of *nemo dat quod non habet*, coupled with the relevant provisions of the Sale of Goods Act 1979 and the Limitation Act 1980.
46 *Anarchy, State and Utopia* p 153.

CHAPTER 16

You really want to know?

The 'American realists'[1]

In the earlier part of this century an assemblage of writers in the United States expressed, on certain aspects of the law, views that came to be regarded as constituting a particular school of thought, a school to which the name 'American realism' came to be applied.

'Realism' is a word with a variety of meanings. As used in philosophy, the word represents the notion, explained in Chapter 1, that universals have an existence distinct from particular instances of a class that a universal represents. Used in another sense, realism means relating to the real world, the world as it actually operates. In this sense it carries the idea of being practical, down to earth, pragmatic. Realism in this sense applied to intellectual matters indicates the testing of theories by measuring them against what is observed in the world, and dismissing theories that fail to match the recorded facts. It is in this second sense that the word 'realism' is used in the phrase 'American realism'.

In this school of jurisprudential thinking certain names stand out, in particular those of Oliver Wendell Holmes (1841–1935), Jerome Frank (1889–1957), John Chipman Gray (1839–1915) and Karl Llewellyn (1893–1962). Here, rather than setting out to paraphrase what each of these writers said – their individual views are best sought in their own writings – we shall seek to set out the principal strands that ran through the thinking of the school as a whole. It must be emphasised, though, that there was never any one corpus of agreed opinion, no central creed, no consensus. There was no more than a

---

1 J W Harris *Legal Philosophies* (2nd edn, 1997) Chap 8; Davies and Holdcroft *Jurisprudence: Texts and Commentary* Chap 5.

series of contributions in books and journals on legal thinking by certain, principally American, writers over a period of years. The link between the ideas of some of them is tenuous. What justifies the notion that they together formed a 'school' is the existence of one common and all-pervading characteristic, namely a determination to look at the law with open eyes, to look, not at the old books, but at the law as it actually operated in everyday practice, whether in the Supreme Court in Washington or the sheriff's court at Jackson Hole, Wyoming. Thus although there was no one shared view, there was a shared attitude, a shared approach.

1 Prediction

It was a remark by Oliver Wendell Holmes that set the ball rolling. 'Take the fundamental question, What constitutes the law? You will find some text writers telling you that it is ... a system of reason, that it is a deduction from principles of ethics or admitted axioms or what not, which may or may not coincide with the decisions. But if we take the view of our friend the bad man we shall find that he does not care two straws for the axioms or deductions, but that he does want to know what the Massachusetts or English courts are likely to do in fact. I am much of his mind. The prophecies of what the courts will do in fact, and nothing more pretentious, are what I mean by the law.' In speaking of the 'bad man' it is clear that Holmes was intending to include any person who is having to contemplate legal proceedings, whether (as a 'bad man') as an accused in criminal proceedings, or a litigant, whether plaintiff or defendant, in a civil action.

If someone who is having to face being a party to legal proceedings consults his solicitor, the principal thing that he will want to know is what his chances are of success – success in the form of an acquittal, or a finding of a defendant to be not liable, or the grant of a remedy sought by a plaintiff. 'How do I stand?' he will ask. 'What's the law on the matter?' In asking the latter question he will think that if he is told the law, he will know the answer to his first question, whether he will win or lose. This is what matters – the outcome of the case. For him, the outcome *is* the law – a finding of guilty and five years in prison; a successful claim for £50,000 in damages. So he presses his adviser. 'Come on, tell me. What's the law. Will I win or lose?'

'Well it's not as simple as that,' his adviser explains. 'We can never be absolutely sure which way a case will go. Your claim is for damages for negligence by the defendant in allowing three Jack

Russell terriers to be at large in her garden when you called at her request to clear her blocked drains. We cannot know for certain whether or not the judge will decide that there was negligence.'

'But I have paid £600 for a barrister's opinion, and this advised me to sue.'

'Yes, but the defendant is denying negligence. So it seems that she has had a barrister's opinion advising her that she is likely to be able to show that she was not negligent.'

'But aren't there *rules* on the matter? I thought that the law *consisted* of rules, rules to which one could refer in order to find out the legal position on any matter. Is that not so?'

'Well, regarding your claim, there is a statute and there are judicial decisions. But the statute is general in its application and the circumstances of one decided case never fit exactly the circumstances of a later one.'

'So the outcome has to be decided afresh each time?'

'If the matter goes to court, yes. Though of course in more cases than not people decide in their own minds what they think the court would decide and settle out of court on the basis of what they assess would be the outcome if the matter proceeded to judgment – abandoning the claim or paying an agreed sum, as the case may be.'

'So in my case, over this attack by those dogs, you cannot tell me what the law is – what the law is for *me* – all you can do is to guess at the outcome?'

'… seek to predict the decision.'

'So,' the would-be plaintiff says, waving his hand round the book-lined office, 'all these books add up to nothing.'

'The best that any lawyer can do is to advise …'

'"Advise" nothing,' exclaims the client, standing up. 'I thought that there was something called "the law", and that you and that £600 barrister of yours could between you tell me what it is. The whole thing's a myth, a guessing game. A game that *I'm* expected to pay for.'

'Of course,' the solicitor says later to his secretary who had come in with a cup of tea and heard the last part of the conversation, 'in a way he's right. The law does not have any teeth until the courts decide something. Indeed, until there is a decision, in way there *isn't* any law. All we *can* do is to predict.'

The limitations of the notion that the essence of law consists of prediction have been well explored. It has been pointed out, for example, that the judicial bodies (whether individual judges or officials such as Masters, or panels of judges) whose decisions are sought to be predicted are established by rules. So not all law is a matter of prediction. That this is so is even clearer when we think of the multitude of matters, particularly in the field of public and administrative law that are properly described as law but which do not lie in the field of litigation and therefore are not a matter of prediction.[2] For example, we could hardly regard a law that laid down that a person was allowed to vote in parliamentary elections when he attained the age of 18 as being in essence a matter of prediction.

A further criticism of the notion that the law is a matter of prediction is that, even if prediction is one function that has to be performed, it is only one of various functions that are performed in the course of the law's operation. If law is seen in terms of the tasks that are performed, then 'the standpoints of all participants in the legal process [eg, the legislator, the advocate, the judge, the jury] would need to be accommodated and the relationship among them indicated'.[3] The standpoint of the would-be litigant alone is not enough for us to understand the nature of the law and its operation.

2 The centrality of the role of the judge

Another strand in American realism, linked with the first but distinct from it, is that which emphasises the significance of the role of the courts in any consideration of the nature of law. It is the role of the judge that is central to a proper understanding.

This view was carried to its limit by J C Gray, who regarded all law as judge-made law. Statutes are not laws by virtue of their enactment. They only become law when applied by a decision of the courts. Only then does a legislative enactment spring to life and acquire actual force. Legislation is therefore no more than a source of law: it is the courts that 'put life into the dead words of the statutes'.[4]

3 Scepticism over rules

The conversation overheard earlier between the solicitor and his client touches on a further strand in American realism: the questioning of the significance of rules. 'All these books,' said the

2 W Twining (1973) 58 Cornell LR 275.
3 Ibid.
4 J C Gray *The Nature and Sources of Law* (2nd edn) p 125.

client, 'add up to nothing.' This aspect of realism Jerome Frank[5] called 'rule scepticism' – a scepticism as to whether rules, if they exist, in practice play the part traditionally ascribed to them. The fact that such a multiplicity of rules exists, and that some can lead to conflicting results may mean that, in practice, in reaching a decision a judge does not explore the whole corpus of the relevant law, the statutes and the earlier cases, and from these by a process of distillation find the principle that guides him to the correct decision. He may pretend to do this, and his judgment may be written in a way that suggests that he has done this. But it may be that what has happened is that the judge has thought about the matter, decided who he thinks has the best case, and then gone to his law books to work out the chain of reasoning that will lead to his predetermined conclusion. Here it will not be the rules of law that settle the outcome but the judge's gut feeling as to which side ought to win, for which he later finds support (or, where the case has been argued before him, adopts the arguments of one counsel or the other). Whether, and if so how often, decisions are reached in this way cannot be known. There is though, for those steeped in the law after years of training and practice, a reluctance to accept that this is how decisions are reached. There is an in-built desire to tell ourselves that it is the rules of law that determine the outcome of issues before the courts, since a belief in all-pervading rules satisfies a need for security. Just as a child's need for security is met by knowing what he can do and what he can't, by knowing where he stands, so in adult life the need for security, albeit intellectual security, can be satisfied to some degree by the apparent logic of the law. 'The language of judicial decision is mainly the language of logic. And the logical method and form flatter that longing for certainty and for repose which is in every human mind. But certainty generally is an illusion.'[6] (The very smell of a law library can impart a feeling of stability, rationality, logic, order.)

But any such sense of certainty and order is, it is argued, an illusion. There *is* no certainty. To the extent that rules exist, they are at best general propositions, incapable of providing a fixed answer to the infinite multitude of possible disputes that can arise in the course of human existence: 'General propositions, "do not decide concrete cases",'[7] said O W Holmes.

This assertion by Mr Justice Holmes brings us to another aspect of the scepticism expressed about the significance of rules. This

5   *Law and the Modern Mind* Preface.
6   O W Holmes *Collected Papers* p 50.
7   Ibid.

concerned the way in which, it was maintained, lawyers had in the past regarded points of law as being deduced, namely by the application of syllogistic logic. This system of reasoning, it will be recalled (by those who have not made the error of omitting to read Chapter 1), is based on the assumption that universal propositions can be posited from which particular conclusions can be drawn. Lawyers had supposed themselves to be reaching conclusions on points of law by the same process: find the relevant general principle and from this could be deduced the subsidiary principle that governed the issue in question. But, Dewey contended,[8] the existence of such general principles was an illusion. Principles, to the extent that such existed, did not pre-exist factual situations. They emerged as statements of the ways in which it had been found that a particular series of cases had been dealt with: there were no 'universals' outside and antecedent to particular cases. (Whether the criticism of how lawyers were said to reach conclusions on points of law is a valid one is for the reader to decide. Some may consider that in practice there is less difference between the traditional approach and Dewey's view of the process than Dewey supposed.)

The strand of realism that denies the significance attached in traditional thinking to rules of law has been subject to various criticisms. Those who were sceptical about the place traditionally ascribed to rules in our law looked, it was said, at too narrow a field. They looked, Jerome Frank pointed out, at the upper, appellate courts (referring here to those of the United States). When we bear in mind the nature of the American Constitution, with its written form, and with the role of the Supreme Court acting not only as the supreme appellate court but also as adjudicator on the validity of legislation passed by the individual states, we can understand the scepticism expressed about the part played by rules in the court's deliberations. In deciding whether a piece of state legislation infringes any of the articles of the Bill of Rights or any of the subsequent amendments, we can see that the court is on its own, being called upon to make decisions in a realm where no rules exist, no rules at any rate of the kind that operate in the sphere, for example, of limitation, or perpetuities, or the attestation of wills. When the Supreme Court is called upon to decide whether the law that prohibits a woman from having an abortion infringes a right conferred by an Amendment to the Constitution, it is being called upon to decide a moral issue. The question may be framed, and the judgments delivered, in a legal

8 'Logical Method and the Law' (1924) 10 Cornell LQ 17.

form, but in reality the court is being required to act as the conscience of the nation: to decide a matter of right and wrong. Previous cases may be cited in argument, but no rules, rules of the traditional kind, exist to guide the court.

This much Frank conceded. But it took, he believed, too narrow a view. When we look at the whole field of law, civil and criminal, public and private, we find a myriad of topics in which rules do exist. Just because there may be uncertainty as to the outcome of the application of a rule does not mean that no rule exists. In the sphere of English land law, an entitlement to a right over another's land can only exist in the form of an easement if the right concerned benefits one piece of land and is a burden on another; there must be a dominant and a servient tenement. Further, the right must be for the benefit of the dominant land, not merely for the benefit of the owner of the land personally. Who can deny that these are rules? The fact that it is for the court to decide, on the evidence, whether the right benefits the land or the owner personally, does not mean that no rule exists. In some spheres rules are so certain as barely to be capable of being the subject of litigation. If a civilian client produces a will signed by only one witness can we say that no rule exists that makes the will invalid? The more we look at the law as it is applied in everyday practice we find that rules exist, rules the application of which entails no question of prediction or, where an element of prediction may enter in, rules that provide a framework within which the court is required to make its decision. Can anyone who has struggled with the rule against perpetuities suggest that rules do not have a significant part in the law's operation?

It is the existence of rules that enables cases to be settled out of court. It is true that if D agrees to pay P a certain sum by way of settlement of a claim this will be because his legal adviser has told him of his prediction that if the matter goes to court the judge would find against him. But it is because of the existence of a rule, for example that a contract can be accepted impliedly by the offeree's conduct, that enables the prediction to be made.

4   Fact scepticism

Despite these objections, however, these protestations that rules do exist and play a significant part in determining the course of the law, some sympathy may nevertheless be felt for the scepticism expressed over the significance of rules when cases are heard by the higher courts of the American system. Jerome Frank referred to this scepticism as 'rule scepticism'. From this he distinguished scepticism over another aspect of the law, scepticism over the possibility of making any realistic assessment of the likely outcome of cases owing to the virtual impossibility of knowing in advance what facts will emerge during the trial and how these will be interpreted by the court. This second group of sceptics Frank called 'fact sceptics'. 'They, too,' he wrote, 'engaging in rule scepticism', peer behind the paper rules. Together with the rule sceptics, they have stimulated interest in factors, influencing upper-court decisions, of which, often, the opinions of those courts give no hint. But the fact sceptics go much further. Their primary interest is in the trial courts. No matter how precise or definite may be the formal legal rules, say these fact sceptics, no matter what the discoverable uniformities behind these formal rules, nevertheless it is impossible, and will always be impossible, because of the elusiveness of the facts on which decisions turn, to predict future decisions in most (not all) lawsuits, not yet begun or not yet tried.[9]

Both the 'rule sceptics' and the 'fact sceptics' expressed their scepticism with regret. They deplored the failure of the system to enable a would-be litigant to be advised with at least a degree of certainly as to the probable outcome of a case. A system that lacked certainty to such a degree was, they contended, defective. Llewellyn wrote,[10] 'The worry is [not about the uprightness of the courts but] instead over *reckonability* of results.... . Results are conceived to be hopelessly unpredictable. It is not mere uncertainty that festers, it is the feeling of hopeless helplessness. That hopeless helplessness wars with an old and not unreasonable tradition that it should not be; that it is wrong for such a thing to be. I am not maundering about "certainty" and womb-yearning or about law "the solid" as a father-substitute or similar unnecessary tripe. I am dealing with the sound and right feeling of the American lawyer and the American law-consumer that the work of his appellate tribunals has no business to be hopelessly unreckonable.'

5 The illusive factors

Recognition of the existence of what Frank called the 'illusive factors', factors that affect the outcome of court cases, together with

9 *Law and the Modern Mind* p viii.
10 *The Common Law Tradition* (1960) p 198.

attempts to pinpoint, and investigate the significance of these, constitutes a further strand in American realism.

Speaking of the prejudices to which a judge or juryman may, albeit unconsciously be subject, Frank wrote: 'Those prejudices, when they are racial, religious, political, or economic may sometimes be surmised by others. But there are some hidden, unconscious biases of trial judges or jurors – such as, for example, plus or minus reactions to women, or unmarried women, or red-haired women, or brunettes, or men with deep voices or high-pitched voices, or fidgety men, or men who wear thick eyeglasses, or those who have pronounced gestures or nervous tics – biases of which no one can be aware.'[11] Here Frank was speaking of the factors that could influence judges and juries in trial courts, prejudices that could affect the credibility accorded to the accounts of witnesses, and so affect what is decided in the minds of the judge and the jurymen to be the facts of the case, and hence the judge's summing up of the evidence and the jury's verdict. The significance of the 'illusive factors' was recognised as being equally important in the judgments of the higher, appellate courts. If a judge of the Supreme Court was called upon to deliver a judgment upon some matter concerning, say, the legality of abortion, no one could imagine that a judge who was a practising Catholic could separate entirely his personal views from the matter before him. (*Muller v The State of Oregon*[12] and *Lochner v New York*[13] provide examples of cases in which it is hard to think that the judges' personal views could not fail to influence the decisions reached.) So important was the belief among the realist school that the attitude of the individual judges influenced the outcome of cases that the personal background of the higher judiciary was examined in minute detail and compared against each judge's track record of decisions, with a view to predicting the outcome of cases that might come before them.

In the light of the power of the US Supreme Court to adjudicate on the legality of state and federal laws, a power that can shape the country's legal future, the appointments made by the President to the Supreme Court were for the realists – and, indeed, continue to be – a matter of the greatest interest. A President cannot be sure that an appointee to the Supreme Court will continue to reflect the same attitudes after his appointment, but nevertheless, by seeking to pick a judge who shares his own viewpoints on crucial issues, a President can indirectly influence the trend of future decisions.

11   *Law and the Modern Mind* p ix.
12   (1908) 203 US 412.
13   (1905) 198 US 45.

Emphasis on the significance of the factors that can influence a judge's decisions – his social background, his cultural and intellectual interests, his relationship in childhood with his parents, and in later life with his wife and children, his political sympathies, his religious views, his financial interests and his psychological make up; even (particularly in trial cases in the lower courts) his frame of mind on a particular day influenced by what he ate for breakfast – emphasis on the significance of all these factors and a study of the extent to which such matters influenced decisions, came to be termed 'behaviouralism'.

6 Look at the whole process

The attempts to elucidate the factors that influence the courts' decisions were one part of a drive towards examining legal processes as a whole. This latter drive forms a fourth thread in American realism – a determination to examine afresh all aspects of the workings of the administration, procedures and practices of the courts at all levels of the system. This all-embracing interest took in such matters as the availability of legal assistance to an accused person, the effects of the availability or non-availability of such assistance on the outcome of trials, the operation of the jury system and the effectiveness of various forms of deterrents.

7 Measure the results

In their methods, some working within the school were following the approach of, and adopting the same techniques as, contemporary sociologists. The operation of the law was to be examined for what it was now seen to be, one aspect of social organisation. In adopting the tools and methods of contemporary sociological research it was natural that attention should be paid to the importance of statistics and, in more recent times, to the analysis of the data so collected by computers. Much faith was placed in the value for jurisprudence of the scientific method. 'Jurimetrics' was the word invented to connote the study of legal processes by scientific means, in particular through the analysis of statistics. 'The next step forward,' wrote L Loevinger, 'in the long path of man's progress must be from jurisprudence (which is mere speculation about law) to *jurimetrics* – which is the scientific investigation of legal problems. In the field of social control (which is law) we must at least begin to use the same approach and the same methods that have enabled us to progress toward greater knowledge and control in every other field.'[14]

8 Shaking the dust off

The attitude of questioning that pervaded the school led to the re-examination not only of the processes of the law but also old established concepts such as sovereignty, *stare decisis* and the 'rule of the law'. Unquestioning acceptance of the old ideas was no longer enough. The traditional notions passed down from one generation to the next must be tested. What did they *mean*? Did they have any meaning at all? Old ideas for so long unquestionably accepted must, if found wanting, be discarded. Writing of the difference between the old approach to jurisprudence and the new study of jurimetrics, Loevinger said, '... the problems of jurisprudence are basically meaningless, since they can only be debated but never decided nor even investigated; whereas the questions of jurimetrics are meaningful since they are capable of being investigated, and ultimately answered, even though we may not know the answers now. Second, the problems of jurisprudence are not truly significant problems, since even if they were "solved", in the only sense in which they could be "solved" – by the giving of authoritative definitions, the "solutions" would have no practical consequences in our lives. On the other hand, all of the questions of jurimetrics are genuinely significant, since even a partial or tentative answer to any one is likely to have far-reaching consequences for society and for the individual. In this sense, jurimetrics is eminently "practical" in its approach, as contrasted with the philsophical speculations of jurisprudence.'[15]

The questioning of old ideas extended to the methods of training lawyers. What was being taught in the law schools? How was the teaching being carried out? What value was there to future practitioners in what was being taught? (It was from this re-assessment of teaching methods that the use of the case-book method evolved.)

So wide, indeed, was the net cast that the movement's concern shifted to an assessment of the place of law generally in contemporary society. The law should no longer be treated as a watertight, self-contained discipline, but should be set, and seen, in its total social and economic context.

14 'Jurimetrics – The Next Step Forward' (1949) 33 Minn LR 455.
15 Ibid.

9 Self-examination

A final strand in or, at any rate, characteristic of American realism was the emphasis placed by writers of the school on the importance of the movement itself. The members of no other school of jurisprudence have devoted so much space to self-examination and congratulation, so many pages to writing about their methods, about the great things that the application of these would achieve and, increasingly, to writing about each other. Much time was spent in front of the looking-glass. Undoubtedly the movement opened windows and let in fresh air, but whether the scepticism and iconoclasm and reformist zeal in fact transformed the processes of the law in the way that was promised is an open question. Nevertheless, even if the operation of the law remained essentially unaltered (and this is a matter of debate), the way in which law was thought about was irreversibly changed. Today we take for granted the presence on the shelves of law libraries books with such titles as 'Law and society' and series such as that published under the title 'Law in Context'. That law is properly seen as a social phenomenon is today a truism. Credit for bringing about this realisation belongs in no small measure to the writings of the realist movement in the earlier part of the century. As has been remarked, 'We are all realists now'.

CHAPTER 17

Northern Light

The Scandinavian Realists

For very many centuries a chasm has existed in philosophy. On one side stand those who maintain that the truth of any proposition is capable of being reached by the application of human reason – by the application of what is termed *a priori reasoning*, in the form, for example, 'Because of X, it follows that Y, because of Y, the consequence must be Z'. For those on this side of the divide, knowledge is capable of being acquired by pure thought, unsupported by experience or experiment. Those who subscribe to this view are termed rationalists, their viewpoint, rationalism.

On the other side stand those who maintain that nothing can be known to be true that does not rest on the experience of the senses.[1] Those in this group are termed *empiricists*.[2] Since empiricists maintain that no knowledge exists other than that which is verifiable by the senses, they deny that there can be any knowledge gained exclusively by a priori reasoning. (A difficulty for empiricists lies, incidentally, in explaining the basis of knowledge the truth of which they do not dispute but which is reached solely by the application of reason alone, unsupported by observation, an example being certain aspects of mathematics.)

European continental philosophy has, broadly, tended to be of a rationalist bent; British philosophy to be characterised by empiricism (as that of Locke, Berkely and Hume).

Empiricist thinking did, however, form the foundation of a school of philosophy that emerged in Vienna in the 1920s and 1930s

---

1 Or on what is expressed in forms of statement that can be observed to be true by the senses.
2 Empirical: relying on observation and experiment, not on theory. OED.

and which came to be known as logical positivism (or logical empiricism or scientific empiricism). The principal interest of those in the Vienna circle lay in the application of scientific thinking to the resolution of the age old disputes of metaphysicians (the resolution being achieved by the issues concerned being blasted out of existence as devoid of any ascertainable meaning).

Hagerstrom

These matters are explained by way of introduction to the work of Axel Hagerstrom (1868-1939), a Swedish philosopher whose feet rested firmly in the empiricist, logical positivist, camp. The strength of Hagerstrom's empiricism lead him to claim that the language in which the concepts of western law have traditionally been expressed amount on examination to mere chimera.

His method was to take a word (or phrase) and then, like someone peeling an onion, to strip away, layer by layer, the meanings that had traditionally been associated with it, discarding as he went those that, when tested against the world of fact, were shown to be devoid of any empirically verifiable meaning. Having done this he gave his own view as to the significance that the word or phrase in practice carried.

What, for example, Hagerstrom asked, is meant by saying that a person has a certain *right?* – a right conferred by a legislator or one that comes into existence as a result of a transaction between citizens, for example the making of a contract. In examining this question he points to the distinction between a person *having* a right (we can imagine a right to fish in a certain river) and his *enjoying* the right (actually fishing there, ie not being stopped from fishing by the owner of the riverbank); and to the converse distinction between a person being under a legal obligation (or duty) (an obligation to let X fish in the river) and the obligation being fulfilled (being compelled to let X fish in the river). Hagerstrom finds that rights are related to the circumstances of the actual world in that when we say that a person has a right we mean that 'he who possesses it either (i) will obtain from the party who is under the corresponding obligation the advantage to which he claims to be entitled; or (ii) will acquire from the courts a power of compulsion, provided that he fulfils their requirements, particularly in the matter of proving facts which the law explicitly states or which custom tacitly implies as conferring the 'right'. If neither alternative is fulfilled, 'there is nothing whatever left of "rights" and "duties"'.[3] Yet, Hagerstrom says, according to the usual way of looking at things, as soon as facts exist that are regarded as conferring a right, or imposing a duty (for example, if a statute conferred a right to walk on land registered under the Commons Registered Act 1965), the right is thought of as a reality, something that actually exists from the moment of, in our example, the coming into force of the Act, and this is so notwithstanding that a 'person who has the right neither actually enjoys the advantage attaching to it without recourse to the courts nor is able to fulfil the conditions required to obtain an equivalent by process of law'[4] (eg does not have the money to obtain an order from the court).

Hagerstrom shows the vacuity of the notion of right in another way. How can a person be regarded as having a certain right, even if he has the money to take court proceedings, if he does not know whether, in the event, the court will in fact find in his favour? How can a right have any existence before a court enforces it?

What is left of the notion of a right if the person who allegedly holds the right neither enjoys the right, nor is capable of enforcing it? (Or, if he has the means of enforcing it, does not know whether the claim will be upheld?) Nothing. The right has no existence in the real world and is seen to have no more than the character of a supernatural power, the notion of 'duty' assuming equally the character of a super-natural obligation.

The power is 'supernatural' in that it refers to 'a reality which is elevated above the physical world'. But at the same time 'every right is supposed to have as its objects an advantage which belongs to the physical world ...' Thus 'the supposed supernatural power or obligation, as the case may be, is a logical absurdity.'[5]

Having demonstrated the emptiness of 'right', Hagerstrom tells us wherein lies the true significance of the notion of rights in a legal system. This lies, he says, in the fact then when the law decrees that something should be so, ie that someone should have right and another should be under a correlative obligation, this serves as psychological means of compulsion towards a certain end.

Here we reach the matter that forms an important thread in the thinking of Hagerstrom and those who were influenced by him in the Scandinavian school of jurists – the significance of the psychological effect of legal concepts on citizens' behaviour. Although the notion of a right may be empty, the fact that a citizen is given to

3   *Inquiries into the Nature of Law and Morals* p 323.
4   Ibid.
5   Ibid, p 324.

understand that he has a right imbues him with a power and strength to employ it. 'We feel that there are mysterious forces in the background from which we can derive support.'[6] The notion of duty similarly carries a psychological effect. It gives rise to a feeling of being under an obligation to act in a certain way.

In finding that the significance in legal concepts lay in their psychological effect, Hagerstrom was not dismissing this effect as unimportant. On the contrary, the psychological effects of legal concepts were important for the part they played in the regulation of society: obedience to the law rests not so much on the knowledge that sanctions exist as on the psychological pressure for compliance that law exerts.

Other concepts analysed by Hagerstrom included the notion of property, the will of the state (embracing here Austin's notion of the command of the sovereign), the binding quality of law. In all these cases his conclusion is that the 'insuperable difficulty in finding facts which correspond to our ideas of such [concepts], forces us to suppose that there are no such facts and that we are here concerned with ideas which have nothing to do with reality.'[7]

From what has been said it will be no surprise to learn that Hagerstrom rejected the notion of natural law as meaningless metaphysics, transcendental chimera. Nor is it any surprise to note that with regard to the existence of values, Hagerstrom was a non-cognitivist – a non-cognitivist not just in the sense of believing that absolutes were unknowable, but of believing that such objective values did not exist. If someone says that a certain course of action is good, what he is saying is that he approves it: that it ought to be. Thus the purported objectivity of the 'is', is no more than an expression of an 'ought', an ought which, being empirically unverifiable, has no meaningful existence.

Hagerstrom's contribution to jurisprudence lay not only in his own writings but also in his influence on others in the Scandinavian school, in particular on Karl Olivecrona and Alf Ross.

Olivecrona

The nature of law

'Every rule of law,' Olivecrona said, 'is a creation of men'.[8] As to its nature, he rejected the notion of law as being a command, since a

6 Ibid.
7 Ibid.
8 *Law as Fact* p 16.

command 'presupposes one person who commands and another to whom the command is addressed'. Clearly, the complex laws of a modern state are not the command of an individual. Nor is it possible to say that the law is the command of "the state" since the state is an organisation and an organisation cannot issue a command. To say that the state issues commands makes sense only if by this we mean that commands are given by an individual active within the organisation.

With regard to content, Olivecrona considered that the content of a rule of law is 'an idea of an imaginary action by a judge in an imaginary situation.'[9] (For example, if a law makes it an offence not to wear a seat belt in a car that is in motion, for Olivecrona the law consists of imagining the action that a judge will take if faced with an accused found not to have been wearing a seat belt.) But, he adds, 'a rule of law is never intended to be regarded in isolation. It is always connected to other rules and its meaning does not emerge unless this connection is observed. The rule about condemning the murderer to death is not only related to the law of procedure where the actions leading up to the judgment are pictured. Many more rules come into play. The accused must have attained a certain age, he must have been of sound mind when he committed the crime, and so on. Thus the picture of the imagined situation in which judgment is given is very rich in detail. Many rules must be put together in order to make a complete picture of the situation and of the action desired.'[10]

Subject to this qualification regarding the number of rules involved in any one situation, Olivecrona reaches the conclusion referred to above, namely that law may be defined as 'ideas of imaginary actions by people (eg judges) in imaginary situations', the application of the law consisting in 'taking these imaginary actions as models for actual conduct when corresponding situations arise in real life'.[11]

How law is expressed

Olivecrona concedes that notwithstanding the nature that he ascribes to them, rules of law are *expressed* in an imperative form. The meaning of a rule is always 'this action shall be performed under such and such circumstances, this right shall arise from such and such facts, this official shall have this or that power'.[12] This does not,

9   Ibid, p 29.
10   Ibid.
11   Ibid.
12   Ibid.

though, diminish his insistence that law cannot be regarded as a command in the normal sense, because in the normal sense a command is given by one person to another. It is true that the same kind of wording may be used in a command by one person to another as in a rule of law – ('Do this', or 'Don't do that'). But in the case of law, the command is made independently of any personal relationship. They are 'nobody's commands ...'[13] For this reason, Olivecrona terms laws *independent imperatives*.

Psychological pressure

The purpose of those who make laws is to influence the actions of citizens. But this can only be done by influencing their minds – by psychological pressure, psychological pressure that arises from the knowledge that something is the law.

For this influence to operate, legislation must be within a constitution which the populace respects and whose rules they habitually obey, accepting without question that those designated as law givers have the monopoly of the power to legislate. The 'effect of [this] attitude towards the constitution is first, that the constitutional law-givers gain access to a psychological mechanism, through which they can influence the life of the country; secondly that only they gain access to this mechanism and that everybody else is debarred from using it or building up another kind of system'.[14]

What is it that fixes in our minds that something is law? What is it that converts – in British law – a Bill into something that we accept as having the binding force of statute? The change is brought about by the performance of a certain formality, in the case of proposed legislation by the vote of an assembly or the signing of a piece of paper by a person in a prominent position. Our knowledge that a certain formality or ceremony has been performed produces the psychological effect of causing us to accept that a legal event has occurred that has binding force – the conversion of a bill into a statute.

The significance of formalities

Here we reach a key element in Olivecrona's thinking – the psychological effect of the performance of legal formalities or ceremonies. He illustrates[15] the point by using the example[16] of the naming of a ship. If, instead, as intended, of the wife of the president of the

13   Ibid, p 43.
14   Ibid, p 55.
15   *Legal Language and Reality* p 177.
16   From JL Austen.

shipping company pronouncing the words, 'I name this ship the *Queen Elizabeth*', someone rushes up, seizes the bottle, cries 'I name this ship *Generalissimo Stalin*' and smashes the bottle against the ship's side, then since the ceremony has not been duly performed (the person designated not having performed the ceremony), the ship would not carry the name *Generalissimo Stalin*. (So Olivecrona says. Yet there is an irony here. The naming of a ship is cited as an example of a case in which the formality has not been duly performed. Yet the strength of Olivecrona's own point about the psychological effect of the performance of a ceremony is illustrated by the fact that a niggling doubt may occur to us. A ship is named by the speaking of certain words and the smashing of a bottle of alcoholic liquid against the ship's bow. *This had happened.* Was the ship's name, however unintended and irrespective of what is painted on her sides, not therefore *really* '*Generalissimo Stalin*'? At the moment the bottle smashed against the side, had the ship not received its name?)

Olivecrona uses a wedding to illustrate the psychological effects of the performance of a legal formality. For the marriage to take place a ceremony occurs, one 'centering upon a few performative words which purport to make the parties man and wife. What happens? The psychological effect is instantaneous, uniform and far-reaching. Everybody falls into line and regards the newly wedded couple as man and wife'.[17]

Force

The fact that a populace and its officials are conditioned by psychological pressures to accept that law is binding does not, Olivecrona recognises, mean that force is not required to ensure compliance with the law. On the contrary, 'In every community force is consistently applied through the officials of the state more particularly in three forms; police measures against disturbances, infliction of punishments and the execution of civil judgments. In all three cases physical violence or coercion is the ultimate expedient.'[18] So crucial, for Olivecrona, is the place of force in the operation of society that for him the conventional view of force as a back up for the law, available as a last expedient, must be rejected. 'It is,' he says, 'impossible to maintain that law in a realistic sense is guaranteed or protected by force. The real situation is that law – the body of rules summed up as law – consists chiefly of rules *about* force.'[19] For

17   *Law as Fact* p 134.
18   Ibid, p 124.
19   Ibid, p 134.

example, 'rules about "rights" and "duties" which are not also rules for the use of overwhelming force are of little avail in actual life'.[20]

Thus instead of accepting the classification of laws which prescribe conduct (eg wear a seat-belt in a moving car) as being primary, and laws about the consequences of disobedience (prosecution, trial penalties) as secondary, Olivecrona regards laws about the application of force as being primary and laws which prescribe conduct as secondary. (The parallel will be noted with Kelsen's view that the law consists primarily of orders directed to officials.)

Law and morality

One other aspect of Olivecrona's thinking needs to be mentioned – his view of the relationship between law and morality. For some people, the order of thinking is that certain things are morally wrong, and out of these the state decrees that certain ones should be made criminal. Olivecrona rejects this view. Everyone, he explains, 'grows up in a community where legal machinery has existed since time immemorial ... The character is formed under the influence of our surroundings ... [A]mong the forces working within society the law is without doubt one of the foremost. The law certainly cannot be a projection of some innate moral convictions in the child, since it has existed long before he was born. The first indelible impressions in early youth concerning the relations to other people are directly or indirectly derived from the law. But the effect is not only to create fear of the sanctions and cause that individual to adjust himself so as to be able to live without fear. The rules also have a positive moral effect in that they cause a deposit of moral ideas in the mind'.[21]

The imperative forms in which the law is expressed – 'Do not steal!' – are taken up and made 'an integral part of our mental equipment.'[22] 'Several things explain how the rules of law can thus be absorbed by the whole people. The suggestive effect of the imperatives is enormous when there is power behind them – here the majestic power of the state, working relentlessly according to the rules about sanctions. This power is surrounded by august ceremonies and met with a traditional and deep-rooted reverence. All this combines to make a profound impression on the mind, causing us to take the fundamental "commands" of the law to heart as objectively binding.'[23] ... 'The individual is caught in [law's] grip

20 Ibid.
21 Ibid, p 153.
22 Ibid.
23 Ibid, p 154.

from the earliest stage in life and his moral ideas are developed under its influence.'[24] Other factors, Olivecrona recognises, are relevant – rules must appear reasonable; the application of sanctions must be regular and impartial; the imperatives of the law must be inculcated by parents teachers and superiors. But nevertheless it is the existence of the law, and the knowledge of the force that lies behind it, that 'is one of the chief factors in the moulding of our moral standards, and not the other way round'.[25]

Ross

The nature of a norm

It is a major concern of Ross in his most recent work, *Directives and Norms,* to find a definition of a norm. The word norm, he says, carries with it the idea of a requirement, a standard that is intended to be observed, and at the same time the idea of something that is normal in the sense of being something that normally actually happens. A definition that covered only one aspect of these two notions would clearly be inadequate. Both aspects must be included – the notion of directive and the notion of directive being observed. Ross therefore proposes that a norm *is a directive which stands in relation of correspondence to social facts.* (We can for the moment think of the definition in terms of a norm as being a rule that is obeyed.) 'It is ... barely questionable that the fundamental condition for the existence of a norm must be that in the majority of cases the pattern of behaviour presented in the directive ... is followed by the members of the society' to whom the directive applies. (For example, a rule requiring shops to close at certain hours is observed by shopkeepers.)

The *social facts* to which Ross refers in his definition include not only the fact that a directive can be seen to be followed, but also the fact that the directive is followed by the populace 'with the consciousness of following the rule and being bound by it' – people must obey a rule in the knowledge that they are complying with a requirement that is binding on them. It is necessary to make this qualification to the definition, Ross explains, otherwise the definition would include various 'observable regularities of behaviour' – things that people in fact do without being bound to, for example following biological patterns of behaviour (such as going to sleep at night); or

24   Ibid, p 156.
25   Ibid.

following directives of a technical nature (such as laying bricks in the proper way to build a chimney); or following social customs (for example 'to wear wedding ring; to serve mustard with boiled cod'[26]). Such patterns of behaviour as these can be seen to be followed but are followed without being 'internalised', without 'being experienced as binding'.

Meaning of 'binding'

This much, Ross believes, is commonly agreed. But agreement comes to an end when the question is raised as to what is meant by calling a pattern of behaviour 'binding'. For some this means that a person experiences a peculiar kind of mental compulsion, a compulsion expressed in such terms as 'it is my *duty* to do so and so'; 'I *ought* to do such and such' with a consciousness that contrary conduct will be met by disapproval.

For others, a pattern of behaviour is binding where its performance is guaranteed by the threat of coercion in the form of state enforced sanctions. A drawback of this view is, Ross maintains, that much of what is indisputably law exists without a sanction existing in the background to enforce it, and he cites constitutional, administrative and procedural law as examples. This complication disappears if we take the position that legal rules are directed at those in authority, the organs of the state; from such directives (eg a direction to a judge to imprison a person found guilty of manslaughter) a citizen knows that it is forbidden to commit manslaughter, the last norm being implied in the first one directed to the courts. 'The upshot,' Ross concludes, ' is that, in describing a legal order, there is no need to employ a double set of norms, one demanding of citizens a certain type of behaviour (eg not to commit manslaughter) and the other prescribing for agencies of the legal machinery under what conditions coercive sanctions are to be applied (eg if manslaughter has been committed).' However, although *logically* there exists only one set of rules, those directed to officials, in practice, psychologically, two sets of rules do exist since citizens feel that there is a set of rules directed to them, rules that are 'independent entities which are grounds for the reactions of the authorities'.[27]

In reading Ross's views on the above topic, the reader will have noted that with regard to the feeling of compulsion, there are, as acknowledged by Ross, parallels with Hart's treatment of the

26 *Directives and Norms* p 83.
27 Ibid, p 92.

internal and external aspects of rules,[28] and that with regard to the law being directed to officials, coincidence with the views of Kelsen.[29]

Common features

Since the writers whose work has been examined in this chapter are spoken of as forming a distinct school of jurisprudence, they share, as would be expected, certain characteristics. Foremost among these is a rejection of what they regard as metaphysics – the dealing with abstract conceptions as if they had some meaningful existence. We have seen this rejection of abstract notions as having any verifiable meaning when dealing with the work of Hagerstrom,[30] and the same view as to the vacuity of metaphysical speculation was shared by others in the school. Since 'What cannot be verified does not objectively exist', to invoke such concepts as justice is meaningless. (To 'invoke justice,' Ross said, 'is like banging on the table.'[31])

For all the Scandinavian writers the empirical method – verification through observation and experiment – was the only means by which the truth of any matter could be established. And since law could only be understood through the observation of facts, law was in this respect as much a science as the physical sciences. No wonder, then, that the abstract concepts in which law has been traditionally expressed were dismissed as 'metaphysical will-o'-the wisps', 'mere fantasies of the mind'.[32]

No wonder either that the Scandinavians rejected equally the existence of objective values of morality, the existence of absolutes such as goodness. Such values were no more than the expression of emotionally prompted feelings of approval or disapproval.

So much for what the Scandinavians rejected. What contribution – if any – of a constructive kind did they make? Is there any way in which we look at the law differently as a result of what they wrote? Perhaps what most sticks in the mind is the emphasis, seen most clearly in the writing of Olivecrona, on the psychological influence of the law. For example, with regard to the relationship between law and morality, might it not be that, as Olivecrona claimed, the fact that something is made illegal *does* tend to lead to a feeling that

---

28 See Chap 4.
29 See Chap 11.
30 See supra.
31 *Law and Justice* p 275.
32 Lloyd *Introduction to Jurisprudence* p 735.

the thing is morally wrong? Consider the wearing of car seat belts. Before legislation was introduced, few would have regarded not wearing a car seat belt as morally wrong – unwise perhaps, but not immoral. Now that, in the United Kingdom, not wearing a seat belt is in law a crime, is there not, at least to an infinitesimal degree, a feeling that not wearing a seat belt is not only unwise but somehow *wrong*?

With regard to formalities, is it not a fact that the formality and ceremony attached to the passage of legislation, culminating in the announcement in the two Houses of Parliament of the Royal Assent, not merely satisfies the requirements of the constitution but also has the psychological effect of imbuing an enacted bill with the aura of validity? Is there not similarly a psychological dimension to the execution of a document as a deed? – or to the pronouncement of a man and woman as man and wife? (And isn't the name of that ship really, *really*, '*Generalissimo Stalin*'? After all, at the *second* that the bottle hit the ship's side …)

Thus, if the Scandinavian jurists are remembered, it is likely to be principally for how they opened our eyes to the need to take into account the possibility that psychological influences may be at work in the operation of the law and on how, in people's minds, it is regarded.

Why realists?

The Scandinavian writers considered in this chapter are customarily referred to as the Scandinavian realists. Why realists? In what sense of realism is the term 'realist' applied to them? It will be recalled (at any rate by those who have not made the mistake of missing Chapter 1) that realism can have more than one meaning. In philosophy, realism means a belief that some kind of thing, or state of affairs, or some kind of fact, has a real existence, ie independent of ourselves and not, eg existing solely in our minds, or as no more than a word in our language. Alternatively, the word can carry the everyday sense of being realistic, concerned with practicalities, adopting a pragmatic approach, looking at the actualities of a situation.

Clearly the Scandinavian jurists are not realists in the first sense of the word. Indeed, in their dismissal of metaphysics concepts such as duties they were the opposite of realist. Their realism can therefore (if indeed the description 'realist' is in fact appropriate) only be that of the second, non-technical, sense of the word.

The Scandinavians and the American realists

It is use of the word realist in this second, everyday, sense of the word that causes the Scandinavian jurists to share the same label as the American realists, treated in Chapter 16. Both schools were realists in the sense of wanting to get behind the curtains they believed concealed the actualities of the law. This much they shared in common. But little else. Although both schools claimed that empiricism was the only approach that could produce meaningful results, it was the Americans who put their empiricism into practice, with detailed analysis of what actually happened in the working of their legal system. For all their stress on jurisprudence properly being a science, the observations of the Scandinavians were made from the armchair rather than in the courtroom. (It may have been noted that the word 'realists' does not appear in the title of this chapter.)

In their objectives, in their methods, in their conclusions (and in the flavour of their writing), a great deal more separates the Scandinavians and the American realists than joins them. This should perhaps not surprise us when we note that while those in the American school were in the main lawyers by training, many of whom with detailed knowledge of the courts, the penal system, the prisons – of how the law *worked* – those in the Scandinavian school were philosophers and academics, theorising from their book-lined studies.

Indeed, in their reliance on a priori reasoning[33] rather than observation, the Scandinavians are perhaps closer to the metaphysicians they criticised than they would like to be suggested.

---

33   See Lloyd *Introduction to Jurisprudence* p 749.

CHAPTER 18

Wholly estimable?

Liberalism

Since the next two topics to be considered, the New Critics and Feminist Jurisprudence, are in some respects rejections of liberalism, it will be pertinent at this point to include a short chapter on the subject of liberalism.

The ideas that go to make up liberalism can (like natural law) be compared to a cord consisting of different coloured strands. At some stages in history, one colour dominates, at other times another; or two or more colours may be equally prominent. Thus liberalism can mean different things at different periods of history, and even at one time it can mean different things to different people.

From the early times, however, one thread runs though the entire cord. This is the assertion of the importance of the individual in relation to the group of which he forms part.

At all stages in human evolution men have lived in groups, whether hunting groups or nation states. In some societies, at some periods, the interests of the group have been regarded as taking priority over those of any one individual within it. The military organisation of Sparta provides an illustration.

But recognition of the significance of human individuality made an early appearance, for example in the Athens of the fourth century, and in the teaching of the New Testament. It was not until after the end of the Middle Ages, with its stratified society, that we find the origins of ideas that were later to develop into what became termed liberalism.

The primacy accorded by Protestantism to the individual conscious and the assertion of the possibility of communication between a person and God without the need for the interposition of the Church that the Reformation brought in its train, were factors that, when coupled with the humanism of the Renaissance, provided a fertile seed bed within which the notion of human individuality could take root. Further, the absolutism of the sovereigns who governed the nation states that emerged with the breakdown of the authority of the church and the Empire provided castle walls against which those who valued individuality could, in the course of time, begin to hurl themselves.

The word liberal did not begin to be applied in the context of party politics until the nineteenth century. But the values of liberalism were to be seen in Britain from at least two centuries earlier as, for example, in the championship of the rights of the individual citizen against the state by John Locke, treated in Chapter 14.

At the heart of liberalism lies a belief in the entitlement of a citizen to manage his own affairs with the minimum of interference by the state. Thus liberalism upholds human rights, and fights oppression by the state. It was liberal values therefore (even if not called liberal at the time) that provided the rationale for the struggles in the eighteenth and nineteenth centuries against such autocracies as those of the Ancien Regime in France and of the Hapsburgs in Austria. Liberal values were those for which the revolutions of 1848 were fought. Liberalism proclaims justice, freedom, liberty and the sweeping away of archaic structures of government.

The liberalism of the early nineteenth century, usually referred to as classic liberalism, was a creature very different from liberalism today. We shall outline the characteristics of classic liberalism before considering how liberalism has changed. It is convenient to deal with the classic liberalism from two viewpoints, political and economic.

Political liberalism

To guard against autocracy, liberalism looked to the establishment of checks and balances under which each of the three arms of government – executive, legislature and judiciary – were kept separate, each acting as a check on the others, as was the purpose, and is achieved by, the constitution of the United States. (In the United Kingdom, although powers of the executive, legislature and judiciary are nominally separate, in practice the executive, through the whipping system and the dispensation of offices and patronage, controlled, as it still controls, the majority party in the House of Commons.)

Political liberalism is a knight in shining armour charging to the defence of the oppressed. Political liberalism is on the side of the angels.

Political liberalism was optimistic. Change was not merely desirable: it was achievable. By amendment here, modification there, things could be changed for the better. Political liberalism thus put its faith in reform. Liberal values stood behind reforms of nineteenth century England – reform of the electoral system, of the police, of the army, of public health, of local government. Not for nothing is the volume of the Oxford History of England that covers the period 1815 to 1870 entitled 'The Age of Reform'.

But reform was not to be equated with intervention. On the contrary, it was a central tenet of liberalism that the functions of the state should be confined to the minimum necessary for the existence of an ordered society. Thus it was Adam Smith's view that the state should be restricted to protecting citizens from outside dangers (ie, by the maintenance of armed forces), to protecting citizens from oppression and injustice (ie, by the provision of a police force and a legal system), and to the maintenance of public works that 'though they may be in the highest degree advantageous to a great society, are however of such a nature, that profit could never repay the expense to any individual, or small number of individuals (eg, street lighting and sewers). (We may note here that in the United States the view expressed by Adam Smith as to the proper functions of the state remain those (with 'public works' including such institutions as schools) held by a significant number within the Republican Party and by a not insignificant number within the ranks of the Democrats.)

Thus liberalism would limit, not expand, the powers and functions of the state. Government might be necessary but, in the word of Thomas Paine, it was a 'necessary evil'.

And democracy? Here Liberalism faced a dilemma. The case for democratically elected governments had influential advocates among liberal ranks. But in practice a problem existed. Since there were more poor people than rich people, if everyone was given the vote, the majority might vote in favour of money being taken way from the rich for the benefit of the poor. In order to prevent such an eventuality, the suffrage could not but be restricted to those who held property of a certain value. Such was the dominant view[1] until the second half of the nineteenth century, only then arguments[2] in support of universal adult suffrage beginning to win ground.

1 Eg, Benjamin Franklin, John Adams, Thomas Macaulay.
2 Eg, Thomas Paine, Jeremy Bentham, John Stuart Mill.

Economic liberalism

In the field of economics, the policies of liberalism were a corollary of those of liberalism in the political sphere. Since liberalism opposed interference by the state, it followed that for liberalism the best results ensued when the market forces are allowed free play. The greatest benefit for any group was to be obtained by allowing each individual to pursue his own interests. Although the individual would promote his own interests before those of others, the group was the gainer since the individual must, in order to gain a benefit for himself, provide a service to others. The individual, 'By pursuing his own interest … frequently promotes that of the society more effectively than when he really intends to promote it.'[3]

Other benefits flowed from the free play of market forces besides that of permitting individual freedom. One was that market forces provided the most effective means of determining what should be produced. This was achieved by the effect of availability on prices. If goods were in short supply, prices would rise. The higher price obtainable would encourage manufactures to produce more of the goods concerned. As more became available, prices would fall, with the result that production would be reduced as resources were allocated to the production of different goods. The price mechanism operated with regard not only to the supply of goods, but also to the provision of services, including an individual's labour. If labour in a trade was in short supply, a worker was free to offer his service to an employer who, to get him, was willing to offer a higher wage. The payment of higher wages in the trade would encourage others to take up the trade, so that in time, with more workers available, and wages as a consequence falling, numbers entering the trade would decline. Thus the different parts of the economy work together with the interconnectedness of the cogs within a clock. But the system would only work effectively if market forces were allowed to operate without restraint, each individual offering his goods or services to the other on an equal footing. Since the combination of workers into unions for the purpose of negotiating wages, disrupted the proper working of the system, trade unions should be proscribed by law (offenders being subject to the penalty of imprisonment or transportation).

The system had the merit that not only did it, though supply and demand, regulate output, it had the further merit of according

---

3 Adam Smith, *The Wealth of Nations.*

rewards to those who most merit them, since what each person received depended on what he could offer.

The system rested on the assumption (the assumption, it will be recalled, from which Bentham started) that people were rational, rational people striving to maximise their gains and to minimise their losses. But for people to have the incentive to maximise their gains they must be secure in the knowledge that what they gained would not be taken away from them. Thus private property was sacred since any move towards the redistribution of property, for example through inheritance tax, would disrupt the operation of the system. If taxes were levied, they should be only those sufficient to cover the cost of the minimum of services a state should properly provide.

The principle of the inviolability of private property was thus buttressed from two directions: by the economic liberalism explained above, and from the assertion that human rights[4] (as proposed by John Locke and as laid down in the constitution of the United States), included the right of private property.

Thus at the heart of liberalism as it existed in the early nineteenth century lay belief in the right of an individual to manage his won affairs; the unfettered operation of market forces, free from intervention by the state; the separation of state powers with the checks and balances that this separation permitted; and the sanctity of private property.

Such was the thinking of classical liberalism in the political and economic spheres, the thinking associated primarily with the Whig party in British politics.

Liberalism changed. It changed because of what people saw to be effects of allowing market forces to have free play. People saw the horrors of the industrial cities; they saw the way in which the theory of the free market resulted in a brutal exploitation of an impoverished workforce and the accumulation of vast wealth in the hands of a few; they came to see the absurdity of asserting that an individual worker was on an equal bargaining position with an individual factory owner, and that the individual consumer was on an equal footing to a commercial company; they began to realise the effects on the economy of failing to educate the mass of the populace in a world where technological training was increasingly needed to compete with rising powers elsewhere; and they saw as soon as they stepped into the street the inability of local government structures that had changed little since the sixteenth century to provide the most elementary necessities of urban life.

---

4 See Chapter 14.

Change, though, was not fast in coming, and opposition to legislation for such purposes as lifting criminal sanctions against trade unions, imposing safety standards in mines and prescribing minimum hours of work for woman and children came from liberal quarters as well as conservative, on the ground that such measures constituted unwarranted state interference with the free play of the market.

By the early years of the twentieth century, however, those characteristics that are generally associated with the word liberal – generosity of spirit, tolerance, sympathy with the oppressed – had sufficiently come to the fore for the Liberal government of 1906 to introduce legislation in the social field that was to be of major significance in British social history. It was, though, the failure of the Liberal party to put forward solutions to the destitution and squalor that was the inheritance from Victorian Britain, coupled with the fact that the party remained one representing essentially middle class interests, that lead to the birth of a party that was to make the improvement of the lot of those at the bottom of the ladder its raison d'être.

Liberalism today

When writers on jurisprudence speak of liberalism it is not so much the liberalism of party politics they refer to but rather the qualities that the word liberalism has come to connote – qualities that people who are politically Liberals would no doubt claim as those for which they stand. What qualities are these?

Foremost stands an abiding respect for human individuality, a respect to which effect is to be given by the recognition that individuals have certain basic rights. High among these are the rights of freedom of expression (including here a freedom from government control of the press), freedom of movement, freedom of assembly, freedom of worship, and freedom to participate in the democratic control of government through free elections; and a right to privacy. It follows that liberalism seeks an end to the persecution of minorities, whether racial or religious; an end to fear of arbitrary arrest and arrest without trial; and freedom from censorship for political purposes. Some qualities are less specific, for example liberalism stands for tolerance of the views of other, as with regard to sexual orientation.

And it stands for the pragmatic approach. Liberalism has no utopian dreams. Liberalism is progressive – it accepts change where change is needed, but moves a step at a time. Liberalism is free from the kind of ideologies that mark the parties which in political terms stand to the left and to the right of it. Liberals want a juster world, but proclaim no all embracing panacea: there is no master plan. Pragmatism, yes. Dogmatism, no.

With such qualities as these who could say that Liberalism is other than estimable? We shall see.

CHAPTER 19

Sez who?

Critical Legal Studies[1]

Fuller has Rex. Dworkin has Hercules and Hermes. Harris has Hero. Now meet Karl – Karl Wurtzburg (born, 1952, Lake Wobegon, Wisconsin).

After graduating at the University of Minneapolis, Karl worked for two years with an insurance company in Chicago. After publishing some well-received papers on maritime insurance, he applied for and was appointed to a lectureship at a university in South Carolina, where he teaches commercial law.

The year is 1979 and it is spring. Sitting at his desk he can see that alongside the roadways of the campus daffodils are coming into flower. Students are making their way to lectures. A workman enters the refectory building carrying a heavy bag. A black woman goes by, pushing a cleaner's trolley. A chauffeur-driven limousine draws up outside the Provost's office. The chauffeur opens the rear door. A smartly dressed man climbs out and goes up the steps. The Provost comes to meet him, ushering him inside. (A businessman the Provost is hoping to get money from, Karl decides.)

Out of doors, the weather is sunny and mild. Karl leaves his desk and goes to the window. 'If only I could *open* it,' he thinks. But the window is sealed. Karl's neck is stiff from the cold air blowing from the vent in the ceiling. There is an On/Off switch by the door, but with the conditioning off, within minutes the room is hot and sticky. 'Trapped. That's what I am,' he thinks. 'Trapped. Trapped in this room. Trapped by the way I am expected to teach. Trapped in this job. Trapped in the system.'

---

1   H Davies and D Holcroft, *Jurisprudence: Texts and Commentary;* Lloyd's *Introduction to Jurisprudence*, ed MDA Freeman.

'Perhaps,' he thinks, 'if I fix something over the vent, it'll deflect the air away from my neck.' It is while he is standing on his desk trying to do this that his friend Mark comes in. 'Coffee?' Mark asks.

Over coffee in the Senior Common Room, Karl explains his woes. 'Trapped,' he concludes, 'in every way, trapped.'

'Of course you are,' Mark says. 'We all are. It's just that most people don't realise they're trapped (like you until now). Some people, it's true, know they're trapped, but don't care. And some people, more and more of us, know we're trapped and object. You should read Gulger – but then you never took legal theory, did you? So you won't know what's been happening. There's a spare place in our allocation for the conference at Savanna next month.[2] I'm going. Why don't you come with me.'

So Karl went.

He didn't understand what all the speakers said, and he noted that there were fierce disagreements. But there were some things that everyone agreed on. For example, when a speaker said, 'No longer can we tolerate the pre-reflective conception of disjoined politico-legal constructs,' everyone clapped loudly, and when he shouted above the applause, 'Especially when the normative contingencies are no more than reciprocal,' everyone clapped louder still and stamped their feet. Karl did not know what the speaker meant but he clapped too. 'Brilliant!' Mark whispered to him. Karl nodded.

In the evenings, after the last session of the day, everyone congregated in the students' union bar. Here the discussion continued, more hotly than ever. Later, when they had walked back to the hall of residence, the kitchens at the end of the corridors were filled with people arguing, agreeing, disagreeing, banging the table in their excitement. It was at these times, not in the formal sessions, that Karl came to understand something of what the loose collection of writers whose work came in time to be referred to as Critical Legal Studies (and the writers the 'Crits'), were seeking to say.

Formalism

What he learned came as a shock. Aspects of law that he had been taught to regard, and hitherto had himself regarded, as among the greatest glories of the common law tradition, were, by the Crits, not merely criticised but damned.

---

2 For the first annual conference on Critical Legal Studies, see Kelman, A Guide to Critical Studies, 1, quoted in Davies and Holcroft, supra, p 471.

For example, Karl had always respected, and tried to emulate, the paths of reasoning by which judges reached their decisions, and academics proposed conclusions on moot points of law. Many times, when reading reports of cases he had come to the end of the summary of the facts and thought to himself, 'I'm glad I didn't have to decide which side ought to win.' Then he would read the judgment and see how the judge, starting with relevant statutory provisions, would look at the object of the legislature in enacting these; consider any matter of construction that arose over the words of the statute; consider pertinent cases, distinguishing those that failed to bear immediately on the point at issue, and noting, in the case of any decision that was relevant, the level of authority of the court concerned; consider any principles of law applicable (a person shall not benefit from his own crime, delay defeats equity, and so on); and so finally, having taken all these matters into account, reach his conclusion – a conclusion that was, Karl almost invariably felt, when you looked at the matter in the way the judge had done, not only manifestly correct, and manifestly in line with the rest of the law in that area, but almost staring you in the face if only you had realised it. (In Dworkinian thinking, the decision had been 'there all the time'.)

Karl's respect for judicial reasoning had been unbounded. But now, he learned, his admiration had been groundless! The notion that there was a form of reasoning that could lead to the correct solution was a sham, the apparent inevitability of the judge's conclusion a façade, behind which was concealed the real position – that decisions were reached in ways that were arbitrary. This was because, throughout the law, principles existed that pulled in opposite directions, one principle favouring one party to litigation, another principle to the other party, which principle a judge adopted being something that could never be predicted.

Conflicting principles[3]

Criminal law

All this Karl found deeply disturbing. But Mark pointed out the evidence. 'Look at criminal law,' Mark told him.

'Kelman[4] uses the example of a wife who, having been battered by her husband, kills him. She pleads the defence of provocation.

---

3   See H Davies and D Holcroft, op cit, pp 479–482.
4   M Kelman, *Interpretive construction in the Substantive Criminal Law*, (1981) 33 Stanford LR 591.

In deciding whether the defence should apply, one approach is to look at the circumstances immediately attending the killing (was the wife being battered at the time?); the other approach is to look at the events leading up to the killing – events during that day, or during the previous week, or month, or longer. Where there has been no battering during, say, the previous three days, whether the judge will accept the plea of provocation will be influenced by which approach the judge adopts, the former leading him to reject the plea, the latter towards accepting it.'

Thus, Mark explained, there is a conflict between the adoption of a narrow 'time-frame',[5] and that of a broader one. But nowhere is guidance given (eg by statute) as to which time-frame is appropriate. Yet which time-frame is adopted decides whether the woman is found guilty.

The narrow/broad time-frame distinction reflects a parallel distinction, that between two views as to what determines human actions. According to one view, people are free to decide their actions: what people do, they intend to do, and so are responsible for their actions. This is the *free will*, or *intentionalist*, view. According to the other view, how a person acts is, to a degree dependent on the circumstances, determined by what has gone before. This is the *determinist* view.[6] It will be seen that the idea of the narrow time-frame approach goes with the intentionalism, the broad time-frame approach goes with the determinism. Crits who have discussed the conflict between the two views have, for example in relation to the case of the battered wife, concluded that it is the intentionalist approach that is most commonly adopted by the courts.

Co-habitation

Another area in which the Crits[7] have seen conflicting principles is that where a woman seeks to enforce an co-habitation agreement against a male partner. Here the conflict is between the (a) common law principle that such agreements (for example that the woman

---

5 Ibid.
6 In its completest form, usually met in the context of theology, the determinist view takes the form of predestination – since God knows everything, he knows what is going to happen, so that everything that happens has got to happen, because it has been in God's mind from the start – with the result, incidentally, that it is already settled who is going to hell and who ('the Elect') are going to Heaven.
7 Eg C Dalton, *An Essay In The Deconstruction of Contract Doctrine* (1985) 94 Yale LJ 997.

should have a half share of the home) are not legally enforceable because of the presumption that such agreements lack the necessary element of an intention to create legal relations (coupled sometimes with the argument that since at the heart of the agreement lies provision by the woman of sex, and since the provision of sex cannot in law form valid consideration, the agreement is unenforceable for lack of consideration); and (b) the principle, arising from public policy, that it is the duty of the courts (in particular the court of equity) to give effect to the intention of the parties. The range of options open to a judge 'makes possible virtually any decision'.[8]

Contract[9]

Other conflicts could be seen in the law of contract, as where the principle enshrined in the maxim caveat emptor (a maxim devised to protect capitalist interests against the interests of the powerless consumer) comes up against the principle that it is the function of the state to intervene to protect the weaker party against exploitation. Which principle a judge would decide should prevail could never be predicted.

Rules v principles

For some[10] writers in the movement, conflict lay at a more fundamental level. For Kennedy[11] the conflict is between those who believe that the law is best framed in the form of rules, and those who would have it framed in the form of standards or principles. Those in the 'rules' camp point to the advantage of certainty – ie the benefit to the citizen of knowing in advance where he stands. Those in the 'standards' camp point to the advantage that law implemented through standards is more likely to achieve the purpose for which the law exists than law framed as a rigid rule, citing here the example of the legal prescription of an age limit designed to protect minors, a limit that may imposed unnecessary restraints on those under the age who do not in fact need the law's protection, and failing to protect those over the limit who, because of their circumstances, still do, the rigidity of the rule thus preventing the achievement of its purpose.

---

8   Ibid.
9   See H Davies and D Holcroft, *Jurisprudence: Texts and Commentary* p 508.
10 But not all. See Lloyd, supra, p 939, for those who do not consider rules and standards necessarily to be in conflict.
11 See H Davies and D Holcroft, *Jurisprudence: Texts and Commentary* pp 484–488. See also M Kelman, op cit.

'So you see,' Mark said, 'when you realise that judges are pulled in different directions by principles that conflict in their result, you can see that the supposed chain of reasoning by which they reach their conclusions is no more than a smoke screen, – how can judges' decisions be inevitable when they are having to decide which of conflicting principles should prevail?'

Ulterior motives

Worse, Karl found, was to come. It was the purpose of some Crits to show how judges were able, by their freedom to chose between conflicting principles, to manipulate the outcome so as to protect or promote the interests of the class from which they came. This was termed 'instrumental analysis', meaning the analysis of decisions to discover the purpose that the decision had been used as an instrument to achieve. 'The goal ... is to show that the conscious or unconscious motive of the judge [is] to further some particular interest, whether of the judge himself or of a group with whom he identified. ... The instrumentalist treats normal rationales of decisions as largely obfuscatory, except when they inadvertently or naively refer to selfish aims.' So instrumentalism 'is concerned with hidden motives that the judges themselves would treat as illegitimate if forced to confront them'.[12]

So what actually happened, the Crits maintained, was that a judge decided which way he wanted a decision to go and then produced an elegant chain of reasoning to lead to his predetermined conclusion – that a judge (or an academic) 'constructs the materials to reach a desired result, and that the result is based on some real interest in winning a certain class of cases, either because they are significant to maintaining economic or political control or because they help solidify a certain ideological story that is helpful to maintaining domination.'[13] So what judges were guilty of was manipulation.

Faced with these arguments, Karl felt that he had no alternative but to accept the Crits' contention that the notion of correct, findable-by-reasoning solutions was a myth, and that a judge's neutrality, his objectivity, no more than an illusion. Law, as Karl had previously viewed it, was turned on its head.

12 D Kennedy *The Structure of Blacksone's Commentaries* (1979) Buffalo LR 209.
13 M Kelman, op cit.

To the barricades?

Listening to the discussions Karl came soon to realise that what motivated those at the conference was not merely a determination to uncover what they believed to be the realities behind the alleged neutrality of the judicial process. What motivated them was a wish to bring about a complete change in the ordering of society. 'They're revolutionaries!' Karl thought, 'Left wing revolutionaries! They're Reds! How did they get permission to hold this conference? What am I doing here? Do the authorities know?'

Remember that in 1979 the Cold War was at its height. Only four years had elapsed since the end of the Vietnam War, in which 58,000 Americans had died in the fight for freedom and democracy. McCarthy might be dead, but American fear of Communism was undiminished. Yet here was a group of academics, some at highly prestigious universities, attacking the very foundations of all that was regarded by right thinking citizens as being best in the American way of life! Why did the authorities not see to it that those in the movement lost their jobs and, as communists had been, hounded into obscurity?

Mark confirmed Karl's fears. Yes, the Crits did condemn capitalism and the free market economy, and the hierarchical society that these produced. They condemned 'liberalism'. They sought a redistribution of social and economic power.

Their role, though, was not (Karl was relieved to hear) actually to call for revolution. That might never be necessary, if only people's eyes could be opened to the realities that the Crits proclaimed. Their special role in this process was to pave the way for change by using their knowledge as lawyers to disclose how the law constituted an impediment to social change: to demonstrate that the law, far from being neutral, formed a buttress to the status quo with all its inequalities.

Legitimation[14]

How the trick was done, Mark explained, could be regarded as taking place in three stages. First the law, for its own convenience, invented categories – employer/ employee, debtor/creditor,

---

14   See H Davies and D Holcroft, *Jurisprudence: Texts and Commentary* p 482.

husband/wife, bailor/bailee, employer/contractor, landlord/ tenant. Secondly, people came to think of themselves as falling into one or other of the various categories that the law had invented. Thirdly, and crucially, people came, because of the respect in which the law was held, to treat the categorisation as part of the natural order of things, as inevitable.

Reification

The complete process the Crits termed *reification*, meaning the turning of something that otherwise has no existence into something that in people's minds has not only a real existence, but a justified existence. The law 'conditions how we experience life. ... [It] construct[s] roles for us like 'Owner' and 'Employee' and then tell[s] us how to behave in those roles ('The person cast as 'Employee' is subordinate. Why? It just is that way, part of the role.'[15]) '[I]n reification we do not simply make a kind of private error about the true nature of what we are talking about, we participate in an unconscious conspiracy with others whereby everyone knows of the fallacy, and yet denies that the fallacy exists.'[16] ' ... each person experiences himself as a thing-like function of 'the system, ... Each person experiences himself in this way because each person is recognised in this way by everyone else, and human beings are such that they experience themselves as they are recognised.'[17]

'I can see what you mean,' Karl said. 'I remember that when you came in to my room on the first day we discussed these things, I had been looking out of the window. The people I watched, I didn't think of as individuals. I thought of them as members of the categories into which they fell – students under a contract with the university, a workman I would have expected to be an independent contractor, a woman I thought of as an employee, a man getting out of a big car I thought of as being an employer, and so on. And all this I accepted as part of the inevitable ordering of things. I didn't *think* about it.'

'That's right,' said Mark, 'and reification extends to the limits of how we talk and think about our society. Listen to this: people learn "that they are all abstract 'citizens' of an abstract 'United States of America", that there exists 'Liberty and justice for all', and so forth – not from the contents of the words but from the ritual that forbids

15 RW Gordon, *Law and Ideology* (1988).
16 P Gabel, *Reification and Legal Reasoning* (1980).
17 P Gabel, op cit.

any rebellion. Gradually, they will come to accept these abstraction as descriptive of a concrete truth because of the repressive and conspiratorial way that these ideas have been communicated (each senses that all the others 'believe in' the words and therefore they must be true), and once this acceptance occurs, any access to the ... forgotten memory that these are mere abstractions will be sealed off. And once the abstractions are reified, they can no longer be criticised because they signify a false concrete. ... The terrible truth of reification is that it is alive within each of us ... .everyone ... knows this, and can do nothing, or almost nothing, about it.'''

'Good God!' exclaimed Karl.

'Exactly,' said Mark, picking up another book. 'Listen to this: "The way law is structured is 'saturated with categories and images that for the most part rationalise and justify in myriad subtle ways the existing social order as natural, necessary, and just."'[18] You see, it's because the law succeeds in getting people to see life and society in its own terms that the law so effectively acts as a legitimising force. "Through law we tell ourselves ... that what is, ought to be."'[19]

'So our thinking about law and society is made up of ideas that inhibit us from realising that things could be different, because we are dependent on our existing ideas to make sense on what we see around us. This is how Robert Gordon puts it. " ... we have to use [our existing ideas] to think about the world at all, because the world makes no sense apart from our systems of shared meanings. ... Yet, if the real enemy is us – all of us, the structures we carry around in our heads, the limits of our imagination – where can we ever begin?"'[20]

The task

'Where do you begin?' Karl asked.

'By not being fooled by what reification does to our thinking, and by refusing to accept that change is impossible – look how your own views have shifted in the past two days. Our task,' Mark said, reading again, "is to unmask the ideological bias behind legal structures and procedures, which regularly makes it easy for business groups to organise collectively to pursue their economic and political interests but which makes it much more difficult for labour, poor people, or civil rights groups to pursue theirs."[21] So what we have got to do is to start by understanding and *disclosing* how law legitimises the existing

18 RW Gordon, op cit.
19 P Gabel, op cit.
20 RW Gordon, *New Developments in Legal Theory* (1982).
21 Ibid.

order of things. And to do this we must not "look only at the un-
deniably numerous, specific ways in which the legal system operates
to screw poor people – though it is always important to do that too...
– but rather at all the ways in which the system seems at first glance
basically uncontroversial, neutral, acceptable ... [so that] both the
dominant and the dominated classes believe that the existing order,
with perhaps some marginal changes, is satisfactory, or at least
represents the most that any one could expect, because things pretty
much have to be the way they are." What we have to do is to "look
closely at these belief systems, these deeply held assumptions about
politics, economics, hierarchy, work leisure, and the nature of reality,
which are profoundly paralysis inducing because they make it so hard
for people (including the ruling classes themselves) to even imagine
that life could be different and better."

"Law, like religion and television images, is [one of a number of]
clusters of belief – and it ties in with a lot of other non-legal but similar
clusters – that convince people that all the many hierarchical relations
in which they live and work are natural and necessary."[22] ... The way
law is written and the way it operates routinely helps "to create and
maintain the ordinary inequalities of everyday social life: the
coercions, dominations, and dependencies of daily relations in the
market place, the workplace, and the family; the ordering of access
to privilege, authority, wealth, power by hierarchies of class, race,
gender, and 'merit'." Indeed, we are brainwashed into accepting that
"if we want to remain prosperous we must endure all the
miscellaneous injustices now in place and even invent new ones".'[23]
Karl looked around nervously. Was the room bugged.

'Do you understand?' Mark asked.

'Yes,' Karl said, 'but I think I'll turn in now.'

Education

The first topic the next day was legal education. From this Karl
learned that it was not only society and the law that was wrong, the
way that law was taught was also at fault. Indeed, by their blinkered
adherence to traditional outlooks, it was law schools that were
especially to blame. It was the law schools that perpetuated the myth
of the neutrality of the judicial reasoning, that concealed the

22 Ibid.
23 RW Gordon, *Law and Ideology* (1988).

conflicts and contradictions that, once the lid was lifted, were revealed as riddling the law. It was the law schools that imbued novice lawyers with the belief that God was in his heaven and that all was well with America, or at least that there was nothing wrong that a little tinkering at the edges could not put right. It was the law schools that were the bastions, the champions, of the great evil – LIBERALISM.

The very nature of the law schools, with their traditions and conventions and hierarchies, mirrored the society whose foundations the schools bolstered by their promulgation of an unquestioning acceptance of the law as encapsulated within a liberal scheme of social organisation. The law schools – self-satisfied, static, conservative – lay at the forefront of the Crits' attack. And 'Since most of the Crits were academics in law schools, they picked first on the targets that were closest to them, the standard ways that other law teachers wrote, taught and talked about first-year legal subjects, such as Torts, Contracts, and Property.'[24] ('Biting the hand that feeds them,' thought Karl.)

What happens in the law schools is 'the inculcation through a formal curriculum and classroom experience of a set of political attitudes towards the economy and society in general, towards law, and towards the possibilities of life in the profession. ... Then there is a complicated set of institutional practices that orient students to willing participation in the specialised hierarchical roles of lawyers.'[25] Not only are students conned into believing that the law emerges from a 'rigorous analytical procedure called legal reasoning'[26], but also, and even more serious, students are bullied into accepting that a distinction exists between law and policy, whereas, for the Crits, 'teachers teach nonsense when they persuade students that legal reasoning is distinct, *as a method for reaching correct results*, from ethical and political discourse in general.'[27]

How do they compare?

By the end of the second day Karl felt that he was beginning to see what the Crits were getting at. How he wondered, as he lay in bed listening to the sounds of Savanna outside the window, did the Crits' views compare with those of writers in other schools?

24 Ibid.
25 D Kennedy, *The Ideological Content of Legal Education* (1982).
26 Ibid.
27 Ibid.

Positivism

With positivists such as Hart and Kelsen, the Crits clearly had no truck. How could they? Any line of thinking that included the notion that the outcome of litigation was decided by the application of rules, could not but be totally at variance with the Crits' view of how the law works. The Crits rejected not only the rules element of positivism, but also the strand of positivist thinking that regarded the law as standing neutral, as being no more than an instrument. Far from standing neutral, for the Crits, the law formed a means by which the status quo in society was perpetuated.

Natural law

Surely the Crits, with their gritty realism, could have nothing in common with the ethereal theorising of the natural lawyers? Certainly the flavour of the writing of the two schools could hardly be more different. But in one respect the Crits, or some of them, did, Karl decided, share with natural lawyers an area of, at the least, sympathy.

The positivist rejects the view that values are capable of being established objectively, maintaining that values are relative, their establishment being arbitrary. The natural lawyer maintains that, at the most fundamental level, values are capable, through human reason, of being ascertained. The Crits would not go all the way with the natural lawyer, but they at least agree with them in rejecting the positivist view of the wholly subjective nature of values, holding firm instead to at least 'the hope that one can transcend the usual distinction between subjective and objective in seeking moral truth…', being committed to at least the ideal 'that we can know social and ethical truths objectively…';[28] that there are indeed 'universal maxims to govern human relationships, practices and laws'[29] This should not surprise us, since, as the Crits make the judgment that the present arrangement of society is wrong, it must be wrong according to some objective standard.

Liberalism[30]

For the Crits 'liberalism' was a dirty word. Under this head they placed all the principal matters that they specially condemned. Thus 'liberalism', for the Crits, includes:

---

28 M Kelman, *A Guide to Critical Legal Studies* (1987).
29 Lloyd, supra, p 940.
30 See H Davies and D Holcroft, *Jurisprudence: Texts and Commentary*, p 513.

(i)   'formalism' (meaning the process by which judges purport, through interpretation of the law, to reach their decisions; coupled with the contention that, as a result of this process, judges' decisions are not political in nature ie favouring a particular policy, but are value free, neutral);
(ii) individualism, within a free market economy)
(iii) the view that values are relative;
(iv) the view that human actions are freely willed (as opposed to being predetermined by what has gone before);
(v) the view that law can be an instrument of social change, as by the securing of legal rights.

The Crits maintain that, on the contrary,

(i)   judges' decisions are not neutral but give effect to values, the supposed interpretative method being a sham;
(ii) collectivism;
(iii) the view that values *can* be objectively ascertained;
(iv) human actions tend to be determined by what has gone before;
(v) the view that, far from being capable of being an instrument of social change, law acts (inter alia, through reification) as an impediment to social change.

American realism

The Crits in some respects can be regarded as continuing the work of the American Realists.[31] They certainly share the latter's critical cynicism. But the differences are greater than the similarities. The Realists minutely scrutinise the law in action so as to be able to tell us how it *works*. The Crits tell us what the law *does* (legitimises and so conserves the status quo).

Language

There was, though, something that Karl still found disturbing . Why was it the Crits expressed their ideas (which, when you understood them, weren't all that difficult to grasp) in such convoluted language? Karl found that when he talked to Mark, he could understand what Mark said. But when he looked at a book or article by one of the Crits, the words swam before his eyes. 'The solution to this dilemma is to

31   See H Davies and D Holcroft, *Jurisprudence: Texts and Commentary* p 471.

be found in the ontological meaning for each person of experiencing the intersubjective movement of socio-economic relations as a political communion of normative subjects.'[32] 'There is no limit to the way that this sense of wholeness and sociality can be expressed, since the historical development of forms of social expression is nothing more than the infinite evocation of social being in the course of its becoming.'[33] 'A complete account of the legal thought would explain the historically determinative association between liberal legalism as denial and liberal legalism as apology.' 'The rationality for which this expanded version of legal doctrine can hope is nothing other than the minimal but perhaps still significant potential rationality of the normal modes of moral and political controversy.'[34] What did it all *mean?*

Karl did not know, but he noticed that the Crits had their own vocabulary – epistemological, contingently, disaggregate, interiorised, conceptualistic, correlative, intentionalistic, quasi/micro phenomenological, hegemonic, objectified, maturation, prereflective, constructs, rhetorical, situationally, relational, dissonant, metaprincipled, arational. Would he be able to become a Crit if he used their words? Hesitantly, he wrote, 'The contingently nonpurposive constucts of nineteenth century liberalism provide uniquely subjective explications for its arational mode of deterministically orientated functionalism.' He stared at the sentence. True, it didn't mean anything. But this did not seem to matter.

Towards the end of a lecture the next day he passed Mark a note. 'Do you think that the speaker is intending to refer to the contingently normative effects of all our politico/legal reciprocities?'

Mark returned the note. At the foot he had written, 'Yes, definitely.'

Karl was puzzled. If the Crits had confidence in their message, why did they muddy the waters with pretentious obscurities? Their way of writing was especially regrettable since there were times when they wrote with clarity and force. For example, Karl was later to read with approval an article debunking Dworkin. '... Dworkin's world ... is the moral terrain of middle America, where a comfortable isolation is interrupted by occasional confrontations that are quickly defused, before life returns quickly to normal.'[35] And, 'The imperial

32 P Gabel.
33 Ibid.
34 Unger, *The Critical Legal Studies Movement* (1983) HLR 579.
35 AC Hutchinson, *Indiana Dworkin.*

foundations, supposedly formed from the hard rock of principle, will be revealed to rest upon the shifting sands of ideological consensus. Dworkin's complacency about that consensus is born of splendid isolation from popular movements. He depends on the moral inertia of the undifferentiated political center and the tyranny of the familiar; "no one really thinks the law wicked or its authors tyrants". Sez who? Has Dworkin spoken to many women, gays, blacks or Indians recently? *Law's Empire* deals with the deprived and the disadvantaged on society by simply pretending that that they do not exist – Qu'ils mangent de la brioche.'[36] Powerful stuff, Karl considered, and something that needed to be said: Dworkin's balloon decisively pricked. If only all CLS writing could have been of this clarity.

Alternatives

'Tell me this,' Karl said to his friend one day after they had returned to their own university, and were having coffee in the Senior Common Room, 'I can understand your objections to what you refer to as formalism. I can understand that you see the law as not neutral but forming a prop to the status quo. I know your disillusionment with the very fundamentals of our liberal, free market, individualistic society. But what would you put in its place?'

'Must dash,' said Mark, 'I have a lecture at two.'

It was only later, when they were in Mark's car on their way to watch the Tigers play the Gamecocks that Karl was able to pin Mark down.

'We need,' he said, 'to replace a society in which individualism prevails with one in which altruism is the hall mark; the pursuit of private gain by one of shared ends. We must recognise that relativism with regard to moral values has had its day, that the attainment of a more equal society is no desert mirage, unattainable, a sad delusion.'

'So, to move to a more equal society, you want to emphasise the importance of people's right, and help the disadvantaged exercise their rights against their oppressors – is that so?'

'Well,' replied Mark, 'some of us[37] are suspicious of the whole idea of rights. The trouble is that when someone claims a right, this assumes that they *need* the right. It presumes the dominance of the person against whom the right is claimed. So if you put it into

36   Ibid.
37   RW Gordon, op cit.

people's heads that they need rights, this reinforces the idea that the status quo is part of the natural order of things. And that's what we're fighting against. In any case, apart from this, rights are usually thought of in terms of individual rights, and this tends to sustain a belief that individual interests are more important than community interests – a view that we certainly do not subscribe to.'

This way of looking at things came as a surprise to Karl, since (remembering the New Deal of the 1930s and the Civil Rights movement more recently) he had always thought that any amelioration of society could be, and *had* been, achieved by, a step at a time, ratcheting up people's legal rights.

'So what *are* you doing towards achieving the new order?'

'We believe that ....'

'No,' said Karl, 'what steps are *you* taking?'

'I'm putting a lot of work into an article for our Law Review,' Mark said, as he blasted the horn returning salutes from fellow Tiger supporters. 'It's on Dissonant correlates in the normative functionalism of non-purposive constructs. I think it will have quite an impact.'

'Will it be methodologically epistemological, or merely residually re-interpretative – in a quasi-reflective sense, of course?' Karl asked.

'I'm not sure,' Mark replied. 'I haven't decided yet.'

('I'm getting the hang of this,' Mark thought, as they turned into the USC[38] campus.)

---

38   University of South Carolina, Columbia, South Carolina.

CHAPTER 20

Close your ears, Mr Knox[1]

Feminism[2]

Lucy is in her final year, reading law, at the University of Melchester. Her friend Paul is in the same class. In the final year Jurisprudence is a compulsory subject. The lecturer is Ms Gilbenkinthorpe.

Today Ms Gilbenkinthorpe announces that having completed her lectures on the New Critics, she will deal with Feminism. Lucy started a fresh page in her notebook and wrote the heading, 'Feminist Jurisprudence'. But, realising that Ms Gilbenkinthorpe had not used the word Jurisprudence, she added a question mark after 'Jurisprudence' and put the word in brackets, like this,

Feminist (Jurisprudence?)

Her interest in the subject, Ms Gilbenkinthorpe said, had been aroused by reading *The Second Sex*, by Simone de Beauvoir. The book, published in 1949, had formed a landmark in the history of the feminist movement.[3] de Beauvoir had not been the first to observe, comment on, or protest about the subordination of women. There had been eminent and influential forerunners, such as Mary Wollstonecraft,[4] Harriet Taylor[5] and John Stuart Mill (whose *The Subjection of Women*, published in1869, advanced the case for women

---

1 c 1514–1572.
2 Carol Smart *Feminist Jurisprudence*, in *Dangerous Supplements*, ed P Fitzpatrick, 1991.
3 Other key landmarks include G Greer, *The Female Eunuch* (1970), *The Whole Woman* (1999).
4 1759–1797: *Thoughts on the Education of Daughters* (1787), *A Vindication of the Rights of Woman* (1792).
5 *Enfranchisement of Women* (Dissertations, vol 2).

to be admitted to the suffrage). But de Beauvoir's book was the first to present a comprehensive and detailed exposition of the position of women down the ages.

The theme of the book came across early: '... man defines woman not in herself but relative to him; she is not regarded as an autonomous being'. Thus, ' ... she is differentiated with reference to man and not with reference to herself; she is incidental, the inessential as opposed to the essential. He is the Subject, he is the Absolute – she is the Other'. So a woman although 'a free and autonomous being like all human creatures ... nevertheless finds herself living in a world where men compel her to assume the status of the Other, – the one that is *different*'. And later, 'From humanity's beginnings, their biological advantage has enabled the males to affirm their status as sole and sovereign subjects; they have never abdicated this position; ... Condemned to play the part of the Other, woman was also condemned to hold only uncertain power: slave or idol, it was never she who chose her lot. ... [W]oman's place in society is always that which men assign to her; at no time has she ever imposed her own law.'[6] ('That figures,' thought Lucy. Paul stirred uneasily.) 'It is male power,' said Ms Gilbenkenthorpe warming to her subject, 'that has enabled women to be treated as the Other, male power that has been the "primary reason for the stunted nature of women's lives".'[7]

So inspired by the book had she been, Ms Gilbenkinthorpe said, that she had become involved in various campaigns within the University and the town to fight cases in which women had suffered discrimination. Women were as much autonomous beings as men, she was convinced, and as such were equally entitled to the rights that men declared were humanity's inheritance. Later, however, although campaigning no less vigorously, she had come to realise that this approach was misguided, being that of someone who accepted the thinking of Liberalism. Liberalism, Ms Gilbenkinthorpe said, was now regarded by the majority of feminists as having proved a false trail and had been largely overtaken by 'Radical feminism'. More recently she had been influenced by a school of thought that had come to be termed Cultural Feminism. She would deal with these various trends in due course but it was important to remember that on the most significant matter of all, namely the fight against patriarchy, feminists were united. In her lectures, she

6 Chapter 2.
7 Robin West, *Jurisprudence and Gender* 55 University of Chicago Law Review 1 (Lloyd, p 1080).

explained, she would be quoting from the works of prominent feminists. [In this book the source of these is given in footnotes.]

Patriarchy

By patriarchy feminists mean the ordering of society under which standards – political, economic, legal, social – are set by, and fixed in the interests of, men, men more highly valued than women. Maleness is treated as the starting point. In a host of matters, of which health, car and household insurance, the majority of sports, military service, job descriptions and job expectations are only a few examples, it is the male that is treated as the norm, the norm to which women, even if not excluded, are treated as the exception. In the study of anatomy, human genitalia are defined in relation to the male form – what men have and women do not. Even God is conceived in the male image – 'God the Father, God the Son ...' In short, patriarchy connotes a 'political structure that values men more than women'.[8]

Law

In law, where patriarchy prevails it is male experiences and per-spectives that are the reference point in relation to which the law is fixed. 'Throughout the history of our Anglo-American jurisprudence, the primary linguists of law have almost exclusively been men – white, educated, economically privileged men. Men have shaped it, they have defined it, they have interpreted it and given it meaning consistent with their understanding of the world and of people "other" than them. As the men of law have defined law in their own image, law has excluded or marginalized voices and meanings of these "others". ... Because the men of law have had societal power not to have to worry too much about the competing terms and understandings of "others", they have been insulated from challenges to their language and have thus come to see it as natural, inevitable, complete, objective, and neutral.'[9] (An example of male experiences and perspectives being regarded as the norm is provided by the way

---

8　Robin West, supra (Lloyd, p 1062).
9　Katherine T Bartlett, *Feminist Legal Methods* (Lloyd, p 1135).

in which work is treated as being that which is 'done for wages outside your own home', the implication being that 'workers are men with wives at home who attend to the necessities of life',[10] and that work done at home by women is not really work at all.)

'Legal language frames the issues, it defines the terms in which speech in the legal world must occur. It tells us how we should understand a problem and which explanations are acceptable and which are not. Since this language has been crafted primarily by white men, the way it frames issues, the way it defines problems, and the speakers and speech it credits, do not readily include women. Legal language commands: abstract a situation from historical, social, and political, context; be "objective" and avoid the lens of nonmale experience; invoke universal principles such as "equality" and "free choice"; speak with the voice of dispassionate reason; be simple, direct, and certain; avoid the complexity of varying, inter-acting perspectives and overlapping multi-textured explanations; and most of all, tell it and see it "like a man" – put it in terms that relate to men and to which men can relate.'[11]

'The claim that law is patriarchal does not mean that women have not been addressed or comprehended by law. Women have obviously been the subjects or contemplated targets of many laws. But it is men's understanding of women, women's nature, women's capacities and women' experiences – women refracted through the male eye – that has informed law.'[12] An example of the male judicial perspective is provided by rape. 'It is the male's view of whether the woman consented that is determinative of consent; it is men's view of what constitutes force against men and forms a resistance by men in situations other than rape that defines whether force has been used against a woman and a woman has resisted; it is men's definition of sex – penetration of the vagina by the penis – rather than women's experience of sexualised violation that defines the crime ... The word "family" and the area of family law is another example. The norm of "family" ... is of a household headed by a man with a wife who is wholly or somewhat dependent on him. Other forms of family – especially those without a man – are regarded as abnormal.'[13]

---

10 Lucinda M Finley, *Breaking women's Silence in Law: The Dilemma of the Gendered Nature of Legal Reasoning, from (1989)* 64 Notre Dame Law Rev 886 (Lloyd, p 1139).
11 Finley, supra (Lloyd, p 1143).
12 Finley, supra (Lloyd, p 1137).
13 Finley, supra (Lloyd, p 1137).

In a patriarchal society the claim by those in power that the law is neutral detached, objective, disinterested, that it looks at matters from the outside, is a sham. Under patriarchy the unwritten message is that 'To be the same as white males is the desired end. To be different from them is undesirable and justifies disadvantages.'[14] This has been the message down the ages. Consider the disadvantages and discrimination that women have had to fight against – over inheritance and the holding of property, over entry to universities, over entry to the professions and judicial office, over jury service, admission to ordination to the priesthood, over rape within marriage, and most fundamental of all, the vote. In all these and a myriad other fields women have had imposed upon them a system of affirmative action in favour of men.[15] Since the law does not recognise women (except as the Other), the law does not protect them. There will be no system that is free from gender bias until women's lives are taken by the law as seriously as men's.[16]

Feminism and Critical Legal Studies

The class would appreciate, Ms Gilbenkinthorpe said, that Feminism shared common ground with aspects of Critical Legal Studies. But there were differences. CLS presents oppression and discrimination in the abstract, and principally from a male point of view. The CLS movement looks down from its academic tower to those who experience oppression and disadvantage. Feminism's starting point is that of the oppressed themselves. Feminism looks upwards, to the patriarchy that must be overthrown. Further, CLS visions of the good society tend to be expressed in general, idealised terms. 'Objectives are often framed in terms of vague, seemingly universal aspirations – such as Roberto Unger's appeal to a world free "from deprivation and drudgery, from choice between isolation ..." Such formulations leave most of the interesting questions unanswered.'[17] Thus CLS visions do not take into account the concerns that Feminists advance. Feminist visions of a better society are more specific, concentrating on the

---

14   Finley, supra (Lloyd, p 1139).
15   Catharine A MacKinnon, *Difference and Dominance: On Sex Discrimination*, from *Feminism Unmodified, Discourses on Life and Law*, Harvard University Press (1987) (Lloyd, p 1084).
16   Robin West, *Jurisprudence and Gender* (1988) 55 University of Chicago Law Review 1.
17   Deborah L Rhode, *Feminist Critical Theories* (1990) 42 Stanford Law Review 617.

values that a good society would have, and the laws and institutions needed if such a society is to be achieved.[18]

The features common to Feminism and CLS are nevertheless important. Of particular significance are a common condemnation of injustice, a common scepticism as to the alleged neutrality of 'the rule of law' and the purported separation of law from politics that this neutrality is claimed to provide, and a shared view on the role that the law has, down the ages, played in conferring an aura of legitimacy on a society's existing laws, institutions and social ordering.[19] Feminism shares with the New Critics the common intention to 'challenge the existing distributions of power'.[20]

Liberal feminism

Earlier, in the 1960s and 1970s, it had seemed natural to feminists that Liberalism should be the appropriate weapon with which to fight for improvements in the position of women. After all, it had been Liberal thinking that had underlain the social legislation passed by Parliament in the United Kingdom before the First World War. It had been Liberal thinking that had formed the intellectual basis of the movement against racial discrimination in the United States, American Liberals calling for the rights conferred by the constitution to be applied equally to all citizens irrespective of their colour or ethnic origin. After massive conflicts, of which the assassination of Martin Luther King had formed one tragic part, advances had been made. And it had been Liberals in American society who had taken a stand against the war in Vietnam.

Liberalism had claimed rights for women, and had secured rights for women. Liberalism worked. Why, then, had many feminists come to regard Liberal thinking as no longer adequate to meet their needs? Why, for the majority of feminists, did Liberalism come to be replaced by Radical feminism?

Radical feminism

The answer, said Ms Gilbenkenthorpe, was best understood by considering the various respects in which Radical feminism differs from Liberal feminism.

18 Rhode, supra (Lloyd, p 1047).
19 Rhode, supra (Lloyd, p 1036).
20 Rhode, supra (Lloyd, p 1036).

1. Liberalism's case rests on rights, and the failure by society to accord women the rights to which they are entitled. For Radical feminists what matters is not the abstruse, ethereal, pie-in-the-sky notion of abstract 'rights', but the fact, the *fact*, of domination of women by men.

Further, Radical feminists are impatient with Liberal feminists over progress. The changes that have so far been achieved by seeking rights bear little relation to the work that has had to be put into achieving them.

What is more, seeking change by securing rights 'too often channels individual aspirations into demands for their own share of protected opportunities and fails to address more fundamental issues about what ought to be protected. Such an individualistic framework ill serves the values of co-operation and empathy that feminists find lacking in our current legal culture'.[21] Thus a 'preoccupation with personal entitlements can divert attention from collective responsibilities'.[22] And further, in practice the rights obtained are all too often ones that do no more than protect predominantly white, middle class interests. It is not surprising, then, that Radical feminists grow restive when Liberals talk about rights.

2. Liberalism accepts without demur the reasoning processes of the law, with its 'Rationality, abstraction, a preference for statistical and empirical proofs'.[23] Radical feminists reject this approach, since 'the reasoning structure of law is ... congruent with the patterns of socialization, experience, and values of a particular group of privileged, educated men'[24] ... 'having been framed on the basis of life experiences typical to empowered white males'.[25]

By way of elaboration, Ms Gilbenkenthorpe quoted from Lucinda Finley. 'As part of this individualistic framework, law is conceptualized as a rule-bound system for adjudicating the competing rights of self-interested, autonomous, essentially equal individuals capable of making unconstrained choices. Because of the law's individualistic focus, it sees one of the central problems that it must address to be enforcing the agreements made by free autonomous individuals, as well as enforcing a few social norms to keep the battle of human life from getting out of hand. It envisions another central task to be eliminating obvious constraints on individual choice and opportunity.

21   Rhode, supra (Lloyd, p 1043).
22   Rhode, supra (Lloyd, p 1044).
23   Finley, supra (Lloyd, p 1137).
24   Ibid.
25   Ibid.

The constraints are thought to emanate primarily from the state or from the bad motivation of other individuals. An individualistic focus on choice does not perceive constraints as coming from history, from the operation of power and domination, from socialization, or from class, race and gender. A final key task for individualistic liberal law is to keep the state from making irrational distinctions between people, because such distinctions can frustrate individual autonomy. It is not an appropriate task to alter structures and institutions, to help the disempowered overcome subordination, to eliminate fear and pain that may result from encounters masquerading as "freely chosen", to value nurturing connections or to promote care and compassion for other people.

'To keep its operation fair in appearance, which it must if people are to trust resorting to the legal method for resolving competing claims, the law strives for rules that are universal, objective, and neutral. The language of individuality and neutrality keeps law from talking about values, structures, and institutions, and about how they construct knowledge, choice, and apparent possibilities for conducting the world. Also submerged is a critical awareness of ... institutional power and domination. There are few ways to express within the language of law and legal reasoning the complex relationship between power, gender, and knowledge. Yet in order for feminists to use the law to help effectuate change, we must be able to talk about the connection between power and knowledge. This connection must be acknowledged in order to demystify the 'neutrality' of the law, to make the law comprehend that women's definitions have been excluded and marginalized, and to show that the language of neutrality itself is one of the devices for this silencing.

'The language of neutrality and objectivity can silence the voices of those who did not participate in its creation because it takes a distanced, decontextualized stance. Within this language and reasoning system, alternative voices to the one labelled objective are suspect as biased.'[26]

Thus by Liberalism objectivity is respected. Liberalism looks at things from the outside and, from what it observes, draws conclusions. Radical feminism embraces subjectivity: it acknowledges without apology that it is involved, interested; that it looks at matters from the inside; that it makes no attempt to 'separate the observer from the observed'.[27] It is true that 'legality has (or should have) certain qualities. There must be something reliable in the system somewhere,

26 Finley, supra (Lloyd, p 1138).
27 Ann C Scales, *The Emergence of Feminist Jurisprudence: An Essay* (Lloyd, p 1060).

there must be indicia of fairness in the system, but neither depends on objectivity'.[28] (Paul looked at Lucy, puzzled.)

3. The focus of attention of the two schools is different. Liberal feminists have tended to concentrate on public issues such as discrimination against woman over pregnancy (whether pregnancy should be a reason for dismissal, whether time off should be given for pregnancy, and the effect of the possibility of pregnancy on job applications and job prospects). Radical feminists, while not discounting the importance of public issues, have looked more towards issues that effect women's private lives, such as protection against harassment, as in the form of being whistled at in the street, degradation and exploitation by pornography, battery and rape within marriage.[29]

Radical feminists have thus paid particular attention to the effect of patriarchy on women's private lives. For example they believe that it needs to be explained '...how it feels to be the person that another has a legal right to invade without her consent. ... – that the harm of invasive intercourse is real even when it does not look like the kind of violence protected by the Rule of Law'.[30] It needs to be shown how patriarchy fails to recognise the economic value of the contribution of women constituted by child rearing and housework. It needs to be shown that abortion is not infanticide but an act by a woman of self defence against the invasion by the other in the shape of the foetus and that seen in this light a woman has a right to be protected against the harm that the foetus does.

4. Regarding pornography, Liberal feminists, while deploring the phenomenon, tend to consider that since suppression would entail restricting individual freedom of choice and form a step towards state control of the press and media, the price of suppression would be too high to pay. Radical feminists have no doubts. Pornography should be outlawed or, at the least, restricted and rigidly controlled.[31]

5. The starting point for Liberalism is the individuality, the separateness, of each human being. Since each person is separate, each person is independent from each of the others in the world. Separation

---

28 Scales, supra (Lloyd, p 1061).
29 See Patricia A Cain, *Feminism and the limits of equality* (1990) 24 Georgia Law Review.
30 West, supra (Lloyd, p 1077).
31 Ibid.

connotes the distinctiveness of each individual's identity and the value of an inner life enhanced by freedom from interference by others. Separateness confers freedom. And 'Because we are all free and are each equally free, we should be treated by our government as free, and equally free. The individual must be treated by his government (and by others) in a way that respects his equality and his freedom. Autonomy, freedom, and equality ... constitute what might be called the upside of ... separation. ... [A]utonomy and freedom both feel very good. However there is a down side to the ...experience of separation. Physical separation from the other entails not just my freedom; it entails my vulnerability. Every other ... individual ... is a source of danger to me and a threat to my autonomy. I have reason to fear you solely by virtue of the fact that I am me and you are you. ... Our ends might conflict. ... In an extreme case, you might even try to kill me – you might cause my annihilation. ... [So] we value the freedom that our separateness entails, while we seek to minimise the threat that it poses. We do so, of course, through creating and then respecting the state.'[32] This is how Liberalism sees things.

For Radical feminists, separateness is not something to be valued. It is not, in Bentham's terms, a pleasure but a pain, entailing as it does isolation, loneliness and alienation. The existence of others they see as being not, as Liberalism does, a threat, but as what gives enrichment, fulfilment, a factor essential to the full flourishing of human life. Thus the Radical feminists turn the Liberal values on their head, seeing individuals not as cherishing autonomy but as striving 'through love, work and government to achieve a unification [with others]. The separate individual seeks community – not autonomy – and dreads isolation and alienation from the other – not annihilation by him.'[33] Thus Liberalism (and those feminists who follow the Liberal path) value separateness, individuality. Radical feminists consider that whatever men may value, it its women's nature to value association, community.

6. Linked with the different attitude to separateness, is a difference between Liberal feminists and Radical feminists as to the nature of human relationships. For Liberalism, since each person is an autonomous unit, relationships between people are contractual in nature, everyone striving for the best terms they can get. Radical feminists say that such a view ascribes to women the objectives that are masculine. Radical feminists see the starting point for women

---

32 West, supra (Lloyd, p 1064).
33 Ibid.

as being not purely an egotistical concern for oneself, but a concern for others, resting on an approach that is caring, giving, nurturing, non-egotistical. Thus while Liberalism sees relationships between humans as contractual, Radical feminists see them as affiliative.[34]

7. Liberal feminists have tended to pay attention to the similarities between men and women, arguing, 'We are in all essential the same as you, we have no less an intelligence, no fewer talents, no fewer capabilities, so why should we be treated differently, as inferiors? Why should women who drive buses get lower wages than men?' Radical feminists point to the weakness of this line of attack – it only holds good in cases where women *are* the same as men, for example as regards physical strength. But men and women are not similarly situated. In particular, women may become pregnant. Why should this difference put them at a disadvantage? So while not rejecting the 'similarity' argument when it is appropriate to do so, Radical feminists focus attention on the differences between men and women, arguing, 'We recognise that differences between men and women exist, but what justification is there for any such differences being treated as reason for women to be disadvantaged?'

8. A further difference concerns the attitude taken towards state power. For Liberalism intervention by the state is something to be resisting as entailing curtailment of individual freedom. For Radical feminists non-intervention can mean no more than the consolidation of the patriarchal status quo. Thus in some cases what is needed is more intervention, not less.[35]

These, said Ms Gilbenkenthorpe, were the principal differences between those who followed the Liberal, and those who followed the Radical, path. But, she stressed, it was a mistake to think of feminist jurists as being divided into exclusive, precisely delimited, camps. The movement was one of individuals expressing their own views. We (Paul kept his head down) feminists are all allies in the struggle against patriarchy. We do not disparage the rights that have been secured, we welcome them. Further, views merge. Thus Radical feminists recognise, as Rhode expresses the point, 'Legal rights have a special resonance in our culture.'[36] For this reason, since '... claims about rights proceed within established discourse, they are less easily dismissed than other progressive demands. By insisting that the rule

34 Rhode, supra (Lloyd, p 1041).
35 Rhode, supra (Lloyd, p 1043).
36 Ibid

of law make good on its own aspirations, rights-orientated strategies offer a possibility of internal challenge that critical theorists have recognised as empowering in other contexts.'[37] ('Claiming rights can get results,' Lucy wrote in her notes.)

Further, Radical feminists recognise that it is patriarchically established rights that can on occasions provide the foundation for a feminist demand. For example, it is the right to privacy recognised within the United States, that underpins the demand in that country that women should be allowed the choice as to whether to abort a foetus.

Thus when Radical feminists attack Liberalism they are attacking a particular form of Liberalism, that in which existing legal structures are embedded, (involving the notions of individuality, autonomy, separateness), and not the efforts made by individual Liberal feminists to challenge the forces that perpetuate women's subordination.

Since the movement is one of individuals expressing their own priorities, it is to be expected that there are wide divergences of opinion among Radical feminists themselves. One such divergence concerns the topic of 'difference'.

Difference

The question here is, how should we respond to the fact that differences exist between the sexes? The question is crucial because it is the difference of women from men that has been used as patriarchy's principal prop. That differences exist – biological, physiological, temperamental – is, said Ms Gilbenkenthorpe, beyond dispute. If we adopt the line that equality is equity, that like cases should be treated alike, how do we deal with the objection that since men and women are *not* alike, there is no reason for them to be treated the same?

One response has been to dismiss differences between the sexes as being of any relevance: women should be treated no differently from men. This line, the line of 'gender neutrality',[38] has produced valuable advances. For example, in the United States acceptance of the principle secured for women the right to administer the estate of a deceased person. It was the line that, in earlier years, secured women admission to universities and the professions. But there can be drawbacks. For example, women may not come up to minimum physical requirements when applying for a job. Especially significant

37 Ibid.
38 Scales, supra (Lloyd, p 1081).

is pregnancy. If we say that men and women should be on identical footing, since men do not get time off for being pregnant, neither should women. If we say that special concessions should be made for women, we can be accused of wanting to introduce the kind of gender discrimination that otherwise we seek to eradicate. Further, placing the sexes on exactly the same footing could work to the disadvantage of women, for example, in custody cases, by men being treated as equally fitted for the upbringing of babies as women.

Another response has been not to dispute that differences exist between men and women. Do not, this line goes, assimilate the position of women to men. Recognise the differences but focus attention on the effect that the differences have and question the justification for these[39]. *Why* should women be disadvantaged at work because it happens that it is women, not men, who become pregnant? If no justification is found, then legislation should be sought to provide compensatory treatment ('special benefit', 'special protection'[40]) for women for the disadvantage they suffer (eg paid leave during the latter stages of pregnancy and the early period of child rearing). (For the more fundamentalistically disposed among feminists, however, this response is flawed in that it falls into the trap of treating maleness as 'the norm of what is human', of 're-enforcing stereotypes about a woman's place'.[41])

Cultural feminism

Just as one way of understanding Radical feminism is to consider the ways in which it differs from Liberalism, so cultural feminism can be understood by considering in what ways this differs from Radical feminism.

For Radical feminists, since differences between men and women have been made the ground for discriminating against women, differences should be treated as irrelevant. For Cultural feminists, women's difference from men is not a source of potential weakness but a source of strength. The difference of women from men is something to be celebrated.

A divergence between Radical feminists and Cultural feminists lies in the fact that Radical feminists 'have chosen to emphasise in their

---

39 Rhode, supra (Lloyd, p 1039).
40 MacKinnon, supra (Lloyd, p 1081).
41 Scales, supra (Lloyd, p 1051).

theory a negative aspect of 'woman' – her sexual objectification – whereas Cultural feminists emphasise a positive aspect – her special bond to others.'[42] With regard to this objectification, for Radical feminists such as Robin West 'violation of a woman's body occasioned by pregnancy and intercourse implies [a] ... violation of her privacy, integrity and life projects'.[43] 'The penis occupies the body and "divides the woman" internally ... in consensual intercourse no less than rape. It pre-empts, challenges, negates and *renders impossible* the main-tenance of physical integrity and the formation of a unified self.'[44] '... an unwanted pregnancy is disastrous, but even a wanted pregnancy and motherhood are intrusive. The child *intrudes*, just as the foetus invades.'[45] 'Intimacy, in short, is intrusive, even when it isn't life threatening ...'[46] 'While women may indeed "officially" value intimacy, what women unofficially crave is physical privacy, physical integrity, and sexual celibacy – in a word, physical exclusivity.'[47] (Paul glanced sideways at Lucy.) 'But the law provides no protection since the law does not recognise the danger of invasion, nor does it recognise the individual's need for ... independence from the intrusion which heterosexual penetration and foetal invasion entails.'[48]

This is not how Cultural feminists see things. For them, and in particular for Carol Gilligan, whose book *In a Different Voice* leads the way, women value intimacy and have a sense of connectedness to life stemming from the fact that 'it is women who are the primary caretakers of young children. A female child develops her sense of identity as "continuous with her caretaker's, while a young boy develops a sense of identity that is distinguished from his caretaker's".'[49] This divergence is reinforced in later life, for boys by fights in the school playground, competitive sports, and competition at work - all experiences that built a sense of the value of autonomy and self sufficiency.

As a result of this childhood, women speak in a 'different voice' from men, a voice that speaks in tones of caring, nurturance, love, and responsibility and concern for others. Thus while Liberal feminists see woman 'defined primarily as someone confined to the private sphere' and Radical feminists see her as man's sexual object,

42 Cain, supra (Lloyd, p 1110).
43 West, supra (Lloyd, p 1071).
44 Ibid.
45 Ibid.
46 Ibid.
47 Ibid.
48 West, supra (Lloyd, p 1073).
49 Ibid.

'Cultural feminists see her as caring and connected to others',[50] and pregnancy, childbirth and child rearing as matters for celebration, not dread and despair.

Further, because of their nature, women have a different moral sense, one arising from attitudes to resolving disputes that differ between the sexes from childhood. Boys treat individuals as autonomous units and in any dispute look for a rule that covers the issue, to see what rights each side has. Boys see a dispute in terms of opposing sides. One side wins, the side that shows the other to be in the wrong. Gilligan terms this the 'ethics of rights'. On the other hand, girls seek solutions not in terms of rights but in terms of seeking to safeguard relationships. Girls do not look for rigid rules but are willing to adopt a different solution for each problem, they seek to settle disputes in a way that shows concern for both sides. They do not ' insist upon uncovering an essence of the problem, but look rather for a solution that is coherent with the rest of experience'.[51] This she terms the 'ethics of care'. Thus morality is seen by women as a matter 'of inclusion rather than the balancing of claims ...',[52] a matter of thinking of the needs of, and responsibility to, others, rather than solely in terms of the rights of others.

Cultural feminists see their task as being to secure due recognition of the authenticity of women's 'different voice' by showing that 'community, nurturance, responsibility and the ethic of care are at least as worthy of protection as autonomy, self reliance and individuation';[53] and that 'the refusal of the legal system to protect those [women's] values has weakened this community as it has impoverished our lives'.[54] What is needed, Cultural feminists say, is a restructuring of law and society to accommodate the nurturant, caring, loving values that are traditionally associated with women.[55]

Connectedness

It is, Ms Gilbenkenthorpe admitted, not easy to give a uniform account of Radical feminist attitude to connectedness. On the one hand, Radical feminists reject the Liberal view of all humans as separate, autonomous units, and instead value association,

---

50   Cain, supra (Lloyd, p 1113).
51   Scales, supra (Lloyd, p 1052) on Gilligan's views.
52   West, supra (Lloyd, p 1067).
53   West, supra (Lloyd, p 1077).
54   West, supra (Lloyd, p 1077).
55   Rhode, supra (Lloyd, p 1039).

affiliation, as preconditions for human flourishing. On the other hand, for many Radical feminists it is the subjugative connectedness inevitably associated with the practical experiences of heterosexual connection – penetration, pregnancy and foetal invasion – that is the source of women's objectification, debasement, powerlessness, oppression, destruction and misery.[56] So women value intimacy but dread the invasion that heterosexual intimacy brings in its wake. ('Rads like connection but not too far', Paul wrote in his notes.)

Feminist tactics

Feminists may be divided in many respects, but they share a common aim – the betterment of women's lot. How is this to be achieved? What is the method to be adopted? Among the courses that Katharine Bartlett proposes is asking 'the woman question'.

The woman question

On this Bartlett says, 'Feminists across many disciplines regularly ask a question – a set of questions, really – known as the "woman question", which is designed to identify the gender implications of rules and practices which might otherwise appear to be neutral or objective ... In law, asking the woman question means examining how the law fails to take into account the experiences and values that seem more typical of women than men, for whatever reason, or how existing legal standards and concepts might disadvantage women ... [T]he purpose of the woman question is to expose those features and how they operate and to suggest how they might be corrected. ... Without the woman question, differences associated with women are taken for granted and, unexamined, may serve as a justification for laws that disadvantage women. The woman question reveals how the position of women reflects the organisation of society rather than the inherent characteristics of women. ...[T]he woman question helps to demonstrate how social structures [for example in 'the workplace, the family, clubs, sport, child rearing patterns and so on[57]] embody norms that implicitly render women different and therefore subordinate.'[58]

---

56 West, supra (Lloyd, p 1069).
57 Bartlett, supra (Lloyd, p 1118).
58 Bartlett, supra (Lloyd, pp 1116-1118).

Incorporationism

But what about seeking practical change? Can it be achieved, as Liberalism has believed, through the process of fighting for legal rights? Radical feminists, as we have seen, consider that this approach has failed to secure, and will fail to secure, the kind of total reappraisal of women's position in society necessary if there is to be an overthrow of patriarchy.

Would another way be to build on the rights approach by combining with this an awareness of women's particular attitude summed up by the phrase the 'ethics of care'? – to integrate the 'ethics of care' with the 'ethics of rights'? This has been termed the 'incorporationist' approach, and for some, in particular Gilligan, it shows good sense, maturity.

But for the true Radical feminist the approach is flawed, amounting to no more than tampering with the problem – the quick fix. It assumes that 'male supremacy is simply a random collection of irrationalities in an otherwise rational coexistence. [It presumes] that instances of inequality are merely legal mistakes – a series of failures to treat equals as equals which we can fix if we can just spot the irrationality in enough cases. As MacKinnon has demonstrated, however, from such a viewpoint we cannot see that male supremacy is a complete social system for the advantage of one sex over another. The injustice of sexism is not irrationality; it is domination. Law must focus on the latter, ... Binding ourselves to rules would help us only if sexism were a legal error.[59] ... [Thus] 'rights-based' and 'care-based' ethics cannot be blended. ... By trying to make everything too nice, incorporationism represses contradictions. It usurps women's language in order to further define the world on the male image; it thus deprives women of the power of naming. Incorporationism means giving over the world , because it means to say to those in power: "We will use your language and we will let you interpret it".'[60]

Unity

That differences of opinion among feminists exist cannot said, Ms Gilbenkenthorpe, be denied. But that this is so must not be allowed to overshadow the fact that on core issues unity prevails. Not only is unity over our objective – the overthrow of patriarchy – but there is

---

59 Scales, supra (Lloyd, pp 1052-1053).
60 C MacKinnon, *Sexual Harassment of Working Women*, p 121.

agreement over our starting point, that we must begin by looking at women's experiences in the real world. There is agreement that our work must be unashamedly 'result orientated'.[61] There is agreement that not only must laws be changed but that the institutions of society must be overhauled with equal thoroughness (for example by ending the overwhelmingly male make up of the judiciary, especially in the higher courts). We are united also in not being deterred by the fact that differences among us exist. Differences of opinion spur further discussion, discussion leading to further insights into the nature of the task ahead.

Criticisms

It would be a sign of weakness, Ms Gilbenkenthorpe said, not to recognise that criticisms of feminist jurisprudence exist. For example, there is agreement, at least by Radical feminists, that the starting point must be women's experiences. But experiences differ, between classes, between races and between those of different sexual orientation and over time. If women's experiences vary, which are to be the experiences from which a degree of generality can be drawn – how is the one 'authoritative female voice'[62] to be discovered? And if it cannot be discovered, how are we to present a credible picture of the shape of the society that we seek?

To this we can reply that 'Although we cannot know a priori what the good society will be, we know more than enough about what it will not be to provide a current agenda. It will not be a society with sex based disparities in status, power, and security'.[63] Indeed it has been a source of strength, not weakness, that feminists have concentrated on concrete issues rather than being drawn into a debate on a vision of utopia, the nature of which would be unlikely ever to secure agreement.

Why should the subordination of women be the subject of special attention, in comparison with the subordination that is based on race, or colour, or caste, or sexual orientation? In parts of Britain's inner cities, which form of discrimination is of most immediate concern, that by men against women, or by the police against blacks? To which we reply that it would be a strange world

---

61 Scales, supra (Lloyd, p 1060).
62 Finley, supra (Lloyd, p 1039).
63 Rhode, supra (Lloyd, p 1048).

indeed in which groups did not find it natural to express their own concerns. The objection, if valid, would mean that protest against injustice never began.

Feminists have come to have a special view of the nature of truth. They, at any rate significant jurists among them, reject the notion of an abstract, neutral truth about any situation: they reject any notion of 'the perfectibility, externality or objectivity of truth'. Instead – according to the view that has been described[64] as 'positionality' – truth is 'situated and partial'. It is situated in that 'it emerges from particular involvements and relationships'. For example the meaning of pregnancy is to be understood not just from the biological facts of the condition, but from the consequences of being pregnant in actual social situations, such as at work, while still at school, or in prison. 'Truth is partial in that the individual perspectives that yield and judge truth are necessarily incomplete. No individual can understand except from some limited perspective.' Thus 'positionality puts no stock in fixed, discoverable foundations. If there is any such thing as ultimate or objective truth, I can never, in my own life time be absolutely sure that I have discovered it. ... There can be no universal, final, or objective truth; there can be only 'partial, locatable, critical knowledge'[65], 'no aperspectivity – only improved perspectives'.[66]

The criticism here, and it is the most serious, is that feminist jurisprudence, to the extent that it accepts positionality, 'destroys the citadel of objectivity and leaves nothing in its place'.[67] Our answer here, Ms Gilbenkenthorpe said, can only be that if in seeking wider perspectives, the truth of any situation may seem to slide from our hands as we grasp at it, this does not alter our goal. That remains constant, the disclosing, and fighting to end all forms of discrimination and oppression based on our gender.[68]

Is it jurisprudence?

'Come on Other,' Paul said after the lecture, 'Are you going to eat?' Later, as they were sitting down, Paul said, 'Is it jurisprudence? I don't think so. It's about changing attitudes and, by doing this,

64   Bartlett, supra (Lloyd, p 1132).
65   Haraway, *Situated Knowledges: The Science Question*, in *Feminism and the Privilege of Partial Perspective* (1998) 14 Feminist Studies 575, 590.
66   Bartlett, supra (Lloyd, p 1133).
67   Scales, supra (Lloyd, p 1060).
68   Bartlett, supra (Lloyd, p 1133).

getting changes in the law. That's not jurisprudence. Jurisprudence is about what law *is*. Austin, Hart, Kelsen, Dworkin, Rawls, that's jurisprudence. What she's been talking about is politics. You wouldn't call Animal Rights jurisprudence, would you? Feminism should be part of sociology, or social history, or politics; not jurisprudence.[69] And I distrust anything that's written in jargon. Plato didn't need to use jargon, did he? He used ordinary language. Who will read this feminist stuff in a thousand years? In the last lecture, do you know how many times she said 'existential'? *Fifty-four!* It's the same in the extracts she hands out – 'existentially', 'contingently', 'epistemologically', 'contextually'; – the words are scattered around like seeds on a bird table. You have to work out what the jargon means before you can understand what they are talking about – that 'reproductive autonomy' means being able to decide whether to have an abortion; that 'adoption of a non-vigilant attitude mode' means not being careful. People who have got anything worth saying don't *need* to write like that.

'Anyway, Feminists are their own worst enemies. They get diverted into all this political correctness stuff instead of seeing the insult that's staring them in the face.'

'What's that?', Lucy asked.

'Public lavatories. Wherever you go, you see women having to queue. Men can just walk in and walk out again. Every stop on a coach holiday women panic that there won't be time for them to go before the bus leaves. It's shameful, humiliating. If Feminists had put all the energy they've put into this "he/she" business into getting a law passed that by such and such a year women's lavatories are to have the same number of cubicles as men have urinals and cubicles, plus 50% (because women take longer), they would have done infinitely more good for women than they ever have done by banging on about political correctness. Think what it was like when we went to Italy. Every stop – it was a nightmare.'

'Well,' said Lucy, 'I know what she would say – that until patriarchy is overthrown none of the disadvantages suffered by women will be properly removed: that women must not be sidetracked from the real objective. In any case, apart from that, it's nonsense to suggest that feminists have not tackled specific issues. In a host of fields feminist campaigns have righted wrongs. As for lavatories, you may be right. But when we went to Italy, what you were worried about was that I would be left behind and you didn't know whether to wait for me or get on the bus. You weren't concerned about women's rights. The

69 See *Dangerous Supplements*, ed P Fitzpatrick.

number of cubicles mattered because *you* were affected. What could be a better example of a patriarchy than that?

'As for feminism not being jurisprudence, those lectures have made me think about what part law plays, and that's jurisprudence, surely? Anyway, if you cut out Feminism, to be consistent you would cut out everything that's been written about the relationship between law and society – you would cut out Marxism, economic views, and you would certainly cut out the New Crits. You would go back to no more than positivism v natural law, and trying to decide what words such as "law", "justice", "rights" mean, which no one will ever agree on. You didn't complain about the New Crits not being jurisprudence, did you?

'And as for jargon, you didn't complain about the way the New Crits wrote, although you told me that they were jargony. No complaints there. And I know why. Because you liked what they said. You're not too keen on Feminism, so you say we shouldn't be doing it. Am I right? Yes I am. Come on. We'll be late. And,' she added, 'you can stop calling me Other.'

'OK,' said Paul. And they went off together for a tutorial on mortgages.

CHAPTER 21

It shouldn't be allowed!

Enforcement of morality[1]

In many, perhaps all, human societies there are standards of conduct fixed by reference to a moral code: there are moral standards – standards by which certain things are regarded as being right to do and things that are wrong to do. These notions of rightness and wrongness may stem from principles expressed in, or inherent in, a society's religion, the moral merit or demerit of certain acts, or certain kinds of acts, emanating from a suprahuman source, perhaps set out in a holy book or manuscript owing its origin, or its authority, to a divine intervention in the affairs of men. Sometimes a society's moral code may be secular in nature, the code being attributable to an accepted body of opinion, a form of social instinct as to what warrants praise and what condemnation, for example as in the case of the belief that it is wrong to attempt to push in front of a queue. Even in such cases, though, the principle behind the belief may owe its origin to a religious precept, for example in the case of queue jumping to the principle of unselfishness that runs through Christianity.

A question that has been the subject of much debate is whether the law should enforce morality. The question can be framed in various ways. Is it the job of the law to secure compliance with a society's moral standards? Is the fact that certain conduct is considered to be immoral a sufficient reason to make it a punishable offence? Is it a proper function of the law to compel citizens to

---

1 J W Harris *Legal Philosophies* Chap 10; R V F Heuston 'Morality and the Criminal Law' (1972) 23 NILQ 274; B Mitchell *Law, Morality and Religion in a Secular Society*; D Lyons *Ethics and the Rule of Law*.

behave in what the society considers to be a morally acceptable way? These are all forms that the question can take, and there are others. We shall, for brevity, refer to the question as being – Should the law enforce morality?

Limits to the debate

We shall, in due course, set out the two sides to the argument. But first, in order to keep the debate from getting woolly at the edges, to put ropes round the ring, we shall set out what the debate is not about.

1. The debate is not over whether absolute standards of morality can be established. Those on each side of the debate assume, for the purpose of the debate, that as a matter of fact in any society certain standards of the kind that we refer to as 'moral' standards exist. Whether such standards, or some of them, can be shown to have eternal validity, or whether such standards are transitory, and relative to changing circumstances, varying from one society to another, and with the passage of time, is not at issue here.

2. The debate is not over whether, if absolute standards of right and wrong exist (standards on which a moral code may be based), these standards, these ethical absolutes, are capable of being known to man. Thus the debate is not between cognitivism and non-cognitivism.

3. The debate is not over whether a law that conflicts with a higher moral code lacks validity. Thus the debate is distinct from that between positivists and those who support the doctrine of natural law (and therefore distinct also from the debate that has come to be termed the Hart–Fuller debate).

4. The debate is not over whether a citizen is under a moral duty to obey the law. This question is part of the debate over whether civil disobedience can ever be justified and is considered in a later chapter.[2]

5. The debate is not over whether it is a proper function of the law to protect the citizen against himself – whether paternalism is justified as an end for the law to act towards.

---

2 Chapter 22.

A note on paternalism[3]

The question here is whether the law should stand aside and allow a person to damage himself, for example by taking drugs, or by smoking tobacco, or to run the risk of suffering damage, for example by failing to wear a seat belt in a car or to wear a helmet when riding a horse or a bicycle.

The fact that certain damaging acts such as taking hard drugs may be considered by some to be immoral is not a matter of relevance. The debate over paternalism concerns the question whether a person should be prevented from doing acts, irrespective of any question of the morality or immorality of the acts concerned, that may cause damage to the person who does them.

A difficulty in the way of any useful debate over whether it is right for the law to have paternalism as an objective is that it is not easy to find instances for debate since whenever an instance is put forward, for example taking hard drugs, it is quickly recognised that there are good reasons on grounds of public policy why the law should intervene in order to prevent (or to regulate) the activity concerned. Thus in the case of hard drugs it can be argued that the damage inflicted on society (in the shape of medical care, police action against associated crime) warrants action by the state to outlaw the use of hard drugs. And if such action is justified on the grounds of public policy, then the matter ceases to be a useful instance over which to conduct the debate over paternalism.

Sometimes euthanasia is put forward as a matter that illustrates the issues in the debate over paternalism – is it proper for the law to seek to protect a would-be suicide by making it an offence for another person to assist him in the act of taking his own life? But here too the view that it is correct for the state to intervene can be justified on the grounds of public policy – that the law should provide protection to those who may be in a position of weakness (from mental or physical causes) from pressure from those who may stand to gain from the death and that this protection can only effectively be provided by making assistance in euthanasia an offence.

Another difficulty in conducting any useful debate over whether paternalism is a proper purpose for the law is that the debate can slide away into an argument over whether a particular instance cited by way of illustration *does* in fact cause damage to the person for whose protection intervention by the state is contemplated. For

3 On paternalism, see B Mitchell Law, Morality and Religion in a Secular Society Chap 5; R E Sartorius 'The Enforcement of Morality' (1972) 81 Yale LJ 891; G Dworkin 'Paternalism in Morality and the Law' (ed Wasserstrom) p 107.

example, if the use of soft drugs is used as an instance, then the argument can cease to be over the issue of the rightness or wrongness of paternalism and go off into the tangent as to whether soft drugs do in fact cause damage to those who use them.

Any attempt to be drawn into an argument over paternalism is thus best resisted until an instance can be found in which paternalism is in fact the point at issue. One such instance in recent years has concerned the refusal of a patient to accept medical treatment. In the case of adults, the common law and statute establish the right of a patient to refuse consent to treatment (and to refuse application of the treatment itself): the wishes of the individual prevail over any paternalistically prompted action for the individual's medical benefit.[4] In 1992, by way of exception, the Court of Appeal held[5] that the court had power, under its inherent jurisdiction to protect minors, to override the refusal of a girl aged 16 to consent to treatment of her condition of anorexia nervosa. In May 1998, the Court of Appeal, confirming the general principle, ruled that the right to refuse consent to treatment applied in the case of an adult woman, of sound mind, who refused permission for her baby to be delivered by Caesarian section, notwithstanding that the refusal of consent endangered her life. In October 1998, the Court ruled that the position was no different where the refusal of permission endangered the life of the baby.[6]

6. The debate is not over whether immoral acts that do manifest damage to society, as by disrupting public order or causing nuisance or outraging public decency,[7] should be made punishable. Those who oppose the enforcement by law of morality do not dispute that such matters are properly the state's concern. For example, instances of conduct that are regarded as infringing the moral code such as polygamy, bigamy, kerb crawling, persistent soliciting, living off the earnings of prostitutes, indecent exposure, incest, the peddling of certain drugs are all matters the outlawing of which is likely to be accepted as being justified, on grounds of public policy, by those whose general position is that it is not the function of the law to enforce morality.

---

4 See *St George's Healthcare National Health Service Trust* (1998) Times, 3 August.
5 *Re J (a minor) (Inherent Jurisdiction: Consent to Treatment)* (1992) Times, 15 July.
6 (1998) Times, 31 July.
7 An offence at common law. In *R v Gibson* [1990] 3 WLR 595 the offence was found to have been committed by the placing on public display of earrings made from freeze-dried human foetuses of three to four months' gestation.

7. Nor is the debate over whether there are connections between law and morality. What has been said in this and earlier chapters will have indicated that the connections between law and morality are legion. A few examples will suffice. (i) A society's legal framework may, and very often is likely to, be based on the society's moral code, legal rules mirroring legal principles (murder being both a moral and a legal wrong; breach of contract corresponding to breaking one's word). (ii) In deciding the level of severity of a sanction to be imposed for breach of the criminal law, the court may be influenced by the moral wickedness of the deed concerned, for example a heavier sentence being imposed for an assault by a twenty-year-old man on a ninety-year-old blind woman than for an assault on a man of the assailant's own age. (iii) A citizen may believe that a law that conflicts with principles of morality lacks validity and that this fact frees him from the duty to obey it. (iv) Another citizen may feel, where a law has been introduced according to the established means, that he has a moral duty to obey it, notwithstanding that he regards the law as harmful or misconceived.

So closely may law and morality be intertwined that in some societies the two may be regarded as not forming separate notions. In the societies of the western world, however, the two spheres have generally been seen, notwithstanding the numerous inter-relationships, as concepts that are distinct.

8. The debate is not over whether the law does enforce morality, by providing for sanctions to be imposed on those who commit what the society regards as moral wrongs. There is a wide range of matters that conflict with the moral code and in respect of which the law imposes sanctions. Murder, rape, theft, assault, cruelty to children or animals are all matters that are contrary to moral values in our present society and which are punishable by law. It is, though, in relation to sexual matters that the question of the enforcement of morality has been especially significant. In the restrictions that are, or have been in the not so distant past, placed on such matters as topless waitresses, live sex on the theatre stage, exhibitions of sadism, massage parlours offering 'extra' services, the public display of pornographic materials, living off the earnings of prostitutes, the law has intervened in order to enforce morality, or at any rate to restrict what is regarded as immoral.

9. Finally, in delimiting the scope of the debate, we must note that in addition to matters that are regarded as both immoral and illegal there are (a) some matters that are regarded as immoral but are not illegal, and; (b) some matters that are illegal but are not

generally regarded as being immoral. There is thus an overlap that can be illustrated like this:

Matters regarded as immoral
(a)

(b)

Matters that are illegal

In category (a) we could perhaps put telling lies (otherwise than in circumstances that constitute misrepresentation in the law of contract). In category (b) we could place forgetting, in the rush to get to Bakewell Magistrates' Court to act as a witness for the police, to get a ticket from a car park 'Pay and display' machine, with a consequent £10 fine.

The debate with which we are concerned is over (i) whether certain matters in category (a) should be made illegal; and (ii) whether certain matters in the area of overlap illustrated above should cease to be illegal.

The debate

Although the debate is referred to as the debate over the 'enforcement of morality', in practice it is not the contention of those who believe that the law should have this role that the law should act positively to 'compel goodness'. There have been times when this view has been held and sanctions imposed for this purpose. For example, during the period of the Commonwealth fines could be imposed on those who failed to attend divine service, and Aquinas had assumed that the state, as official representative of the community, had authority to 'compel right living'.[8] But in more recent times it is with the imposition of sanctions for doing certain acts that are regarded as immoral that the debate has been principally concerned; enforcement of morals has been about punishing acts of moral badness, not punishing the failure to perform acts of moral goodness.

Since the 1960s the debate over whether it is a proper function of the law to enforce morality has sometimes been referred to as the Hart–Devlin debate, from the names of two protagonists who entered the lists during this period. The debate has it origins, however, much earlier. An appropriate starting point for our purposes is provided by the views of John Stewart Mill. Mill did not write specifically on the question that we are considering, but the

---

8 Summa Theologica QU 90 Art 3.

thesis put forward in his essay *On Liberty*[9] constitutes an important argument on the anti-enforcers' side.

John Stuart Mill

The subject of the essay, Mill explained, was the nature and the limits of the power, which can legitimately be exercised by society over the individual. In earlier times this contest was one between government and subjects, liberty meaning protection against tyranny by the establishment of limits to the power that rulers could exercise over the community. After tracing the process by which government came to be accountable to the people, Mill says that it came to be 'perceived that such phrases as "self-government", and "the power of the people over themselves", do not express the true state of the case. The "people" who exercise the power are not always the same people as those over whom it is exercised; and the "self-government" spoken of is not the government of each by himself but of each by all the rest. The will of the people, moreover, practically means the will of the most numerous or the most active part of the people – the majority, or those who succeed in making themselves accepted as the majority; the people, consequently, may desire to oppress a part of their number, and precautions are as much needed against this as against any other abuse of power.'[10] It follows that '"the tyranny of the majority" is now generally included among the evils against which society requires to be on its guard.'[11]

Thus tyranny is not only that which is capable of being exercised by government – society is itself capable of being the tyrant. 'Society can and does execute its own mandates; and if it issues wrong mandates instead of right, or any mandates at all in things with which it ought not to meddle, it practises a social tyranny more formidable than many kinds of political oppression, since, though not usually upheld by such extreme penalties, it leaves fewer means of escape, penetrating much more deeply into the details of life, and enslaving the soul itself. Protection, therefore, against the tyranny of the magistrate is not enough; there needs protection also against the tyranny of the prevailing opinion and feeling, against the tendency

---

9 See the Introduction by G Himmelfarb to the Penguin edition (1974).
10 *On Liberty* p 62. (The page numbering is from the Penguin edited by G Himmelfarb, 1974.)
11 Ibid.

of society to impose, by other means than civil penalties, its own ideas and practices as rules of conduct on those who dissent from them; to fetter the development and, if possible, prevent the formation of any individuality not in harmony with its ways, and compel all characters to fashion themselves upon the model of its own.'[12]

The limit to interference

Therefore there must, Mill believed, be 'a limit to the legitimate interference of collective opinion with individual independence; and to find that limit, and maintain it against encroachment, is as indispensable to a good condition of human affairs as protection against political despotism.'[13]

The practical question is 'where to place the limit – how to make the fitting adjustment between individual independence and social control ...'[14] Since certain restraints on the actions of other people are essential for society to operate: 'Some rules of conduct must, therefore, be imposed – by law in the first place, and by opinion on many things which are not fit subjects for the operation of the law. What these rules should be is the principal question in human affairs ... No two ages, and scarcely any two countries, have decided it alike; and the decision of one age or country is a wonder to another. Yet the people of any given age and country no more suspect any difficulty in it than if it were a subject on which mankind had always been agreed. The rules which obtain among themselves appear to them self-evident and self-justifying. This all but universal illusion is one of the examples of the magical influence of custom ...'[15]

Likings and dislikings

The practical principle that guides people 'to their opinions on regulation of human conduct is the feeling in each person's mind that everybody should be required to act as he, and those with whom he sympathises, would like them to act. No one indeed, acknowledges to himself that his standard of judgment is his own liking; but an opinion on a point of conduct, not supported by reasons, can only count as one person's preference; and if the reasons, when given, are a mere appeal to a similar preference felt by other people, it is still only many people's liking instead of one. To an ordinary

12   Ibid, p 63.
13   Ibid.
14   Ibid.
15   Ibid, p 64.

man, however, his own preference, thus supported, is not only a perfectly satisfactory reason but the only one he generally has for any of his notions of morality, taste, or propriety, which are not expressly written in his religious creed, and his chief guide in the interpretation even of that. Men's opinions, accordingly, on what is laudable or blameable are affected by all the multifarious causes which influence their wishes in regard to the conduct of others, and which are as numerous as those that determine their wishes on any other subject. Sometimes their reason; at other times their prejudices or superstitions; often their social affections, not seldom their antisocial ones, their envy or jealousy, their arrogance or contemptuousness; but most commonly their desires or fears for themselves – their legitimate or illegitimate self-interest.'[16]

'The likings and dislikings of society, or of some powerful portion of it, are thus the main thing which has practically determined the rules laid down for general observance, under the penalties of law or opinion ... The only case in which the higher ground has been taken on principle and maintained with consistency, by any but an individual here and there, is that of religious belief ... It is accordingly on this battlefield, almost solely, that the rights of the individual against society have been asserted on broad grounds of principle, and the claim of society to exercise authority over dissentients openly controverted'[17] (ie by Protestants who challenged the authority of the Catholic church at the time of the reformation; and, later, by non-conformist groups which challenged the established Protestant churches).

From the circumstances of English history, 'though the yoke of opinion is perhaps heavier, that of law is lighter than in most other countries of Europe; and there is considerable jealousy of direct interference by the legislative or the executive power with private conduct ...'[18] However, there is 'no recognised principle by which the propriety or impropriety of government interference is customarily tested. People decide according to their personal preferences.'[19]

The principle

It is to fill the void left by this absence of principle that the essay is undertaken. And at this point Mill states what this principle should

16 Ibid, pp 64–65.
17 Ibid, p 67.
18 Ibid.
19 Ibid, pp 67–68.

be. In a passage of crucial importance he writes that the object of the essay 'is to assert one very simple principle, as entitled to govern absolutely the dealings of society with the individual in the way of compulsion and control, whether the means used be physical force in the form of legal penalties or the moral coercion of public opinion. That principle is that the sole end for which mankind is warranted, individually or collectively, in interfering with the liberty of action of any of their number is self-protection. That the only purpose for which power can be rightfully exercised over any member of a civilised community, against his will, is to prevent harm to others. His own good, either physical or moral, is not a sufficient warrant. He cannot rightfully be compelled to do or forbear because it will be better for him to do so, because it will make him happier, because, in the opinions of others, to do so would be wise or even right. These are good reasons for remonstrating with him, or reasoning with him, or persuading him, or entreating him, but not for compelling him or visiting him with any evil in case he do otherwise. To justify that, the conduct from which it is desired to deter him must be calculated to produce evil to someone else. The only part of the conduct of anyone for which he is amenable [ie answerable] to society is that which concerns others. In the part which merely concerns himself, his independence is, of right, absolute. Over himself, over his own body and mind, the individual is sovereign.'[20]

... and its limits

Having laid down the principle, Mill at once explains its limits. The 'doctrine is meant to apply only to human beings in the maturity of their faculties. We are not speaking of children or of young persons below the age that the law may fix as that of manhood or woman-hood. Those who are still in a state to require being taken care of by others must be protected against their own actions as well as against external injury.'

From Mill's general principle it follows that 'there is a sphere of action in which society as distinguished from the individual, has, if any, only an indirect interest: comprehending all that portion of a person's life and conduct which affects only himself or, if it also affects others, only with their free, voluntary, and undeceived consent and participation.... This, then, is the appropriate region of human liberty. It comprises, first, the inward domain of consciousness, demanding liberty of conscience in the most comprehensive sense, liberty of thought and feeling, absolute freedom of opinion and sentiment on

20 Ibid, pp 68–69.

all subjects, practical or speculative, scientific, moral, or theological....
Secondly, the principle requires liberty of tastes and pursuits, of
framing the plan of our life to suit our own character, of doing as we
like, subject to such consequences as may follow, without impediment
from our fellow creatures, so long as what we do does not harm them,
even though they should think our conduct foolish, perverse, or
wrong. Thirdly, from this liberty of each individual follows the liberty,
within the same limits of combination among individuals; freedom
to unite for any purpose not involving harm to others: ...

'No society in which these liberties are not, on the whole,
respected is free, whatever may be its form of government; and none
is completely free in which they do not exist absolute and un-
qualified. The only freedom which deserves the name is that of
pursuing our own good in our own way, so long as we do not attempt
to deprive others of theirs or impede their efforts to obtain it. Each
is the proper guardian of his own health, whether bodily or mental
and spiritual. Mankind are greater gainers by suffering each other
to live as seems good to themselves than by compelling each to live
as seems good to the rest.'[21]

Opinions

In Chapter 2 of the book Mill deals with liberty of thought and
discussion (a sphere in which less difference of opinion exists today,
at any rate in most western societies, than in Mill's time), concluding
that 'it is imperative that human beings should be free to form
opinions and express opinions without reserve'.[22] In the third
chapter he considers whether 'men should be free to act upon their
opinions – to carry these out in their lives without hindrance, either
physical or moral, from their fellow men, so long as it is at their own
risk and peril.' The proviso, he recognises is indispensable. 'No one
pretends that opinions lose their immunity when the circumstances
in which they are expressed are such as to constitute their expression
a positive instigation to some mischievous act. An opinion that corn
dealers are starvers of the poor, or that private property is robbery,
ought to be unmolested when simply circulated through the press,
but may justly incur punishment when delivered orally to an excited
mob assembled before the house of a corn dealer, or when handed
about among the same mob in the form of a placard. Acts, of
whatever kind, which without justifiable cause do harm to others
may be, and in the more important cases absolutely require to be,

21 Ibid, pp 71–72.
22 Ibid, p 119.

controlled by the unfavourable sentiments, and, when needful, by the active interference of mankind. The liberty of the individual must be thus far limited; he must not make himself a nuisance to other people. But if he refrains from molesting others in what concerns them, and merely acts according to his own inclination and judgment in things which concern himself, the same reasons which show that opinion should be free prove also that he should be allowed, without molestation, to carry his opinions into practice at his own cost.... As it is useful that while mankind are imperfect there should be different opinions, so it is that there should be different experiments of living; that free scope should be given to varieties of character, short of injury to others; and that the worth of different modes of life should be proved practically, when anyone thinks fit to try them. It is desirable, in short, that in things which do not primarily concern others, individuality should assert itself.'[23]

However, in practice 'individual spontaneity is hardly recognised by the common modes of thinking as having any intrinsic worth, or deserving any regard on its own account. The majority, being satisfied with the ways of mankind as they now are (for it is they who make them what they are), cannot comprehend why those ways should not be good enough for everybody ...'[24] But '[h]uman nature is not a machine to be built after a model, and set to do exactly the work prescribed for it, but a tree, which requires to grow and develop itself on all sides, according to the tendency of the inward forces which make it a living thing.'[25]

As the splendid passages roll past few can fail to be carried along by Mill's argument for individualism and his attack on 'the engines of moral repression'.[26] But, as so often is the case, it is when we look up from the book at the world beyond that the strength of the thesis may begin to seem less secure than it had appeared on the printed page. Does Mill's formula – that one should be entitled to do anything that does not harm others – work? How is the theory to be applied?

Application

That difficulties can arise over the practical application of the thesis Mill readily accepts and in the final chapter of the book he deals with certain specific matters such as the sale of poisons, drunkenness and offences against decency (which he counts as coming within

23   Ibid, pp 119–120.
24   Ibid, p 120.
25   Ibid, p 123.
26   Ibid, p 72.

the category of offences against others and therefore rightly prohibited).[27] A further problem he admits to is this: 'In cases of personal conduct supposed to be blameable, but which respect for liberty precludes society from preventing or punishing because the evil directly resulting falls wholly on the agent; what the agent is free to do, ought other persons to be equally free to counsel or instigate?'[28] For example, in Mill's day fornication was considered (and Mill did not dispute the view) to be a moral wrong. Under Mill's thesis the state had no business to prohibit the activity. But should a person be free to advocate fornication? Mill concludes that he should: 'whatever it is permitted to do, it must be permitted to advise to do'.[29] A doubt remains, however, Mill concedes, where 'the instigator derives a personal benefit from his advice, when he makes it his occupation, for subsistence or pecuniary gain, to promote what society and the State consider to be an evil. Then, indeed, a new element of complication is introduced – namely, the existence of classes of persons with an interest opposed to what is considered as the public weal, and whose mode of living is grounded on the counteraction of it. Ought this to be interfered with, or not? Fornication, for example, must be tolerated, and so must gambling; but should a person be free to be a pimp, or to keep a gambling house? The case is one of those that lie on the exact boundary line between two principles, and it is not at once apparent to which of the two it properly belongs. There are arguments on both sides.'[30]

After marshalling the arguments on each side Mill is unable to decide which set of arguments prevails, concluding 'I will not venture to decide whether they [the arguments that support the prohibition of advocating or encouraging moral wrongs for personal profit] are sufficient to justify the moral anomaly of punishing the accessory when the principal is (and must be) allowed to go free; of fining or imprisoning the procurer, but not the fornicator – the gambling-house keeper, but not the gambler.'

If Mill is unable here to give us an answer, what expectation can we have that his thesis will provide the key to the dilemmas with regard to what should and what should not on moral grounds be permitted that have beset our own age? – dilemmas that exist, for example, in the sphere of euthanasia, the possession, use and sale of soft drugs, the use of human embryo tissue in research, in vitro human

27 Ibid, p 168.
28 Ibid.
29 Ibid.
30 Ibid, pp 168–169.

fertilisation and surrogate parenthood. Nevertheless, despite difficulties of application, as a champion of the principles of human freedom and individual liberties, Mill's great work, in its clarity, logic, vigour and conviction, stands unequalled in English writing.

Stephen

A view that ran directly counter to that of Mill was expressed by J F Stephen in 1874 in his *Liberty, Equality and Fraternity*.[31] For Stephen there are some acts that are of so outrageous and gross a wickedness that they must be prevented at any cost. Whether the acts are the cause of damage to anyone other than the person who does them is of no relevance. The prevention of immorality is a proper end in itself and justifies action by the state, action that Mill would contend lies outside the sphere of the state's legitimate concern. For Stephen the morality that it was the law's duty to enforce was to be determined by reference to the unanimous opinion of society. Where there was strenuous and unequivocal condemnation of certain conduct, then this should be proscribed. Stephen gave no indication of recognising that moral codes vary from one society to another, and from one age to the next within any one society. It is clear that by morality he was thinking of the moral code ordained (if not observed) by the ruling section of society of his own day.

Wolfenden

In 1957 the debate over whether the law should properly concern itself with the enforcement of morals received a focal point with the publication of the Report[32] of the committee established by the Home Office and the Scottish Home Department, under the chairmanship of J F Wolfenden, to consider, inter alia, the law and practice relating to homosexual offences and the treatment of persons convicted of such offences by the courts, and to report what changes if any, were considered desirable.

The conclusion reached by the committee was that 'Unless a deliberate attempt is to be made by society, acting through the agency

31   For an analysis of Stephen's thesis, see R A Samek (1949) Can Bar R 188 at 200–208.
32   Cmnd 247.

of the law, to equate the sphere of crime with that of sin, there must remain a realm of private morality which is, in brief and crude terms, not the law's business. 'To say this is not to condone or encourage private immorality.'[33] Therefore, 'It is not the duty of the law to concern itself with immorality as such ... it should confine itself to those activities which offend against public order and decency or expose the ordinary citizen to what is offensive or injurious.'[34] The committee accordingly recommended[35] that homosexual behaviour between consenting adults in private should no longer be a criminal offence. The recommendation was implemented as regards persons over 21 by the Sexual Offences Act 1967.

Devlin

Two years after the publication of the Wolfenden report, Lord Devlin undertook an assessment of the issues that underlay the report in his book *The Enforcement of Morals.*[36] 'What is the connection,' he set out to discuss, 'between crime and sin and to what extent, if at all, should the criminal law of England concern itself with the enforcement of morals and punish sin or immorality as such?'

In answering this question Lord Devlin posed three subsidiary questions. The first, which is in two parts, is this: 'Has society the right to pass judgment at all on matters of morals? Ought there, in other words, to be a public morality, or are morals always a matter for private judgment?' Lord Devlin's conclusion is that there is such a thing as public morality and although he fails to deal as specifically with the questions he posed as would have been helpful, we are left with the impression that since, in Devlin's view, there is such a thing as public morality, society does have the right to pass judgments on matters of morals, and that morals are therefore not always a matter for private judgment.

The second question is this: 'If society has the right to pass judgment, has it also the right to use the weapon of the law to

---

33 Ibid, para 61.
34 Ibid, para 257. The passage relates to the committee's consideration of the law relating to prostitution. But it is clear that the principle was one that guided the committee in dealing with homosexuality.
35 Ibid, para 355.
36 For assessments of Devlin's views, see Williams 'Authoritarian Morals and Criminal Law' [1966] Crim LR 132; R Dworkin 'Lord Devlin and the Enforcement of Morals' (1966) 75 Yale LJ 986; G B Hughes 'Morals and the Criminal Law' (1962) 71 Yale LJ 662.

enforce it?' Devlin's answer here is that society does have such a right since 'a recognised morality is as necessary to society as, say, a recognised government' and that 'society may use the law to preserve morality in the same way as it uses it to safeguard anything else that is essential for its existence'.

At this point Devlin steps aside to consider an additional question. 'How are the moral judgments of society to be ascertained?' He answers that immorality 'for the purpose of the law is what every right minded person is presumed to consider to be immoral' and he adopts here the view of Pollock on what that writer called 'practical morality' – that based not on philosophical or theological foundations but 'in the mass of continuous experience half-consciously or unconsciously accumulated and embodied in the morality of common sense'. So in determining the content of public morality the law is not looking for 'true belief' but 'common belief'.

The third question is this: If society has the right to use the weapon of the law to enforce morality, 'ought it to use that weapon in all cases or only in some; and if only in some, on what principles should it distinguish?' Devlin recognises that a citizen cannot be expected to surrender to the judgment of society the whole conduct of his life. 'It is the old and familiar question of striking a balance between the rights and interests of society and those of the individual.' It is not possible to put forward any general statements about how in our society the balance ought to be struck. But nevertheless there are, Devlin believes, certain principles that the legislature should bear in mind when it is considering the enactment of laws that enforce morals.

One is that there must be toleration of 'the maximum individual freedom that is consistent with the integrity of society.... Nothing should be punished by the law that does not lie beyond the limits of tolerance.'

But '[n]ot everything is to be tolerated. No society can do without intolerance, indignation and disgust; they are the forces behind the moral law, and indeed it can be argued that if they or something like them are not present, the feelings of society cannot be weighty enough to deprive the individual of freedom of choice.' However, 'before a society can put a practice beyond the limits of tolerance there must be a deliberate judgment that the practice is injurious to society.'

The second thing that the legislature should bear in mind when it is considering the enactment of laws that enforce morality is that the limits of toleration shift. By this Devlin does not mean that standards of morality of any one society shift ('at any rate so far as they come from a divine source they do not'), but 'the extent to which society will tolerate – I mean tolerate, not approve – departure from moral standards varies from generation to generation'. For this reason the law should be slow to intervene in the sphere of morality, because what may not be tolerated in one generation may come to be tolerated in the next, 'the swell of indignation having abated, leaving the law without the strong backing that it needs'.

The third matter that the legislature should bear in mind, something that Lord Devlin advances more tentatively, is that as far as possible privacy should be respected.

The answer to the third question (ought the law to enforce morality in all cases or only in some) is thus that there are no hard and fast rules. Each instance must be considered separately and a judgment reached after taking into account the three matters he has stated. In reaching the judgment the principle must be that the law's proper purpose is the protection of society. It is with regard to the purpose of the law that Devlin believes that the thinking of the Wolfenden report is mistaken. The error of the report is that it finds that 'the single principle to explain the division between crime and sin is that criminal law exists for the protection of individuals'. The law should not stop here. 'The law does not discharge its function by protecting the individual from injury, annoyance, corruption and exploitation; the law must protect also the institutions and the community of ideas, political and moral, without which people cannot live together.... What makes a society is a community of ideas, not political alone but also ideas about the way its members should behave and govern their lives.' It is society in this form that it is the proper function of the law to protect.

In summary form Lord Devlin's argument is thus that a society's morals are part and parcel of that society. Its moral standards are the standards of conduct of which the reasonable man approves. The law should enforce morals in those circumstances in which this is necessary for the preservation of society. Where any matter is regarded with intoleration, indignation or disgust, then it is right that it should be prohibited by law since, if it is not, moral judgments might be confused as a result of people seeing moral wickedness going unpunished, thereby bringing the law into disrepute, with a consequent weakening of society. In deciding in specific cases whether moral wickedness should be punished, the 'legislator must gauge the intensity with which a popular moral conviction is held, because it is only when the obverse is generally thought to be intolerable that the criminal law can safely and properly be used.'[37]

---

37 *The Enforcement of Morals* p 95.

In the final chapter of the book Lord Devlin makes an additional point. Since the law does take into account moral turpitude in fixing the punishment for a crime it is reasonable that the law should be equally concerned with moral turpitude in deciding whether a particular act should be a crime.

A significant difference between the position of Stephen and that of Devlin has been pointed out by Professor Hart. For Devlin the law should enforce morality as a means of protecting the fabric of society, of which a shared morality is an integral part. For Stephen the preservation of morality is an end in itself and one that justifies legal enforcement, irrespective of the fact that immoral acts harm no one directly, or indirectly by weakening society.

Hart

Lord Devlin's views have had their supporters and their critics. Among the earliest of the latter was Professor H L A Hart in his book *Law, Liberty and Morality*, published in 1962. Before setting out his arguments against Devlin's thesis, Hart makes two preliminary points. The first is that he raises no objection to the law prohibiting immoral acts on the ground that the commission of the act causes an offence to others of a degree that turns the matter into a public nuisance. He cites bigamy as an example. Some people may consider that 'in a country where deep religious significance is attached to monogamous marriage and to the act of solemnising it, the law against bigamy should be accepted as an attempt to protect religious feelings from offence by public act desecrating the ceremony.' Hart does not reject this contention but maintains that it is important that, although the law is intervening in order to protect religious sensibilities from outrage by a public act, the bigamist should be seen to be punished, not as being irreligious or immoral, but on the grounds of nuisance. For the law, in proscribing bigamy, is dealing with the offensiveness to others of the bigamist's public conduct, which, because of the element of public nuisance involved, is its proper concern, not with the immorality of the conduct, which is not. Thus the 'example of bigamy shows the need to distinguish between the immorality of a practice and its aspect as a public offensive act or nuisance.'

But what, Hart turns to consider, about immoral acts that are done in private? It could be argued that such acts should be forbidden by law by virtue of Mill's principle that coercion is justified to prevent harm to others, the harm in this case being the distress caused to others by the thought of what is being done behind closed doors. Hart rejects this view, and the rejection lies at the core of his argument. 'To punish people for causing this form of distress would be tantamount to punishing them simply because others object to what they do; and the only liberty that could coexist with this ... is liberty to do those things to which no one seriously objects.' This is the kernel of Hart's thesis: we have a right to be protected against shock or offence to feelings by some public display. But we have no right to be protected from distress caused by knowing that certain things are done in private. A right 'to be protected from the distress which is inseparable from the bare knowledge that others are acting in ways you think wrong, cannot be acknowledged by anyone who recognises individual liberty as a value.'

In support of this thesis, Hart proceeds to make certain supplementary points. First he challenges Devlin's view that offences against the moral code weaken a society. This is no more than an assumption: '... no evidence is produced to show that deviation from accepted sexual morality, even by adults in private, is something which, like treason, threatens society. No reputable historian has maintained this thesis, and there is indeed much evidence against it. As a proposition of fact it is entitled to no more respect than the Emperor Justinian's statement that homosexuality was the cause of earthquakes.' Devlin, Hart says, 'moves from the acceptable proposition that some shared morality is essential to the existence of any society to the unacceptable proposition that a society is identical with its morality as that is at any given moment of its history, so that a change in its morality is tantamount to the destruction of a society.'[38] The former proposition might be accepted but the latter is 'absurd'. 'Taken strictly, it would prevent us saying that the morality of a given society has changed, and would compel us instead to say that one society had disappeared and another one taken its place. But it is only on this absurd criterion of what it is for the same society to continue to exist that it could be asserted without evidence that any deviation from a society's shared morality threatens its existence.'

Next Hart turns to the means of enforcement: coercion. There is, he says, 'little evidence to support the idea that morality is best taught by fear of legal punishment. Much morality is certainly taught and sustained without it, and where morality is taught with it, there is the standing danger that fear of punishment may remain the sole motive for conformity.' If the threat of coercion does not teach people to behave morally, justification for coercion could be sought in the retributive theory of punishment – that punishment is the appropriate return for the evil committed. But a 'theory which does not attempt to justify punishments by its results, but simply as something called for by the wickedness of a crime, is certainly most plausible, and perhaps only intelligible, where the crime has harmed others, and there is both wrongdoer and a victim' – when it is felt 'that it is right or just that one who has intentionally inflicted suffering on others should himself be made to suffer'.[39] But the basis of the thinking is dependent on there being a victim as well as an offender. Where, as in the case of an immoral act committed in private, there is no victim but only a transgressor of a moral rule, the view that punishment is still called for lacks a valid basis.[40] 'Retribution here seems to rest on nothing but the implausible claim that in morality two blacks make a white: that the evil of suffering added to the evil of immorality as punishment makes a moral good.'[41]

Next Hart considers the view that apart from any justification that can be found for the punishment of immorality on the grounds of retribution, punishment can be justified on the ground that it has value as denunciation. Stephen, Hart says, 'sometimes writes as if the function of punishment were not so much retributive as denunciatory; not so much to gratify feelings of hatred or revenge as to express in emphatic form moral condemnation of the offender and to "ratify" the morality which he has violated'.[42] Those who believe that the law should properly fulfil this denunciatory function in reality are saying that the law should act to instil and strengthen respect for the moral code.[43] But the moral code of any society changes with time, following the process of discussion and self-criticism, a process that is curtailed or at any rate inhibited by the enforcement of the existing code by legal sanctions. 'The use of legal punishment to freeze into immobility the morality dominant at a particular time in a society's existence may possibly succeed, but even where it does it contributes nothing to the survival of the animating spirit and formal values of social morality and may do much to harm them.'[44]

Hart's argument is, therefore, that the views put forward by both Stephen and by Devlin are equally untenable. Stephen is in error

39 Ibid, p 60.
40 Ibid.
41 Ibid.
42 Ibid, p 63.
43 Ibid, p 66.
44 Ibid, p 72.

since to 'use coercion to maintain the moral status quo at any point in a society's history would be artificially to arrest the process that gives social institutions their value'.[45] Devlin is in error since 'there is no evidence that the preservation of a society requires enforcement of its morality "as such".'[46]

Professor Hart does not dispute that members of a society should be encouraged to abide by its moral standards. But this should be achieved by discussion, advice and argument, not by legal coercion. The use of coercion to secure compliance with a moral code involves elements that are contrary to the spirit of moral value – enforcing conformity through fear; gratification of feelings of hatred by retributory punishment; infliction of punishment as a symbol of condemnation, and the insulation of a society from modification in its moral values. The price of seeking to impose adherence to moral values by legal sanctions in terms of human misery and the loss of freedom is too high.[47]

Other protagonists

The exchange between Lord Devlin and Professor Hart sparked off much discussion, some commentators supporting one or other of the viewpoints of the two main protagonists, others adding neutral comments.

Writing in 1962 *G Hughes*[48] pointed to the weaknesses in Devlin's use of the judgment of the right-minded person for determining what matters should be proscribed by law. 'The yardstick is to be the feeling of right-minded people, though we are not told who are to be considered "right minded". Without qualification, this remarkable statement has a frightening evocation of the notorious Nazi law of 1935 that empowered the judges to punish acts that deserved punishment "according to the healthy instincts of the people".[49] ... The weakness of Lord Devlin's position ... is perhaps demonstrated by a curious passage at the end of his lecture where he discusses the crime of abortion. "[A] great many people nowadays," he complains, "do not understand that abortion is wrong." (The use of the word "understand" here would seem to indicate

---

45 Ibid, p 77.
46 Ibid, p 82.
47 Ibid, p 83.
48 (1962) 71 Yale LJ 662.
49 Ibid, p 675.

some revelation granted to the author and which many people have not enjoyed.) ... But since he has admitted that many people do not think abortion is wrong, it is evident that by morality here he does not mean commonly shared attitudes of approval and disapproval but rather the morality of a Church group.'[50]

In Hughes's view, 'The examination of existing law and the debate about proposed laws should be conducted by making as explicit a statement as is possible of the values that the law is designed to protect, by a careful investigation of the harm done to those values by the conduct prohibited or which it is sought to prohibit, and by a careful consideration of the probable efficacy of legal prohibition. In this debate the prevalence of feelings of disgust or revulsion in the community towards given conduct is one factor to be considered and no more than that. It can never replace careful investigation of the social consequences of conduct and criminal prohibition, and if that careful investigation returns a verdict contrary to that of the disgusted majority, then that majority feeling must be ignored, unless to ignore it would lead to disturbance of a kind more harmful than the prohibition in question. The legislator cannot be wiser than he is, but he does not have to be as stupid as the stomach of the man in the street.'[51]

In 1966 *Professor Dworkin* discussed[52] the validity of the assumption made by Devlin that a society has a right to protect its basic social institutions against conduct that the majority of its members disapprove of on moral grounds. The weakness, he found, lay in the uncertainty that must exist as to whether a legislator can in fact satisfactorily assess whether a consensus of opinion exists and, if such a consensus is found to exist, whether the opinion is based on rational grounds. As to Devlin's own views on what is and what is not immoral, Dworkin comments, 'What is shocking and wrong is not his idea that the community's morality counts, but his idea of what counts as the community's morality.'[53]

In *Law, Morality and Religion*, published in 1967, *B Mitchell* concluded that the function of the law is not only to protect individuals from harm, but also to protect the essentials of a society. The law cannot, he maintained, remain neutral as regards morality since in protecting the institutions of a society, it presupposes certain 'universal values of morality' and in carrying out the task of pro-

---

50 Ibid, p 680.
51 Ibid, p 682.
52 'Lord Devlin and the Enforcement of Morals' (1966) 75 Yale LJ 986.
53 Ibid p 1001.

tection the 'reinforcement of morality' is sometimes justified. Thus Mitchell leans towards Devlin's thesis that a society has a right to protect itself. But he makes important provisos. The morality that the law presupposes should be open to criticism and debate carried out in the light of the fullest use of social reason, and it is vital that privacy should as far as is possible be respected.

In 1971, *R A Samek*[54] threw fresh light on the debate when he pointed out that 'enforcement of morality' could have four meanings, meanings which had been 'telescoped' together in the Hart–Devlin controversy. The four possible meanings were as follows:

1. that every immoral act should eo ipso also be an illegal act;
2. that some immoral acts should qua such acts also be illegal;
3. that the immorality of some acts should be the decisive factor in making them illegal;
4. that immorality of an act should be a relevant factor in deciding whether to make it illegal.

Samek commented that 'We may say that [Devlin] is not really advocating the enforcement of morals as such as an end, but only the enforcement of morals in the weaker sense as a means to the end of preserving the existence of a society. However, given the ambiguity and dubiousness of that end, the means tend to become the end; Lord Devlin's belief in the instrumental value of enforcing conventional morals tends to become a belief in the value of enforcing conventional morals as such. The value of enforcing a specific moral code is at least capable of rational examination, but there is no way of examining the value of enforcing conventional morals as such. It is no accident, I think, that Lord Devlin in practice advocates the enforcement of a moral code of which he approves'.[55]

Samek's own view is that the enforcement of morality is justified in the fourth sense that he distinguished – that the immorality of an act should be a relevant factor in deciding whether to make it illegal. 'The immorality of an act should never be the decisive factor in making it illegal, since the appropriateness of a moral sanction does not entail the appropriateness of a legal sanction. What is grist to the fine mill of morality, may well escape the clumsy engine of law or be mangled by it. But any attempt to exclude the immorality of an act as a relevant factor in deciding whether to make it illegal, is both dangerous and futile. It is dangerous because it leads to the illusion that a legal system can function without the foundation and

54 (1971) 49 Can Bar R 100.
55 Ibid, p 215.

the frame of reference of a moral system, and it is futile because moral values have a way of infiltrating into even the most antiseptic legal system.

'But a word of caution is necessary here. We must not think of law as taking over moral rules lock, stock and barrel. Even if moral rules could be formulated with sufficient precision, they would still have to be adapted from their moral environment to serve the special end of legal enforcement. It is more fruitful to think of legislators and judges as craftsmen who work up moral and other values into the form of law for the benefit of the society they serve.'[56]

R V F Heuston,[57] writing in 1972, pointed to two particular weaknesses in Devlin's argument. Devlin, Heuston said, failed to prove that moral disintegration in fact leads to political disintegration, that enforcement of all aspects of a moral code is in fact essential to the existence of a society. Devlin also failed to take into account that within a nation state at the present day there may well be a plurality of moralities (as where, we might add as an example, to one group a book might seem unexceptionable to the point of dullness, and yet to another group execrably blasphemous and immoral).

In 1977 *N B Reynolds*[58] added weight to the anti-enforcers' case by pointing out the practical disadvantages of laws that have as their object the suppression of matters that are considered by some to be immoral. He listed these.

1. Many acts commonly treated as being examples of immorality, if made criminal, are victimless. Victimless crimes tend to be difficult to enforce.

2. The cost of enforcing laws against victimless crimes tends to be high. Police are forced to use legally and morally questionable techniques in carrying out investigations. Society is damaged by the creation of black markets as the price of illegal goods and services is forced up, and by the crime associated with the running of these markets. [In 1998 it was estimated that 40% of robberies are made to fund the purchase of drugs; that in the UK drug addicts steal £2 billion a year to fund their habits, and that the cost to the state of (unsuccessfully) fighting the drugs trade amounts to £500 million a year.[59]]

56   Ibid, p 221.
57   (1972) 23 NILQ 274.
58   (1977) 11 Georgia LR 1325.
59   *The Times*, 2 April, G Seargeant.

3. Citizens who commit acts they find in no way immoral are arbitrarily degraded when the law makes the acts concerned illegal.
4. Administration of laws against what the state has made illegal on moral grounds results in the less well defended segments of society being discriminated against. Police can choose arbitrarily against whom to act.
5. This arbitrary power leads to corruption and exploitation as officials become subject to bribes, thus bringing the system of criminal justice into disrepute.

Conclusion

By way of conclusion the following points can be made.

1. The starting point for the debate over the enforcement of morals is that there *is* such a debate. We make this assumption because this book is published in the United Kingdom at the end of the second millennium. It should be remembered, however, that in a world-wide context, no such assumption is to be made: in some countries there is no debate because it goes without saying that it is the proper function of the state to enforce morality, to ensure, for example, respect for Allah and His Prophet, or to uphold the doctrines and social teaching of the Holy Catholic Church. The debate as we know it, has no place.

2. It might be thought that, in many western societies, during the twentieth century the tendency has been for the law to play a lesser part in enforcing morality. Perhaps this is so. But another interpretation is possible. When the law has been changed so that certain acts, previously prohibited on grounds of morality, cease to be illegal, what may be happening is not that the law has ceased to enforce morality, but that the acts concerned have ceased in the mind of the community to be regarded as immoral. People who say that the law has no business in enforcing morality by proscribing pornography[60] may in fact be saying no more than that they do not find that pornography offends their conscience. Thus it may be that it is the boundaries of what is considered immoral that have moved

60 Obscene Publications Act 1959.

rather than that there has been any significant change as to whether the law should enforce.

3. So rapidly and so radically has public opinion on matters of personal conduct changed that a question that now comes to the fore is - Do standards of morality with a sufficient level of general acceptance for it to be useful to continue to talk of the state enforcing morality any longer exist? In 1997 a report conducted for the Broadcasting Standards Commission concluded that there was no national agreement on what is unacceptable, unsocial or even shocking. As a correspondent in *The Times*, in speaking of television, summarized the position, 'We live in two nations, one utterly appalled by the entertainment that the other half cannot get enough of'.[61]

4. Be that as it may, the fact is that cases involving morality continue to come before the courts. A jurist may reach the conclusion that there are two sides the argument, but the legislature and the judiciary have to make decisions.[62] The issue can arise, for example in the context of blasphemy, as in 1996 when the European Court of Human Rights was called upon to rule on the legitimacy of the banning within the United Kingdom of a video, *Visions of Ecstasy* which depicted St Theresa of Avila in erotic scenes with the crucified Christ. (The ban was upheld.[63]) The arguments on either side can arise equally in the context also of the question as to whether it is a proper function of the state to act against the availability of material considered to be pornography (In 1998 the West Midlands police raided the library of the University of Central England and confiscated a book celebrating the work of the photographer Robert Mapplethorpe).

During the past decade it has been prosecutions for certain practices in private that have focused attention on the issues at stake in the Hart – Devlin debate. In 1990 twelve men were charged with causing actual bodily harm and with aiding and abetting the causing of actual bodily harm. The twelve had been

---

61 The conventional 'Devlinian' view continues, however, to be affirmed, as by George Carey, Archbishop of Canterbury, writing in 1998: 'Yet most of us recognize that no society can survive for long unless it is held together by standards that transcend the individual. Values and morals are social, not merely individual'.

62 See *Shaw v DPP* (1962) AC 220.

63 (1996) Times, 5 December. See also *R v Gay News* [1979] 1 All ER 898 (HL); *Otto-Preminger Institut v Austria* (1994).

members of a sado-masochistic group which had carried out a variety of bizarre practices.

Some of the men were charged with, pleaded guilty to, and received sentences (including prison sentences) for certain other offences committed in the course of the group's activities, including possessing drugs, keeping a disorderly house where men came to have sex with animals, having obscene photographs for publication for gain and sending an indecent photograph through the post.

With regard to the sado-masochistic practices, it had been held in *R v Donovan*[64] in 1934 that where an assault causing actual bodily harm took place, the fact that the persons harmed had, expressly or impliedly, given their consent was not to be a defence except in a limited number of circumstances, including those where a person gave consent to the performance of surgery, or where consent was given (impliedly) for any damage that might be caused in the course of playing 'manly sports'.

Since the defendants had pleaded guilty either to causing actual bodily harm (the sadists) or to aiding and abetting the causing of actual bodily harm (the masochists), no question of guilt arose to put to the jury and the judge proceeded to pass sentence.

But what sentence? The interest of the case lay in the attitude of the judge to the pleas in mitigation. Counsel for the defendants pointed out that the accused had all been of full age, and that those on whom harm had been inflicted had given their full and express consent. The activities had been conducted in total privacy, and no money had changed hands. Any injuries had healed quickly, none having required hospital treatment (with the charge on the public purse that this would have incurred).

If the judge had been minded to follow the principle at the heart of Mill's essay on liberty, considering that how people conducted themselves in private with no harm to others was their own concern, it would have been open to him to pass token, or suspended, sentences. If he had been minded to follow the views of Lord Devlin regarding the suppression of vice being as much the law's business as the suppression of subversive activities, he would consider that the conduct ought not to go unpunished, consent and privacy being irrelevant.

In the event, the sentences imposed showed that the judge's views reflected those of Devlin, not Mill. 'Much has been said [at the trial] about individual liberty', he said, 'but the courts must draw

64   [1934] 2 KB 498. See also *A-G's Reference (No 6 of 1980)* [1981] 2 All ER 1057.

the line between what is acceptable in a civilised society and what is not.' The assaults had been 'lewd, immoral and unnatural' and could not be condoned. In respect of those sentenced for sado-masochistic practices only (and not for these practices coupled with other offences such as possessing drugs or keeping a disorderly house) the prison terms imposed were of either three years or two years nine months. Those whose part had been solely masochistic received suspended sentences.

It is possible that the judge's attitude was influenced by circumstances surrounding the group's activities. One of the defendants was found to have helped to corrupt a teenage boy, another to have 'brought a lot of people into the S&M [sado-masochistic] scene', the one who kept a disorderly house where men came to have sex with animals was a retired pig breeder, the group had recruited scores of 'slaves' for their activities by inserting advertisements in the 'gay' press, a defendant who had been witnessed by the court on a home made video was a lay preacher, the animals had included a donkey and a dog. None of these circumstances, individually or collectively, should perhaps have been allowed to decide the outcome, but their mere recital shows a background that it would perhaps have been difficult for any judge not to be influenced by.

Yet not one witness could be produced by the prosecution, after extensive investigations, who had not given his full consent to what was done. With regard to majority of the defendants no persons had been involved who were not of full age. And the activities had been entirely in private. The convictions were nevertheless upheld by the House of Lords,[65] which held (by a majority of three to two) that consent to sado-masochistic practices was no defense to charges of wounding or assault causing actual bodily harm. The defendants appealed to the European Court of Human Rights on the ground that the verdicts of the British court infringed their rights under Article 8 of the European Convention on Human Rights which provides that 'Everyone has the right to respect for his private and family life, his home and his correspondence'. The Court found that the prosecution had been justified by virtue of exceptions to the principle in Article 8 relating to 'the protection of health ... '

In 1996 the Law Commission, in a consultation paper 'Consent in the Criminal Law' discussed whether, if adults are willing to be hurt or injured in the course of sport or sexual activity, it was proper for the criminal law to intervene The paper considered not only

---

65   *R v Brown (and others)* [1993]2 All ER 75 (HL).

sado-masochism but also such topics as short-pitched bowling, religious scourging, cosmetic piercing, female circumcision and Thai kick boxing. The Commission's provisional conclusion was that while acquiescence should not be a defense where there was 'serious disabling injury', the law should not prevent adults from consenting to damage or pain for religious or sexual purposes.

The Commission's conclusion has not been followed by legislation. But that public opinion is changing, and that the authorities are aware of this, has been reflected when a decision has been taken not to prosecute, or by the leniency of a sentence, or by an appeal against conviction being allowed. For example, in 1996 a night-club manager who ran monthly 'Club Whiplash' evenings, was cleared by the jury of the charge of keeping a disorderly house; also in 1996 the Court of Appeal allowed an appeal by a husband charged with assault for searing his initials into his wife's bottom (the branding having been carried out at the wife's request and being regarded by the couple as external evidence of their mutual love); and in 1998, suspended sentences only were imposed in a case in which seven men, the 'Bolton Seven', were charged with gross indecency in the form of group homosexual sex, the offence having been committed by virtue of the fact that one of the men was six months short of his eighteenth birthday and that sex had occurred when three men had taken part or been present, (homosexual sex being lawful only if no more than two men take part and both are of full age).

5. It will have become apparent during the course of this chapter that it can sometimes be difficult to prevent the debate over whether it is a proper function of the state to enforce morality from becoming entangled with one or more of the separate debates referred to at the start of the chapter. The issues raised by *R v Brown* discussed above illustrate this point: the matter of sado-masochism between consenting adults in private raises the question as to whether such practices are immoral; if they are considered to be immoral, whether it is the function of the state to prohibit them; and, if they are not regarded as immoral or if the court takes no view on the matter of morality, whether it is nevertheless the function of the state to prohibit them on grounds of paternalism or on some other ground of public policy, for example, the possibility of expense of medical care. (It will be noted that although *R v Brown* is commonly cited as an illustration of the issues raised in the debate over whether it is a proper function of the state to enforce morality, the decision of the European Court did not rest on morality, but on public policy – the protection of health.)

6. *R v Brown* illustrates not only that a discussion on whether the law should enforce morality needs, to be meaningful, to stick to the point at issue, but also the fact that the subjects that are conventionally discussed within jurisprudence do not form exclusive compartments, since the case could provide a focus for discussion in a variety of spheres. Is the conduct concerned an example of something that is contrary to *natural law* according to traditional theories; or according *to Finnis* ? Is there a *right* to conduct oneself as one wishes in private? Does prescription of such conduct run counter to any pertinent Declaration of rights such as that of the United Nations? Does the conduct provide an illustration of an instance in which *paternalism* by the state is justified? How would such conduct be treated in a society governed by the principles of *utilitarianism*? Would such conduct be outlawed in a society in which *justice* prevailed? The chapter divisions of a book on jurisprudence have no place in the world outside its covers.

7. The debate between Hart and Devlin took place in the 1960s. In the light of trends since that time, it might seem that it is the views of Hart that have had the greater support. Even bearing in mind the point made above about changes in public opinion as to what is immoral, perhaps this is correct – that the anti-enforcers have had the best day. This does not mean, though, that morality is no longer a concern of the law. The criminal law is dependent on acceptance that things that the law prohibits are not justified. Where the law is considered to prohibit something without justification, then the law is brought into disrepute and, in the event of law being disregarded (as in the case of the Sunday shop closing legislation) the system weakened. Conversely, where something causes wide-spread 'intolerance, indignation and disgust' and the law fails to act, demands for change can arise of an insistence and strength that no government can indefinitely ignore (demands, for example, with regard to animal welfare, or the ability of police officers to escape disciplinary hearings by taking ill health retirement, or the possession of hand guns). Thus even if Hart's view is regarded as that which finds the most general acceptance, this is very far from meaning that in the context of the law, morality has ceased to be of relevance.

Indeed, with the incorporation into law of the principles of the European Convention on Human Rights that the Human Rights Act effected, the question of morality now expressly finds a further[66]

---

66   Ie in addition to the common law and statutory offences of conspiracy to corrupt public morals. See *Knuller v DPP* [1973] AC 435.

place within the structure of UK law by reason of the provision in Article 10, which confers a right to freedom of expression, that exercise of the right should be subject to such restrictions as are necessary in a democratic society in the interests of the protection of, inter alia, 'health or morals'.

Postscript – Analytical and normative jurisprudence

In paragraph 6 above we noted that the issues raised in a case such as *Re Brown* could find a place in discussion of other areas of jurisprudence, such as natural law, or paternalism. But discussion of the issues raised by *R v Brown* would have no relevance when considering the work of Austin, or of Hart in his *Concept of Law*, or of Kelsen in his analysis of the nature of a legal system. Why is this? The answer lies in distinction that runs through much of jurisprudence, the distinction between jurisprudence that is analytical in character, and that which is normative. Normative here means relating to a norm in the general sense of 'a rule for behaviour, or a definite pattern of behaviour, departure from which renders a person liable to some kind of censure'.[67] Thus normative jurisprudence is concerned with the content of law, what the law ought to be; analytical jurisprudence is concerned with determining what law (or a particular legal concept) *is*. Thus Hart, in presenting his scheme, is not concerned with the content of law; his aim is to present us with a scheme that holds good irrespective of whether the legal system is that of liberal democracy or a tyrannical dictatorship.

A topic may be approached from either angle. Consider justice (Chapter 15). Perelman's approach is analytical. Rawls's approach, at the outset, is analytical. But where he begins to lay down restrictions on what people in the original position may, in his view, opt for, he moves over to a normative approach. Nozek's approach is wholly normative.

---

67   *The Oxford Dictionary of Philosophy*, S Blackburn.

CHAPTER 22

Having one's cake?

Civil disobedience[1]

The question here is whether circumstances can exist in which disobedience to the law is justified, or whether, given the existence of a legal system, a political obligation (meaning an obligation to obey the law) exists. Of almost daily occurrence reports appear of acts of civil disobedience in protest against such matters as the building of new roads (as at Twyford Down and the Newbury bypass); the construction of new or extended airports (as at Manchester in 1997);. abortion; the transport of live animals; the use of animals for research; the culling of animals (such as seals); the dumping on land or at sea of toxic waste, or structures containing toxic waste; the export to tyrannical regimes of arms, or implements capable of use for torture; the manipulation of the genetic make up of plants or animals; or the use on agricultural crops of insecticides that, by destroying all insect life, affects the food chain of the adjacent natural environment, or of herbicides that affect human health.

It has been not only at the present day, but from the earliest times that occasions have arisen when people have felt justified in refusing to obey the law. In this chapter we consider the grounds on which disobedience to the law has been sought to be justified.

'*Sought*'? – 'Sought to be justified'? 'Sought', the past participle of the verb 'to seek', carries the sense of to 'attempt', a word the use of which indicates that an attempt is considered necessary. Use of the phrase 'sought to be justified' fails to stand neutrally. It

---

1 P Singer *Democracy and Disobedience* (1974); K Greenawait *Conflicts of Law and Morality* (1987); *Civil Disobedience and Violence* (ed Murphy); *Civil Disobedience, A Casebook* (ed Crawford, 1973); H A Bedan *Civil Disobedience: Theory and Practice* (1969).

assumes that the law ought to be obeyed and that people who disobey it are under a burden of proof to justify their disobedience.

The notion of onus of proof can be useful here. For some the starting point is that a moral duty to obey the law exists, the onus of proof resting on those who would disobey the law to justify their action. For others, no moral duty to obey the law, merely because it is the law, exists: for these, the onus of proof rests on those who say the law ought to be obeyed to justify their claim.

The majority of writers have stood in the former camp. Even the natural lawyers, as we saw in an earlier chapter, stopped short of allowing their doctrine to be carried to its logical conclusion – that a law that infringed natural law could be disobeyed as being invalid.

In everyday life, away from the realms of the legal philosopher, a duty to obey the law is for many people the starting point of their thinking. If asked why a moral obligation existed to obey the law, a man in the street might well reply, 'I don't see it as a question of morals. It's a matter of common sense. We live in a complex society. If people declined to obey the law there would be chaos, a chaos from which I would suffer. It is in everyone's interests, including mine, that the law is obeyed.' If the man was asked why he was refusing to pay a particular tax he might reply, 'Ah, there's special reasons for that', thus accepting that special reasons were needed, that the onus of proof was on him to justify his action.

The limits of the debate

In preparation for the debate over whether disobedience to the law is ever justified, certain points need to be clarified – points of clarification as to what the debate is, and is not, about.

(a) The debate is not over whether there can be justification for disobedience in the form of a challenge to the whole of a society's laws, ie, in an attempt to overthrow an existing regime or system of government and the establishment of an alternative in its place. Disobedience directed to such an end constitutes rebellion. Whether such revolution can be justified is the subject of a separate debate.[2] (In the debate those who seek to justify rebellion would be likely to point to the contract theories of Locke and Rousseau.) Nor is the

2 See T Honoré 'The Right to Rebel' (1988) 8 OJLS 34.

debate over disobedience aimed at securing self-determination for a particular group by re-drawing a country's boundaries so as to result in the creation of a new, independent , sovereign territory. This too is a separate debate. (Those supporting secession perhaps pointing to the wording of the American Declaration of Independence of 1776.)

Our question is: Can there be justification for disobedience to one law (or group of laws) while not denying that obedience remains due to others? Can there be circumstances when a person can be justified in saying 'I'm not obeying *that* law' – in believing himself to be entitled to pick and choose as to which laws he will obey and which he won't?

(b) Nor is the debate over whether violence can be justified in the course of disobeying the law. This again is the subject of a separate, subsidiary, debate – if a person is justified in disobeying the law, are there circumstances in which violence is justifed? If so, what are these circumstances and what degree of violence do the circumstances warrant? To bring into our debate the question of the use of violence muddies the waters. This is because if violence is used, the obeyer can point to the circumstances of the violence (eg damage to neutral bystanders) as an argument against disobedience to the law. So the main issue is obscured, ie whether disobedience per se can be justified.

(c) Nor is the debate over whether disobedience is justified in a society in which no constitutional means exist by which citizens can secure a change in the law. In the debate which is the subject of this chapter the assumption is that some form of democratic government prevails. Whether disobedience is justified in a dictatorship is yet another separate debate – a debate in which the disobeyer may perhaps have an easier task in justifying his action than he does where at least some means are open to him to achieve the ends he seeks. But he will not necessarily have a walkover: there are those who argue that even where no democratic form of government exists disobedience to the law cannot be justified (foremost among the arguments being that of Thomas Hobbes in *Leviathan*).

(d) Finally, we should note that the debate is not concerned with justification for disobedience to the law solely for the purpose of gain or profit, disobedience for example, in the case of a private individual, in the shape of theft, escaping from custody, parking on a double yellow line, or evading tax; or, in the case of a commercial concern, disobedience in the shape of refusal to comply with the laws[3] that require certain classes of shops not to open on Sundays. We are thus talking about disobedience for some wider purpose than the disobeyer's gain. Generally the disobeyer's wider purpose is that of protest, the disobedience being of the law protested against, or of some other law that is disobeyed in the course of making an act of protest, for example failing to disperse when called upon to do so by the police. However, provided that the protest is based on principle, eg the unfairness of a tax, we need not exclude from the debate protests which, if successful, would benefit those who make the protest (eg by lifting the imposition of a tax).

Since we are concerned with disobedience grounded on principle we can include among the group of disobeyers with which we deal those who disobey on grounds of conscientious objection, noting merely that here the purpose of the refusal to obey is generally not principally to secure a change in the law, but stems from a refusal to participate in some action (eg joining the armed forces) to which the disobeyer objects on grounds of conscience. Disobedience may, it is true, sometimes have mixed motives. For example, the occupation of an empty building by squatters may be for the purpose of both protesting against buildings being left empty when people are homeless, and giving the squatters a roof over their heads. But the fact that borderline cases may exist need not distract us from the question at issue.

In practice the kind of disobedience that is the subject of this debate generally involves a breach of a criminal law. But the law broken need not necessarily be criminal; it can be civil, as where walkers, in protest against the withdrawal of rights of access following the sale of land by the Forestry Commission into private hands, express their indignation by walking across the land, thereby committing the civil wrong of trespass.[4]

Since the act of disobedience may, and perhaps most commonly will, involve a breach of the criminal law it might seem strange to speak of the present debate as being over the question of 'civil disobedience'. The word 'civil' here is used, however, not in contradistinction to 'criminal', but to 'military', indicating that the debate is not over justification for revolution, with gunfire in the jungle, the seizure of presidential palaces and the overthrow of governments, but over the parameters which have been indicated under (a) to (d) above.

Civil disobedience generally involves action by a group of people. But disobedience by an individual on grounds of principle is not

3 Shops Act 1950, s 47.
4 See also the terms of the 'Rivington Pledge', p 172 supra.

excluded from the terms of the present debate. Thus a single conscientious objector who refuses conscription to the armed forces' ranks for the purpose of our present debate is committing an act of civil disobedience as much as does a crowd of people which sits down outside, and refuses to move from, the embassy of a foreign country in protest against that country's use of poison gas to suppress a minority population.

Civil disobedience generally involves an element of publicity. But we can include under civil disobedience acts done in private, unknown to the authorities, provided that the object is protest not private gain. For example, if abortion is forbidden in a society, or forbidden except in certain circumstances, and abortions are carried out, without charge, in private, in defiance of the law by someone who opposes the law, then the same arguments (or at any rate a number of them) are as relevant as where the defiance is carried out in public.

Our purpose in placing the limits on the debate set out under (a)–(d) above has been not merely to prevent the blurring that occurs when overlapping issues are debated at the same time. The purpose has been to prevent the contestants raising arguments that take the debate away from the core of the issue. Thus by excluding the use of violence we prevent the obeyer from raising the argument 'look at the damage you have caused' (ie the damage, or the possibility of damage, cancels out any possible justification for disobedience that might otherwise have existed). By excluding the rebel we have made the disobeyer face the question whether he is entitled to disobey one law while taking advantage of the rest. By circumscribing the debate we have placed ropes round the ring.

Although we have said that the most generally held assumption is that the onus is on the disobeyer to prove his case, and so, in a court of law, it would be for the disobeyer to speak first, for our present purposes it will be convenient to state first the principal reasons that have been advanced in support of the notion that a duty to obey the law exists, and then let the disobeyer give his reply. The arguments in the debate have been rehearsed by many writers. They can be marshalled under seven headings.

1 Gratitude

Socrates, under sentence of death is urged, by his friends on the grounds of the injustice of the sentence, to escape and flee to another country. In his reply, recounted by Plato in *Crito*,[5] he refuses

---

5   Printed in *Civil Disobedience and Violence* (ed Murphy) p 12.

to do so on the ground, inter alia, that by doing so he would be showing ingratitude to the state that had, by marrying his mother and father, brought him into existence, had regulated his education, provided for his training in the accomplishments of music and gymnastics, ingratitude to the state that had been as a parent to him, whose benefits he has accepted, to whom he has owed all that had been of value to him in his life. Injustice no more entitled a citizen to strike against the state than a child to strike back against a parent.

The disobeyer responds: loyalties can be cancelled by later conduct of the one to whom loyalty was at one stage owed.

2 Breach of contract

Disobedience to the state constitutes breach of the contract that underlies government – the contract by which citizens give up certain rights in return for the greater benefit of living in an ordered society. This is the notion of contract that has had a central place in European political thought, the ancestry of which can be traced back through Rousseau, Jefferson, Locke, to the ancient world, where Plato, in *Crito*, speaks (through the mouth of Socrates) of the citizen as having entered into an implied contract that he will do as the state commands; and in *The Republic*, Glaucon says 'And now for ... the nature and origin of justice. What they say is that it is according to nature a good thing to inflict wrong or injury, and a bad thing to suffer it, but that the disadvantages of suffering it exceed the advantages of inflicting it; after a taste of both, therefore, men decide that, as they can't evade the one and achieve the other, it will pay to make a compact with each other by which they forgo both. They accordingly proceed to make laws and mutual agreements, and what the law lays down they call lawful and right. This is the origin and nature of justice'.[6]

Thus governments should be obeyed because their authority is derived from the people.

The disobeyer responds: the notion of contract is a fiction. Even if a society was originally based on a contract (and no evidence of this has been produced) no one since that time has agreed to join the association; the terms of this notional contract are undefined; no one can, in practice, leave the association. Participation in government, for example by voting in elections, cannot be construed as implied acceptance of the alleged contract, since such participation can be attributable (and is realistically to be attributed)

6   The translation is that in the Penguin edition by D Lee.

to making the best of what is available. Since no consent to be bound has been given, no breach of any contract occurs if the law is disobeyed.

3 Snatching two pieces of the cake

In a democracy all have an equal opportunity to influence decisions. The disobeyer accepts the majority view when it suits him, so he should accept the majority decision when it does not. Acceptance of majority decisions, giving no advantage to any one person, is a fair way of resolving differences and distributing benefits. The citizen who declines to abide by majority decisions is abrogating to himself the decision-making process, he is seeking to impose his own views on others, to obtain a greater say than that enjoyed by his fellows. He is acting like a person who agrees that everyone should have an equal piece of the cake and then snatches two pieces. Even if participation in voting does not signify the existence of a contract on which a government is based, voting does signify an implicit promise to abide by the outcome.

The disobeyer responds: the state in which I live is referred to as a democracy by those in whose interests it is to maintain the state in its existing form. But in this 'democracy', not everyone *does* have an equal chance of influencing decisions by their vote. True, there is universal adult suffrage, but there are ways and means of securing access to those in power that are available to people with money and connections that are not open to the ordinary citizen. Such people have an immeasurably greater chance than I do to influence the course of events.

Even if no such means of behind-the-scenes influence existed, groups representing particular interests have an influence on the course of events far greater than that which can be exercised by the individual citizen. There is no fair division of power.

Even if all citizens did have an equal opportunity to influence the course of events, by the nature of present day constitutional arrangements, this influence is exercisable only at times of elections. Between elections governments are able to act as elected dictatorships. Any notion of government decisions being made democratically is a fiction. Only if a referendum was held on every issue could decisions be regarded as being made democratically.

Further, government decisions are by no means all carried out in fulfilment of promises made in manifestos published before elections. *I* did not vote as to whether measurements should be metrified. *I* did not vote as to whether a motorway should be built through the Dartmoor National Park. The decisions were made by the government. *I* did not vote as to whether Great Britain should construct the atom bomb and build a processing industry for the purpose of producing the necessary materials. (Not even the cabinet voted on, or was informed of, the matter.)

So, not having participated (not having even had a chance to participate), I cannot be held to be morally bound to accept the decisions concerned.

Even if a particular matter was the subject of a vote (for example, as being a key issue in an election, or the subject of a referendum) and I participated, this fact does not by itself make me morally obliged to accept the outcome, since by voting I am not to be taken as agreeing to injustice, and the fact that a decision is that of a majority does not mean that it is just. (Fifty-one per cent of a black population could agree that the forty-nine per cent of the white population should work at lower rates of pay than black people.)

4 Weakening the system

We live in an imperfect world. No true democracy has ever existed. Despite its imperfections our democracy provides a system that approximates as closely to fairness as, bearing in mind realities, we are likely at present to achieve. Disobedience weakens the system, and opens the way for the introduction of a system that lacks all the advantages of the existing one.

The disobeyer responds: this is a matter that I concede I must take into account. I recognise that there may be worse systems than ours. But I believe that my protest over one matter is not going so to weaken the system as to lay the way open to its being overturned in favour of a worse one. To the extent that such a risk exists, the strength of my feeling is such that this is a risk that I am prepared to take.

5 What if everyone ...?

If you claim that you are right to break the law to secure the ends you seek, you are in no position to deny the same right to others. What's sauce for the goose is sauce for the gander. If everyone did as you did, no form of democracy, whether an imperfect one such as ours, or an ideal one of your choosing, could operate.

The disobeyer replies: what you say is true, and I accept that I would not like it if others, by taking the law into their own hands, forced a change that I was opposed to (though I believe that in a fairer system of democracy the likelihood of disobedience would be less). But my reply must be the same as before: that others might follow my example is a risk that, such is the strength of my feeling, I must take. (And I must tell you that in practice I think the risk is small. In response to my occupation of the offices of a nuclear power station, you say what if everyone did that kind of thing? My reply is that I assess the risk of everyone doing the same as being so small as to be of no relevance.)

6 Use of existing means to secure change

Our society provides ways in which the law can be changed. Changes are being made all the time. It is incumbent on the citizen to use the means that exist under the present system, not to have recourse to methods of his own choosing. Democracy is better served if government decisions are made as a result of reasoned persuasion, not as a result of intimidation – intimidation, you should note, that could be used by others to secure ends to which you are opposed.

The disobeyer responds: existing means? What means? Writing to one's MP? Standing on a soap box at Speaker's Corner? Joining an amenity group that writes letters to the newspaper? That means exist for changing the law is in reality a myth. What opportunity do objectors, in practice, have of influencing a decision over the building of a motorway, when the procedure for an inquiry precludes objectors from questioning the Ministry's forecast of traffic increases on which the need for a motorway is based? When the objectors' resources for legal advice and advocacy are minuscule compared with those of the promoting department of government? When a decision to build a motorway has never been the subject of a decision of Parliament or the electorate? To the extent that means exist for securing a change, I have exhausted them. Here are the replies I have received from my MP, word-processed stock letters prepared by civil servants. It is because I have exhausted all existing means that I take the action I do.

7 The risk of anarchy

The stability of our society is a façade. The riots in Bristol, Toxteth, Brixton, showed how quickly law and order can break down. It is easy for the idea of 'law and order' to be derided, but the fear in the faces of innocent people caught up in the shambles of street-fighting shows that the values of orderliness and respect for the law are not to be sneered at. Mob rule, arson, lynch law, the disintegration of society do not lie as far beneath the surface as we would like to think. Disobedience to the law is the first step down a road that can lead not to the improvement you claim to seek, but to evils of an immensely greater magnitude than any that exist at present.

'For all its trappings and majesty the law is a fragile instrument, and if it is broken – in whatever cause – something very much more important than the trappings and majesty is lost. Our law is the lifeblood of our democracy, and we live under the law's shadow. Through the centuries our law has been, however imperfect, the one thing that has stood the test of time. Shall we break it now? I tell you that if you do so, you will never be able to put it together again.'[7]

The disobeyer responds; I will make three points. First, your use of the phrase 'law and order' suggests that law and order break down at the same time. This is not so. There may be disorder without a breakdown of the law. If officials continue to obey commands and have sufficient force, through the police or the military, to retain or regain control, there is no breakdown of the law. My action may, it is true, in certain circumstances, affect public order. But if it does, it does not affect order generally. At most it will affect order in a particular locality. And in many instances, for example where protesters block an outlet from which toxic waste from a nuclear power station is discharged into the sea, the action, being confined to a specific objective, cannot be regarded as amounting to a break down in public order. Your contention that my action forms a threat to 'law and order' does not stand up.

Second, you speak of the stability of our society. Society is not threatened by action such as mine – action that is public, open for all to see. The threats to our society are insidious ones. Cities controlled by drug barons (as reported of Dublin in 1997). Interference with jurors. Intimidation of those who would assist the police. Corruption within the police. The imprisonment for long periods of persons whose convictions are known by those in authority to have been obtained on grounds that are unsafe, relevant evidence having been withheld from the defence. The cynicism caused by complaints against the police being investigated by other police; and by police accused of wrongdoing being permitted to take ill-health retirement on full pensions. The ease with which the proceeds of crime are laundered into legitimate outlets. The failure of prosecutions for financial fraud; or, where such prosecutions succeed, the lightness of the sentences imposed, or the early release of those imprisoned. The absence of effective protection for those who blow the whistle on corruption or other malpractice. Threats to due administration in local government as when officers of a National Park Authority

---

7 Bernard Levin, *The Times* (1995) 21 February.

ignore the resolution of an authority committee.[8] Threats to parliamentary democracy constituted by the flouting of parliament's intention when a Minister, having exercised a discretion to defer the introduction of a scheme approved by parliament, proceeds to introduce in its place, under common law powers, a radically different scheme; or when the supremacy of parliament as the law-making body is challenged by publication by a Minister of 'guidance' that takes effect with legal force without the approval of Parliament; or when, carrying shades of 1642, an officer of the executive declines to comply with an order made by the court. Besides such threats as these, any threat posed by our action – in public, for all to see - pales into insignificance.

Third, who spoke of violence? By the terms of our debate we are speaking of peaceful protest. If any action leads to others using my protest as a means of causing violent disruption then this I regret and the forces of law will have my support in arresting the malefactors. But I cannot allow the fact that there are evil people in society to be a reason for preventing me from making the protest my conscience bids me make.

8 No valid distinction between violent and non-violent action

That a distinction can be drawn between violent and non-violent action is an illusion. Violence connotes the application of force. The physical damage that is done in such cases as where protesters break into premises therefore constitutes violence. Even where no physical damage is done, protesters who fail to comply with an order to desist from their action will be removed by the police by means that will unavoidably involve the use of force.

The disobeyer responds – My action in lying down in the road was peaceful. It entailed no violence. What follows is not my concern. I defend my own action alone.

'Political obligation'

Your acceptance that something is the law of itself entails an obligation (sometimes referred to as political obligation) to obey.

---

8 As when officers of the Peak Park Joint Planning Board (as it was then) failed to implement a Resolution of the authority's Park Management Committee that a Public Path Creation Order should be made creating a footpath link at the end of the Monsal Trail near Monsal Head, Little Longstone, Derbyshire, notwithstanding that the Resolution was prefaced by the words, 'Having carefully considered all the objections and the statutory requirements including the expediency of the proposal it was: RESOLVED ...'

The disobeyer responds; your contention is flawed on two counts. First, I do not accept that my acceptance that something is the law entails an obligation of obedience. The link constituted by your word 'entails' does not exist. Second, as the Scandinavians showed, 'obligation' is one of those words whose meaning dissolves when subjected to analysis. Without more, the word tells us nothing. This is because, as seen in Chapter 1, when the word 'ought' or 'obligation' is used a relationship is proposed between a certain action and compliance with a particular standard or criteria. If you say that I ought to obey the law, I am entitled to enquire what standard or criteria you refer to. Is it that I ought to obey the law if I am not to endanger the stability of society? If so, that point has already been dealt with. If you are saying (as I think you are) that I ought to obey the law if I am to abide by your own moral code, then there is no point in pursuing the matter further since this is what our disagreement is about – the morality of civil disobedience.

For the reasons I have given, the obeyer concludes, in particular concerning two bites of the cherry, I maintain that you are under a moral obligation to obey the law; and, further, that because of the risk of producing a greater evil than that which you confront, it is in your own best interests to obey the law.

The disobeyer responds: for all the reasons I have given, even if such an obligation as you postulate exists (which I dispute), and even if the risk you speak of exists (which I question), I do not accept that there can never be circumstances in which this obligation ceases to apply.

Practicalities

Turning from the arguments to matters of fact, three points may be made.

1. The arguments advanced to justify civil disobedience are of practical importance since the existence of these arguments, coupled with the cogency with which they are advanced, can affect the turn of events. The fact that people hear and note the arguments can overcome an inherent unease at breaking the law. Waverers who otherwise would have stayed indoors may join in the action.

2. A further matter of fact is that it is the common experience that those who commit acts of disobedience *feel* that the onus is on them

to justify their action. The person who moves on when instructed to do so by the police is unlikely to feel that he needs to justify this action. The man who refuses to do so does: as he is carried away by the police he cries out to the crowd to explain the reason for this action.

That the civil dissident can be uneasy in this action has been demonstrated by R A Wasserstrom.[9] The moral justification by civil dissidents has, Wasserstrom points out, in various instances taken the form of claiming that the law disobeyed, under natural law principles, is not really valid law at all. Thus the dissident is not *really* breaking the law. The argument that the disobeyer is not really breaking the law has been based also on the argument that the law disobeyed is invalid as being contrary to the constitution (as in the case of protests against segregation in the 1960s in the United States), or contrary to the principles of natural justice (as in the case of protests at certain motorway inquiries in England in the 1970s and 1980s) or in breach of some alleged 'natural right'. So in cases where he seeks to show that he is not *really* breaking the law, the civil dissident thereby tacitly recognises that disobeying the law, if it *is* the law, is something that he should not do.

3. Finally we may note that the decision whether to take part in an act of civil disobedience can be influenced by a range of factors. These are likely to include the following:

i.   an assessment of the merits of the existing society;
ii. an assessment of the likelihood that the act of disobedience will endanger the stability, or even continued existence, of the society whose law is disobeyed;
iii. regard for the possible consequences personally for the disobeyer (imprisonment, fines, loss of employment, social stigmatism, embarrassment or distress to relatives or friends);
iv. an assessment of the likelihood of the act of disobedience securing the objective desired;
v.   an assessment of the likelihood of the desired objective being achieved by other means;
vi. the degree to which the potential disobeyer is swayed by the arguments of those who assert the existence of a moral duty to obey the law, and of those who assert the rightness in some circumstances of disobedience;
vii. finally, and crucially, the degree of indignation felt over the matter protested against.

---

9   R A Wasserstrom 'The Obligation to Obey the Law' in *Essays in Legal Philosophy* (ed R Summers, 1968).

Whether or not a person takes part in an act of civil disobedience will be decided, consciously or unconsciously, by weighing up the facts that pull in one direction or another. For example, we can imagine someone who does not feel particularly strongly about an issue taking part in civil disobedience when he has little to lose (being unemployed and homeless); and we can imagine a Church of England archdeacon for whom the factors listed at i–v above sway him against disobedience and whose feelings on vi are neutral, but who decides to defy the law because his indignation is so strong that this outweighs the factors that pull him against taking action.

Who wins?

In the debate that has been the subject of this chapter, who wins? – he who asserts that circumstances can exist in which disobedience to the law is justified, or he who denies this assertion? We cannot say. There is no yardstick labelled 'Justification' – a standard measurement, like some rod of iron under a glass case in the vault of some government office, the length of which constitutes a 'yard'. So the contestants in the debate are not in a position to cry out, 'Look! My arguments exceed the standard; we win!' or, recognising that their arguments fall short, admit defeat. But this is what we should expect since in jurisprudence, as in philosophy, no one ever 'wins' (which is as well, since if one side won, this would put an end to the game).

CHAPTER 23

The man on the beach

The only tool?

No, there is no rod of iron under a glass case. But in conducting the debate (and the other debates that have been the subject of this book), we do have tools: the words we use.

'*Word*' – the most elusive, the most magical, the most important word of all. More important than 'justice', 'truth'; 'existence'; 'God', 'consciousness'? Certainly, because 'word' describes the things without which nothing can be discussed. Indeed, without words, not only would we be unable to discuss the meaning of such matters as what it means to be conscious,[1] but the word conscious would not exist to be discussed (and neither would the word 'word').

And the next most important? There is no second most important word, but there is a second most important thing: the order in which words are arranged.

It is by words and their arrangement that we are able both to give expression to what we understand our senses tell us exists outside our bodies, and to express our response to words arranged in groups that others put to us. Even scientists, whose assertions are expressed in equations and formulae would be hard put to it to propound their theories without words. It is our possession of the combination of words and their arrangement that distinguishes us from amoebas.

Is this no more than saying that without words and their appropriate arrangement there can be no such thing as thought?

---

1 Danniel Dennet, *Consciousness Explained; Kinds of Minds;* David Chalmers, *The Conscious Mind*; F Crick, *The Astonishing Hypothesis: scientific search for the soul*; R Penrose, *Shadows of the Mind: search for the missing science of consciousness.*

No. Words are not a prerequisite for thought. When I think 'I could do with a coffee', I can have the thought without putting the thought into words. When I think, 'I feel ill,' or 'I'm late,' or 'I hate him,' I *may* express the thought in words, I may use the words to myself 'I feel ill,' but I do not need to for the thought to be there. That words are not necessary for thoughts to exist is known to anyone who has had a dog. Just because a dog does not have words does not mean that it cannot think, 'I want to be taken for a walk,' 'It is time for my meal,' 'Go on, throw it!' When the dominant male gorilla, Frodo, watches his younger brother Biscuit, he can think 'He is getting uppity. Unless I do something soon, he will challenge my position,' without (as far as we know) the use of words to express his thought.

Is it words and their combination that alone enable us to convey our thoughts to others? No, thoughts can be conveyed by gestures, expressions. A raised eyebrow, a girl's sideways glance, a shrug of the shoulders, a wave of the hand, a nod, wide-opened eyes, a dropped jaw, clenched teeth, and Frodo's brandishing of a stick – all can convey a thought without the use of words.

It is the function of words and their arrangement, the combination that makes language, to provide a precision in the conveyance of a message that gestures and expressions alone cannot provide, and to provide a vehicle for the expression of concepts that, without language, could not be expressed. (Could the concept 'law', or 'rule', or 'justice', or 'grundnorm', exist without language?)

At the far, western, end of the Edale valley in Derbyshire lives and works a young man who earns his living by making wooden bowls, using a foot-driven pole lathe of a kind used by the former Chiltern bowl turners, members of a craft that had roots of unknown antiquity. To shape the block of wood on his lathe, he uses one or other of sixteen chisels, each two foot long, and each with a different curve to its cutting tip. With these he can make a bowl of any shape that the nature of wood and the power of the lathe permits. He made the tools himself, having learned sufficient of the blacksmiths trade to do so, and learning the shapes needed from visiting craft museums where old tools are preserved, and from his experience on the lathe. The tools need to be kept sharp, the cutting edge of each precisely preserved. With fewer tools he could still make bowls, but with each additional tool available, the range and variety of bowls that he can make increases.

The analogy, of course, is with words. Each noun, adjective, verb and adverb in a language has its function, to convey a meaning. A language with a hundred thousand words can convey a wider range of meanings than one with ten thousand words. No language in the western world has words designed to convey so great a variety of shades of meaning as English – so great a variety of cutting edges. If we are able to express ideas with greater precision than was possible in Anglo-Saxon England, it is because of the expansion of our vocabulary by the inclusion of words from Norman French and Latin. (Consider whether the ideas in any chapter of this book would have been capable of being adequately expressed in Anglo-Saxon.) It is therefore to be regretted when the language's tool kit of words is eroded by the distinction between words being lost as a result of the illiteracy of people in a position to affect public understanding of the language.

The process is witnessed daily. Often the misuse is prompted by a desire to show off, the writer or speaker, aware of his lack of education, too insecure to use a simple word, employing a word he believes will impress.[2] For example, we hear 'substantive' used when what is meant is 'substantial'; we hear emotive for emotional; divisive for divided; governance for government; simplistic for simple; proven for proved; stadia for stadium; angst for anger; arcane for archaic; eschew for forego; empathise for sympathise. Sometimes the error is due, not to a wish to show off, but merely to ignorance, as when the difference is not known, for example, between malingerer and malcontent; between reticence and caution; adverse and averse; such as and like; emblem and symbol; ascribe and subscribe; militate and mitigate; castigate and chastise ('Madam Speaker chastised Members for their unruliness'); disinterested and uninterested; impunity and immunity; forgive and condone; prompted and provoked; anticipate and expect; improve and enhance; deem and think; imply and infer ('Are you inferring that I am not telling the truth?'); deny and dispute; dispute and refute. Just as each day the planet's bio-diversity is reduced as the number of species diminishes, so the language's precision, its diversity, its ability to convey meaning is diminished by the misuse to which it is daily subject.[3]

In seeking to comprehend, to express, words are the only tool. They are being thrown away.

The only tool? At present, yes. But think about this. Suppose that a man is sitting alone on the seashore thinking about the American constitution. What happens at the second of time that the word

---

2 And perhaps being under the impression that all words listed as alternatives in a computer's Thesaurus carry the same meaning.

3 Eg, by sports commentators.

4 Francis Crick, *The Astonishing Hypothesis.*

'constitution' forms part of a sentence in his thoughts? What *happens*, inside his brain.[4] Something, but what?

Here we reach one of what are generally regarded as the five great unsolved mysteries of the world – whether there is a law that overarches the existing laws of physics; the origin of the universe and the nature of the Big Bang (if there was a Big Bang); the origin of life; the capacity of strings of DNA to carry the blue print for the construction of the hardware and the software[5] of a living creature; why is it that when an adaptation to a creature's physical characteristics would, because of changed circumstances, make the creature better able to survive, out of the trillions of mutations that could occur, it has been, over evolutionary time, the advantageous mutation that does occur; and, as with the man on the beach, the physical nature of thought – the physical, testable, verifiable, ascertainable nature of what happened in our material universe when the man thought 'constitution', the thing that *did not happen in the case of the pebble at his foot.*

This brings us to the thread – not yet even a frail rope bridge – across the divide that separates philosophy and neurology – the world of thought from the world of the touchable, grey, porridgy mass inside our skulls.

Neurologists are able[6] to pinpoint the parts of the brain responsible for the execution of various functions, and parts where various emotions occur. For example, they can tell us the area in which we remember how to do things automatically, such as walking;[7] in which we register sensory stimuli, such as sight, hearing, smell, touch;[8] in which sensory perceptions are processed and interpreted; in which appropriate response to incoming stimuli are generated (to jump out of the way of a bus);[9] in which we retain our memory of objects temporarily out of sight;[10] in which short term memories are stored;[11] in which is located our long term memory;[12] in which negative emotions including fear are generated;[13] in which we control emotions;[14] in which we are able to plan and choose between different

---

5 Eg, that which enables a bird to fly.
6 See Rita Carter, *Mapping the Mind.*
7 Basal Ganglia.
8 Thalamus.
9 Dorsolateral prefrontal cortex.
10 Upper right hemisphere of the prefrontal lobe.
11 Hippocampus.
12 Frontal and temporal cortical areas.
13 Amygdala.
14 Cingulate cortex.

courses of action;[15] in which incoming words are comprehended[16] (including, even, the area in which consonants are detected), in which lies the bridge between the visual recognition of words and the rest of the language process; in which (or roughly in which) words are given meaning;[17] and in which speech is articulated.[18]

All this is known by three means. First by seeing, if an area of a person's brain is damaged (from an accident, or a stroke, or disease), what effect this has on the person's abilities or character, for example by the loss of long term or short term memory, or the loss of speech, or the loss of fear, or by an inability to control emotions. Secondly, by watching, by brain imaging, which areas of the brain are shown as being electrically active (lit up) when a particular action is undertaken or emotion experienced (for example as when, for experimental purposes, fear is generated). Thirdly, by noting the effect on a person's capacities and personality if a piece of brain is removed by surgery.

When the man on the beach thought the word 'constitution' what happened was that he remembered the meaning of the word (or, at any rate, the meaning for him). So he was retrieving an item from his long term memory and bringing it in to play - like a fresh member of a team being brought on to the field to replace one that goes off. In terms of brain activity, a memory is an 'association between a group of neurons [brain cells] such that when one fires, they all fire, creating a specific pattern',[19] a pattern repeated each time the group is activated.

Would it be possible to construct a movie camera that took many pictures a second (like the kind that take pictures of the wings of a humming bird in flight) and use this to see what happened at the second at which the man thought 'constitution', so that we could see what actually happened at that second?

The difficulties in the way of achieving this are formidable. Areas of the brain are linked: activity does not take place in one isolated area at a time. The brain has about 100 billion active cells, the neurons, each one linked with up to ten thousand neighbours. The possible permutation and combinations of links between neurons run in to millions of trillions.[20]

---

15 Dorsolateral prefrontal cortex.
16 Wernicke's area.
17 Angular gyrus.
18 Brocca's area.
19 Carter, op cit, p 159.
20 Even the links that connect the right and left hemispheres of the brain number approximately 80 million.

But we might ask, even if not practical, would it not theoretically be possible, since electricity follows a path, for the neural connections to be presented like road directions? – after one mile, take the turning on the left, take the second right after that. In half a mile bear right on to a narrow lane. Proceed until the lane joins a dual carriageway. Turn left until the third roundabout, and so on.

By way of reply, we would be told that even if a camera was invented that took a million pictures a second, further problems exist. One is that so far we do not know the area of the brain in which structure is imposed on incoming speech – where the individual words of a sentence, because of their order, acquire meaning. Identifying this area would be a prerequisite for identifying the physical result of the man thinking 'constitution'.

A further difficulty is that words do not occur in the brain in isolation but in association with emotions or thoughts. For example, one person's thought 'constitution' might be accompanied by a feelings of stability, continuity, worthiness; another person thought of 'constitution' might be accompanied by a feeling of rigidity, conservatism, resistance to change, frustration; another person's thought of 'constitution' might be accompanied by a feeling of panic arising from the fact that 'constitution' was the kind of thing he had never understood.

Even if a way was found of filtering out the baggage that a person carries in his mind associated with a particular word, a further difficulty is that brain activity is not solely electrical: it is chemical also, through the operation of neurotransmitters,[21] chemical signals which pass from one cell to another at the points of contact (synapses) between them.

But supposing that a million pictures a second camera was constructed, one that could record chemical reactions as well as electrical pathways and that a three dimensional movie was made of the man's head as he sat on the beach, would this not mean that it would then be possible to know in *physical* terms what happened when he thought 'constitution'?

The movie, we would be told, would only be capable of being recorded by computer, and the computer code would be longer than the distance round the edge of our galaxy.

But supposing, we ask (never giving up), some way was devised of compressing the code, in a similar way to that in which computer files are zipped, so that the record of what occurred was to reduced to manageable proportions, say a hundred thousand London

21 Eg, dopamine, serotin, noradrenaline, endorphin, acetylchrorine.

telephone directories. This would mean, surely, that it would then be possible to record what happened in the physical world when the man on the beach thought the word 'constitution'? Such a course is, of course, beyond the realms of credibility, just as it is impossible that a machine should carry a hundred people across the Atlantic at faster than the speed of sound. The idea is absurd. (As absurd as the idea that dust should be collected from the tail of a comet in outer space and, after a journey of four billion miles, brought back to earth for analysis? As absurd as that a device could be bought from a shop in the high street capable of performing a million transactions a second?)

But suppose that the world is not hit by an extinction-sized comet or asteroid or meteorite during the next thousand years and science continues to advance at its present rate, and that by the end of that time the electrical and chemical track through the brain of a thought can be recorded in ten thousand London telephone directories. This would mean that it would then be possible to record both what happened in the physical world when the man on the beach thought the word 'constitution', and what happens when you, the reader, think the same word. And to compare the two records. We would then know whether the man on the beach meant the same thing as you did. And he would know what you meant. You might, after reflection, decide that his meaning was better and decide that in future you would instruct your brain to adopt the path followed by his track instead of what had been your own.

If this came to pass we would know what words – including words such as law, justice, right, morality, obligation – meant to each of us. And if we agreed on an authority, for example the editors of the Oxford English Dictionary, we could have a dictionary that defined the meaning of words, not by using other words, but by computer records of trackways through the brain.

Until this time is reached, our only tool is to define the meaning of words by using other words, words that themselves require definition by still other words. Fortunately, the meaning of words in the English language is still sufficiently precise to be used without misunderstanding in general discourse. But each word represents a chisel with a differently shaped tip. It is sad when daily the tips are broken, when our only tools for conveying meaning are broken, our language mutilated by the ignorance, or the conceit, or the laziness, of those whose position gives them the power to spread their illiteracy over the population at large.

Index

Eleustic
 meaning, 11
Empiricism
 British philosophy, in, 234
 Hagerstrom, of, 235-237
 logical, 235
 meaning, 11
 nature of, 234
 scientific, 235
Epistemological
 meaning, 11
Equality
 treatment, of, 104, 198. *See also*
  JUSTICE
Erastianism
 meaning, 11
Eristic
 meaning, 11
Ethics
 Bentham, of, 155
 current issues, as to, 150, 151
 Darwinism shaping, 161
 definition, 150
 fundamental question of, 148
 hedonistic, 160
 metaethics-
  debate on, 151-153
  good and evil, distinction
    between, 152, 153
  scope of, 150
 natural law as foundation of, 70
 normative-
  debate on, 153
  scope of, 150
 principles, application of, 150, 151
 private morality, applying in, 158,
  159
 purpose of, 150
 reasons for observing, 166
 relation of morality to, 159
 utilitarianism as branch of, 164
**European Convention for the
 Protection of Human Rights
 and Fundamental Freedoms**
 British law, adoption in, 195
 rights in, 193
Euthanasia
 paternalism of law, 293

Feminism
 campaigns, 271
 core issues, unity on, 286, 287
 Critical Legal Studies, and, 274,
  275

Feminism-*contd*
 criticisms of, 287, 288
 cultural, 271
  differences between men and
    women, approach to,
    282
  radical feminism, divergence
    from, 282, 283
  task of, 284
  women, view of, 283, 284
 differences between men and
  women, approach to, 281,
  282
 incorporationism, 286
 jurisprudence, whether, 288-290
 law, language of, 272-274
 liberal-
  connectedness, view of, 283, 284
  focus of, 278
  human relationships, nature of,
    279
  objectivity, respect for, 277
  pornography, view of, 278
  radical feminism, differing
    from, 275-281
  reasoning processes of law,
    acceptance of, 276-278
  rights-
    case resting on, 276
    claiming, 275
  separateness, view of, 278, 279
  similarity between men and
    women, attention to,
    280
  state power, view of, 280
 liberalism, and, 271
 nature of truth, view of, 288
 patriarchy, view of, 272
 radical-
  'connectedness', 284, 285
  cultural feminism, divergence
    from, 282, 283
  differences between men and
    women, attention to,
    280
  focus of, 278
  heterosexual intimacy, view of,
    285
  human relationships, nature of,
    279
  incorporationist approach, view
    of, 286
  liberal feminism, differing
    from, 275-281